MARY-LE-PORT, BRISTOL

EXCAVATIONS 1962 – 1963
by
LORNA WATTS and PHILIP RAHTZ

with contributions by

D. Bramwell
L. A. S. Butler
J. Casey
M. D. Crane
D. Dawson
R. H. M. Dolley
D. Fowler
A. Goodall
I. Goodall
C. E. Gowenlock
L. V. Grinsell
R. G. Jackson
R. H. Leech
J. Litten
D. Moore

F. Neale
B. Noddle
D. O'Connor
M. W. Ponsford
J. Rackham
S. E. Rigold
A. Saville
J. H. Thornton
D. Tweddle
A. Vince
A. R. Williams
B. Williams
D. F. Williams
C. Wilson
C. Witt

Cover illustration: Mary-le-Port ruins by John Piper, courtesy of the Tate Gallery, Catalogue no. 5718.

Frontispiece: view of Bristol from the Robinson Building c.1963 with St. Mary-le-Port Church tower under scaffolding on the right.

ISBN 0 900199 26 1

First printed 1985 by the City of Bristol Printing and Stationery Department (M4499).

Designed by Kate Gilmour, City of Bristol Museum and Art Gallery.

Foreword

Professor Philip Rahtz's excavations at St. Mary-le-Port in the early sixties were among the earliest post-war projects of real significance in Bristol and I am delighted to be able to associate the City of Bristol Museum and Art Gallery with the publication of his findings. Detailed excavations of medieval churches continue to be rare in Britain and Professor Rahtz's work on the remains of this once-charming church is doubly welcome. We are very glad to be able to add the report to our growing monograph series which, at present, constitutes our primary outlet for the publication of major rescue excavations undertaken by, or on behalf of the City Museum and Art Gallery. And we are particularly pleased to have been allowed by the Trustees of the Tate Gallery to reproduce on the front cover John Piper's beautiful and typical painting of the church as it lay in ruins shortly after the Second World War.

I take this personal opportunity to thank my colleagues, David Dawson (Curator of Archaeology and History) and Mike Ponsford (Field Archaeologist in that Section) for the considerable amount of work they have shouldered in seeing the manuscript through the press; and I thank my old friend Philip Rahtz, and Lorna Watts (his wife), for being such sympathetic and patient authors. I am indebted, also, to Kate Gilmour, in our Design and Production Section, for her work on the design and preparation of the complex manuscript for the printers; as always we have enjoyed our collaboration with the Printing and Stationery Department of Bristol City Council in the production of yet another important addition to this Monograph series.

Once again, the City Museum and Art Gallery is indebted to the Historic Buildings and Monuments Commission for England—English Heritage—for assessing the report and then giving us a considerable grant-in-aid towards its cost of publication.

Nicholas Thomas
Museum Director
City of Bristol Museum and Art Gallery
May 1985

Editors' Note

References to accession numbers of items in the collections of the City Museum and Art Gallery, Bristol, and to monographs published by the Museum are prefixed with the abbreviation BRSMG, our international museum code.

Chapter 1: Summary

This report, in printed version and accompanying microfiche, concerns the church and street of St. Mary-le-Port, Bristol. It is principally a description and discussion of the data from excavations in the area in 1962–1963. The area has also been put into a wider context by some discussion of the relationship of the work to the archaeology and history of Bristol. There is a detailed exposition, in written and graphic form, of the development of properties in the Mary-le-Port area and their relationship to the church, from early medieval times to the present day. Frances Neale has compiled this from written sources and suggested correlations with the archaeological evidence as now expounded in this report.

Mary-le-Port Street and the church may both have had their origins at least as early as the tenth century. They may be part of an early gridded layout located to the north or north-west of an important bridge crossing the river Avon, or may have developed on the west edge of a pre-Conquest nucleus in the Castle area.

The street route developed into a hollow way. Some evidence for domestic and industrial activities on either side of it in late Saxon and early medieval times is afforded by archaeological finds relating to the working of metals (mainly iron), leather, animal bone, ?wood and ?textile, to the consumption of food and to the disposal of waste. Broadly contemporary with these activities was a timber building set in the angle between the western part of this street and the church.

In the thirteenth century, or later, apparently in an act of corporate or collective town-planning, the hollow way was filled up and paved. The make-up may have been derived from the digging-out of cellars in this part of Bristol. The Timber Building was succeeded by a complex of stone walls, enclosing the north-east corner of the northern churchyard.

The church of St. Mary-le-Port was certainly in existence by the later twelfth century, but the earliest features found in excavation could be of an earlier church, contemporary with the hollow way, possibly before the Conquest.

The church of the twelfth century had a rectangular nave and chancel, but was probably aisleless; transepts, and the north aisle (and possibly also a south aisle) were added in the thirteenth century, together with a longer chancel. The church reached its maximum development in the later fifteenth century; there was certainly a double arcade at this time. The north aisle was widened and a substantial western tower was added. A cellared property was built in the north-east angle of nave and chancel, which was probably the medieval parsonage referred to in written sources.

In the early sixteenth century the tower was modified, any south aisle demolished and the cellared property incorporated into the church. By the mid-seventeenth century, the narrow space between the north side of the church and the street had been built on by multi-storeyed properties, which effectively hid the church from this side; access to its north porch was by an arched entrance through these.

Burial on the north side of the church ended before 1648; to the south it continued to the last century. Inside the church, graves, notably vaults of the eighteenth and nineteenth centuries, destroyed virtually all the archaeological stratification.

The sixteenth-century church, with successive restorations, continued in use to modern times. Together with the seventeenth-century buildings erected against its north wall, it was destroyed in 1940 by German bombing in a night in which all this part of Bristol was largely obliterated.

Finds from the excavation include a few pre-medieval finds, of ?prehistoric and Roman date and also objects with Anglo-Saxon and Viking parallels; architectural fragments, sculpture, tomb-fittings and tools of stone; objects of burnt or fired clay, including plain and decorated floor tiles; an important series of eleventh-century and later pottery; some window and vessel glass; some tools and other objects of iron, copper alloy, lead and bone; coins including two of the third century and one of Harold II of 1066; metal-working residues; and an informative group of faunal remains, of cattle, sheep, goats, pigs and birds.

The evidence of the human remains were not realised, nor has there been a proper integration of the standing structure of the ruined church with the evidence of below-ground archaeology. In spite of these serious omissions, which would be unthinkable in a modern excavation, the work in the Mary-le-Port area has given a valuable insight into the development of a church and street in an early area of Bristol—the first of its kind in the city.

Portable 'finds' and the site archive are stored at the City of Bristol Museum and Art Gallery (BRSMG:29/1984). 35 mm. colour slides of the excavations are stored at the Department of Archaeology, University of York.

Chapter 2: List of Contents

MF: microfiche only
  S: summary only, full version in microfiche

Chapter 6: Excavation method, recording and stratification   57

Chapter 7: Chronological summary, street and church   59

Chapter 8: Mary-le-Port Street East   63

Chapter 9: Mary-le-Port Street West   71

Chapter 10: St. Mary-le-Port Church 89

Chapter 11: Artefacts and samples   131

2.1   List of Figures

(MF = microfiche only)

2.2 List of Plates

(68 plates; 76 photographs) (MF = microfiche only)

There are additionally many photographs which exist as (a) colour slides in the collection of the Department of Archaeology, University of York (from which some of these monochrome prints have been made); (b) monochrome negatives; (c) monochrome prints of which the negatives have not been found (see 14.1 for list).

No. of Plate		Scale in photograph	Negative No.	Colour Slide No.	Source or Remarks	Page No./ MF No.
1	View of Bristol from Robinson Building, c.1963, with St. Mary-le-Port on right.	—	—	12,625	Mono copy.	Frontispiece
2	Ricart's 'Bristol', 1479, enlarged area of Mary-le-Port.	—	—	—	MacInnes and Wittard eds., 1955, frontispiece.	31
3	Part of Millerd's Plan of Bristol, 1673.	—	—	—	Bristol City Museum facsimile.	35
4	Mary-le-Port Street from west, with west side of St. Mary-le-Port church tower in background; monochrome photo from painting ?c.1800.	—	—	—	Bristol City Museum unnumbered (Braikenridge).	50
5	Mary-le-Port Street, south side, from north-east; church tower in background; monochrome photo from painting of c.1800.	—	—	—	Bristol City Museum M 2801.	52
6	Mary-le-Port Street, south side, from north-east; church tower in background; painting by E. A. Phipson 1907.	—	—	8,115 or 12,679	Source unknown; mono copy.	53
7	Mary-le-Port Street, south side, from north-east; church tower in background; drawing ?c.1910.	—	—	—	Bristol City Museum Mb 3229.	54
8 MF	Mary-le-Port Street, south side, from north-east; painting ?c.1910.	—	—	—	Bristol Record Office Postcard 99c.	10/8
9	Mary-le-Port Street, south side from north-east; photograph ?c.1910. Fred Little postcard.	—	—	12,667	Source unknown; mono copy.	55
10 MF	Mary-le-Port Street, south side, from north-east; church tower in background.	—	—	—	Bristol Record Office.	10/10
11 MF	Ditto, but with names of shops, etc., written in on negative; postcard.	—	—	8,118	Source unknown.	10/11
12 MF	Mary-le-Port Street, south side from north-east; photograph 1931.	—	—	—	Source unknown.	10/12
13 MF	Mary-le-Port Street, south side, Jones' Brush 'Factory'; photograph ?c.1930.	—	—	8,117 and 12,674	Source unknown.	10/13
14 MF	Area 106, Timber Building, from south-south-east.	feet and inches	—	8,125	Mono copy.	10/14
15	Area 106, Timber Building, from south-west.	feet and inches	—	12,667	Mono copy.	81
16 MF	Area 106, wall 106.4, from north-east.	inches	—	12,691	Mono copy.	10/16
17 MF	Area 106, wall 106.4, detail from south-south-west.	inches	—	12,692	Mono copy.	10/17
18	Pier complex, features F45, F47, F56, F57, F58 and F63, from south-west.	feet	B25	—	—	101
19A MF	Wall F81 from south-east, pier F14 behind.	feet	B22	—	Negative lost.	10/19
19B MF	Wall F81B from east, vault behind.	inches	B33	—	Negative lost.	10/19
19C MF	Piers F31 and F23 from north, F20 above.	feet	A25	—	Negative lost.	10/19
19D MF	Piers F57, F58 and F63, from south-east.	feet	B19	—	Negative lost.	10/19
20	North-east corner of chancel, from south-west; foundations F135, F137, F131 and F55; vault on right.	feet and inches	C13	—	—	103
21	Stucco screen base F176, from north-west.	inches	C8	—	—	106

No. of Plate		Scale in photograph	Negative No.	Colour Slide No.	Source or Remarks	Page No./ MF No.
22 MF	Column-base F133, block F132 and foundation F136, from south-west.	feet and inches	C11	—	—	10/22
23	Detail of Millerd's Plan of Bristol, 1673—St. Mary-le-Port Church.	—	—	—	Bristol City Museum facsimile.	109
24 MF	Monument F186 of early sixteenth century; monochrome copy of painting.	—	—	12,673	Source unknown.	10/24
25	Mary-le-Port Street, south side; church north porch right of centre; drawing ?early twentieth century.	—	—	—	Bristol Record Office postcard 98e.	112
26 MF	Mary-le-Port Street, south side; Beehive boot shop and church north porch; photograph c.1908.	—	—	—	Reece Winstone 1957, plate 11; cf. ibid. 1879–1874, plate 33.	10/26
27 MF	Mary-le-Port Street, south side; Haynes umbrella shop and church north porch; photograph of 1931.	—	—	—	Source unknown.	10/27
28	St. Mary-le-Port Church from south-east, Buttermarket Passage in foreground; painting by S. Jackson 1825; monochrome photo.	—	—	—	Bristol City Museum M 2789 (Braikenridge).	114
29	St. Mary-le-Port Church interior, from west; painting by I. Johnson 1828; monochrome photo.	—	—	—	Bristol City Museum M 2791 (Braikenridge).	115
30 MF	St. Mary-le-Port Church, plan of proposed alterations 1842.	—	—	—	Bristol Record Office negative 7963/1.	10/30
31 MF	Ditto, projected restoration 1861, plans before and after.	—	—	—	Ditto negative 7963/6.	10/31
32 MF	St. Mary-le-Port Church, projected restoration 1875, completed 1877—ground plan including seating.	—	—	—	Bristol Record Office negative 7963/2.	10/32
33 MF	Ditto, details of tower in plan and elevation.	—	—	—	Ditto, negative 7963/4.	10/33
34 MF	Ditto, roofing plan.	—	—	—	Ditto, negative 7963/9.	10/34
35 MF	Ditto, details of heating system.	—	—	—	Ditto, negative 7963/3.	10/35
36 MF	Ditto, details of gables and guttering.	—	—	—	Ditto, negative 7963/8.	10/36
37 MF	Ditto, details of windows and arcade.	—	—	—	Ditto, negative 7963/5.	10/37
38 MF	Ditto, details of bench-ends and window design.	—	—	—	Ditto, negative 7963/7.	10/38
39A MF	St. Mary-le-Port Church interior, looking east; ?1930s. Fred Little postcard.	—	—	—	Source unknown.	10/39
39B MF	'Ancient Iron Chest found with valuable documents in the cellar of Mary-le-Port church Bristol' (caption on Fred Little postcard).	—	—	—	Source unknown.	10/39
39C MF	'Brass eagle lectern in St. Mary-le-Port church' (caption on postcard).	—	—	—	Source unknown.	10/39
40 MF	St. Mary-le-Port Church from south-east, churchyard railings in foreground; photo 1931.	—	—	—	Source unknown.	10/40
41	St. Mary-le-Port Church, from south-east, with south churchyard.	—	—	—	Bristol Record Office postcard 98D.	117
42 MF	St. Mary-le-Port Church from south-west, after the blitz, 1940.	—	—	—	Shipley and Rankin, 1945, 22.	10/42
43	St. Mary-le-Port Church, interior, from east, after the blitz, 1940.	—	—	—	Shipley and Rankin, 1945, 22.	118
44 MF	Tower of St. Mary-le-Port Church from east-north-east; probably 1950.	—	D.o.E. B3492	—	Note facing below roof-line.	10/44

No. of Plate		Scale in photograph	Negative No.	Colour Slide No.	Source or Remarks	Page No./ MF No.
45 MF	Ditto, from north-north-west; 26.5.51.	—	D.o.E. A1272/1	—	—	10/45
46 MF	Ditto, east side below roof-line; 30.3.50.	—	D.o.E. A832/4	—		10/46
47 MF	Ditto, stair turret, from east-north-east; 30.3.50.	—	D.o.E. A832/3	—	—	10/47
48A MF	St. Mary-le-Port Church tower, east face from west; August 74.	—	D.o.E. A9213/1	—	—	10/48
48B MF	Ditto, north face from north; August 74.	—	D.o.E. A9213/2	—	—	10/48
48C MF	Ditto, west face from west; August 74.	—	D.o.E. A9213/3	—	—	10/48
48D MF	Ditto, south face from south; August 74.	—	D.o.E. A9213/4	—	—	10/48
49 MF	St. Mary-le-Port Church, south face of tower from south, with entrance to churchyard (note buttress cut-back at ground level); drawing ?late nineteenth century.	—	—	—	Bristol City Museum Mb 2968/75.	10/49
50 MF	Cellar window F138, from north.	feet	C25	—	Negative lost.	10/50
51 MF	Tower area from south-east before excavation 1962.	—	B4	—	Negative lost.	10/51
52 MF	West Cellar, south wall from north, showing two phases of wall—steps F141 in foreground.	feet	D68	—	—	10/52
53 MF	West Cellar from south-west with blocking wall F140.	feet	C32	—	—	10/53
54 MF	East Cellar from south.	feet	D42	—	—	10/54
55 MF	East Cellar, detail of chute at east side.	feet	D40	—	—	10/55
56	Angel sculpture ST 1; cf. figure 66.	inches	C16	—	—	133
57 MF	Romanesque capital ST 8; cf. figure 67.	inches	C23	—	—	10/57
58	Graveslab effigy ST 16; cf. figure 70.	inches	C21	—	—	138
59	Minety-type ware pot; cf. figure 80.107; restored in Bristol City Museum.	—	—	—	—	157
60	Breastplate 1786, CA 13; see figure 88.	—	—	—	—	168
61	Motif from coffin-lid, eighteenth century, CA 14, length 28 cm.	—	—	—	Now lost.	170
62	Grip plate, eighteenth century, CA 17; cf. figure 89.	—	—	—	—	171
63 MF	Plate from ?pew-end 1799, CA 22; cf. figure 89.	—	—	—	—	10/63
64 MF	Coffin-handle, eighteenth century, CA 15; cf. figure 90.	—	—	—	—	10/64
65 MF	Coffin-handle, nineteenth century, CA 20; cf. figure 90.	—	—	—	—	10/65
66	Breastplate, 1803, CA 21; cf. figure 91.	—	—	—	—	175
67 MF	Exhumation of a corpse, 1814, below monument of early sixteenth century (F186); monochrome copy of painting in notebook, drawn by Henry Smith.	—	—	12,678	—	10/67
68	Corpse and coffin of 1814; monochrome photo from painting.	—	—	—	Bristol City Museum M 2793 (Braikenridge).	182

2.3 List of Tables

2.4   List of Appendices

(all Microfiche only)

		MF No.
MF 14.1	List of photographs.	9/E1 – E6
MF 14.2	Church—opinions on architectural dating.	9/E7 – E10
MF 14.3	Correlation lists between former and final numbering of contexts:	
	MF 14.3.1 MLPS East.	9/E11
	MF 14.3.2 MLPS West.	9/E12 – E13
	MF 14.3.3 Church.	9/E14
MF 14.4	Equivalence lists of archival numbering and published numbers of artefacts.	9/F1 – G3
MF 14.5	Pottery, equivalence list of former and published fabrics.	deleted
MF 14.6	Detailed pottery correlation lists between former and published fabrics; also dating details:	
	MF 14.6.1 MLPS East.	9/G4 – G12
	MF 14.6.2 MLPS West.	9/G13 – 10/A7
	MF 14.6.3 Church.	10/A8 – 10/A12

2.5   Form of report

In accord with current (1983) trends, and with the policy of the Department of the Environment in its grant-aiding for publication, this report is presented in two complementary versions. This is the printed version; a much fuller version, much expanded in text, figures and plates, is appended as microfiche. The latter was written first and is the definitive text and illustration for the dedicated student. The printed version, while serving as a convenient summary of the report for the general reader, also acts as a guide and an index to the microfiche version, and it includes full contents lists. In general it does not give the full authority for many statements made, nor the detailed evidence on which they are based. It is essentially a précis, with one exception: Frances Neale's Chapter 5 is reproduced in full in the printed version with all its figures. This is because it has a wider interest than the other parts of the report, not only intrinsically for students of medieval and later Bristol, but also for its methodological interest in its use of written sources and their relation to topography and to the archaeology.

Some archaeological reports currently being produced use microfiche in a rather different way: they use it only for those parts of the report which are too long, detailed, or indigestible to go into the printed version. We believe however that the microfiche should be complete in itself, so that it can be used independently by those with readers and, if necessary, converted into a print-out. For the more general reader the printed version (with appended microfiche) is available at a price very much less than a full printed version would have cost.

In the printed version, the same numbering has been kept for chapters, divisions within the chapters, figures, plates and tables. Reference is made only to those illustrations or tables which are retained in the printed version, unless it is felt that reference to the microfiche is important in certain cases. The retention of the same numbering system means that the reader can easily refer to the same expanded version in the microfiche.

There is a danger in producing a summary report of this kind that many of the ambiguities and shades of probability become ironed out. Statements of possibility sound like facts; tenuous evidence assumes undue significance, e.g. 'evidence for leather-working' turns out to be a few off-cuts of leather and a possible tool. Readers of the printed version must be on their guard, and be hesitant in taking bold statements at their face value without reference to the full data in microfiche.

Chapter 3: Introduction

3.1 Circumstances of research

This report concerns a series of rescue excavations in the centre of Bristol in 1962 – 1963, on the north side of the river Avon, within the parishes of St. Mary-le-Port and (marginally) St. Peter. The area explored comprised the church of St. Mary-le-Port with most of Mary-le-Port Street on its north side, extending to the east as far as Dolphin Street (figure 23). The church and the street were the only areas in this part of Bristol where archaeological stratification survived. Large areas on all sides had long since been destroyed to well below the level of undisturbed bedrock as the basements of pre-Second World War stores. After wartime bombing and the subsequent clearance of rubble, these areas were made into car parks, leaving church and street isolated; the former as a derelict ruin, the latter as a raised causeway.

The eastern part of the historic centre of Bristol, comprising the Mary-le-Port area, St. Peter's Church and the Castle was, in the early 1960s, destined for redevelopment as a new museum complex for the city, with large new buildings and massive landscaping. In the event the development never took place, although some landscaping and destruction of archaeological levels did take place in later years. It was against this background that rescue excavations were arranged by Bristol City Museum, with financial support from the then Ministry of Works (now the Historic Monuments and Buildings Commission England). There had been limited excavation in the Castle area in the late 1940s, under the aegis of the 'Ancient Bristol Exploration Fund' (cf. Ponsford, 1979, 82), and, in the late 1950s, at Baldwin Street by one of the present writers (Rahtz, 1960) and at Back Hall (Barton, 1960). The Mary-le-Port excavation was however the first relatively-large-scale modern excavation in Bristol, although the quality of the work was low, and resources inadequate. Subsequently, in the later 1960s and 1970s, archaeology in Bristol was better organised and funded, leading to the extensive excavations under the auspices of the City Museum, principally under the direction of M. W. Ponsford.

Not only were the excavations important in the development of archaeology in Bristol, but also in the context of both urban and church archaeology. The major excavations in such British towns as Winchester and York were still to come; and church archaeology had hardly advanced beyond its long-established basis of art and architectural history (Rodwell, 1981, Chapter 1). Even less appreciated in the early 1960s was the importance of medieval Christian graves, a factor among others (10.10) which resulted in the low priority given to them in the Mary-le-Port excavation.

3.2 Mary-le-Port and the early history and archaeology of Bristol

Bristol is a settlement of medieval origin, but the early details of its history are still obscure, both in terms of precise dating and even of location, in spite of extensive excavation in the area of the city centre. There are no local pre-Conquest written sources, but references to Bristol do occur in the Anglo-Saxon Chronicle and in Domesday Book (Lobel and Carus-Wilson, 1975, *passim*). The principal evidence for the city's importance is numismatic; at least six moneyers were working in Bristol before the Conquest, and minting may have begun as early as the reign of Aethelred II (cf. Ponsford, 1979, Chapter III.A.1). Archaeology has complemented this evidence of activity in late Saxon times, but precise dating by decade is still elusive.

Although there are some flints from excavations (e.g. in this report, 11.3), none is from a context which might encourage belief that the spur of land between the rivers Avon and Frome was a prehistoric site of any consequence, least of all an Iron-Age promontory fort, for which its topography might seem appropriate (cf. figure 1).

Roman finds and buildings have been found in numerous places in what is now Bristol, including the recent discoveries at Greyfriars (Ponsford, undated), but there is no nucleus in the area of the ancient city which might suggest that Bristol had Roman origins; the nearest settlement or fort of any size is at Sea Mills *(Abonae)*.

Anglo-Saxon sites in the area include such well-known places as Westbury-on-Trym, Pucklechurch and Cheddar. Excavations at the latter have demonstrated the existence of structures earlier than *c.*A.D. 930

(Rahtz, 1979, Period 1); but finds, even of the tenth century, are rare. It is clear that the area was virtually aceramic before *c*.A.D. 940, and even after that pottery is sparse until the late eleventh and twelfth centuries (Rahtz, 1974). Under the circumstances it is not surprising that so few middle and late Saxon sites are known in the area. Even if Bristol did have its origins in the tenth century, which is not yet demonstrable (though likely, 12.1), it would be difficult for archaeology to prove it; precise scientific dating evidence is needed rather than the relative sequences such as those described in this report, and found elsewhere in Bristol in recent years.

Several models for the origins of Bristol have been suggested in recent years. In 1971 Walker discussed, retrospectively from the documentary evidence for the medieval period, all the factors which were favourable to its prosperity, notably its defensive position and its port; the latter especially for its Irish connections. He was nevertheless unable to explain why Bristol should have such relatively late beginnings compared with numerous other towns of Roman or later origin—notably those that formed part of the Alfredian and Edwardian urban network of the later ninth and tenth centuries.

For Walker 'the Saxon borough, which has traditionally been identified with some confidence' lay in a loop formed by the river Avon and its tributary, the Frome (1971, 6). It centred on the crossroads where the later High Cross stood and included Mary-le-Port within it. This was apparently influenced by the early archaeological investigation of this area, and one of the present writers (P.A.R.) is embarrassed by the weight Walker placed on the brief interim report on the Mary-le-Port excavations published in *Medieval Archaeology* (8(1964), 264–265) (also see Chapter 4 below). This included the suggestion that a deep deposit found in a borehole near St. Peter's Church was in a defensive ditch. This, it was suggested, formed the eastward defence of the promontory-neck site of earliest Bristol with its 'planned layout' around the crossroads, where the medieval High Cross later stood (figure 1). The north-south elements of this, in this argument, led down to Bristol Bridge, believed to be the site of the bridge after which *Bricgstow*, 'the place of assembly by the bridge' (cf. Lobel and Carus-Wilson, 1975, 2–3) was named (cf. 12.1).

In the event, this hypothesis has had to be abandoned, partly because other excavations in the area did not find any evidence of such a major ditch, but more particularly because of the discovery of extensive pre-Conquest deposits in the Castle area by Ponsford, to the east of the Mary-le-Port area (Ponsford, 1979) (see below). Some of these had already been found under the Castle eastern defences by the time that Walker wrote, but he accepted uncritically the then provisional view (influenced presumably by the strength of the tradition of the location of the earliest nucleus around High Cross and by the topography of the naturally 'moated' area (cf. Lobel and Carus-Wilson, 1975, 3)) that these discoveries represented an 'industrial suburb' (Walker, 1971, 6).

These ideas have been modified by models developed independently by M. Ponsford and F. Neale, stimulated both by more recent excavations, and by reconsideration of wider documentary sources.

Neale suggests *(in lit.)* an important explanatory model for the origins of Bristol—that it was originally a mercantile centre for the royal estate of Barton, a paired relationship similar to that of Cheddar and Axbridge (cf. Rahtz, 1979), and other palaces and burhs. She asks whether, by the early eleventh century, Bristol, on the edge of the Barton estate, had developed as a port and a market centre to such an extent that it 'overshadowed the royal base it had originated to serve'; and whether the rationale behind the siting of the subsequent Norman castle was control of the by-now significant settlement by the river crossing. Since she is looking at Bristol from the east in this context rather than from the river confluence, she too emphasises the importance of the eastern ridgeway leading into the settlement.

Excavation has enabled Ponsford to fill in some of the details about this early settlement. His excavations in the Castle area led him boldly to claim that the origins of Saxon Bristol lay here, and that the medieval crossroads were the centre of a later walled expansion to the west. These acquired, he suggested, an independent nucleation when the Castle was built, destroying much pre-Conquest property (cf. Ponsford, 1979, Chapter III.A.1; *contra* Walker, 1971, 8). This hypothesis is wholly consistent with Frances Neale's of an eastern approach into and through the town being 'shut off' by the erection of the Castle.

Discussion continues to refine these last ideas, especially about how far west Saxon settlement spread. It may have continued beyond the Mary-le-Port area, but there is as yet no evidence that it did. Mrs Neale summarises *(in lit.* 1983) the current stage of a continuing debate as:

1. The earliest, Saxon, settlement was on the narrowest part of the ridge; ?vestigial remains of a planned gridded layout associated with this survive; the bridge was possibly slightly upstream of its later position; there was possibly a wharf area around this, with Mary-le-Port on its fringes (cf. Neale, 1974). Both Mary-le-Port and St. Peter's were, in this view, within the *western* limit of the settlement.

2. The Norman Conquest resulted in a movement of the focus of the settlement westwards, with a new

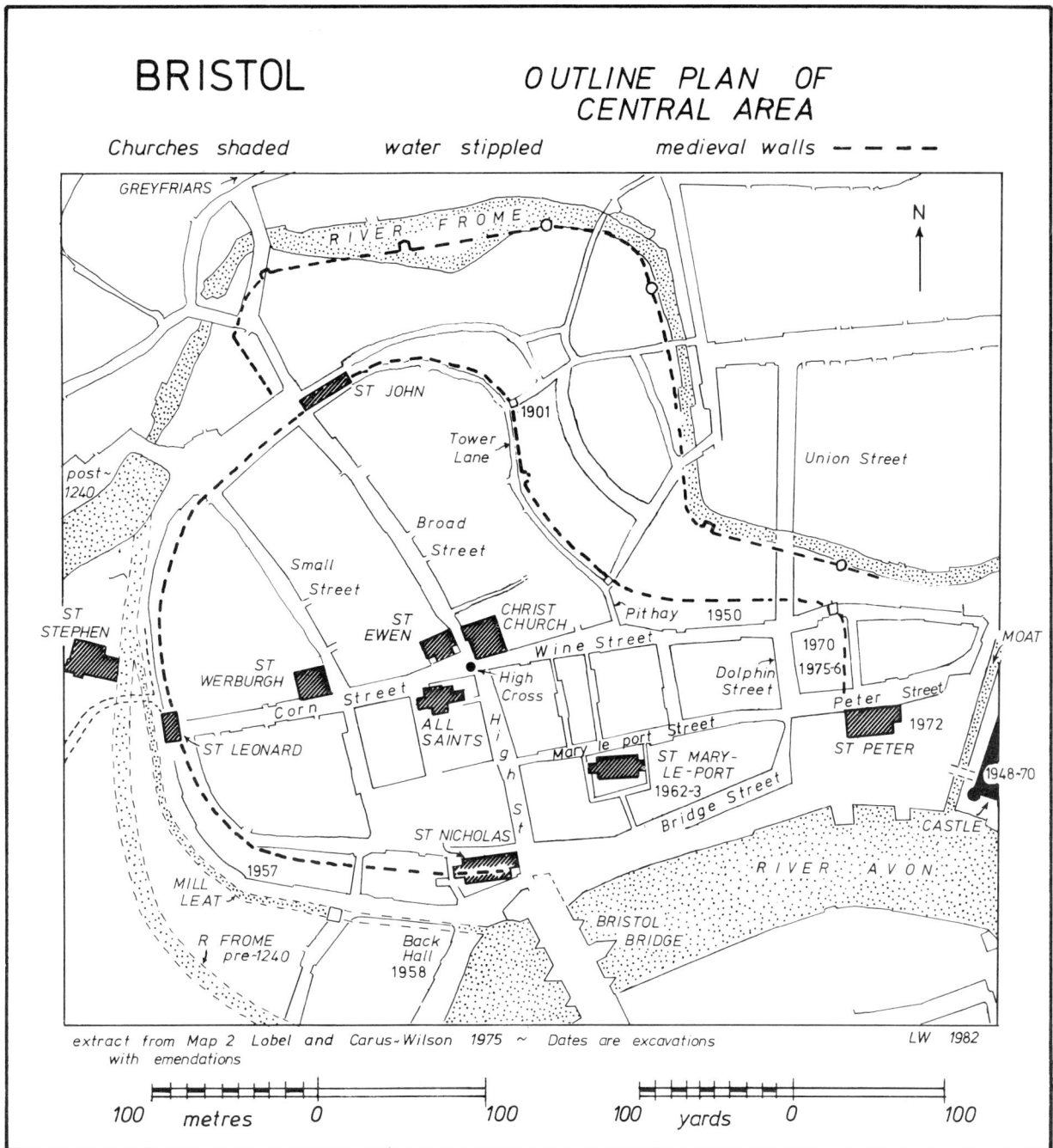

Figure 1.

symmetrical plan, the shift being necessitated by the building of the Castle; the bridge now crossed in its present position, which is clearly related to the Norman plan. Mary-le-Port was now on the *eastern* edge of the town. This sequence places Mary-le-Port on the edge of both developments.

3.   There follows the accepted sequence of various suburban developments (cf. Lobel and Carus-Wilson, 1975).

The most recent discussion on the history and topography that has been published is that in the *Atlas of Historic Towns, 2* (Lobel and Carus-Wilson, 1975). Although published too early to include the results of the important recent excavations referred to above, the text, and especially the maps, provide an accessible background to the general topographical history of Bristol, even if details have since been shown to be incorrect.

3.3   The Mary-le-Port area

The foregoing details and hypotheses are fundamental to any consideration of the origins of the Mary-le-Port site and to the dating of the structures and deposits described in the present report. They are also relevant to any wider discussion of Bristol's parish boundaries and of its churches (figure 2). Of especial interest in relation to the latter is St. Peter's, claimed in the twelfth century by the Bishop of Worcester to be the oldest church of Bristol (cf. Lobel and Carus-Wilson, 1975, 5). If Bristol did originate in the Castle area, extending westwards to High Street, then St. Peter's and Mary-le-Port would have been in the central part of the bigger area. St. Peter's may have been the church of Bristol which had three hides of land in 1086; St. Peter's is thought to have been the parish church of Barton Manor (Neale *in lit,* and Walker, 1971, 6); or was the 1086 church St. Mary-le-Port, where pre-Conquest material, possibly as early as the tenth century, and apparently earlier than the Castle area (11.10.4) has now been found? St. Peter's Church has not yet been excavated, so we do not have an archaeological data-set to compare with that from St. Mary-le-Port described in this report.

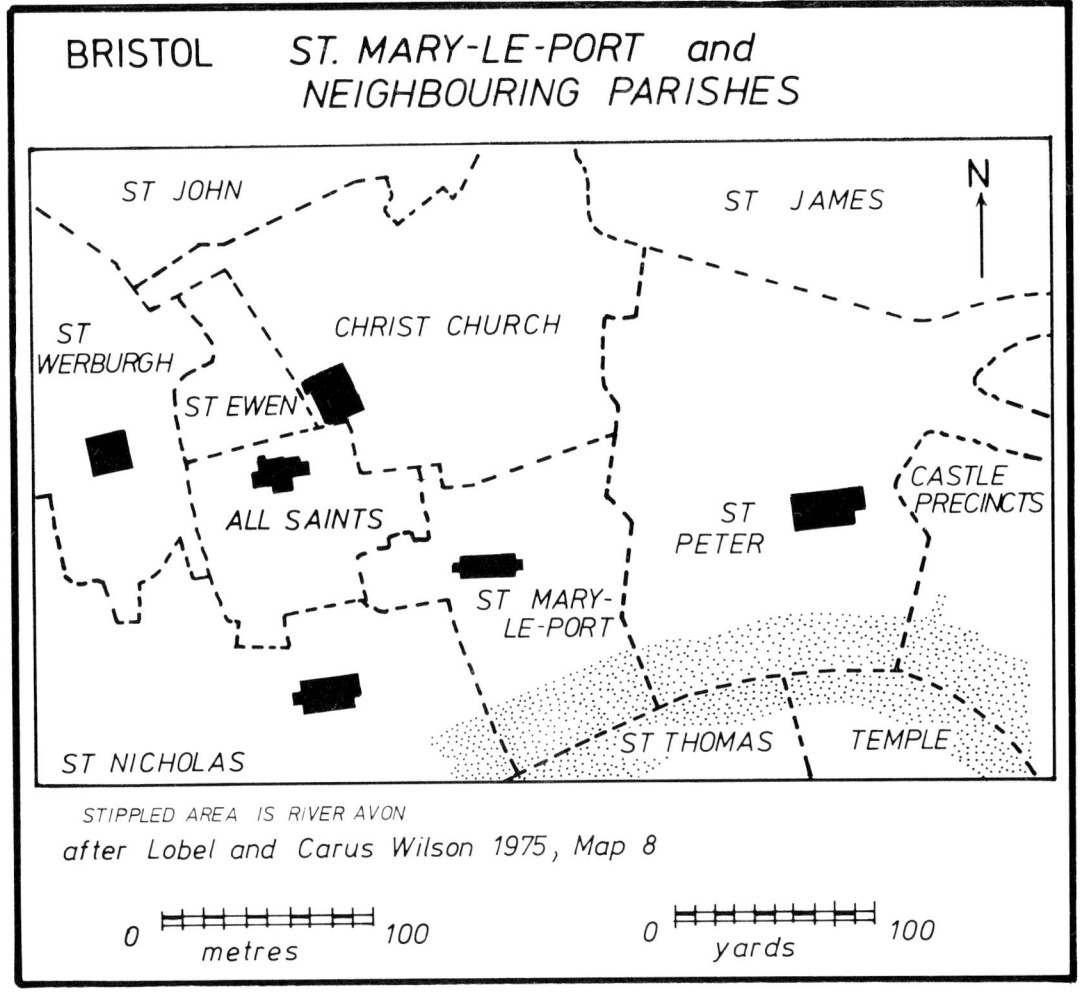

Figure 2.

The background of the history of the church of St. Mary-le-Port, its parish (figure 3), and its neighbours have been studied by Frances Neale, and her account appears in Chapter 5 below. She has also constructed a hypothetical model of the development of the church and surrounding area which can be compared with the archaeological evidence. Her delineation, in written and graphic models, of the property and street relationships (part of her wider study of Bristol) is of the greatest value. Not only does this give some flesh to the battered remains found in excavation, but it also provides in a model form (using 'model' now in a different sense) a realisation of a difficult body of material, which has been done for few other cities. Derek Keene has attempted something similar for Winchester (Keene, forthcoming) and has begun similar work in London. Sarah Croney is beginning a similar study of York (Croney, forthcoming).

3.4   St. Mary-le-Port Church

Archaeological evidence for the successive phases of the church is in general slight and of poor quality, and is confined to below-ground elements. It does nevertheless provide new evidence for the medieval development of a church which hitherto was known and studied only in its final composite state, principally of late Perpendicular style.

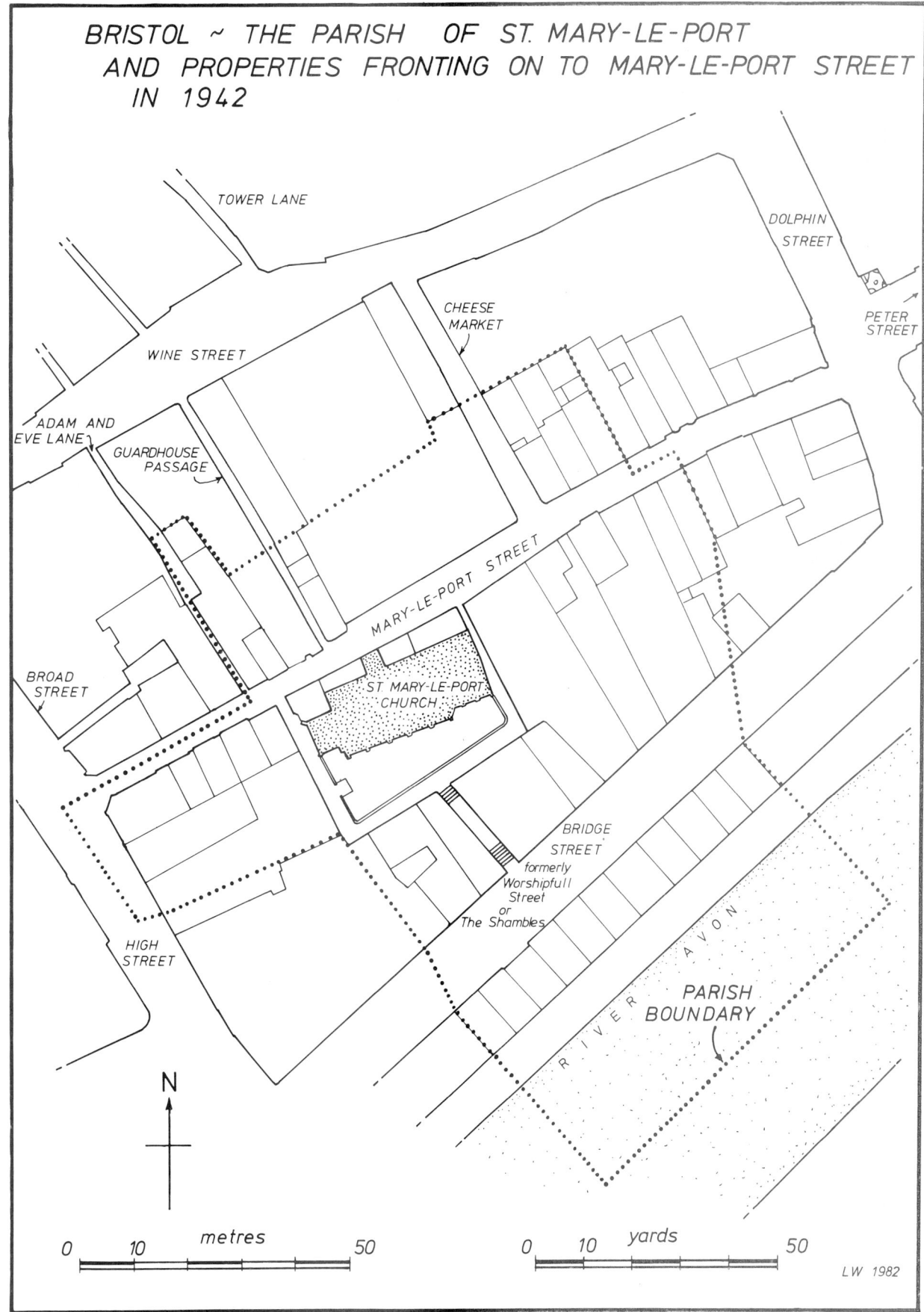

BRISTOL ~ THE PARISH OF ST. MARY-LE-PORT
AND PROPERTIES FRONTING ON TO MARY-LE-PORT STREET
IN 1942

TOWER LANE

DOLPHIN STREET

PETER STREET

WINE STREET

CHEESE MARKET

ADAM AND EVE LANE

GUARDHOUSE PASSAGE

MARY-LE-PORT STREET

BROAD STREET

ST MARY-LE-PORT CHURCH

BRIDGE STREET
formerly Worshipfull Street or The Shambles

RIVER AVON

HIGH STREET

PARISH BOUNDARY

N

0   10   metres   50

0   10   yards   50

LW 1982

Figure 3.

The latter has been partially described by numerous writers, and illustrated with greater or lesser detail in maps, engravings, and pictures (Chapter 10 below; see also Neale in Chapter 5). There are also transcriptions in secondary sources of documents, some of which were destroyed in the church in 1940, including the churchwardens' accounts (Nicholls and Taylor, 1881, II, 225 – 229). There are also descriptions of fittings, such as the great 283.5 kg. brass eagle lectern, as well as of other more permanent features such as tombs, which may be more easily related to archaeological discoveries than the movable objects. The pre-war appearance of the church is indicated in some detail by surviving faculties, drawings and photographs.

The church was partly destroyed by bombing on 24 November 1940. Photographs taken then (e.g. plate 41) show that more remained after the blitz than survived at the time of excavation. It appears that a considerable part of the walls were dismantled in the 1940s by the City Council because they were unsafe. In 1962 a 'bite' was taken out of the south wall to accommodate a corner of the new Norwich Union building (figure 45), a piece of inexcusable vandalism which typified the neglect of the archaeology and architecture of cities in Britain at that time (cf. Rodwell, 1981, Chapter 2). By the early 1960s the ruin was an overgrown mass of rubble and rubbish, with human bones dropping out of the exposed section of the churchyard by the Norwich Union. It was a daunting sight for a modern excavator with limited time and resources. After the completion of such excavation as was possible, the church was to some extent protected. The vicissitudes of Bristol's planning in subsequent years are no part of the present report. At one time the church and its surroundings were to be swept away as part of extensive clearance for the new museum! Happily it still, in 1983, survives; it has been adequately consolidated by the City of Bristol and can still yield valuable information to future archaeologists.

3.5 Acknowledgements

The excavation was initally directed by P. A. Rahtz for the then Ministry of Works and the City Museum, Bristol, but pressure of other excavations increasingly prevented his day-to-day participation; the direction gradually passed into the hands of assistant directors; Ronald Lampert (now Keeper of Anthropology at Sydney Museum) became heavily involved in the later stages, and, with Brian Arthur (then of the City Museum), did some of the initial post-excavation work. The labour force consisted of a small team of Bristol Corporation workmen, and some volunteer helpers, among whom we may single out Frances Neale, Margaret Gray and Jim Hancock for their invaluable help.

Mechanical help was provided by the City Engineer's Department for clearance of rubble and removal of the modern upper surfaces of Mary-le-Port Street and for boreholes near St. Peter's Church (4.1); workmen were used to move spoil; most of the careful digging was done by volunteers. Details of recording are given elsewhere (Chapter 6).

Other commitments (including P.A.R.'s removal to academic life) delayed the writing-up of the excavations for over a decade; in the later 1970s, Daryl Fowler began work on the report as the basis for an M.A. thesis, but ill-health and pressure of other work prevented him from making much progress with finds and records. These had by this time become very disorganised; many items had been lost, and the pottery especially had suffered by being sorted, re-sorted, and over-handled. The task of compiling the present report has been formidable. It has been undertaken by Lorna Watts, under the general supervision of P. A. Rahtz, with the help of grants provided by the Department of the Environment.

We are grateful to those whose help is acknowledged in the foregoing paragraphs, and also to the following: Alan Warhurst, then Director, Bristol City Museum; Daryl Fowler, who has made his analyses freely available to us; Helen Humphries and Frank Gardiner, for help with finds drawings; Nicholas Thomas, currently Director of Bristol City Museum, for the support of his staff and his museum facilities; Francis Neale, whose section in this report is of outstanding quality and value to students of Bristol; the specialists who have contributed to, or commented on, other sections; they are separately listed below; and to L. Biek, T. Dyson, P. Greene, J. G. Hurst and R. Morris for discussion and information.

Our best thanks must however go to Mike Ponsford, who, over several years, has given very freely of his time and expertise, and saved us from very many errors.

Specialist reports and comments have been generously provided by the following:
D. Bramwell.
Dr L. Butler, Department of Archaeology, University of Leeds.
Dr J. Casey, Department of Archaeology, University of Durham.
Dr M. D. Crane, Assistant Curator of Geology, City of Bristol Museum and Art Gallery.
D. P. Dawson, Curator of Archaeology and History, City of Bristol Museum and Art Gallery.
R. H. M. Dolley, then of the British Museum.
D. Fowler.
A. Goodall, York.

Dr I. Goodall, R.C.H.M., York.

C. E. Gowenlock, then of the Department of Chemistry, University of Bristol.

L. V. Grinsell, then of Bristol City Museum.

R. G. Jackson, Bristol.

R. H. Leech, Director of Cumbria and Lancashire Archaeological Unit.

J. Litten, Department of Prints and Drawings, Victoria and Albert Museum.

D. Moore, Department of Mineralogy, British Museum (Natural History).

F. Neale, formerly of the Bristol Record Office.

B. Noddle, Department of Anatomy, University College, Cardiff.

D. O'Connor, Department of the History of Art, University of Manchester.

M. W. Ponsford, Field Archaeologist, City of Bristol Museum and Art Gallery.

J. Rackham, D.o.E. Research Fellow, Department of Archaeology, University of Durham.

The late S. E. Rigold, then of the D.o.E.

A. Saville, of Cheltenham Museum.

J. Thornton, formerly of Department of Boot and Shoe Manufacturers, Northampton College of Technology.

D. Tweddle, Assistant Director, York Archaeological Trust.

Dr A. Vince, then of Department of Archaeology, University of Southampton.

Dr A. R. Williams, then of the Institute of Science and Technology, University of Manchester.

B. Williams, Assistant Field Officer, City of Bristol Museum and Art Gallery.

Dr D. F. Williams, D.o.E. Ceramic Petrology Project, University of Southampton.

Dr C. Wilson, then of the Centre for Medieval Studies, University of York.

C. Witt, Curator of Applied Art, City of Bristol Museum and Art Gallery.

Chapter 4: Boreholes and Mechanical Excavation in the Areas of St. Peter's Church, Bridge Street, and the Castle (figure 4)

4.1 St. Peter's Church area

In the Mary-le-Port excavations, the work on the eastern part of Mary-le-Port Street posed again the problem of the eastern boundary of the late Saxon and medieval town, believed at that time to have developed around the High Cross junction (figure 1) (cf. 3.2 and 5.2). The edge of a north-south linear feature was indeed found at the eastern limits of the excavation area, under the western pavement of Dolphin Street (8.5.1). This could not be followed under Dolphin Street itself, but the availability of a diamond-drill boring apparatus (c.50 mm. bore) enabled us in 1963 to test the stratification east of Dolphin Street, in the area around St. Peter's Church. Four years later, in 1967, the City Engineer's Department made further borings in the same area, some details of which were made available.

The results are shown diagrammatically in figure 4. The profiles indicate the depths and character of the geological strata underlying the St. Peter's area, and are presumably similar to those under St. Mary-le-Port church itself.

In most of the holes all the levels above the disturbed natural were of modern debris—the filling-up after the Second World War of cellars under bombed properties. This was done as part of a tidying-up process, but made archaeological excavation of a normal kind impractical. The profiles do indeed indicate the problems attending any future work in this area. Ponsford's subsequent work further to the north, on the other side of Peter Street, showed that far more archaeological evidence survived there (*Medieval Archaeol.* 20 (1976), 187 and 21 (1977), 242).

In general, the level of the natural, as encountered in the boreholes, has been truncated by man-made disturbances. It is likely that the original ground surface in the area was at c.18 m. above O.D. (c.60 ft. A.O.D.); it survives to this level at the east end of the Mary-le-Port Street East excavation. Elsewhere its former elevation must remain uncertain; it has been truncated by terracing, by the digging of cellars, and by a deep feature in borehole 1, which will be further discussed below. Truncation varies from 1 – 2 m. in some holes to 6 m. or more in holes 1 and 6. In the latter case, the depth was due to a deep cellar terraced down near the water frontage.

In the case of hole 1, however, an anomalous result was found: below c.2.5 m. of modern rubble and concrete, a wall was encountered—alternate layers of Pennant Sandstone and soft pink mortar—whose courses or foundation extended for over 2 m. in depth; below this was a further 2 m. or more of very dark-brown silt with animal bones and preserved twigs. It was postulated in 1963 that this lower organic fill might be the silt of a massive ditch extending north-south across the Bristol 'promontory'—a major defensive work protecting the early pre-Conquest town to the west (see 3.2 above). It was thought possible that the ditch extended under the Dolphin Street area and might be related to the north-south linear feature encountered in excavation by its west edge (see 8.5.1). It was further postulated that the massive (probably medieval) wall built above the ditch silt was a replacement of the earlier ditch line in stone, in perhaps the twelfth or thirteenth century, delimiting the town from the Castle area.

Other holes did not confirm this hypothesis. Holes 3 and 7 might have been beyond the ditch's eastern edge, and the southern part of the ditch might have begun to turn westwards before hole 2, which was relatively shallow. Subsequent holes by the City Engineer in the area of the curve of Dolphin Street did not encounter any silt or wall layers, and natural was reached at no more than 2 – 3 m. below that in Mary-le-Port Street. The hypothesis therefore appears to have been refuted; indeed subsequent work by Ponsford has cast doubt on the existence of any defensive work in this area (Ponsford, 1979). There have also been informative excavations in the area to the north of Peter Street (Boore, 1982).

Alternative explanations have therefore to be found for the anomalous stratification encountered in hole 1, and for the linear feature by the west edge of Dolphin Street. The latter will be discussed in later pages (8.5.1). Hole 1 may have encountered some localised feature, such as a well or a deep cesspit, above which a wall was later built; or did the drill penetrate slightly obliquely, cutting first through the steining of a medieval well or pit and then breaking through into its silt?

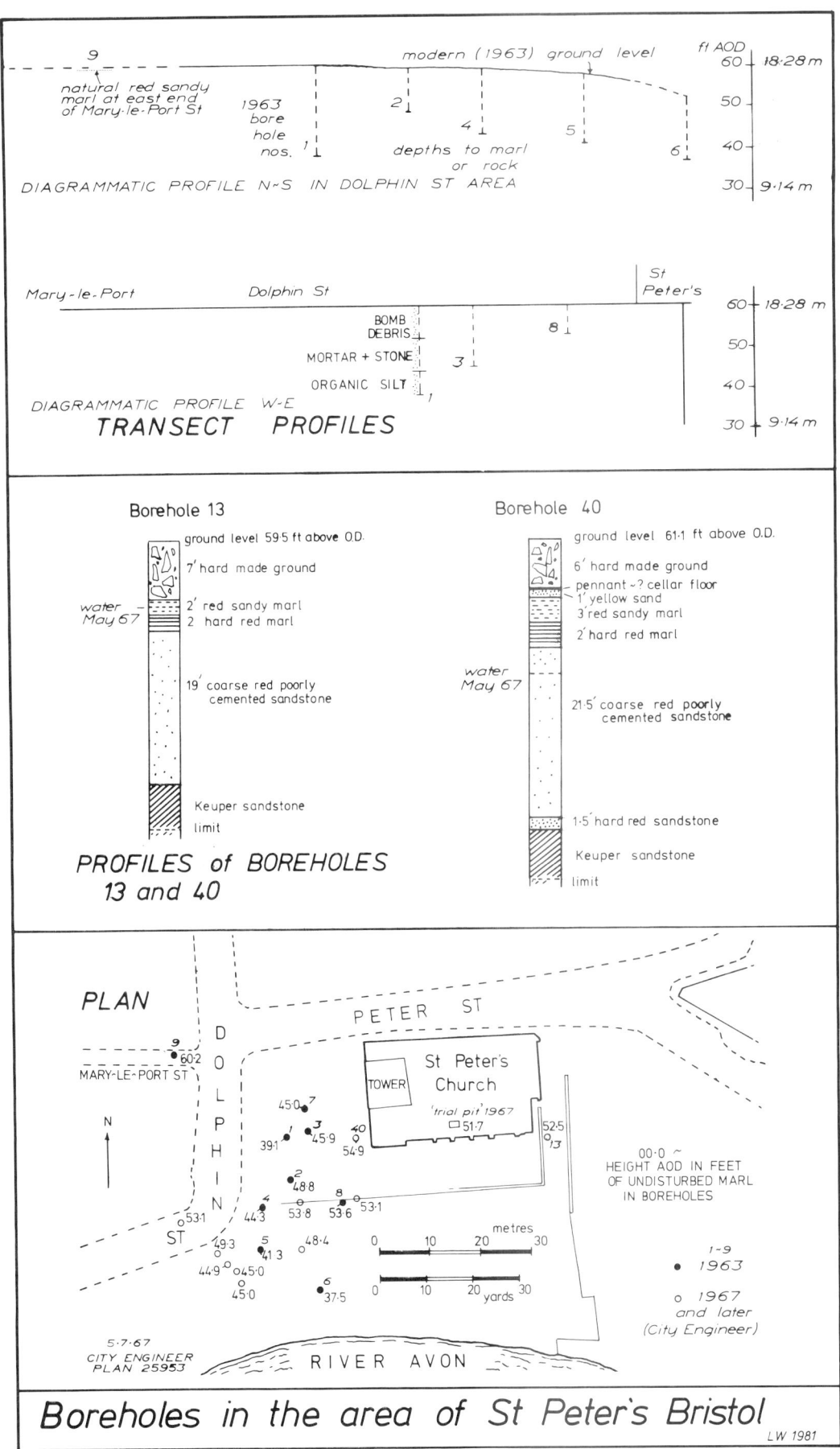

PROFILES of BOREHOLES
13 and 40

PLAN

Boreholes in the area of St Peter's Bristol

LW 1981

Figure 4.

4.2 Bridge Street

Two cuttings were made mechanically in the sloping bank between Bridge Street and Lower Bridge Street in an unsuccessful attempt to locate the line of any south town wall. A depth of 5 m. of loose brick rubble was removed but it was too dangerous to excavate below this.

4.3 The Castle area

Observations were made on the line of the southern curtain wall, but the dubious results obtained have been superseded by the later work of Ponsford in this area.

Chapter 5: The Mary-le-Port Area, Historical and Topographical Survey

by Frances Neale, B.A., A.K.C. (formerly Assistant Archivist at Bristol Record Office) (written 1969 – 1970, revised 1983)

5.1 Introduction

There has been much past theorising about the layout of early Bristol, including its streets, early church dedications, parish boundaries and their relationships with town walls. There is still, however, basic information to be deduced about the early plan of the settlement, from such clues—archaeological, physical or documentary—as survive. Correlation of all these types of evidence can make the best use of their often inevitably meagre and patchy nature. St. Mary-le-Port Church, its site, street and parish, is an intrinsic part of the central town plan. Because excavation revealed, for the first time, physical evidence of Saxon settlement and roadline, it offered a worthwhile opportunity to attempt such a correlation for this site.

The results of this attempt to match the documentary evidence with the structures and the chronological sequence of the excavation are described elsewhere in this report (Chapter 12). In addition to the documents referred to there, there are many more property deeds, especially of the fifteenth century, which relate to Mary-le-Port Street. These may, with continuing research, ultimately fit into a larger 'jigsaw' documentary reconstruction of the whole area; but at the time of writing they could not be fixed in relationship to the church or its immediate surroundings. These deeds do, however, provide a valuable, factual framework to the background history of the development of the street. The relevant documentary or other evidence has been brought together with the main archaeological phases of both church and street sites to which they relate, as 5.2 – 5.14 below. Where documentary evidence enables a discussion by topic to be made in any period, these are listed as 5.3.12a, etc.

While no examination of documentary evidence can ever be guaranteed complete, and more references may always come to light, all the appropriate manuscript sources at the Bristol Record Office have been thoroughly examined, with two exceptions, which are the post-medieval Council Proceedings and the Bargain Books—both unindexed.

5.2 Topography and history

Mary-le-Port Street, within the heart of the town of Bristol, opened off the eastern side of the High Street and extended to Dolphin Street (cf. figure 1). It ran parallel to, and south of, Wine Street, between that and the River Avon. The church was situated on the south side of the street, but not parallel to it. There was a small churchyard on the south side of the church, with an alleyway surrounding both church and churchyard and opening onto Mary-le-Port Street at either end. Various alleys linked Mary-le-Port Street with Wine Street to the north, while another connected the churchyard alleyway to Worship Street on the south side. Worship (alias Worshipfull) Street was the garbled version of an earlier street-name of uncertain origin (cf. 3.2 above and Neale 1974). By the sixteenth – seventeenth centuries it was known as The Shambles; and after the removal of The Shambles and the reconstruction of the area, it was renamed Bridge Street.[1]

The principal area excavated (figure 23) (Chapters 9 – 10) comprised the interior of the church, the wedge-shaped area of land between the north wall of the church and Mary-le-Port Street, including part of the street itself, and extended eastwards as far as the churchyard alleyway; a further area was excavated in the eastern part of Mary-le-Port Street (Chapter 8).

St. Mary-le-Port is one of the five ancient central Bristol churches (figures 1 and 2), three of which are dedicated to principal Christian figures (Holy Trinity (later Christ Church), All Saints and St. Mary), two of which have dedications of twelfth-century, or earlier, origin (St. Ewen, St. Werburgh). Three of the churches (All Saints, Christ Church and St. Ewen) are centred upon the main crossroads of High Street, Broad Street, Corn Street and Wine Street which formed the focal point of the medieval city layout (figure 1)—a layout certainly in existence by the fourteenth century. They are thus to be closely associated with a basic street plan, whatever its date of origin, by which the principal road from the bridge over the River Avon (which gave Bristol—*Bricgstow*—its name) across to the River Frome, met the east-west road along the spine of this ridge of land between the two rivers. St. Werburgh was set halfway down the western arm of this crossroads. Mary-le-Port Street, in its medieval form at least, formed a 'back lane' to Wine Street—the eastern arm—and was therefore an intrinsic part of the crossroad layout (cf. 3.2 above).

The boundaries of the parishes attached to these ancient churches are aligned not by reference to the thirteenth-century town wall, but to the natural lines of the Rivers Avon and Frome, suggesting the possibility of a pre-thirteenth-century date. These boundaries are also, in the cases of St. Ewen, Christ Church and All Saints, aligned with parts of Broad Street, Corn Street and Wine Street. It is also of interest that the eastern boundaries of St. Mary-le-Port and Christ Church parishes make an apparently deliberate alignment across the narrowest part of the neck of land between Avon and Frome (figures 1 and 2), considerably west of St. Peter's church, Dolphin Street and the disputed eastern town limits.[2] The four quadrants into which the crossroads divided the area were already established as the four secular Quarters, later the Wards, of Holy Trinity, St. Mary in Foro, All Saints and St. Ewen's as early as 1295.[3] The basic road plan is therefore an intrinsic part of both secular and ecclesiastical organisations which were fully operational by the thirteenth century and probably earlier.

On the ecclesiastical side, the existence of Mary-le-Port Street in 1245 is implied in the reference by name to the 'way of the blessed Mary',[4] and St. Ewen existed in the mid-twelfth century,[5] so that the existence of the accompanying parishes and, by implication, the other parishes and road layout might be deduced thus far back. Hitherto, however, this has marked the earliest limit of direct evidence about the layout of ancient Bristol. Some earlier authorities[6] assumed that the dedications to the seventh-century St. Ewen, bishop of Rouen, and the tenth-century Mercian princess St. Werburgh proved that the churches and thereby the settlement and its main roads were Saxon in origin. St. Ewen's, however, was founded by the Norman, Robert, Earl of Gloucester, c.1130 – 1140, and it is not unlikely that he chose a patron saint from his homeland for the dedication.[7] A case has been made that the dedication to St. Werburgh may also be of late eleventh- or early twelfth-century date; the result of a revival in the cult of that saint centred upon Chester—a port with which Bristol would have had much contact through trade.[8]

Perhaps one of the most important results of the Mary-le-Port excavations has been that physical evidence has been found of a date earlier than any documentary record; evidence both of an eleventh- or earlier twelfth-century church (and possibly an earlier one), and an eleventh-century or earlier street. We know also that a bridge must have been in existence by c.1000, from the *Aelfwerd on Bric* coin of the early eleventh century. And if one of the ancient central churches and one of the streets is eleventh century, could this imply a similar date for some of the others, closely correlated as they are? While evidence of 'Saxon' church dedications should probably be discounted, archaeological evidence for the late Saxon layout of Bristol has taken their place. Now that it has the possible backing of archaeological evidence, this basic street plan of Bristol begins to bear comparison with the grid-layout of earlier Saxon *burhs* (cf. Rahtz, 1977, figure 22) (but cf. 3.2 above).

Early references to the church of St. Mary-le-Port are invariably just to the Blessed Mary, or St. Mary in Foro (in the market place, i.e. the market within the town as opposed to Old Market, outside the walls in the Manor of Barton). The gradual appearance, c.late fifteenth century, of the term St. Mary-le-Port is therefore using 'port' in the sense of market and is not a reference to the proximity of the docks. The two terms 'St. Mary de Foro alias St. Mary le Port' continued in use, sometimes together, as late as 1690.[9]

5.3   The archaeological and historical sequence

For discussion of the archaeological data assumed here, see Chapters 7 – 10; also see chronological summary figure 24.

5.3.1   PREHISTORIC AND ROMAN
The discovery of flints and Roman finds on the site yielded potential evidence of prehistoric and Roman occupation on this site between the two rivers (cf. 11.3); see also now Boore, 1982, for further finds in the area north of Peter Street.

5.3.2   HOLLOW WAY
Sealed and protected by the later Mary-le-Port Street, a hollow way is the earliest roadway yet found within the city; there were indications of fenced properties and craft working on both sides (MLPS East and West, earliest phases, Chapters 8 – 9).

The hollow way appears to be on the same general line as the later street; it was thus the forerunner of the later Mary-le-Port 'back lane', possibly implying the existence of the other main streets as early as this one (cf. 5.2).

5.3.3 TIMBER BUILDING

The late Saxon or early Norman timber building is one of the earliest structures found in Bristol, with pottery, hearth, cesspit and iron-working residues (9.6.2).

There is other early evidence in this area from an excavation in 1950 on the north side of the street, adjoining the Cheesemarket (i.e. a little east of the 1963 site). This yielded 'Saxon' pottery from a rubbish-pit. These must have been the first possibly pre-Conquest sherds found stratified in Bristol and the writers were at that time understandably cautious about believing it.[10] There is now also further evidence from the area north of Peter Street (Boore, 1982).

5.3.4 CHURCH PHASE 1

Alongside 5.3.3 was the first possible church of St. Mary-le-Port: features of what may be a plain rectangular late Saxon/early Norman building with stone foundations (Phase 1, 10.3.1). Various implications should be noted:

(i) Why are the church and street at such a curious angle to one another? Neither is related to true east.

(ii) If St. Mary-le-Port Church and Street are of eleventh- or early twelfth-century origin, what are the implications of this for the other (a) streets, (b) churches, (c) parish layouts, the topography of which are all so closely related?

(iii) If the building of Phase 1 was a church, this would seem to contradict the theory that it was 'founded' c.1166 – 1170 by William, Earl of Gloucester (see 5.3.6).

5.3.5 STONE WALLS

The timber building went out of use; on the line of its east and north sides were built stone walls, enclosing the north-east corner of the northern churchyard (9.6.3).

5.3.6 CHURCH PHASE 2, TWELFTH CENTURY

This was the first definite church; if the features of Phase 1 do represent a church, this is an enlargement of it, in sub-phases 2A and 2B (Phase 2, 10.3.2 – 2B).

The church of Phase 2 could be contemporary with the grant of St. Mary-le-Port Church by William, Earl of Gloucester, to Keynsham Abbey which he founded c.1166 – 1170.[11] The chief authority for the foundation and endowment of the abbey is a confirmation of 1318[12] but a payment out of St. Mary-le-Port certainly appears among the endowments of the abbey in 1291, as does the church of St. Werburgh.[13] Earlier authorities[14] have tended to attribute the actual foundation of the church to William as well, but this need not have been the case.

5.3.7 PAVING OF HOLLOW WAY, THIRTEENTH CENTURY OR LATER

The hollow way was filled up, sealed and paved with substantial cobbles (basically becoming the street which survived until 1940) (MLPS East and West, later phases, Chapters 8 – 9).

5.3.8 CHURCH PHASE 3, THIRTEENTH CENTURY

The church was enlarged; north and ?south aisles were added (Phase 3, 10.3.3). The north aisle was presumably well provided with windows; this would assume that, at the time of their construction, the space between the church and street (in the main excavation area, MLPS West) must have been open and free from buildings (cf. 5.3.12, 13).[15]

5.3.9 WINDOW OF A STONE ?HOUSE, LATE THIRTEENTH CENTURY (10.3.3d)

A late thirteenth-century stone window frame (found re-used in a later cellared property, see below) may have been from a stone house in the area; or it may have come from the Phase 3 church.

(i) These archaeological phases indicate that the area is changing in character. The shift from unmade to cobbled roads, for example, reflects increasing local prosperity and status. It is surely not a coincidence that in 1245 (i.e. about one generation after these developments might be supposed to have gained momentum) the first document for the area survives.

(ii) In 1245 William son of Henry Langbord leased Walter de Panes a shop in the way of the Blessed Mary, next to the shop of his brother Henry Langbord.[16] The lease does not give any details that can be plotted on the ground; it is, however, the first documentary proof of the existence of Mary-le-Port Street; it indicates a street with shops, and a local family of sufficient standing to own two of them. No trades are given; but Henry Langbord the father was a burgess of Bristol; and Henry Langbord the brother appears as a Moneyer in the 1248 writ issued to Bristol for minting the new Henry III long-cross coinage.[17] Robert de Kylmeynam, one of the witnesses of this deed and a reeve of Bristol, was a Custodian of the Mint under the same writ (there spelt Kilmain), suggesting prosperous local connections. Such documentary details support the archaeological evidence of improvements to the area.

(iii) The appearance of the 'church of St. Mary' in the Taxatio Ecclesia of 1291, and of the St. Mary in Foro Quarter in 1295,[18] confirm the existence of both the ecclesiastical and secular administrative units by this time.

5.3.10 CHURCH PHASE 4, LATER FIFTEENTH CENTURY

Further improvements were made to the church, including the rebuilding of the chancel and the construction of the tower at the west end (Phase 4, 10.3.4).

5.3.11 CELLARED PROPERTY

A cellared property was built into the north-east corner and later integrated with the church (Phase 4, 10.3.4).

There is a possibility that this house may have been the parsonage (cf. 5.3.13).

5.3.12 CHURCH PHASE 5, EARLY SIXTEENTH CENTURY

The north arcade was rebuilt, together with the north aisle, any south aisle was demolished, and a new south wall to the church was built (Phase 5, 10.3.5). Part of the cellar of the house (5.3.11) was filled in. The eastern part was retained and indeed continued in use until the twentieth century, latterly as a stoking room (East Cellar, 10.7).

The fourteenth – sixteenth centuries see a steady increase in the quantity of documentary evidence which refers to Mary-le-Port Street, mostly in the form of original or enrolled property deeds, and some wills. A study of these documents has, however, revealed two major limitations:

(i) That property ownership in Mary-le-Port Street was divided up among a wide variety of owners: numerous private individuals, the Abbey of St. Augustine's and the Chapel of the Assumption on Bristol Bridge. The feoffees of St. Mary's and St. Peter's parishes acquired a few properties. The Corporation only seems to have acquired two properties, traceable from the eighteenth century only, on the north side of the street. One individual sometimes owned several houses scattered along the street. This mixed ownership has prevented the survival of any sufficient block or sequence of deeds, rentals or surveys which might enable lengths of the street to be reconstructed at any one period. The fragmentary plotting of buildings that has been possible is dealt with as Appendix A, and the greater part of the documentary evidence is therefore here used as general background to the archaeological remains, as it cannot be correlated exactly with them.

(ii) In addition, the wedge-shaped area of land between the north wall of the church and the street, upon which excavation was concentrated, was an open unbuilt space throughout this period. The presumed windows of the north aisle have already assumed this (5.3.8). It is also reflected by the fact that not one document makes any reference to buildings abutting against the church; no document can be related to the building with any degree of certainty. The first buildings on this area are not recorded until the seventeenth century. Prior to this it was used as part of the churchyard; the burials found here (5.3.13) must ante-date the seventeenth-century buildings (cf. 9.10). The larger area of ground south of the church served as the principal churchyard. Several properties are described as backing onto, or situated next to, the churchyard,[19] but in practically every case these properties either front onto Worship Street or are associated with other properties that do so, indicating that the churchyard concerned is the main one to the south of the church and outside the excavation area. Only one deed,[20] of 1394, describes a row of premises including shops and a garden, fronting onto 'Saint Maristrete' and flanked on one side by the cemetery of that church; this could therefore be a reference to the northern burial ground area, although whether the property lay to the east or west side of it is not clear. Because this was an open space and a church burial ground, none of the surviving property documents of this period relate to this particular area of ground. One will of 1471 refers to property 'opposite the church'.[21]

The documents of the fourteenth – sixteenth centuries do serve, however, to give considerable background detail, placing the Phase 4 cellared property (5.3.11) in its setting of the rest of the developing street; and showing the alterations to the church (5.3.10 – 12) as a reflection of its prosperous parishioners. This background material is here treated by subjects, and the fragmentary plotting of buildings is described separately (Appendix A, p. 36ff).

5.3.12a BUILDING AND DEVELOPMENT: DOCUMENTS

Perhaps most noticeable is the fact that from 1304 onwards,[22] properties in Mary-le-Port Street are always flanked on both sides by other buildings, never by open spaces; the only exception is the deed of 1394 referred to above, which mentions the cemetery. There are a few references to new buildings, as in 1387 when a property on the corner of the High Street is situated between tenements and shops of William Somerwell in St. Mary-le-Port Street and a messuage (presumably fronting High Street) 'lately built' by Hugh Carleton,[23] or later in 1460 when the feoffees of St. Peter's parish leased to William Clerk, merchant, a new tenement' in St. Mary-le-Port Street.[24] There is, however, no indication whether these were the first buildings on their respective sites or merely replacements. More meaningful is the total disappearance of any mention of gardens after the fourteenth century. In 1387 a rent of assize of twelve silver pence was payable out of a garden in St. Mary-le-Port Street[25] and in 1394 two shops and a garden stood on the south side of the street.[26] With the fifteenth century, in contrast, except for one reference in 1433 to a messuage backing on 'a certain open place of the land of John Berton behind',[27] all properties are hemmed in on three sides by other houses.

5.3.12b   BUILDING AND DEVELOPMENT: MAPS

This is certainly the impression of the area given by Robert Ricart in his map of Bristol drawn in 1479[28] (plate 2)—a map which, despite some medieval fantasy, contains much precise and vivid detail. The area

Plate 2.   Ricart's 'Bristol', 1479, enlarged area of Mary-le-Port.

east of High Street is close-packed with houses, through which pokes a small church tower. The tower (A on plate 2) is almost lost behind two fairly large buildings (B and C), either of which might be intended as the church; both have bellcote-like structures on their roof, but it is the one further from the tower (C) which appears to have the lead-sheet roofing characteristic of churches and other important buildings on Ricart's map, so this point remains unsolved (cf. 10.3.4b). The houses have tiled roofs, jettied upper storeys (indicated by a double line) and, in some cases, tall chimneys. In contrast it is more difficult to know how far to trust either William Smith's map of Bristol in 1568 or Hoefnagle's in 1581;[29] the former is on a very tiny scale, and the latter contains many obvious inaccuracies in the representation of known buildings. Smith gives the impression of a wholly built-up area around St. Mary-le-Port, whereas Hoefnagle shows gardens in the centre of the blocks of houses. Both show an alley running straight past the west end of the church, south to Worship Street, in place of the churchyard alley with its right angles. The disadvantage of all these maps, together with that of Millerd in 1673 (see 5.3.13) is that, being 'oblique views', the elevation of St. Mary-le-Port Church itself effectively obscures the site of the excavation.

5.3.12c BUILDING CONSTRUCTION
The houses themselves might be most typically illustrated by a 1472 building contract[30] for a house in the High Street nearby. The timber-framed building, on a site 10 ft. 4 in. (3.15 m.) wide and 19 ft. 5 in. (5.92 m.) deep, was to consist of a shop, a hall above with an oriel window, a chamber above the hall also with an oriel window; and another room above that. Prints of Mary-le-Port Street show numerous four- or five-storey jettied, timber-framed buildings on a similar narrow 10 ft. (3.05 m.) frontage, mainly of sixteenth – seventeenth-century date but continuing this late fifteenth-century building tradition.

5.3.12d SHOPS
Mary-le-Port Street was a street of shops throughout its documented history, from the first recorded pair owned by the Langbord brothers in 1245. William Somerwell had a tenement, a messuage and five shops all adjoining each other, in 1388,[31] and thereafter shops are frequently mentioned. William King held at least four shops in St. Mary-le-Port Street in 1394,[32] two of which he sold to James Cokkes. James Cokkes in turn, by his will of 1423,[33] owned seven messuages and six shops in the street, in which he also mentions a stable. Thomas Frome, selling a messuage to Hugh Escote in 1412,[34] is the first to specify that it had a shop *in front,* but probably this was usually taken for granted. The deeds of a messuage 1443 – 1446[35] are the first to describe it as having a shop in front and a cellar below.

5.3.12e CELLARS
Such cellars were a feature of the area; some still survive under High Street, by the Norwich Union Building. They were described in 1480 by William Worcestre who, in listing the 'vaults, arches and cellars made of stone and roofed with boards and timbering', noted that 'in Seynt Marye Port-strete on either side of the road are 15 vaults and cellars'.[36] The vaulted cellar excavated (5.3.11) would have been one of these.

5.3.12f ROADS
William Worcestre also gives a street measurement involving St. Mary-le-Port Street, of '560 gressus'.[37] Taking a 'step' as measuring two feet, heel to toe, and equal to approximately 21 in.[38] (53 cm.), this gives a length of 326 yds. 2 ft. (298.7 m.). The measurement is in fact 'from the inner side of Newgate past the keep of Bristol and past the church of St. Peter and St. Mary de la Port', which, as a combined measurement along Peter Street and St. Mary-le-Port Street together, does give the correct length. About ten years later, in 1491, Ricart's Kalendar records that 'This yere dyvers stretes in Bristowe were new paved' including 'Seynt Mary Strete'.[39]

5.3.12g CHURCH
William Worcestre, that inveterate measurer of Bristol, also estimated, c.1480, that 'the church of St. Mary de Port contains with its tower in length 60 steps'[40]—a length of 35 yds. (32 m.) which agrees closely with the 35 yds. 1½ ft. (32.50 m.) internal length of the Phase 4 church. Any improvements to the church in the fifteenth century might be equated with bequests made by its prosperous parishioners, such as James Cokkes who in 1423 left monetary bequests both to the rector and to the fabric of the church.[41]

The first known reference to a chapel of St. Katherine is in the will of Martin Boucher in 1411, in which he expresses his wish 'to be buried in the chapel of St. Katherine in the church of St. Mary-le-Port'.[42] It is again mentioned in the will of Adam Inhyne, 27 January 1418/19; he is to be 'buried before the altar of St. Katherine in St. Mary-le-Port, beside his late wife Maud'.[43]

William Innyngh in 1447 left property on the Weir,[44] and John Innynge in 1457 granted shops and property in Bear Lane, to the church,[45] both making further references to the chapel of St. Katherine in the church. In 1451 Alice Escote had left a messuage in Mary-le-Port Street itself to feoffees of the church.[46]

A chapel of the Mayden Uncumbre, otherwise called Wilgeforte is mentioned in the will of John Newman; in 1518 he gave the rent of his house in The Shambles to provide an *obit* in this chapel which had just been built.[47] St. Uncumber is the English name for this saint who was the daughter of a king of Portugal, where she was known as Wilgefortis. The story told of her is that she took a vow of virginity, and when her father desired her to marry the King of Sicily, in self-defence she grew a beard and her wooer promptly withdrew.[48]

5.3.12h INDIVIDUAL HOUSES

Of houses in Mary-le-Port Street to leave any individual record, three were inns. The Repersynne (John Culver, hosteler) existed at the back of one property *c.*1443 – 1446,[49] but whether to the north or south side of the street is not clear. The Cardinal's Hat stood second from the west in a row of six houses in 1460, noted as being 'opposite the church' in 1471.[50] The Swan first appears in 1463[51] and again in 1579 – 1580[52] although it is impossible to make sense of the compass points of the latter, since The Swan can be securely located on the south side of[53] Mary-le-Port Street, at its east end on the corner of Dolphin Lane, where it stood unaltered until its demolition in 1936; it seems to have been the only building in the street to retain much of its fifteenth-century exterior fabric.[54] Of the other houses, the earliest reference is to the messuage called 'Le Thorowhowse' which stood in Mary-le-Port Street between Richard Shirwyn's stable and a house occupied by Robert Haselwell, turner, and which James Cokkes left to his younger son John in 1423.[55] This stood on the north side of the street, since in 1480 William Worcestre describes 'The way called le through-hows in the centre of the way of Wynch-strete, by Haddon-tanerie to the way of Seynt Mary port-strete' as being 90 steps (52½ yds.) (48 m.) in length (almost precisely the length of Adam & Eve Lane, Guardhouse Passage or the Cheesemarket: cf. Ashmead's Plan of Bristol, 1828—cf. figure 21) and four steps (7 ft.) (2.13 m.) wide 'in the centre of the way'.[56] In 1491 – 1492 and 1511 – 1512 there was a somewhat mysterious 'house called Seynd' or 'Seind' over against the churchyard, next to which was an accessway for use of which the churchwardens of St. Mary-le-Port paid St. Augustine's Abbey 2*s.* per annum.[57] Unfortunately, there are really no grounds to justify identifying this with the house in the north-east angle of the church (5.3.11 – 12) and the churchyard alleyway adjoining it; it could just as well refer to the southern, main churchyard. Thirdly, and also of fifteenth – sixteenth-century date, a house on the south side of Mary-le-Port Street, west of the church and about 65 ft. (19.81 m.) from the High Street corner, which later became nos. 44 – 45, contained an elaborate plaster ceiling and a magnificent stone chimneypiece with the Cordwainers' Arms upon it.[58] J. E. Pritchard, reporting this when the building was demolished in 1920, suggested that since there were no personal coats of arms on the chimneypiece, it might have been the hall of the Bristol Cordwainers' Company. In this connection, there were a remarkably high proportion of shoemakers and cordwainers working in the street in the seventeenth century (see 5.3.13e below). William Worcestre (1480) also makes a somewhat obscure reference[59] to 'three fine houses of great height called le Saynt Mary port with deep vaults arched over with stone down below', and about 40 steps (just over 23 yds. (21.03 m.) in length); but since he adds that the distance from The Shambles to the entrance into the three houses was only 18 yds. (16.46 m.), they must have been situated in the vicinity of the south churchyard.

5.3.12i PEOPLE: OCCUPATIONS AND STATUS

The chief impression made by the owners and tenants of property in Mary-le-Port Street is that of an extremely mixed community, in no way segregated by class or trade as has been suggested elsewhere in the city. In this they bear a close resemblance to the Lower Brook Street, Winchester, community with merchants and artisans living alongside one another.[60] William Somerwell (holding property *c.*1386 – 1388),[61] James Cokkes (ditto *c.*1394 – 1423)[62] and the Escote family (ditto *c.*1395 – 1451)[63] were persons of substance and the last two at least would appear to have lived in their Mary-le-Port properties. Other property-holders included Maurice de Berkeley in the fourteenth century,[64] Dame Joan Brooke in 1423,[65] John and Robert Poyntz in 1451 – 1471 and in 1517,[66] Thomas and John Aldworth in 1562.[67] Merchants appear frequently: Thomas Berkeley in 1443 – 1446,[68] John Sherpe and William Clerk in 1460,[69] William Joce in 1463,[70] Thomas Kempe in 1553,[71] Nicholas Shee in 1557,[72] George Snigge senior in 1575,[73] and Philip Langley in 1584.[74] At the same time, between 1423 and 1584 the surviving records list a turner, a currier, a baker, four brewers, two tailors, a haberdasher, a shoemaker, a draper, a plumber and a mercer.[75]

5.3.13 NORTH BURIAL GROUND, PRE-1648; AND SEVENTEENTH – EIGHTEENTH CENTURIES

The area north of the north aisle and that in the angle between the chancel and the north aisle were used as a burial ground. Minor repairs were made to the church, but no structural alterations.

The first documents which relate directly to the wedge-shaped area of ground between the north wall of the church and Mary-le-Port Street are dated 1664; they refer back to the erection of the first building on this ground *c.*1648. The burials in this area should thus be dated as prior to 1648.

5.3.13a BUILDINGS: LOCATION

In June and August 1664 the Bishop of Bristol, the patron, and the incumbent of St. Mary-le-Port issued two leases, to John Gamlen, cordwainer,[76] and to Elizabeth Stretton, widow,[77] respectively, of the properties which had been built on hitherto 'void ground', 'about sixteen years since during the recent usurpation', i.e. c.1648, when the living had fallen vacant. One area of void ground had originally been leased to Gamlen and to James Sharpe, flax-dresser, who had erected several buildings on it; but by 1664 these 'said severall buildings' were 'all reduced into and used as one Messuage', then occupied by Edward Pierce, cordwainer. It was this house and ground which was leased by Gamlen himself in 1664. The parsonage and another area of void ground, described more precisely as adjoining the parsonage and extending from the church porch to the upper (i.e. eastern) end of the church, had originally been leased, c.1648, to Elizabeth Stretton's father, Thomas Harris, brewer. He built two tenements on the open area; and by 1664 the ex-parsonage and these other two houses were occupied by two grocers, an ironmonger and a tailor. These two leases provide documentary evidence of the first erection, in the seventeenth century, of buildings against the north wall of the church, eventually blocking its windows (cf. 9.12). The church porch opened from the centre of the north wall onto Mary-le-Port Street. Thomas Harris's plot must therefore have been on this north side of the church, extending east from the porch to the end of the church itself, and to the churchyard alley. This in turn suggests that the parsonage which they adjoined may well have been the surviving part of, or on the site of, the medieval building (5.3.11) in the north-east angle of the church. No other reference to the whereabouts of the parsonage has been found; and if it in fact went out of use in the seventeenth century, this would form part of a typical pattern of reorganisation which occurred in many other city parishes in the seventeenth – eighteenth century. By the time detailed directories appear, in the nineteenth century, the incumbent of St. Mary-le-Port is established in Berkeley Square, Clifton.[78] Gamlen's building plot is less precisely described; but the two 1664 leases are so similar that it would seem reasonable to suggest that it was the other half of the wedge-shaped area, to the west of the church porch. This is the smaller, narrower half of the wedge which would seem in keeping with the smaller property and single occupant of 1664.

5.3.13b BUILDINGS: APPEARANCE

These seventeenth-century buildings became nos. 38 – 42 Mary-le-Port Street, and their subsequent history can be traced through prints, photographs and directories.[79] Nos. 38, 39 and 40 were to the east of the church porch, and nos. 41 and 42 to the west; but 40 – 41 in fact formed one triple-gabled building that completely straddled and enclosed the church porch. No. 39 had been demolished by the 1890s, but the other houses remained as handsome five-storeyed jettied half-timbered buildings, steeply gabled, and with impressive bay windows. Nos. 38 and 40 (those, significantly, built by Thomas Harris, brewer, c.1648) carried armorial bearings of the Brewers' Company on their frontages; a carved stone chimneypiece with these same arms existed in no. 19, on the north side of the street between Cheesemarket and Dolphin Lane.[80]

5.3.13c MAP

The other principal source of evidence for the area in the seventeenth century is Millerd's map of Bristol in 1673 (plate 3). Its pictorial layout unfortunately hides the north side of the church; the accuracy of some details is questioned below, especially in relation to the south aisle (10.3.5a). Its general impression of the area is however useful. The churchyard alleyway separates the church and its ground from the neighbouring houses. Except for the churchyard on the south side of the church, the area is entirely built up. On the south side of Mary-le-Port Street, the houses are close packed, gable-end to the street, with the exception of the larger Swan Inn on the corner of Dolphin Street. On the north side of Mary-le-Port Street, however, there would seem to be a slightly more spacious layout, with some houses presenting wider frontages to the street. A courtyard, surrounded by a covered way between Mary-le-Port Street and Wine Street and opening into the latter, is identified as the Meat Market; the alley between Wine Street and Mary-le-Port Street which was later known as Cheesemarket, is shown but not named. An unknown number of houses on the north side are obscured by the church tower; but the numbers of houses shown east and west of the church, on the south side of Mary-le-Port Street, in 1673, correspond remarkably closely to the numbers indicated on Ashmead's plan of 1828 (cf. figure 21) and in later directories. East of the church in 1673 are shown six houses and the larger Swan. Ashmead shows twelve properties; but of these, the directories show that at least two constituted the former Swan premises and that eight others were at times held as pairs—i.e. in all probability being only four buildings—giving, again, a total of six buildings plus the Swan. West of the church, Millerd shows three houses, of which the westernmost faces into High Street. In 1828 Ashmead shows four properties and this is borne out by later directories, no. 46 on the corner often having several occupants: a discrepancy of only one building.

5.3.13d DEEDS: PLOTTING

The two leases of 1664 are the only surviving documents that appear to be located with certainty in the area of the excavation (cf. 5.3.13a). The problems of mixed, scattered ownership and of consequent

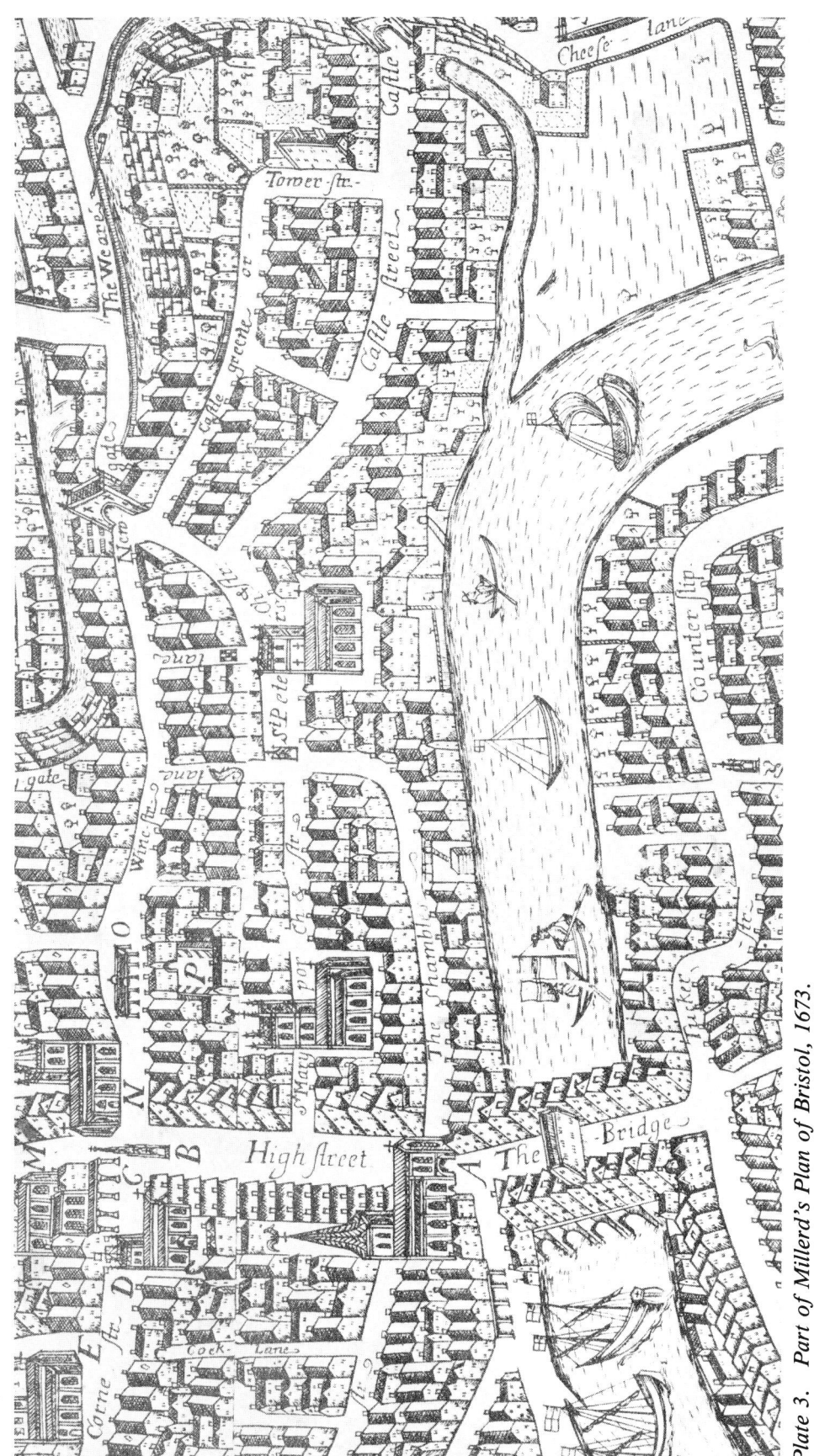

Plate 3. Part of Millerd's Plan of Bristol, 1673.

fragmentary topographical information which were found in 5.3.10 – 12, apply equally to this later phase: for which, in fact, fewer deeds seem to have survived. This fragmentary information is therefore collected separately, as Appendix B (p. 44ff).

5.3.13e OCCUPATIONS
Seventeenth-century deeds do, however, continue to add information about the nature of the street. Its character obviously changes, from the medieval community of mixed status, to a street of small artisans. Between 1664 and 1680 only one merchant, John Walter, is recorded;[81] otherwise there are six shoemakers or cordwainers, seven involved in the food trades (five grocers, a baker and a butcher), and one apiece of seven miscellaneous trades: ironmonger, tailor, cook, bodicemaker, flaxdresser, apothecary and buttonmaker.[82] The back-references to c.1648 in the 1664 leases would add a brewer and a second flaxdresser. The high proportion of shoemakers and cordwainers adds interest to the discovery of the stone chimneypiece decorated with the Cordwainers' Arms, in an elaborate room at nos. 44 – 45[83] (cf. 5.3.12h).

5.3.13f EARLY EIGHTEENTH-CENTURY DEEDS
Eighteenth-century documents are meagre, but continue to show a crowded street of small shopkeepers. The Olive Tree stood on the north side of the street towards its eastern end, and the Three Pigeons somewhere on the south side, both in 1708.[84]

5.3.13g EIGHTEENTH-CENTURY MAP
John Rocque's map of Bristol in 1742 shows the area in a simplified form that does not add much new information. Adam & Eve Lane, The Guard House, and the Corn [sic] Market link Mary-le-Port Street to Wine Street. A lane is shown linking the south-west corner of the churchyard alleyway to the High Street; this does not appear on other maps.

5.3.14 NINETEENTH – TWENTIETH CENTURIES
Late eighteenth- and early nineteenth-century brick burial vaults were constructed beneath the church, destroying most of the levels within the building, but leaving sufficient small undisturbed areas between to make possible the archaeological interpretation of the earlier church structures. An extensive restoration of the church took place in 1877 (10.3.6).

Ashmead's Plan of Bristol in 1828 (cf. figure 21) shows the area in great detail, with indications of individual properties along the street frontage. These can be matched with the nineteenth- and twentieth-century directories so that the street can be reconstructed from c.1860 onwards. The two sources together show that the site to the north of the church, between the two ends of the churchyard alleyway, was occupied by nos. 38 – 42; the cellar to the west of the church porch would have belonged to no. 41 (see Appendix C, p. 48ff).

In 1864 no. 38 is not mentioned, but no. 39 was occupied by S. and C. Nosworthy; no. 40 by Harris; no. 41 by P. Bevan, brushmaker, and no. 42 by S. Bennett. By 1868 Eliza Trapnell, hosier and draper, had taken no. 39 and the Lamb, prop. R. J. Cowderoy, was at no. 42. In 1870 J. Jones & Co., brushmakers, occupied no. 38; Eliza Trapnell was still at no. 39; J. E. Tucker, baker and confectioner, was at no. 40, while Bevan and Cowderoy still held nos. 41 and 42. By 1901 Jones, the brushmakers, had taken over both nos. 38 and 39. H. Leonard's Progressive Boot Company owned no. 40; J. Walklate, chemist, was in no. 41, and Mills and Jewell, fruiterers and fishmongers, were at no. 42. The occupants and usage of each individual building can be traced in this way right up to the outbreak of the Second World War. In 1937 only Jones & Co., brush-factors, remained, of the older shops, at nos. 38 – 39; Mrs E. Haynes was at no. 40; Campbell's, wallpapers, at 41, and J. F. Liddington, confectioner, at no. 42.

The end of the area came in November 1940, when the body of the church and nos. 38 and 42 were totally destroyed by enemy action, and the rest of the street subsequently demolished.

5.4 Appendix A Fourteenth – Sixteenth Centuries (figure 5)

Schedule of references, with plans where appropriate, to properties in Mary-le-Port Street.

As with the other appendices, the latest-known occupants are nearest the street frontage; the progressively earlier occupants further from the frontage, within each property. Where, however, the side of the street is unknown, the latest occupants are at the top of the diagram and earlier ones towards the bottom.

Name in CAPITALS are the owners; Names (thus) are of lessees or other occupants. Mortgagors and attornies are omitted.

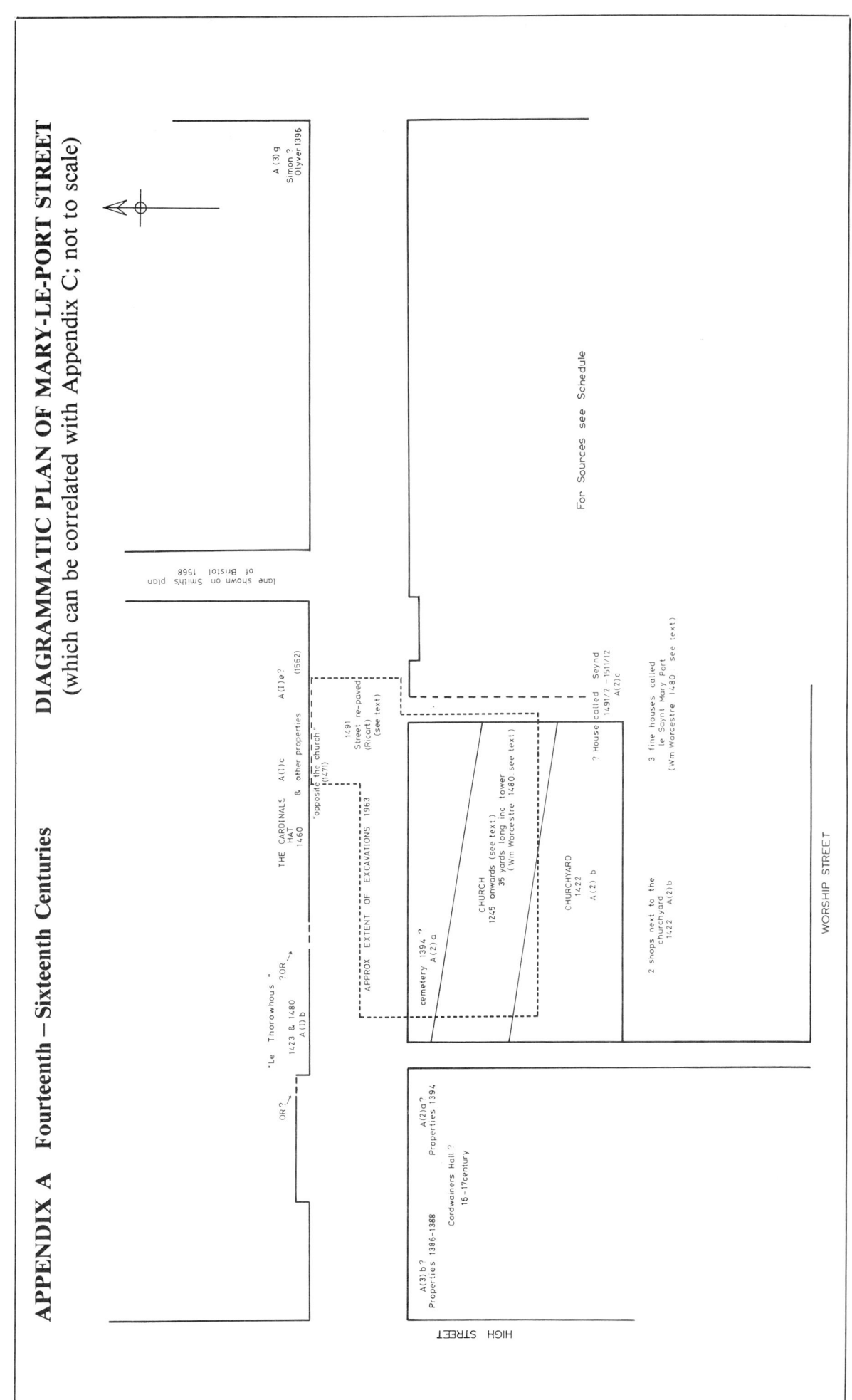

APPENDIX A   Fourteenth – Sixteenth Centuries

DIAGRAMMATIC PLAN OF MARY-LE-PORT STREET
(which can be correlated with Appendix C; not to scale)

A (3) g
Simon ?
Olyver 1396

lane shown on Smiths plan
of Bristol 1568

THE CARDINALS   A(1)c
HAT   & other properties
1460

A(1)e?
(1562)

"opposite the church"
†(1471)

1491
Street re-paved
(Ricart)
(see text)

? House called   Seynd
1491/2 – 1511/12
A(2)c

3 fine houses called
le Saynt Mary Port
(Wm Worcestre 1480 see text)

"Le Thorowhous"
?OR →
1423 & 1480
A(1) b

OR ? →

APPROX EXTENT OF EXCAVATIONS 1963

cemetery 1394 ?
A(2)a

CHURCH
1245 onwards (see text)
35 yards long inc tower
(Wm Worcestre 1480 see text)

CHURCHYARD
1422
A(2) b

2 shops next to the
churchyard
1422 A(2)b

For Sources   see   Schedule

WORSHIP STREET

A(3) b?
Properties 1386–1388

A(2)a ?
Properties 1394

Cordwainers Hall ?
16–17century

HIGH STREET

Figure 5.

A(1) North Side of Street

A(1)a 1304.

Bristol Record Office: P/St. Philip and Jacob D/1(c).

This shows St. Augustine's had property on both north and south sides of street (cf. A(2)a and A(3)b).

Tenement in Mary-le-Port Street
owned by John le Tannar, burgess,
occupied by Roger le Barbar
with Mary-le-Port Street in front
extending to Wynchestreet behind
tenement of Thomas Mounserel on one side,
tenement of St. Augustine's Abbey
on the other
granted to Jordan Broun, burgess.

A(1)b 1423 – 1480.

Wadley, 1886, 112.

On north side of street, probably bridging a lane to Wine Street—cf. William of Worcestre in Dallaway, 1834, 98.

Messuage called 'le Thorowhouse' in
Mary-le-Port Street
owned by James Cokkes: left to son John
between stable of Richard Shirwyn
and messuage occupied by Robert Haselwell,
turner.

A(1)c 1443 – 1471.

Bristol Record Office: P/St. Philip and Jacob D/1(i).

Ibid. All Saints P/BS A3 (260).

Veale, 1950, 171.

Wadley, 1886, 146.

The crucial entry is in the will of John Gaywod, 1471: tenement opposite the church.

Possibly adjacent to property A(1)e, if chapel properties are one and the same?

John Berton: cf. A(1)d.
Chapel ref. also A(3)o.

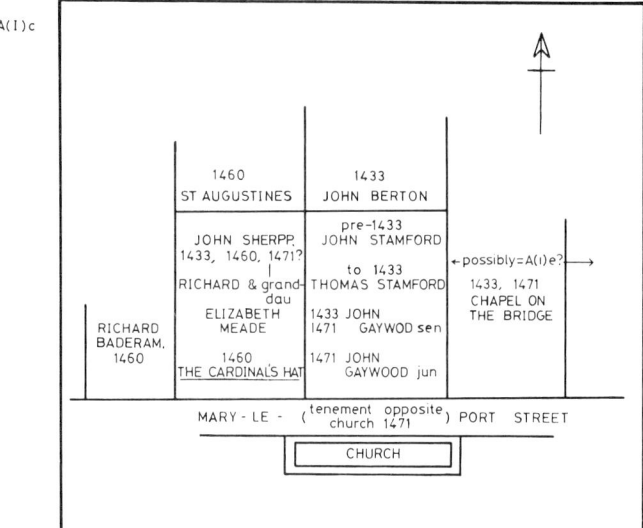

Figure 6.

A(1)d 1463.

Veale, 1950, 149.

This hinges upon the same John Berton holding land at the back of both A(1)c and d; this places A(1)d on north side of street. Thus this reference is added to A(1)f and B(2)a, for a Swan Inn on the north side of the street.

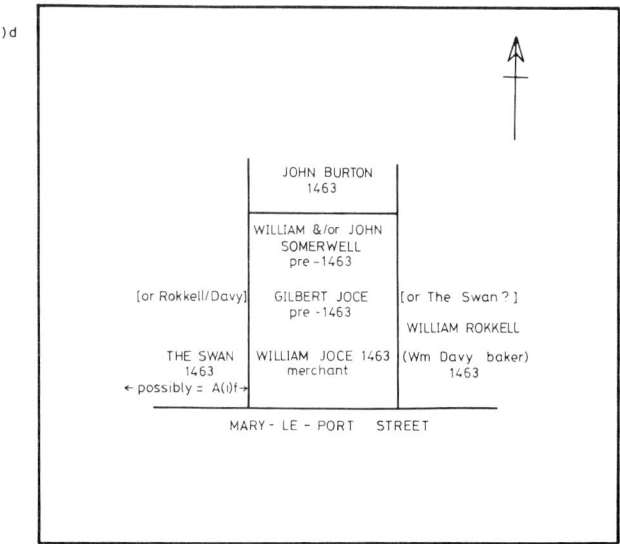

Figure 7.

A(1)e 1562.

Bristol Record Office: Latimer's Mss. Calendar, 126.

No clues *re* east-west: but if chapel property were on west side, this might tie-in with A(1)c.

Half-tenement in Mary-le-Port Street owned by Thomas Durban, occupied by Jenkin Dye, shoemaker, granted to Jenkin Dye between house of Thomas and John Aldworth, Esq's, on one side and one lately of the Chapel on the Bridge, now occupied by Jenkin Dye, on the other extending behind to tenement in Wine Street occupied by Richard Marten, haberdasher.

A(1)f (1543), 1579 – 1580.

Bristol Record Office 01150 (8,12,16).

The compass points on this deed do not make sense unless one takes Mary-le-Port Street as running north-south (Dolphin to High Streets): in which case, taken together with the Trinity Hospital connection, this is probably the same property as that in Appendix B(2)a (Bristol Record Office, 00700 (1 – 2)).

Cf. A(1)c,d.

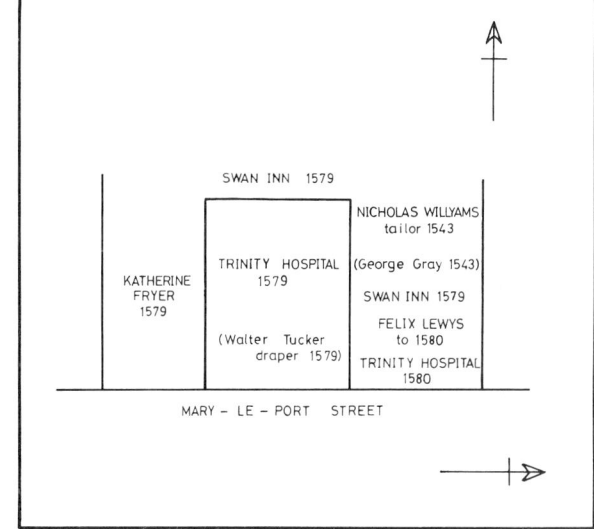

Figure 8.

A(2) South Side of Street

A(2)a 1394.

Veale, 1933, 213.

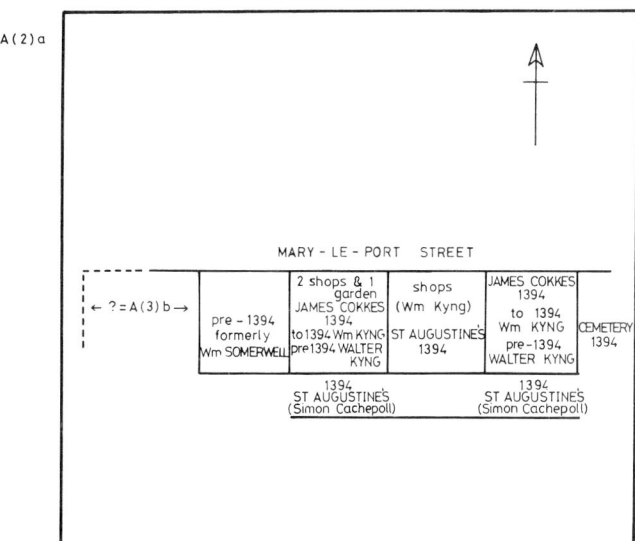

Figure 9.

This sequence makes two major assumptions:
(i)   that since premises fronting Mary-le-Port Street adjoin the cemetery, the latter is the northern graveyard area;
(ii) that Somerwell's premises are the same as those mentioned at the eastern end of the A(3)b sequence: when in fact it is not altogether certain that A(3)b is on the south side of street,
with the result that it is suggested these premises (A(2)a and A(3)b) together run from the northern graveyard westwards to High Street corner.
Either assumption could be wrong: the premises could have turned a corner down the churchyard alleyway, either east or west of the church, and so be adjoining-cum-fronting the southern churchyard.

There are no east-west indications; so that if this is so, and the Somerwell connection is wrong, the whole sequence could be reversed (i.e. cemetery at west end of the line).

If A(3)b is on the south side as well, Simon Cachepoll might be the successor to Hugh Carleton (note the similar long property running behind Mary-le-Port Street ones) or his neighbour at back.

A(2)b 1422.

Bristol Record Office: P/ST MP/D 14.

As other property in this grant includes what is apparently the main house (cf. also Wadley, 1886, 112) in the area between Worship Street and the southern churchyard, it seems most probable that these two shops adjoin the southern churchyard, south of the relevant area.

Two shops next to the churchyard of St. Mary-le-Port owned by James Cokkes granted to Thomas and Joan Fisshe (son-in-law and daughter: cf. Wadley, 1886, 112).

A(2)c 1491/1492 – 1511/1512.

Beachcroft and Sabin, 1938, 94 – 99.

A tenement called Seynd or Seind over against the churchyard and one tenement in the churchyard owned by St. Augustine's Accessway adjoining Seynd, used by churchwardens of St. Mary-le-Port.

A(2)d 1553 – 1557.

Bristol Record Office: ST P/MP/D 26 and Latimer's Mss. Calendar 120.

This sequence is based on the assumption that '-Launsdon' in 1553 is the same person as Thomas Lamesden of 1557, the dates and names being so similar. Otherwise, Robyns-Lane/Shee Lamesden of 1557 must be regarded as unlocated.

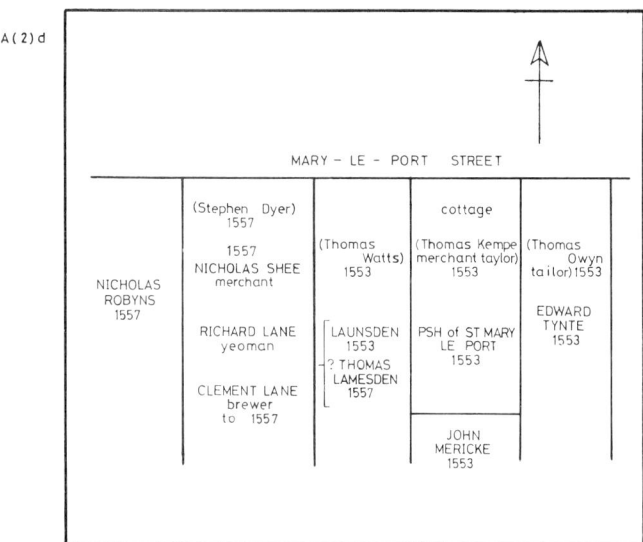

Figure 10.

A(3) Unlocated Buildings (no evidence *re* north or south side of street)

A(3)a Fourteenth century.

Bickley, 1900, 14.

Also A(3)h, 1.

A certain tenement in Mary-le-Port Street held by Maurice de Berkeley occupied by Walter Goby.

A(3)b 1386 – 1388.

Veale, 1933, 199, 200, 203, 205, 213.

From these references alone, it is not possible to settle whether the properties run from the north or south corners of Mary-le-Port Street and High Street.

If it is acceptable for the east end of this sequence (Somerwell) to match the west end of A(2)a (also Somerwell; and note St. Augustine's Abbey in similar position to both) then the south corner (as indicated) is the more probable—and a complete run of properties from the corner to the church is established for the 1380s – 1390s.

The suggested position of Hugh Carleton's tenement, fronting High Street and running back at right angles to the others, is reinforced by his reappearance behind Somerwell's properties.

A(3)c 1387.

Veale, 1933, 204.

Possibly also south side, through association with Arthur family of A(3)b?

Ref. also to William Frome: A(3)h.

A(3)d 1388.

Veale, 1933, 213.

Possibly connected with A(2)a, but cannot be proven; Somerwell refs. also A(3)b; cf. A(3)h.

A(3)e Fourteenth century.

Bickley, 1900, 13.

Cf. A(3)f: Spert family.

A(3)f 1395.

Wadley, 1886, 52.

Possibly connected with A(3)e in some way; refs. also to Walter Escote A(3)1, Escote family A(3)h.

John Bruer: cf. Bernard and Walter Brewer, A(3)h.

Simon Olyver: cf. A(3)g, but this cannot be the same property because A(3)g requires Dolphin Street to east.

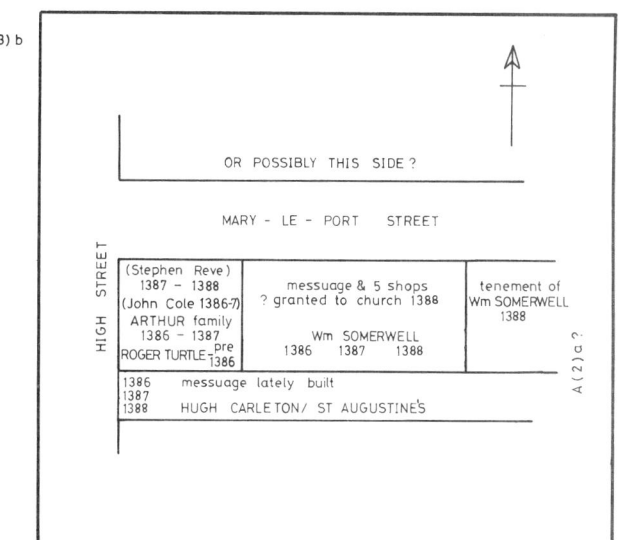

Figure 11.

A garden in St. Mary de Foro street held by Edmund and Isabella Arthur occupied by William Frome.

Tenement in Mary-le-Port Street held by William Somerwell occupied by James Cokkes granted to two chaplains (for parish?) between shop of Walter Denyas and tenement lately of Walter Kyng.

A certain tenement in Mary-le-Port Street held by Bishop of Worcester occupied by Robert Spert.

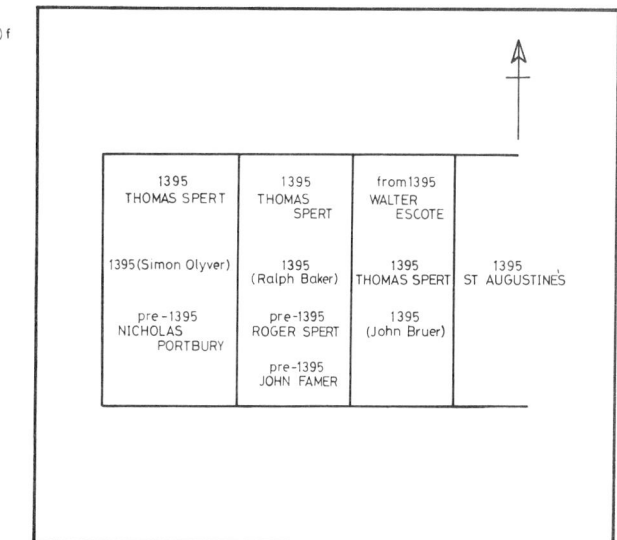

Figure 12.

A(3)g 1396.

Bickley, 1900, 24.

Possibly on the corner of Mary-le-Port
Street and Dolphin Street, but no
indication of north or south side; northern
corner is slightly more 'opposite' St. Peter
Street.

One tenement in Seintmaristrete
held by Simon Oliver
opposite the church of St. Peter
in the way which leads towards
Wynchstrete.

A(3)h 1412 – 1517.

Bristol Record Office: P/ST MP/D 2, 4, 9,
10 – 13, 53.

Wadley, 1886, 112.

No east-west or north-south points are
given for three central properties: all are
therefore interchangeable! But since the
properties to east and west of Escote had
identical occupants from John Cokkes
onwards, this hardly matters.

Note resemblance between the alternating
Cokkes properties here, and in A(2)a,
though there is no mention of St.
Augustine's here, and a connection cannot
be proved; it might however suggest that
this sequence is also on south side of
street.

James Cokkes left two distinct messuages
in 1423:
(i) owned James Cokkes, left to wife with
mess. of James Cokkes occ.
John Bern on one side, mess. of Hugh
Escote on other;
(ii) owned James Cokkes, left to son John
mess. of Hugh Escote on west
mess. of Bernard Brewer on east.
Provided that the messuage of Hugh
Escote in (i) and (ii) is one and the same,
these 1423 details are so similar to the 1412
and 1451 layouts as to justify their
incorporation in the same plan. The only
major conjecture is that James Cokkes
acquired Thomas Frome's property
between 1414 and 1423.

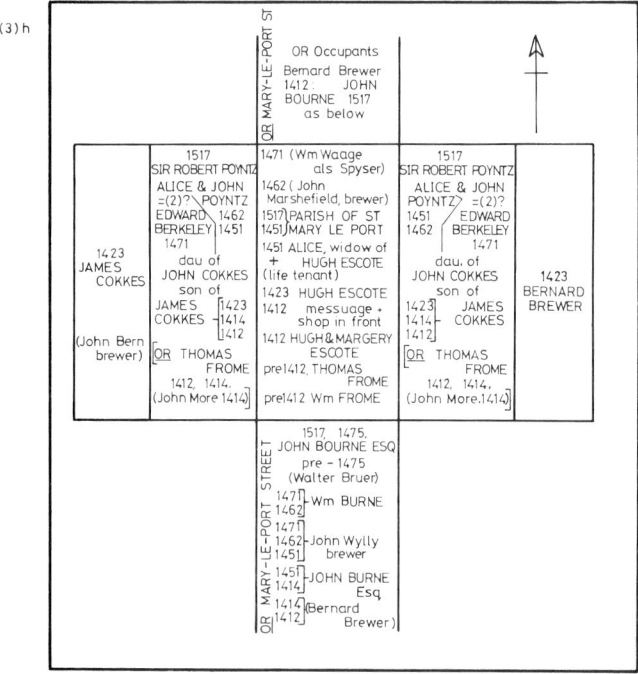

Figure 13.

A(3)i 1423.

Wadley, 1886, 112.

Possibly ties in with A(2)a?

Messuage and shop in Mary-le-Port Street
owned by James Cokkes: left to wife
occupied by John Grove
between messuage of St. Augustine's
on east
and messuage of Dame Joan Brook
on west.

A(3)j 1423.

Wadley, 1886, 112.

This is a separate bequest, and therefore a separate property from A(3)i; but possibly also ties in with A(2)a? Reflects the scattered tenure of individual houses by Cokkes, cf. A(3)h.

Messuage in Mary-le-Port Street
owned by James Cokkes: left to wife,
messuage of St. Augustine's on one side,
messuage of Dame Joan Brook on other.

A(3)k 1423.

Wadley, 1886, 112.

No details given.

One messuage and two shops in
Mary-le-Port Street
owned by James Cokkes: left to wife.

A(3)l 1443 – 1474.

Bristol Record Office: 5163(150); 26166(1443 – 1446).

Cf. Walter Escote A(3)f; Berkeley cf. A(3)h.

Messuage with shop in front and cellar
below in Mary-le-Port Street
owned by Thomas son of Robert Ledbury,
granted to John Moret, burgess (1443),
and by him to St. Peter's parish (1446)
between tenement late of Thomas
Berkeley, merchant, now of
William Moret on one side
and tenement of Walter Escote, occ.
Richard Payne, currier, on other
extending to Rypersynne (John Culver,
hosteler) behind.

A(3)m 1460.

Keele Univ., Staffs, M72/16/24.

New tenement in Mary-le-Port Street
owned by Feoffees of St. Peter's
leased to William Clerk, merchant,
between tenement of William Kayleway
on one side
and tenement of John Clyve of Old Sarum
on the other
from street in front
to tenement of Edward Lord Cobham at back.

A(3)n 1575.

Bristol Record Office: Latimer's Mss. Calendar, 140.

House and loft in Mary-le-Port Street
owned by George Snigge, merchant,
granted to son George Snigge,
adjoining tenement of Robert Risbit.

A(3)o 1584.

Bristol Record Office: Latimer's Mss. Calendar, 162 – 164.

Chapel had land on north, and possibly on south side of street: A(1)c,e.

Tenement in Mary-le-Port Street
owned by Edward Longe, plumber,
late occupied by Philip Langley, merchant,
granted to Thomas Colston, mercer,
adjoining tenement lately of Chapel on
Bridge.

5.5 Appendix B Seventeenth – Eighteenth Centuries (figure 14)

B(1) Diagrammatic plan of Mary-le-Port Street, which can be correlated with Appendix C (below)

Note: in this and the plans below, as Appendix C, the latest noted occupants are nearest the street frontage within each property; earlier occupants are progressively further from the street frontage.

Names in CAPITALS are of owners or principal lessees; Names (thus) are of other occupants.

B(2) North Side of Street Unlocated Buildings

B(2)a 1679 – 1730.

Bristol Record Office 00700 (1 – 2).

These deeds would seem to identify a Swan Inn on the north side of the street: cf. the known Swan Inn on south side at Dolphin Street end (Winstone, 1957, plate 8).

Cf. A(1)d, f.

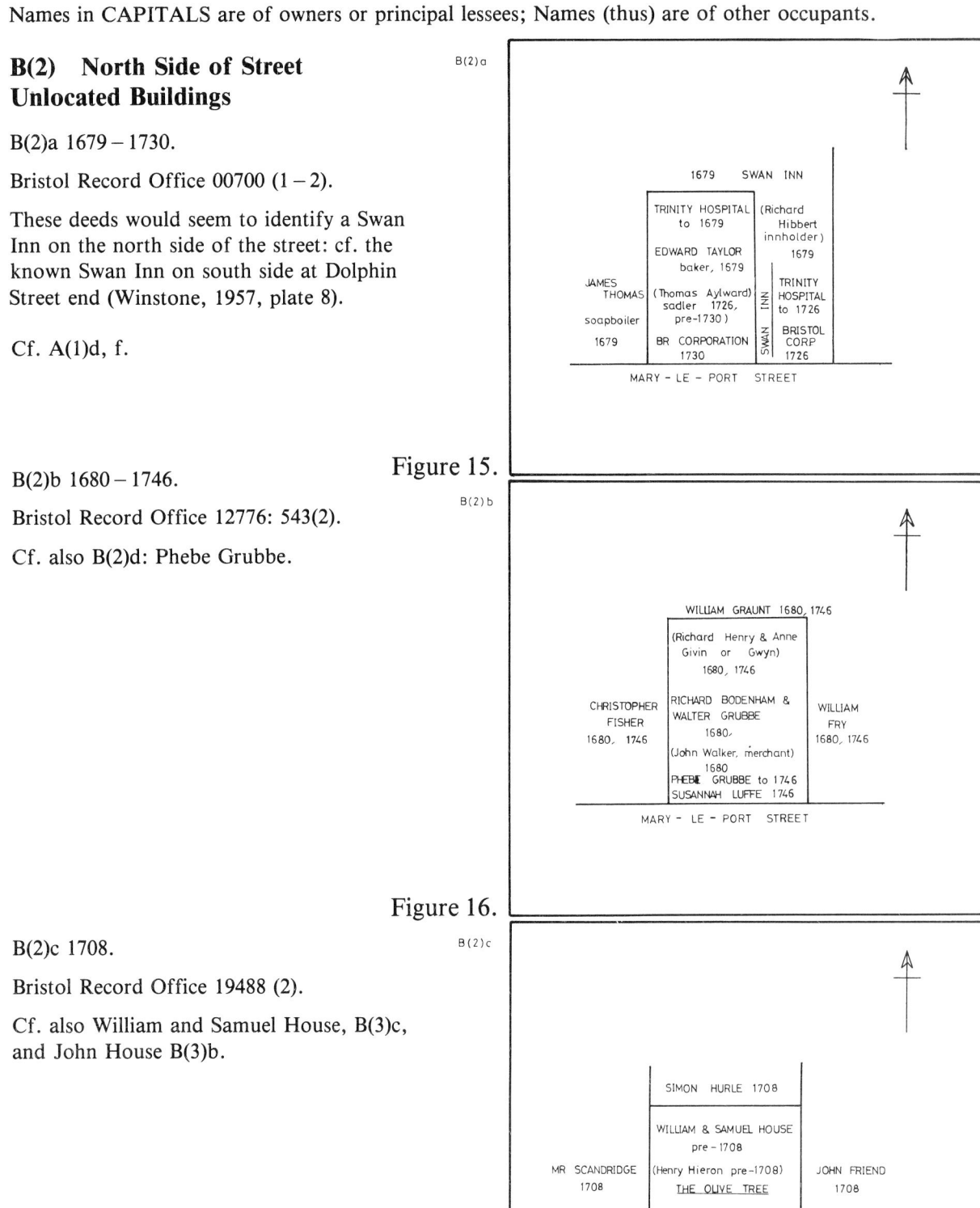

Figure 15.

Figure 16.

Figure 17.

B(2)b 1680 – 1746.

Bristol Record Office 12776: 543(2).

Cf. also B(2)d: Phebe Grubbe.

B(2)c 1708.

Bristol Record Office 19488 (2).

Cf. also William and Samuel House, B(3)c, and John House B(3)b.

APPENDIX B(1)   Seventeenth-Eighteenth Centuries   DIAGRAMMATIC PLAN OF MARY-LE-PORT STREET
(which can be correlated with Appendix C; not to scale)

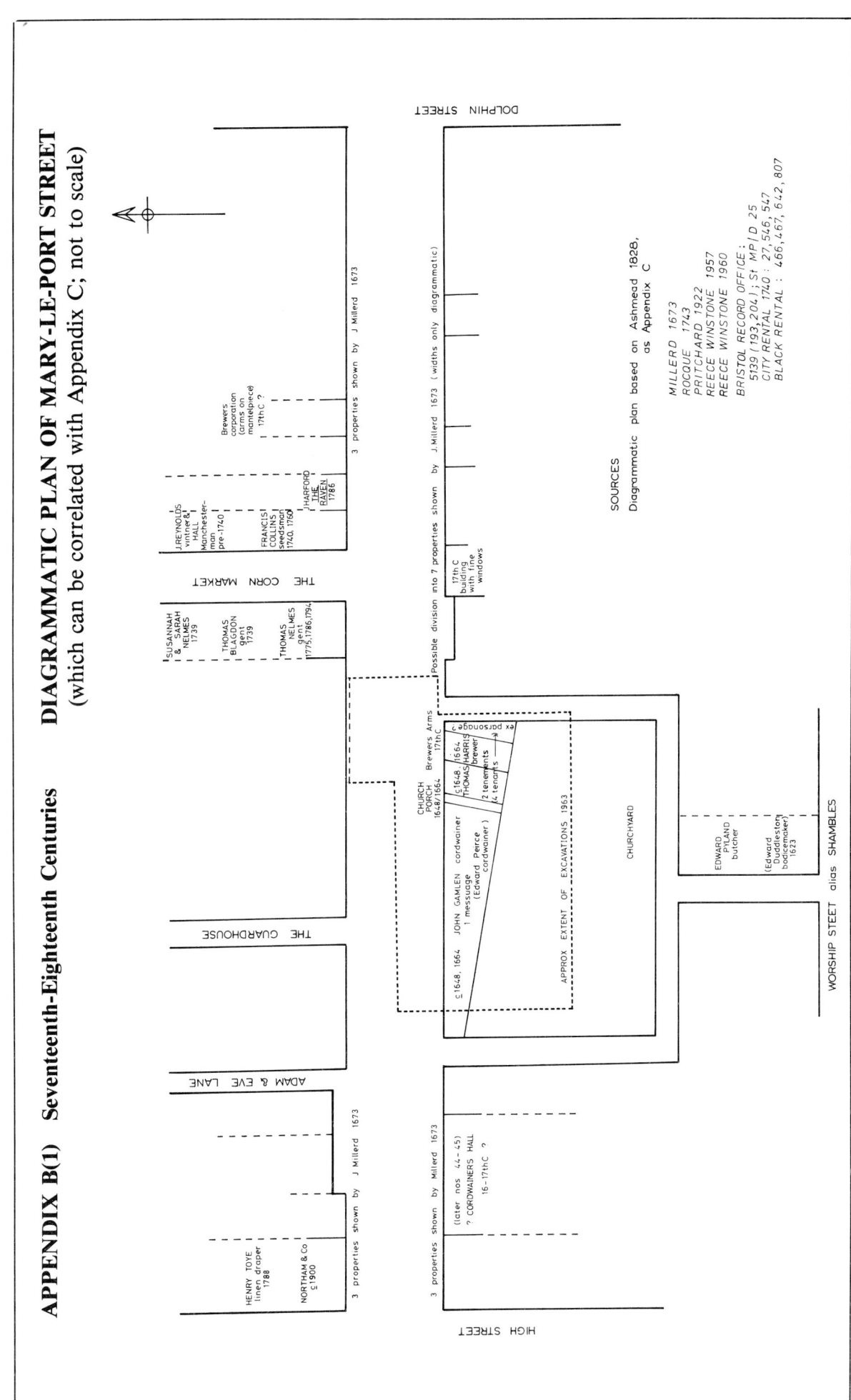

Figure 14.

45

B(2)d 1746.

Bristol Record Office 543(1).

Situation of (2) proves that (1) must be on north side of street; probably close to B(2)b, from similarity of tenants.

Two messuages:
(1)   in St. Mary-le-Port Street; owned by Phebe Grubbe; occupied successively by John Ford, cook dec'd; John Walter dec'd; and John Mott dec'd; leased to Mrs Luffe;
(2)   behind (1) in lane leading to Wine Street.

B(3)   South Side of Street:Unlocated Buildings

B(3)a 1606.

Bristol Record Office 5139 (349).

'Two houses now one'.

B(3)a

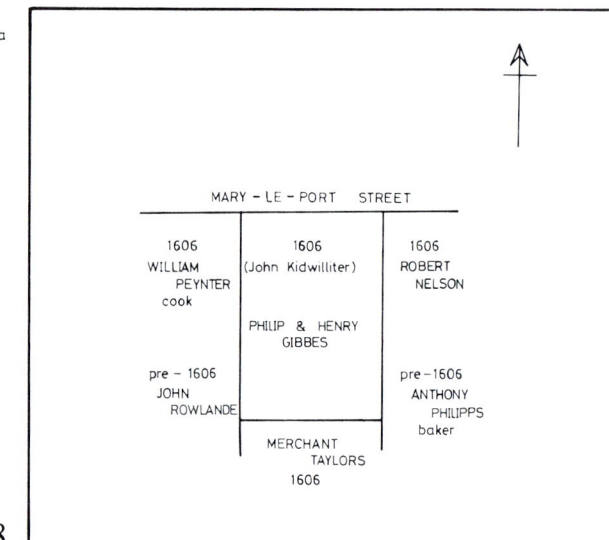

Figure 18.

B(3)b 1652 – 1670.

Bristol Record Office 14531 (2,5); 26166 (for 1660).

B(3)b

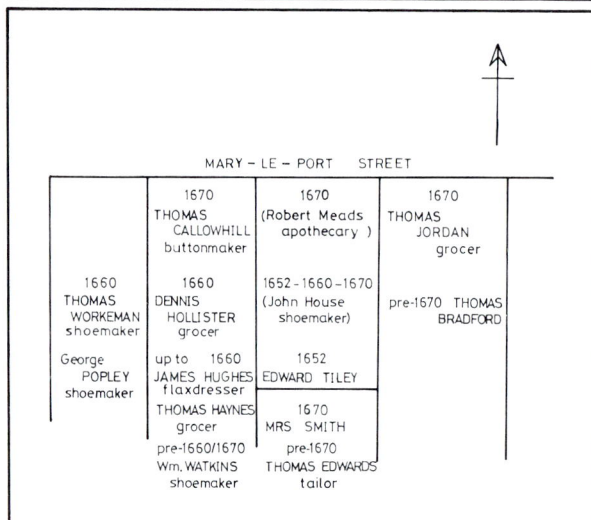

Figure 19.

B(3)c 1708.

Bristol Record Office 19488(2).

This appears to have no western neighbour; so possibly a corner property, later no. 37 or on corner of High Street. It cannot be the later no. 42, since that would have the church on its south side.

B(3)c

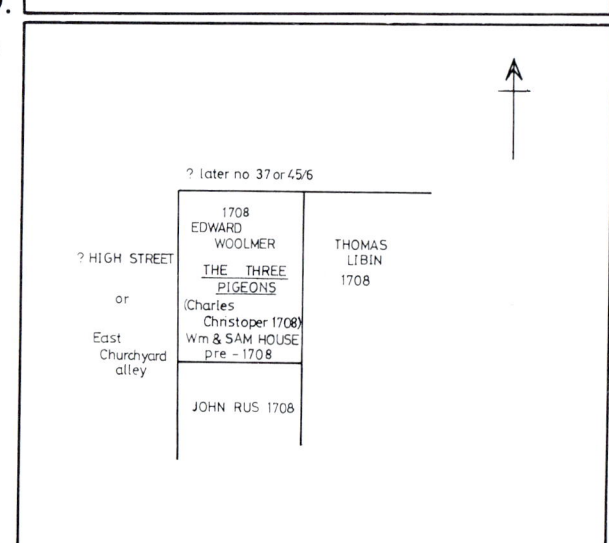

Figure 20.

5.6   Appendix C   Nineteenth – Twentieth Centuries (figures 21 – 22)

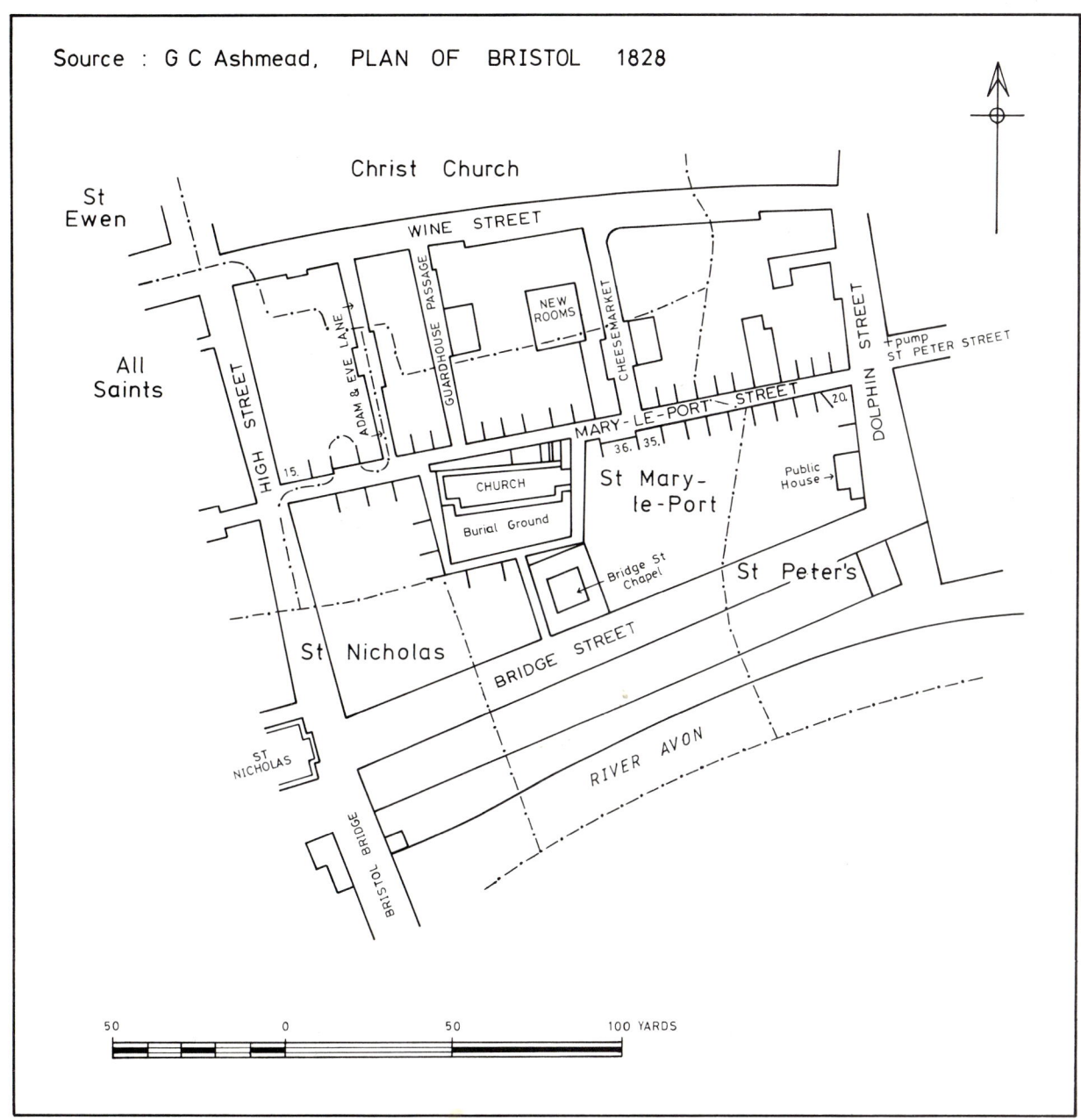

Source : G C Ashmead, PLAN OF BRISTOL   1828

Figure 21.

Figure 22 is a diagrammatic plan of Mary-le-Port Street. It is based on Ashmead's plan of 1828, with the help of the other sources listed below. It shows the premises and their successive occupiers. The plan is not to scale. The property divisions are as shown by Ashmead, but their relative widths are not necessarily accurate.

Sources: Ashmead, 1828.

A selection of four Directories of Bristol, of 1864 (1868), 1870, 1901 and 1937.

Photographs: 1880s, in Reece Winstone 1962
  1890s, in Reece Winstone 1960
  *c.*1900, in Reece Winstone 1957
  1902, in ibid.
  1908, in ibid.

Leases: Bristol Corporation Leases
  1 Black Rental, 463, 467; Printed Rental, 39
  2 Black Rental, 466, 1065; Printed Rental, 39
  3 City Rental, 1740, 27; Black Rental, 642
  4 City Rental, 1740, 27; Black Rental, 807.

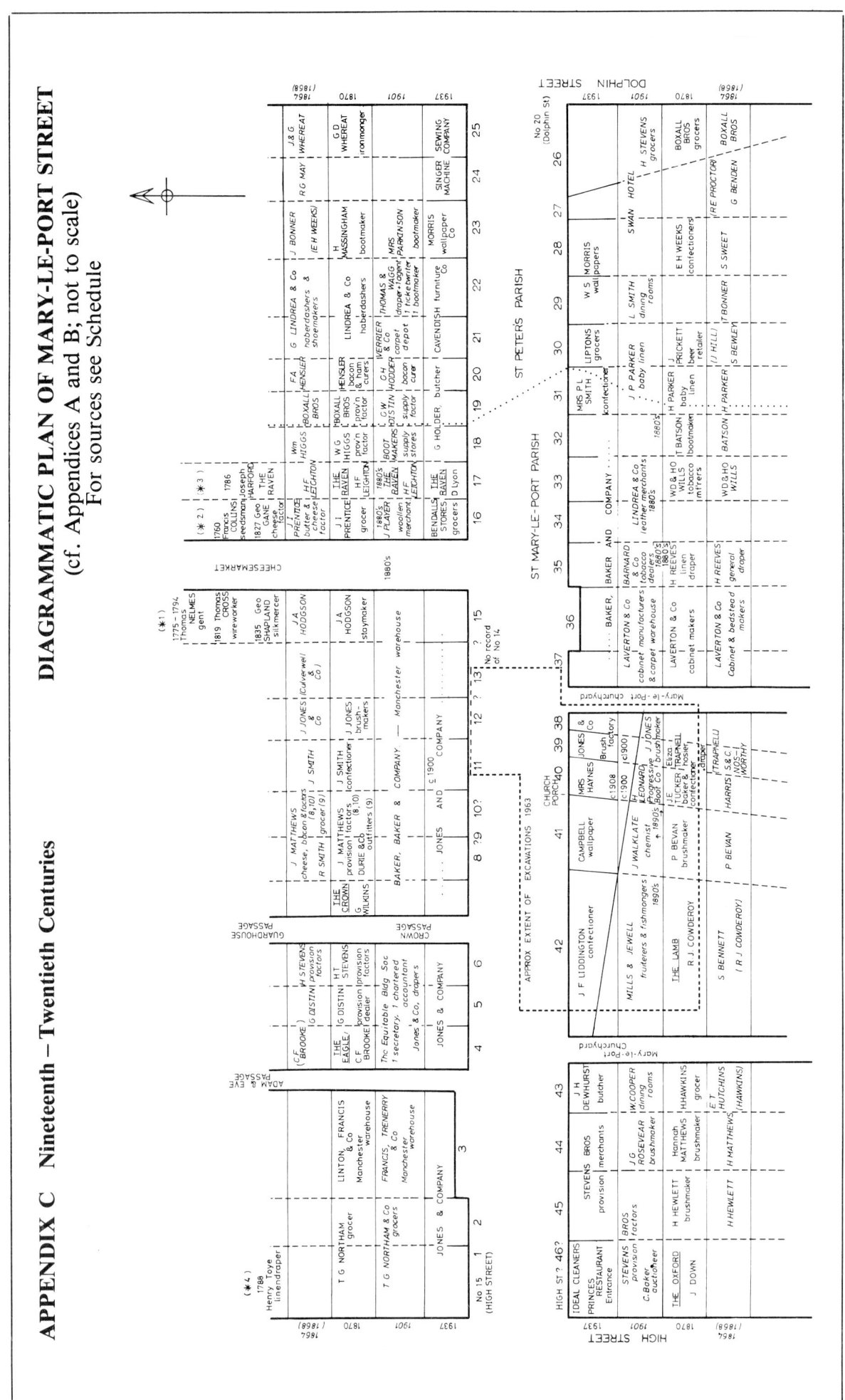

DIAGRAMMATIC PLAN OF MARY-LE-PORT STREET
(cf. Appendices A and B; not to scale)
For sources see Schedule

APPENDIX C Nineteenth – Twentieth Centuries

Figure 22.

Street numbers are indicated for the first of these directories in which they appear, although the proof of their exact position often depended on the details in later directories. The church porch was situated between nos. 40 and 41; the 1901 directory is proved wrong by Reece Winstone's photograph, 1957, plate 11.

The parish boundaries are after Ashmead and the Directories. The 1937 Directory places them wrongly, one house too far west.

5.7 References

1. See Ashmead, 1828; cf. figure 21.
2. Cf. Chapters 3 – 4 and Lobel and Carus-Wilson, 1975, Map 8.
3. Veale, 1931, 5.
4. Bristol Record Office: P/St MP/D 1.
5. Bristol Record Office: P/St E/A1, St. Ewen's parish records: Charter of Theobald Archbishop of Canterbury (1140 – 1162) to John Turstin, priest at St. Ewen, granting him the church.
6. And more recently: Little, 1954, 18.
7. Ralph, 1960a.
8. Greening, 1966, 20 – 22; Ralph, 1960b.
9. i.e. Bristol Record Office, 5139 (208).
10. Marshall, 1951, 35 – 37.
11. *V. C. H. Somerset* 2 (1911), 129.
12. Cat. Pat. 1317 – 1312 (Rec. Comm.), 68.
13. *Taxatio Ecclesiastica* 1921 (Rec. Comm.), 220. *V. C. H. Somerset* 2 (1911), 129 is wrong in saying that St. Mary-le-Port does not appear in 1291.
14. Robinson, 1915, 184.
15. The existence of these blocked north windows was revealed in later restoration (cf. Shipley and Rankin, 1945 and Nicholls and Taylor, 1881, 2, 229). The documentary evidence implies that they remained open until the seventeenth century (see 5.3.13).
16. Bristol Record Office: P/St MP/D 1.
17. Grinsell, 1962, 14.
18. *Taxatio Ecclesiastica* 1291 (Rec. Comm.), 220; Veale, 1931, 5.
19. Bristol Record Office: P/St MP/D 14: grant of property by James Cokkes to Thomas and Joan Fisshe (son-in-law and daughter), 1422; cf. Worship Street area properties described in his will of 1423 (Wadley, 1886, 112). Refs. also in 1491 – 1492, 1511 – 1512 Beachcroft and Sabin, 1938, 94, 95, 99). Also in 1623: Bristol Record Office, P/St MP/D 25.
20. Veale, 1933, 230.
21. Wadley, 1886, 146.
22. Bristol Record Office: P/St. Philip and Jacob D/1(c), 1304. This is the second oldest surviving property deed, P/St MP/D 1 being the oldest.
23. Veale, 1933, 203.
24. Keele University, Staffs: M 72/16/24 (catalogue: Bristol Record Office).
25. Veale, 1933, 204.
26. Veale, 1933, 230.
27. Bristol Record Office: St. Philip and Jacob D/1 (i).
28. Bristol Record Office: Robert Ricart, The Maire of Bristowe is Kalendar; reproduced in Toulmin-Smith, 1872 and as frontispiece to McInnes and Wittard, 1955.
29. View of Bristol by William Smith, 1568; reproduced as frontispiece to Bickley, 1900; View of Bristol by J. Hoefnagle, 1581.
30. Bristol Record Office: All Saints Parish deeds P/A5 HS C9 (m.).
31. Veale, 1933, 213.
32. Veale, 1933, 230.
33. Wadley, 1886, 112.
34. Bristol Record Office: St MP/D 2.
35. Bristol Record Office: 26166 and 5163 (150).
36. Dallaway, 1834, 52.
37. CCC MS 210 p 88, transcribed and translated by FN: *'Via de jnteriori parte de la Newgate per turrim Bristollie & per Ecclesiam sancti petri ~~ad~~ [sic] et Sancte Marie de la port continet nonies 60.20 gressus.560 gressus'.*
'The road from the inner side of Newgate past the keep of Bristol and past the church of St. Peter to

Plate 4. Mary-le-Port Street from west, with west side of St. Mary-le-Port church tower in background; monochrome photo from painting ?c.1800.

[*deleted*] and St. Mary de la Port measures nine times 60 & 20 steps: 560 steps'. Note: Dallaway 1834, 29, following Nasmith, has printed a completely garbled version in which this and the previous entry have been accidentally run together, giving a reading that is topographic nonsense.

38. See Harvey, 1969, introduction.
39. Bristol Record Office: Robert Ricart, The Maire of Bristowe is Kalendar (Toulmin-Smith, 1872, 48).
40. Dallaway, 1834, 87—he quotes this correctly.
41. Wadley, 1886, 112.
42. Bristol Record Office: P/St MP/D 63 and Wadley, 1886, 87.
43. Wadley, 1886, 102.
44. Veale, 1937, 205 – 206.
45. Bristol Record Office: P/St MP/D 50.
46. Bristol Record Office: P/St MP/D 9.
47. Bramble, 1884 – 1888, 138 – 139.
48. Bramble, 1884 – 1888, 139n; also Ralph, 1961.
49. Bristol Record Office: 5163 (150), and 26166.
50. Veale, 1950, 171; Bristol Record Office, All Saints Parish Records P/AS BS A3 (260) (catalogue, 140); Bristol Record Office, St. Philip and Jacob P/St PJ D/1 (i); and Bristol Record Office, Latimer's Mss. Calendar, 126; Wadley, 1886, 146.
51. Veale, 1950, 149.
52. Bristol Record Office: 01150 (8, 12, 16).
53. Subsequent evidence of a Swan Inn on north side of street—see Appendices A – B.
54. Pritchard, 1922, 87 – 88; Reece Winstone, 1957, plate 8.
55. Wadley, 1886, 112.
56. Dallaway, 1834, 98.
57. Beachcroft & Sabin, 1938, 9, 94, 95.
58. Pritchard, 1922, 88 – 92.
59. Dallaway, 1834, 55 – 56.
60. *Winchester Studies* 5 (forthcoming).
61. Veale, 1933, 4, 200, 203, 213, 214, 230.
62. Veale, 1933, 4, 230; Bristol Record Office: P/St MP/D 2, 4; and 14; Wadley, 1886, 112. Note also that James Cokkes' son John was styled a 'gentleman' in 1451: P/St MP/D 10.
63. Wadley, 1886, 52; Bristol Record Office: P/St MP/D 2, 4, 9 and 10.
64. Bickley, 1900, 14.
65. Wadley, 1886, 112.
66. Bristol Record Office: P/St MP/D 10, 11, 12 and 53.
67. Bristol Record Office: Latimer's Mss. Calendar, 126.
68. Bristol Record Office: 26166.
69. Veale, 1950, 171; and Bristol Record Office: All Saints Parish records P/AS BS A3 (260) (catalogue, 140); Keele University, Staffs: M72/16/24 (catalogue in Bristol Record Office).
70. Veale, 1950, 149.
71. Bristol Record Office: P/St MP/D 26.
72. Bristol Record Office: Latimer's Mss. Calendar, 120.
73. Bristol Record Office: ibid., 140.
74. Bristol Record Office: ibid., 162 – 164.
75. Wadley, 1886, 112.; Bristol Archives Office: 5163 (150) and 26166; 01150 (8, 12); P/St MP/D 11, 26; and Latimer's Mss. Calendar, 126, 162 – 164. Veale, 1950, 149.
76. Bristol Record Office: 5139 (204).
77. Bristol Record Office: 5139 (193).
78. Bristol Directories, 1870 and 1901.
79. Pritchard, 1920, 139; Reece Winstone, 1962, plates 37 – 38; 1960, plates 52 – 53; 1957, plates 9, 11; also cf. MF 9.12.
80. Pritchard, 1922, 87 – 88; Reece Winstone, 1957, plate 11. Robinson, 1915, 186 states that the Brewers' Corporation arms appeared on nos. 36 and 38, but Pritchard and Winstone together probably provide a more accurate source of information.
81. Bristol Record Office: 12776.
82. Bristol Record Office: 5139 (143, 204, 349); 12776; 14531 (2, 5); 26166; and P/St MP/D 25.
83. Pritchard, 1922, 88 – 92.
84. Bristol Record Office: 19488 (2).

Plate 5. Mary-le-Port Street, south side, from north-east; church tower in background; monochrome photograph from painting of c.1800.

MARY-LE-PORT STREET, BRISTOL.—A relic of the old Guild houses
of Bristol Merchants.

Plate 6. Mary-le-Port Street, south side, from north-east; church tower in background; painting by E. A. Phipson 1907.

Plate 7.   Mary-le-Port Street, south side, from north-east; church tower in background; drawing ?c.1910.

Plate 9. Mary-le-Port Street, south side, from north-east; photograph ?c.1910; Fred Little postcard.

Chapter 6: Excavation Method, Recording and Stratification

Details of excavation and of recording are given in Chapters 8 – 10, together with the conditions of stratigraphic survival, in the sections dealing with the three major units of excavation, Mary-le-Port Street East, Mary-le-Port Street West and St. Mary-le-Port Church. The location of all three areas excavated (figure 23) was dictated by the ground available and by the survival of pre-modern stratification.

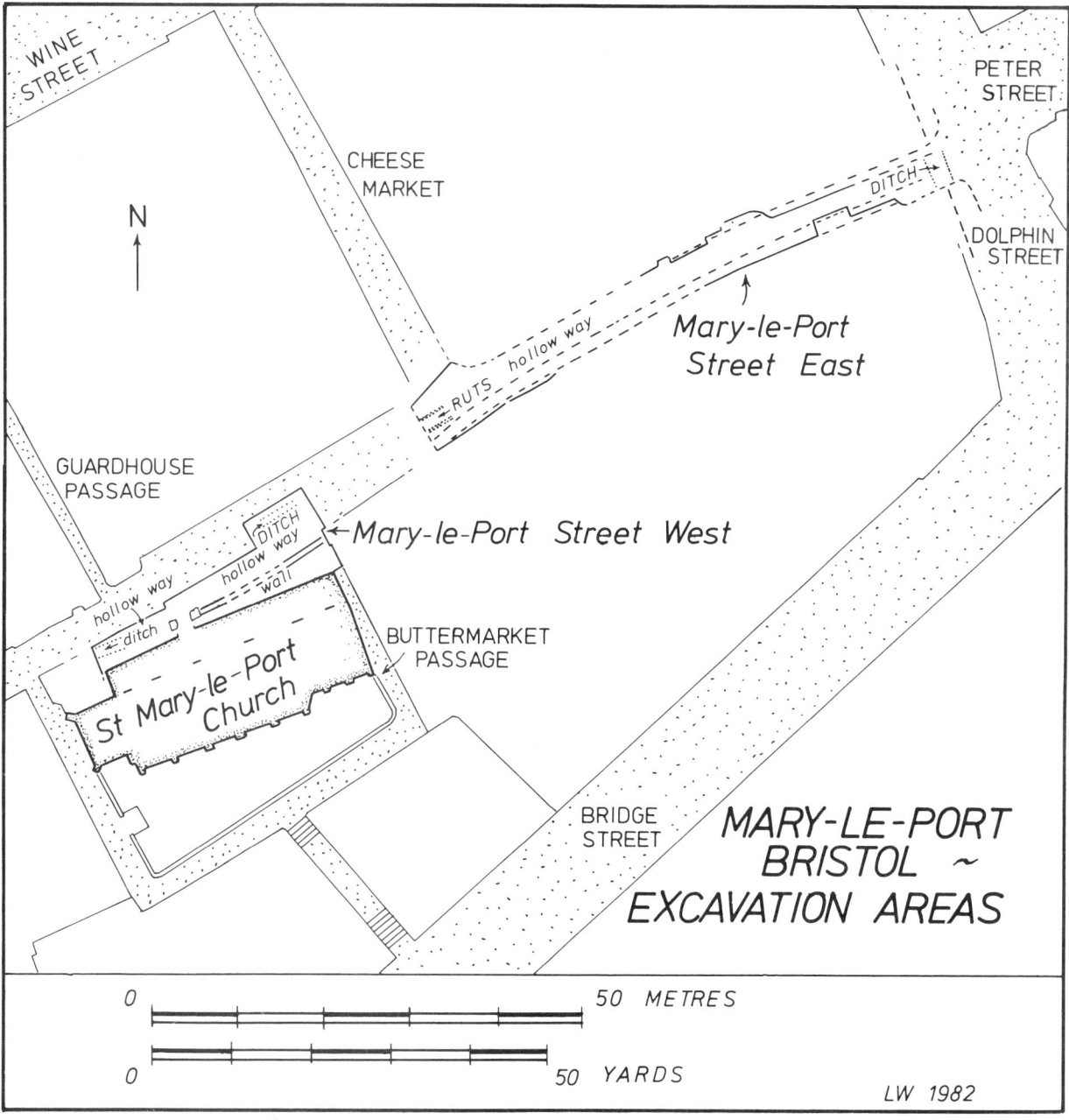

Figure 23.

In all areas the upper levels were cleared mechanically, to the surface of the latest medieval paved road in the street, or to the pre-modern floor levels in the church. This policy was adopted because of the effects of war damage and subsequent measures to 'tidy up' before redevelopment; it was also necessitated by limited time and finance and determined by contemporary expectations of this type of site.

Apart from the outlying boreholes in the St. Peter's area (drilled with a 50 mm. diamond-drill borer), excavation was based on open area methods, although this was frequently severely confined by the ground available. The three major excavation units were themselves composed of sub-units and were not continuous areas of excavation. The causeway of MLPS East was separated from the rest of the excavation by a gap of *c*.16 m. where no archaeological stratification remained. The church and MLPS West comprised an isolated, partially surviving, block of ground, but even here there were a few links between the church and street or between their individual components. The twelve areas within the church consisted in the main of no more than slender 'pillars' of intact strata, or blocks of composite piers, cut away all round by later vaults. Each area was excavated independently. No above-ground recording was undertaken beyond superficial photography. Master phasing and correlation across the site is very much a tentative and interpretative product of subsequent analysis.

Total excavation was usually not possible—many areas were not taken down to the natural substratum. Very little of any buried ground surface was seen. Large areas had already been destroyed before excavation—by cellars, drains, and cisterns in MLPS West and by burial vaults within the church. Many walls were not removed, which might have clarified both the local and general sequence. Not all excavation was done by the archaeological staff, notably the removal of skeletons from the interior of the church, which was done by Corporation workmen. Other Corporation workmen (an average team of four) did the heavy work of the excavation, the more skilled trowel and brush work being done either by the staff (two or three people) or by local volunteers (averaging three or four).

Excavation method was thus adapted to conditions of what would now be called salvage archaeology. This was reflected too in the written records made at the time. Drawings did however go some way towards compensating for and clarifying these. Detailed stratifiction tables (cf. table 1 MF, etc.) could subsequently be compiled only because the basic excavation data had been recorded; a detailed presentation of data such as these tables is a reflection of the methodology and requirements of the 1980s rather than those of twenty years ago. These now form the primary written records of the excavations, on which the descriptions and interpretations of the main report are based. Phasing has been established on the basis of stratigraphical relationships, which were then tested against the artefactual material.

Chapter 7: Chronological Summary, Street and Church

Chapters 8 – 10 that follow deal with the three separate areas of excavation of Mary-le-Port Street East (MLPS East), Mary-le-Port Street West (MLPS West), and St. Mary-le-Port Church (figure 23). These areas were not only separate campaigns of excavation, but were stratigraphically discrete (Chapter 6 above). Each area was separately recorded and phased. The phase sequence in each street area (Arabic numerals 1 – 6 in MLPS East, and 1 – 8 in MLPS West) could be reasonably linked in 'Master Phases' (Roman numerals I – VII), representing major 'events' in the street's history. No such confident equation could be made between these street Master Phases and the church Phases 1 – 6, nor need any exact correlation be expected. There are however likely to be broad correlations between church and street history, not only in absolute chronological terms, by century or decade, but also in terms of periods of major topographical changes, themselves related to socio-economic factors common to the whole of early Bristol. These are discussed in Chapter 12, when all the evidence has been marshalled, but the diagrams of summary phasing in church and street are here appended as figures 24 and 25 to give the reader a conceptual anticipation of the framework discussed in the following pages.

In Chapters 8 – 10, the discussions of finds are deliberately not in general integrated with the discussions of phasing, which was established in the first place by analysis of stratigraphic relationships. This is partly to keep the latter argument independent, but also so that the artefacts may be considered as a whole: their function and their social, dating and other attributes being considered in relation to each other, rather than as mere appendages to the phases with which they are associated.

To enable the sequence proposed in Chapters 8 – 10 to be better visualised, the outline of the changing relationships between church and street from the earliest pre-urban landscape to the dense urban one destroyed in 1940 will be summarised here. The comments that follow should be read in conjunction with the phase correlation diagram of figure 24 and the complementary plan sequence of figure 25.

In very small areas, both inside the church and alongside the street, patches of buried soil survived. These serve to indicate former minimum height of ground surfaces above O.D. in specific places, which must in essence be earlier than the late Saxon and medieval levels which properly begin the archaeological sequence. They also represent soil that formed the surface of the landscape in prehistoric, Roman and earlier Saxon times. While none of these patches yielded material of these early periods, the presence of flints, Roman and ?Saxon finds in later levels may hint at contemporary occupation, however slight, associated with this landscape.

The features preceding the hollow way may also be earlier than the late Saxon period. The bottom fill of the 'double ditch' at the east end of MLPS East was aceramic; the finds from the upper fill, after the disuse of the ditches, are of late Saxon – early medieval date.

The very small areas in the church that could be earlier than even the putative church of Phase 1 could also be earlier than the late Saxon period; or late Saxon, but preceding any major stone-based structure here. The site of the church was also of course part of the earliest landscape.

The hollow way, the Timber Building, and the earliest ?church Phase 1 appear to be broadly contemporary but cannot be directly linked. It should be noted that the hollow way as defined with its metalling and dirt must be secondary to a 'missing' stage, when linear movement was taking place along this line, initially (perhaps only vaguely defined) at the level of the surface of the earlier landscape, but gradually wearing down the surface into a hollow way. In other words the hollow way as archaeologically defined in MLPS Master Phase III is already of some antiquity; the time span involved must also have included events in the earliest ?church or pre-?church phases.

By the end of the twelfth century there was clearly a definite church, which must have at least from its inception have radically affected the character of the area, even if there had been no earlier church in church Phase 1. The first certain church is represented archaeologically by church Phase 2, and documentarily by the reference of c.1170. This must coincide at least in part with some part of the hollow way sequence—its life, its filling and finally its paving.

The enlarged church of Phase 3 flourished before and after the street was paved. All later churches had the paved road to their north; there is written evidence both that the church of Phase 4 existed by 1480, with its cellared ?parsonage and north churchyard; and that the street was paved (or re-paved) shortly before 1491.

CORRELATION of PHASING of MARY-LE-PORT STREET and ST. MARY-LE-PORT CHURCH

Mary-le-Port, Bristol

Street
MLPS EAST AND WEST

DESCRIPTION AND DOCUMENTATION	MLPS EAST PHASE	MLPS WEST PHASE	SUGGESTED DATING	MLPS MASTER PHASE
Natural substratum and disturbed top of buried soil	0~1	0~1	Geological and pre~Saxon	I
Pre-hollow-way events	1	2	Late Saxon or earlier	II
Hollow-way, timber features, street residues	2 a~f	3~4	Late Saxon to c 1300	III
Street with shops by 1245				
Make-up for street paving ~?cellars	3 a~b	5	Late 13th ~ 14th century	IV
Stone walls ~cemetery by 1394				
Paved road ~ by 1491	4 a	6	Later 13th century plus	V
Dirt above paved road	4 b	7	Later 13th century plus	VI
All late and post-medieval contexts; buildings on north side of church by 1648	5~6	8	Late- and post-medieval	VII

Church

CHURCH PHASE	SUGGESTED DATING	DESCRIPTION AND DOCUMENTATION
0~1	Geological and pre~Saxon	Natural substratum and disturbed top of buried soil
0~1	Late Saxon or earlier	Pre-church events
1	Late Saxon or early post-Conquest	? Church
2	12th century	Norman church ~ by 1170
3	13th~ later 15th centuries	Early English church; cemetery by 1394
4	Later 15th century	Perpendicular church and cellared property ~ by 1480
5	Early 16th cent.	Modifications to 4
6	Early 16th century 1940+	All later features to 1940 ~northern cemetery ceased by 1648

BROAD DATING

Prehistoric, Roman, pre~Saxon	
Late Saxon or earlier	
Late Saxon	
to	
13th century	
....	
14th century	
to	
15th century	
16th-20th centuries	

LW 1982

Figure 24.

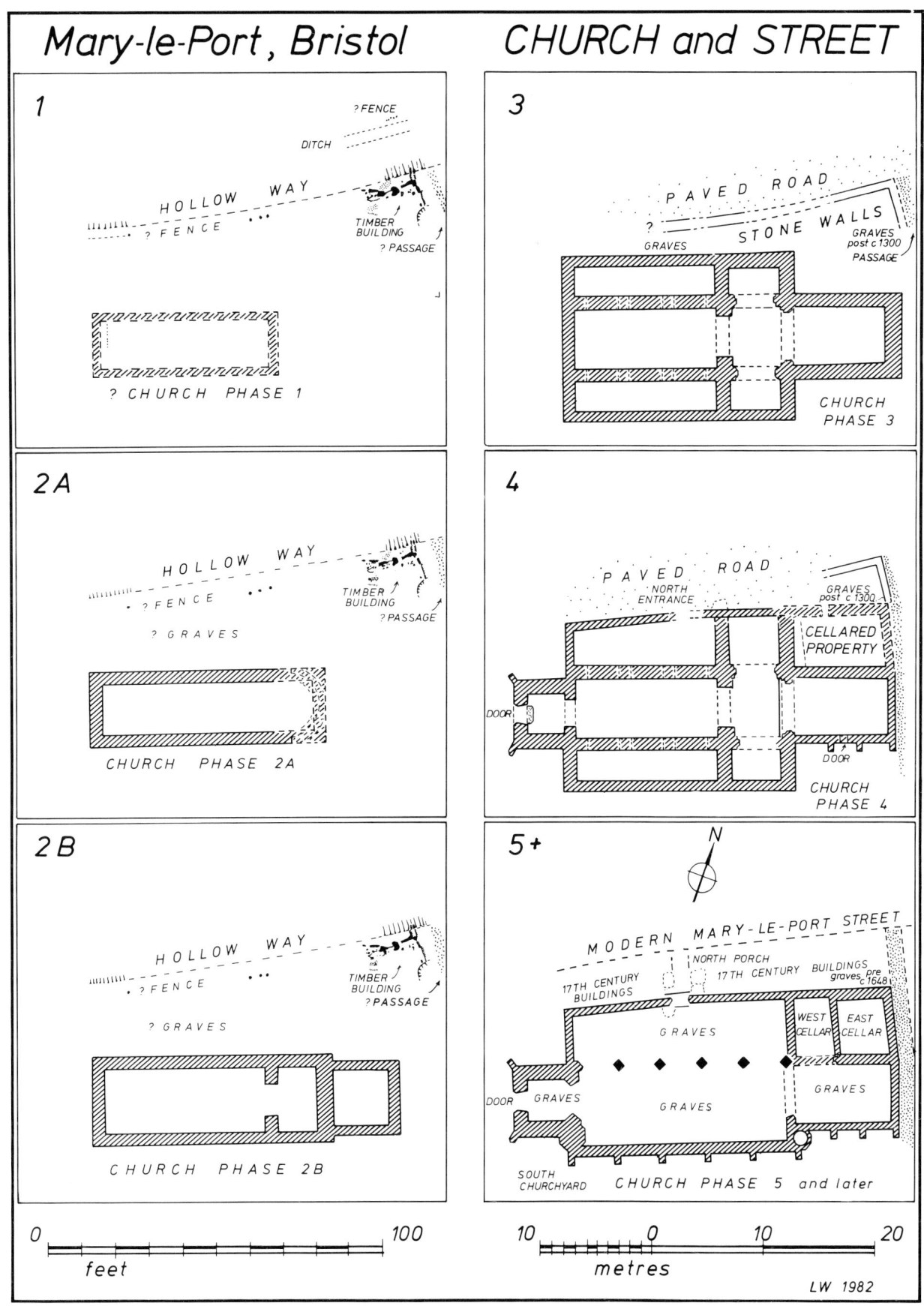

Figure 25.

It is unfortunate that the church and street sequences cannot be more closely linked. Initially church and street were separated by areas of secular occupation, including the Timber Building; later by a small northern churchyard in which burials were being made before the Phase 3 church, and continued until some time prior to 1648. After the latter date, the church was intimately connected to (or disconnected from) the road by buildings packed against it; but below-ground disturbance ultimately associated with these severed nearly all possible links that there might have been between church and street.

The church as it was known in modern times was essentially that of Phase 5, of the early sixteenth century. For a century or more it stood in this state to the south of the paved street, dominating the local landscape, its north frontage still presumably lit by windows. The buildings of the earlier seventeenth century effectively completed the Mary-le-Port sequence, creating the dense urban landscape which survived in this form to within at least one of the authors' memory.

Chapter 8: Mary-le-Port Street East

8.1 Summary of phasing

(see Chapter 7 for integration of these with MLPS West and church)

Phase 0	natural substratum.
Phase 1	pre-hollow way events.
Phase 2a – f	hollow way and fillings and associated events.
Phase 3a – b	levelling material, etc., prior to paving.
Phase 4a	paving.
Phase 4b	dirt levels above paving.
Phases 5 – 6	all late- and post-medieval contexts and unstratified material.

8.2 Introduction (figure 26)

This part of the report deals with the road area of Mary-le-Port Street to the east of the church, extending as far as the junction with Dolphin Street (= MLPS East). This is of course a continuation of that part of Mary-le-Port Street which ran past the north side of the church precinct.

8.3 Method

Before excavation, the road existed as a causeway some 5 m. wide between car parks on either side. The surface of the road was 90 cm. higher at its west end than by its junction with Dolphin Street. The road survived as a raised linear feature between lowered car parks, formerly the basements of stores. There was surprisingly little disturbance by mains services, as Mary-le-Port Street had remained a back lane rather than a main thoroughfare in recent centuries (see Chapter 5). There was a sewer underneath the road, but fortunately it had been tunnelled for parts of its length. The tarmac and post-medieval levels below it were bulldozed away, down to the medieval paved surface which survived in places.

8.4 Recording

The length of the road (c.66 m.) was divided into areas A – F, J and Z (figure 26), in some cases arbitrarily, in other cases because of their isolation by modern disturbances. In each area, layers were designated numerically, A1, 2, 3 . . ., B1, 2, 3 . . . Areas A – J + Z are shown altogether in figure 26, and A – C in more detail in figure 27. Not all the areas were excavated to natural, but total profiles were obtained at certain points (e.g. figures 28 and 31).

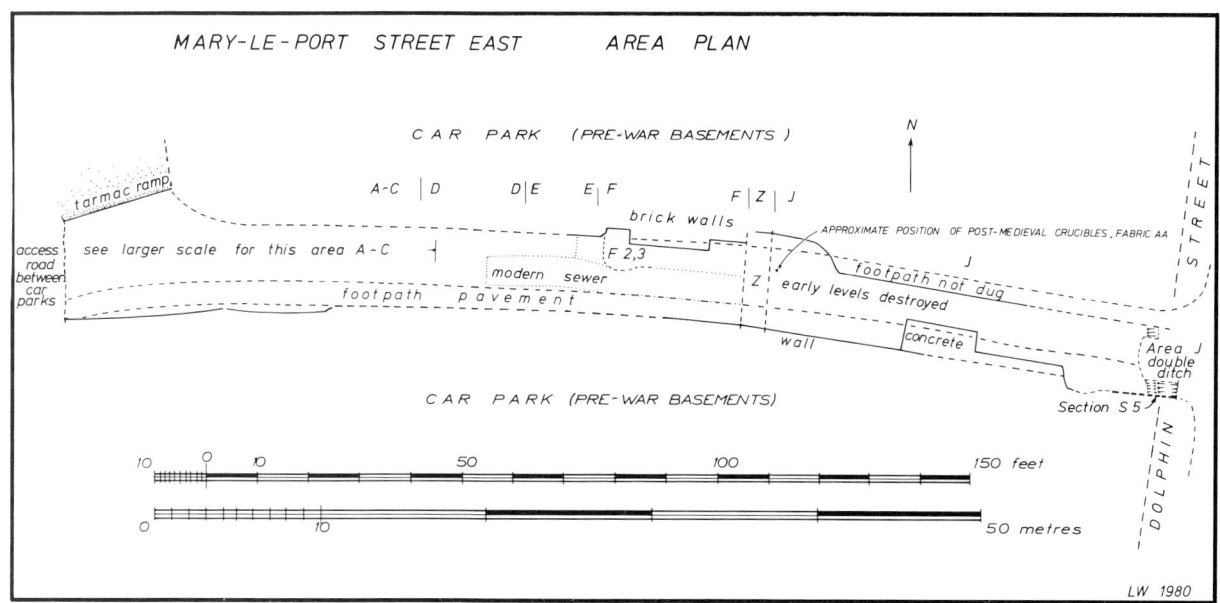

Figure 26.

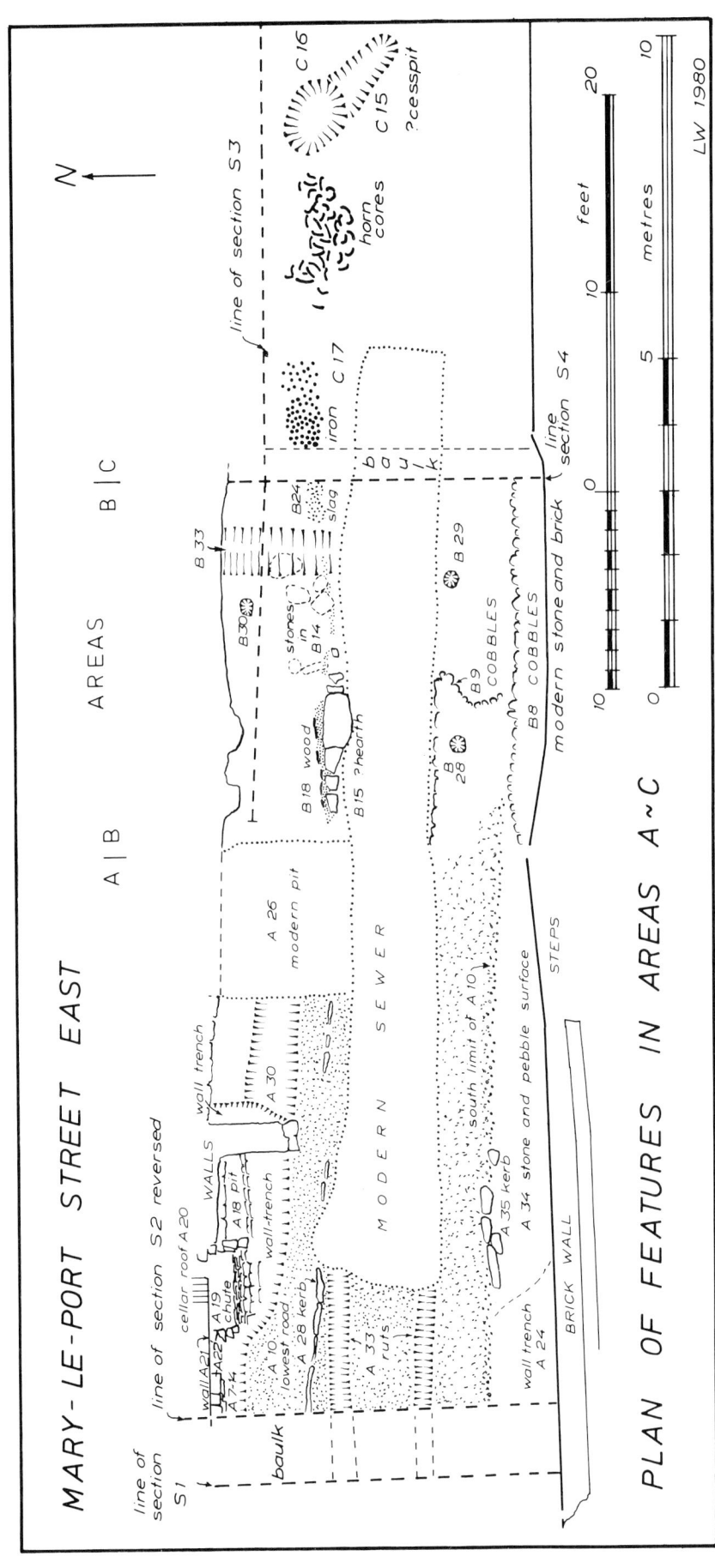

MARY-LE-PORT STREET EAST

PLAN OF FEATURES IN AREAS A~C

Figure 27.

LW 1980

8.5 Phasing

(plans, figures 26 and 27; sections S5 and S2, figures 28 and 31)

Thirteen definable groupings of stratigraphical units could be defined on the basis of the drawn sections and recorded notes (= MLPS East Phases 1 – 6, with sub-units) (cf. 8.1).

8.5.0 PHASE 0

The natural layers here are sands and gravels overlying red clay marl. ?Buried soil was seen only on the west side of the double ditch (J9 in S5). It is apparent from the depths of the former that any layer interpreted as upcast containing red clay would have to be derived from a depth of at least half a metre into the subsoil (if of local origin).

8.5.1 PHASE ?1/2a

In most areas examined the earliest phase of Mary-le-Port Street was a hollow way. The only feature which may be earlier than this is the 'double ditch' complex of two phases (i.e. a ditch of two distinct phases) at the east end of MLPS East, close to Dolphin Street (figures 26 and S5; cf. 4.1). The only reason to think this may be earlier than the hollow way is that it was sealed, after it had silted or been filled, by a ferruginous-concreted layer (at base of layers J3 and J4 in S5) which was very like the hollow way surface further west. Since the ditch is clearly re-cut (the eastern deeper member being later), it would appear that there was for some time a north-south boundary in this area, before the line of Mary-le-Port Street was established; indeed its very existence appears to preclude a contemporary road here, unless the latter was a cul-de-sac, or crossed the ditch by a bridge.

The ditch in either or both phases may have had a bank on its west side; it may have been the levelling of this/these back into the ditches (= Phase ?1/2a) which accounts for their fill of J5 – 8. This fill also includes in the later phase some occupation dirt and 'cess' (J6), which implies occupation in the area; the ditch was possibly levelled to allow the road to extend towards the area of St. Peter's Church (but also cf. 3.2).

The finds from these layers are of broadly similar late Saxon/early medieval date to material associated with the use of the hollow way elsewhere. They are however all in the upper layers of the fill of the

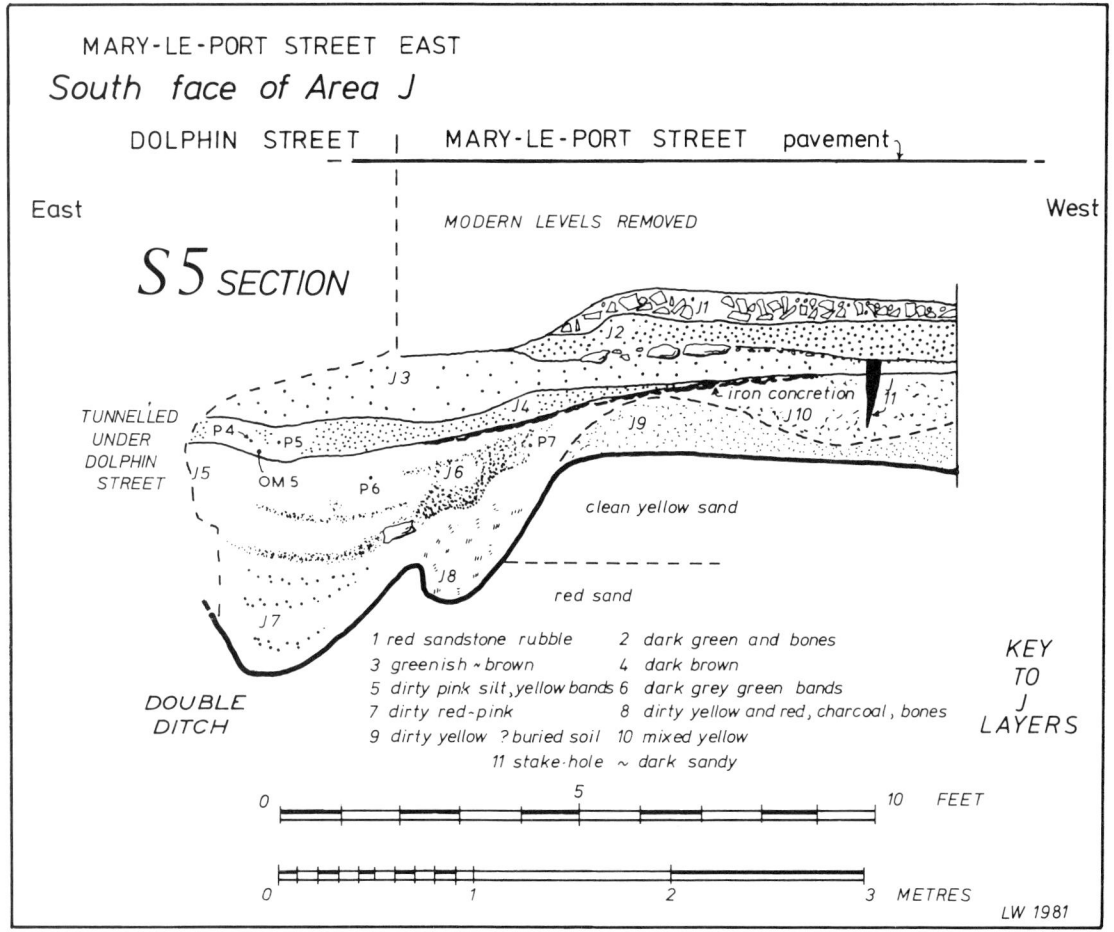

Figure 28.

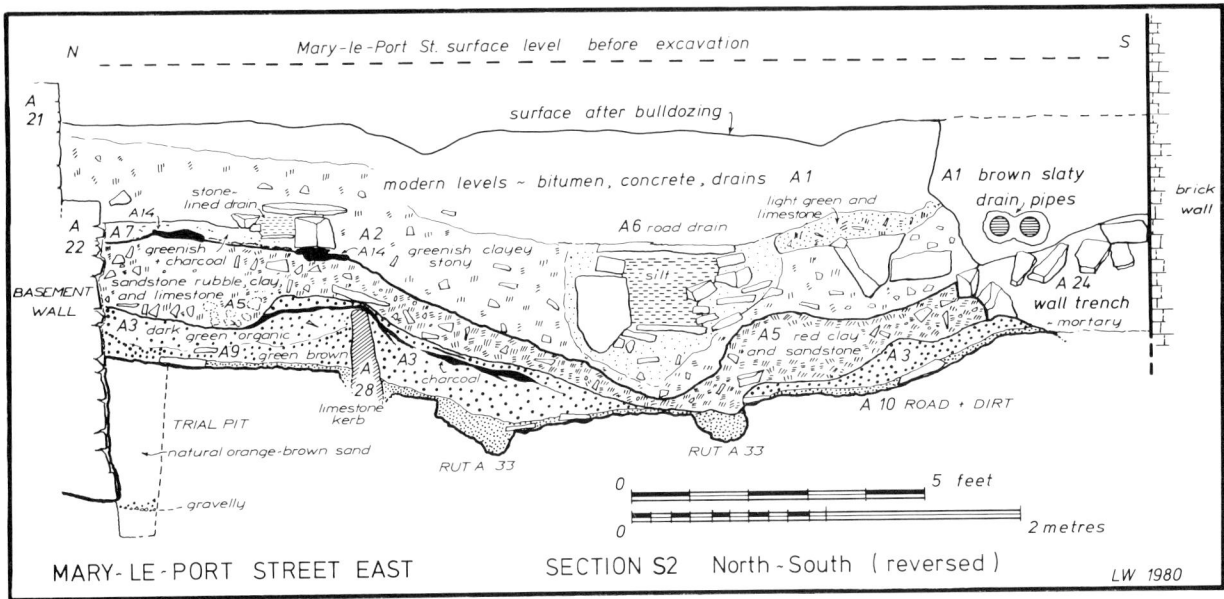

Figure 31.

'double ditch', and clearly secondary to its functional use. While the negative evidence of the absence of material from J7 and J8 should not be exaggerated, it is not inconsistent with these ditches belonging to the earliest (?aceramic) occupation of the area, before Mary-le-Port Street developed. The finds in the upper levels may only have been deposited when the ditches were levelled off as a prelude to road development (cf. 8.6.1 below).

The ditch in either or both of its phases, with or without a bank, may have been a property or public area boundary, perhaps before Bristol was a defended town at all. If this were true, it might be suggested that Dolphin Street developed along its eastern side, either on open ground, or between this ditch/bank and a similar boundary forming the west side of the St. Peter's area. In either case, we may suggest that Mary-le-Port Street (unless it were a cul-de-sac) is not a primary feature of the layout of this area, but that it, and the properties on either side, were developed only after a period in which the area was open, or had scattered occupation with a boundary to the east. St. Mary-le-Port Church may however have been in existence from the time of this earliest phase.

8.5.2 PHASE 2

8.5.2a PHASE 2a
The hollow way (A10, etc.) as excavated consisted of an irregular east-west linear hollow (cf. figure 27 and S2), 30–40 cm. deep; its base was a ferruginous concretion of pebbles and stone. There is no reason to think that this was deliberately laid; it is more likely to be the result of the compression of dirt and stone by human, animal, wheel or sled traffic, concreted over time either by iron-pan or industrially-derived ferrous residues in the area. How long a time was needed to wear the hollow way to this depth is uncertain, but some interval must be allowed between the inception of the road-zone as a route and any layers or features which were associated with its final lowered surface, as defined in excavation. These are accordingly attributed to the next sub-phase.

8.5.2b PHASE 2b
The earliest definable features of the road itself, apart from its lowered concreted surface were two ruts (A33, cf. figure 27 and S2), of normal cart width of c.1.3 m +. These were defined only in the western 3 m. of the part of the road examined; they were cut in a hollow way which was c.3.25 m. wide, as defined in section S2. The limit of the roadway to the north was indicated by a series of kerb stones (A28). As seen, these were c.35 cm. high (see S2); to their north was a more level surface, which was however in other respects similar to that of the roadway itself. Associated with what appeared to be the earliest definable phase of this was a ditch or timber slot (B33, figure 27), presumably associated with occupation on the north side of the road. It was filled and sealed by layers of dirt, elsewhere lying directly on the earliest surface, and assigned to the next phase, 2c.

On the south side of the hollow way there was no kerb, but there was an edge to the road and flat ground beyond (cf. S2).

8.5.2c PHASE 2c

This phase comprises soil layers on the lowest road (A10a, B16). These had a high organic content, ash and charcoal, with some stones; a feature of this and most other 'dirt' layers to be described from the road was the greenish tinge frequently associated with cess, of animal or human origin.

Although this dirt is stratigraphically later than the road and associated surface, it is thought to represent at least partly the mud continually present when the road was in use, rather than a deposit accumulating subsequent to the abandonment of the surfaces (Noddle however suggests that the animal bone is a secondary dump in the road, cf. 11.21.2). There can be little doubt that the entire length of the road was normally covered in mire—a condition made worse as the roadway was more and more eroded; and that this probably extended around adjacent properties on either side.

8.5.2d PHASE 2d

Of the occupation and buildings by the lowest road, only small areas survived. There were post-holes (B28 – 30) and deposits of iron slag, leather, wood, and horn-core (B24, possibly industrial debris *in situ;* C14; C17, ?a working area for horn industry; C24; E4). While some of this material might be domestic midden, it seems more likely that it represents industrial waste and concretion, indicative of the craft processes that were taking place at various points alongside the road. The data indicate the potential of roadside archaeological deposits in reflecting what was carried on in the adjoining properties, here alongside Mary-le-Port Street in the late Saxon and/or early medieval periods. We may cite in this case iron working, including smelting; leather and bone working; and ?spinning (cf. 8.6.2).

The survival of substantial amounts of these materials suggests that they represent the last phase of such activities before the ground-level began to rise.

8.5.2e PHASE 2e

Further dirt sealed these deposits (A3, A9, etc.) but was itself associated with further roadside features. These include a possible hearth (B15), the stones of which were bounded on the north side by a possible timber fence (B18, figure 27).

This dirt was accumulating not only on the areas beside the road, but also in the hollow way. This is seen clearly in section S2 where the dirt (A3, A9), accumulating finally to bury the kerb A28, spread also over the hollow way, to a depth of 20 – 30 cm.

It may be that we are seeing here a rapid worsening of road conditions, perhaps resulting from increasing density of domestic or industrial activity in the vicinity, or from a severe recession in whatever private or public cleaning mechanisms that had formerly been practised. There had clearly been a dramatic change from a road which was gradually being lowered by wear and scouring to one which was being filled up.

8.5.2f PHASE 2f

Were it not for the presence of features associated with these dirt layers, the latter might have been interpreted as dump, filling up the hollow way in anticipation of the proper paving of Phase 4. That they were not is reinforced by the position of the features (a trench or slot A30 and a ?cesspit C15 – C16) stratified in the *surface* of these dirt layers immediately below the make-up that followed.

By now the original surfaces of the hollow way and adjacent areas, and the dumps of waste on them, were deeply buried; there was still perhaps something of a hollow way. Although this appears self-evident from the profiles of the layers as seen in section S2, we must allow for subsequent subsidence right down to recent times. There can be no doubt however that the hollow way was at least partly filled up, but that there had also been a rise in the level of the adjacent areas, presumably outside or inside properties. Finds associated with the levels of Phase 2 are discussed in 8.6.2 below.

8.5.3 PHASE 3

8.5.3a PHASE 3a

At this point in the stratification there is a dramatic change, a hiatus in dirt deposition, and an event which appears to have been virtually simultaneous throughout the length of the street. This is the dumping of sand, red clay, and stone debris (A5, etc.) which must have amounted, over the whole length, to hundreds of tons. It contained very little occupation material except a scatter of sherds (cf. MF 8.6.3 – 4), its suggested sources being from the excavation of natural layers and from builders' waste. It implies building operations in the vicinity associated with excavations into the natural strata of sand, stone and clay. The suggested context is the construction of cellars. These were in the medieval period and later a feature very characteristic of Bristol. Many such cellars survive today, still used for storage or converted into bars or restaurants (cf. 5.3.12e). It seems most likely that the cellars in this case were those under properties adjoining Mary-le-Port Street. The archaeological evidence does not permit a direct association because of subsequent rebuilding and disturbance, but there were medieval cellars on either side of the street which were destroyed for pre-Second World War basements. The entrance to one survived on the north edge of Area A (see 8.5.5 below), although it is uncertain whether the stonework observed was the original medieval structure. A further cellar by the church, and demonstrably of (later) medieval date, is described with the church area in later pages (10.6 to 10.7).

If the dumping did occur along most of the street, then we may interpret this phase of the archaeological record as a remarkable example of communal planning, an agreed concerted action (if not necessarily of cellar building) of the dumping of spoil in the old hollow way, now demonstrably a rather unpleasant place, at least judged by later standards. Whether this was a private agreement among a group of merchants or shopkeepers, or whether a public act of a more central urban authority cannot of course be demonstrated archaeologically and any opinions on this point must be based on historical criteria related to urban government and planning.

It would seem however that it can only have taken place in an area of general prosperity and expansion. Neither in this levelling material nor below it are there any finds which need be dated to later than *c*.1300 (cf. 8.5.4b).

On this basis we might date the filling and paving of the road to the thirteenth century—a period when there is ample evidence from other sources for Bristol's rapid growth (cf. 5.3.9 and church Phase 3). This is indeed the dating preferred in this report. A cautionary note must nevertheless be sounded: the lack of definable fourteenth- and fifteenth-century pottery in these levels is at best negative evidence, the more so as the pottery changes in Bristol between the later thirteenth and later fifteenth century are ill-defined (but cf. subsequent sequence also). This might seem an unnecessary qualification were it not for two indicators which might point to a fifteenth-century dating for the filling of the hollow way and the paving of the street.

One is that Mary-le-Port Street is described as 'newly-paved' in 1491 (5.3.12f); the other is that as far as we are aware most if not all of the known cellars in Bristol are of fifteenth-century date; and so indeed apparently (but not certainly) is that excavated by the church (the cellared property of church Phase 4). Neither of these is a serious objection: 'newly-paved' might well mean re-paved; the destroyed cellars either side of Mary-le-Port Street (fifteen cellars and vaults were certainly in existence by 1480, cf. 5.3.12e) may have been of pre-fifteenth-century date (cf. the ?re-used thirteenth-century window, 10.3.3d); and even if they were as late as this, the explanation of the make-up of clay and sandstone as having come from cellar excavation may be erroneous; there were other major works in progress in Bristol at this period which would have made such material freely available for road-filling, such as the foundation trench for the town walls in the eleventh – twelfth century or the re-direction of the river Frome in the mid-thirteenth century (cf. Walker, 1971, 8 and 22).

It is possible that the re-organisation involved not only road-paving (and possibly the building of stone cellars), but also a major change from timber to stone buildings in this part of Bristol.

8.5.3b PHASE 3b

There must also be a presumption in this hypothesis that the road was to continue in use but at a higher level than before. There is no evidence of any surface to the dumped material of 3a. In very small surviving areas, the paving of Phase 4 was laid directly on the dump; elsewhere however there were intermediate layers of dirt.

8.5.4 PHASE 4

8.5.4a PHASE 4a

It is suggested that the layers of 3a and 3b were deposited in a relatively short time—perhaps a matter of months—and that there was from the start of this operation an intention to raise the street level and to improve it beyond recognition by paving as represented by Phase 4a.

The earliest surviving paving was in places quite substantial but where the road levels were stratified the lower surfaces (notably A34) were of rough stone and small cobbles. A34 was however only defined as such in the south edge of the area, and appeared to be bounded by a kerb A35. This suggests that the paved road itself at this stage was hardly wider than the hollow way had been (cf. figure 27).

The upper surfaces were very much more systematically laid, large stone being pitched, and covered with paving of further blocks; and it seems probable that the paved road in its mature form extended over the whole area between properties on either side; it was probably up to 6 m. wide (i.e. wider than the maximum width excavated).

8.5.4b PHASE 4b

None of the levels so far described contained any finds datable later than *c*.1300; Phase 4b (the paving) contained a single sherd with a maximum *currency* lasting until *c*.1350 (cf. MF 8.6.4). Above the paved road, and in all features cut through it, modern finds were present. One post-medieval survival was a group of ?seventeenth-century crucibles in a disturbance (figure 27 and 11.10).

The paved road clearly remained in use for a very long period, perhaps several hundred years, and acquired very substantial wear. The post-road stratification, mostly removed mechanically, is illustrated in S2.

8.5.5 PHASE 5

It would appear that in pre-modern times there was a considerable accumulation of cess and other debris (cf. A2), and there were stone-lined drains, which must have been buried underneath surfaces which, by the time of excavation, had long since been destroyed.

Throughout this period, the cellared properties on either side were presumably in continuous use. As already suggested, they may have had their origins in the thirteenth century; it is possible that some phase of the walls, chute and cellar arch seen on the north side of Area A was medieval; post-medieval finds were made in the wall-trench on the south side of A19 and A18, but they may have been deposited during rebuilding or repair processes. The wall-trench A24 on the south side may also be medieval; there were no later finds in it, and it could have been stratigraphically linked to Phase 4 layers.

8.5.6 PHASE 6

The later history of the street is one of continuous disturbances and stone and brick building, often massive. By modern times Mary-le-Port Street was an asphalt road with a pavement sidewalk on its south side separated from the road by steel edging. The final road surface was over 1.75 m. above that of the lowest level of the hollow way, and it is to this that we owe the preservation, at least in small areas, of the important early medieval layers below.

The archaeological evidence for the properties on either side is slight, but does give some hint of their nature, especially in the eleventh – thirteenth centuries for which documentary data is lacking. For later times the written sources are of course very detailed and the tenement sequence is discussed by Frances Neale in Chapter 5.

8.6   Artefacts from MLPS East

8.6.1 PHASE ?1/2a

In the ditch fills were sherds of Saxo-Norman Fabric A (including one of the P6 sherds in J5; S5); J5 also contained a sherd of Fabric E (glazed), current c.1080 – 1200. OM5 comprised runnels of waste lead, possibly from metal working.

8.6.2 PHASE 2

Finds from this phase include flints, Roman pottery, metal objects, animal bones. The flints include utilised pieces (cf. 11.3). Roman finds comprise a tegula and brick fragments, two third-century coins and perhaps two glass beads and a piece of ?window glass. The metal objects include several iron tools (clench bolt, hammerhead, ?leather-working awl, an ?early medieval horseshoe); of copper-alloy, a buckle frame and part of a set of balances; and of stone, spindle whorls and a piece of *porfido verde antico*.

Manufacturing processes suggested by Phase 2 artefacts are spinning, leather, bone and metal working. The animal bone data link the first three. Horn fragments came from C31 of Phase 2a and from C17 of Phase 2d; dirt on the hollow way (Phase 2c) yielded c.1500 pieces of bone (c.127 kg.), and bird bone. Noddle's report (11.21) examines alternative interpretations of these, as consumers' waste or butchery for example, and how they are likely to have accumulated; she suggests they are a secondary dump in the road. Most are from cattle and sheep, with some pigs and goats and a few fragments of horse, dog and cat. Beef forms the bulk of the meat. The horn debris indicates horn working, and parts of three bone combs may suggest bone working. The bird bones (11.21.3) include goosander, wigeon (from waterfowling), domestic goose and fowl.

The evidence for spinning is a series of spindle whorls, of stone and pottery. Leather working is represented by offcuts of sheep or goat (and cf. iron awl above).

Iron working is indicated by ore, slag and furnace lining, from smithing rather than smelting (cf. 11.18.1); there is also some cupreous slag and crucible fragments.

Pottery from Phase 2a is all of Fabric A; that from Phase 2c is more numerous and extends the range of currency into the thirteenth century, with a variety of fabrics and forms, from local, middle-range and long-distance trade; that from Phase 2e includes a sherd compared with a Cheddar fabric of suggested late tenth- to eleventh-century currency and Ham Green ware current c.1225 – 1300.

8.6.3 – 4   PHASES 3 – 4

There are few finds in Phases 3 – 4 by comparison with those in the dirt of the hollow way. There are from 3a floor-tile fragments of ?late thirteenth – early fourteenth-century date; pottery of a similar range to previously; and a sherd from a pottery lamp. Phase 4 includes ceramic roof furniture and a sherd of a later fabric (current *c.*1250 – 1350). A residual find here was a copper-alloy hooked fastener (CA23) of possible pre-Conquest date.

8.6.5 – 6   PHASES 5 – 6

The only finds of interest from the upper levels of the roads are the group of ?seventeenth-century crucibles already mentioned, a group of glass vessels from A18, a cellar fill of Phase 5 (see 12.5 also) and one (probably two) hone of Norwegian Ragstone. There were also two more residual ?pre-Conquest finds: part of a horseshoe (IR1) and a copper-alloy faceted pin (CA10).

Chapter 9: Mary-le-Port Street West

9.1 Summary of phasing
(see Chapter 7 for integration of these with MLPS East and church)

Phase 0 natural stubstratum.
Phase 1 disturbed top of substratum, ?buried soil.
Phase 2 pre-hollow-way events.
Phase 3 hollow-way and timber features (including Timber Building).
Phase 4 fill of hollow way.
Phase 5 levelling material prior to paving.
Phase 6 paving and stone walls.
Phase 7 dirt levels.
Phase 8 road, all late- and post-medieval contexts, and unstratified material.

9.2 Introduction (figure 34)

MLPS West comprises parts of Mary-le-Port Street and the narrow range of buildings that lay between the church and the street. Excavation of the early levels at the east end included a complete section of the hollow way. Its fill contained a coin of Harold II (1066). A timber building was overlaid by stone walls, boundaries of the northern churchyard. These were broadly contemporary with the paving of the hollow way. A cellared property associated with this sequence was built in the north-east angle of the nave and church; it was subsequently fully integrated with the church and is thus described in Chapter 10.

Until the Second World War a dense series of buildings constructed against the church towered up above Mary-le-Port Street. Some of these were four – five storeys high and largely hid the church behind them. They were however astonishingly limited in width, with no more than 4 m. between the church and the street edge.

The site was mechanically stripped before excavation to the level of the medieval street and the tops of associated structures. It was evident at this stage that most stratification had been destroyed by cellars and cisterns and that only three areas would be worth investigation. The most westerly, Area 101, was excavated to natural; the next, 102, a narrow strip between a cellar and the street, was left in the main unexcavated; 103, the area outside the church's north door, was excavated only partly, to define medieval road surfaces clearly, together with some associated and underlying structures. The eastern area (104 – 106) was mostly excavated to natural, extending southwards as far as the church.

There were few stratigraphic links between the street, its associated building area and the church. For most of it length, the north wall of the church (in its Church Phase 4 form) marked a hiatus between church and exterior; but at the east end there were some structural links between the buildings outside the church and the church itself, including the cellared property mentioned above.

The phasing of Areas 104 – 106 can be linked to that of 101 – 103 only by the principal medieval paved-street levels, though a general correlation can be made between the pre-paved-street 'dirt' levels at each end of the street. Because a phased sequence can be defined for Area 104 – 105, this will be described first. Sections in MF figures provide supporting data for those areas. Discussion of the phasing of other areas is in 9.8; an interpretative summary of phasing is contained in figure 36 MF.

9.3 Areas 104 – 105
(north and east part of excavated areas, plans figures 34 and 35, section S8, figure 39)

9.3.0 PHASE 0
Natural substratum.

9.3.1 PHASE 1
The earliest archaeological stratum in this area is 105.15N, seen only in the extreme northern area as shown on the left of S8. This was similar in texture to the natural reddish sandy, but was green-stained,

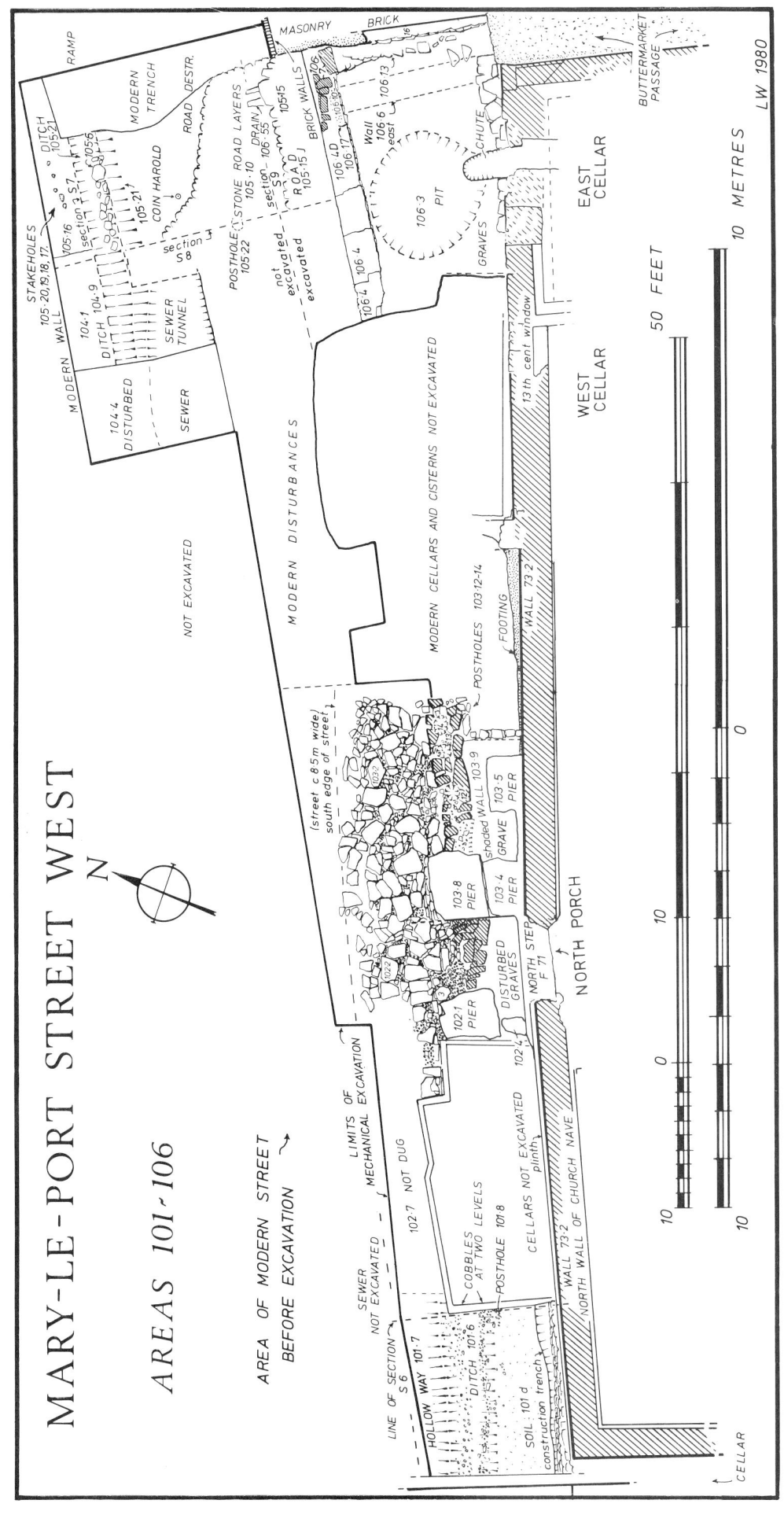

MARY-LE-PORT STREET WEST

AREAS 101–106

N

AREA OF MODERN STREET
BEFORE EXCAVATION →

RAMP
MASONRY
BRICK
MODERN TRENCH
MODERN WALL
ROAD DESTR.
DITCH 105.21
10.56
section S7
STAKEHOLES 105·16
section S8
105·21
COIN HAROLD
STAKEHOLES 105·20,19,18,17.
DITCH 104·9
104·1
10.4·4 DISTURBED
SEWER TUNNEL
SEWER

POSTHOLE 105·22
STONE ROAD LAYERS 105·10
section 106·55
ROAD 105·15 J
DRAIN S9
10545
BRICK WALLS
106·3
106·17 LD
106·13
Wall 106·6 east
106·4
106·4
106·6
PIT 106·3
not excavated
excavated
not excavated
excavated

NOT EXCAVATED

MODERN DISTURBANCES

MODERN CELLARS AND CISTERNS NOT EXCAVATED

(street c 85m wide)
south edge of street
POSTHOLES 103·12–14
shaded WALL 103·9
103·5 PIER
103·8 PIER
GRAVE
103·4 PIER
1021 PIER
DISTURBED GRAVES
102·4
1032
1022
FOOTING
WALL 73·2
13th cent window
CHUTE
GRAVES

EAST CELLAR
WEST CELLAR
BUTTERMARKET PASSAGE

NORTH STEP F 71
NORTH PORCH
NORTH WALL OF CHURCH NAVE

LIMITS OF MECHANICAL EXCAVATION
102·7 NOT DUG
COBBLES AT TWO LEVELS
POSTHOLE 101·8
CELLARS NOT EXCAVATED
plinth
WALL 73·2

LINE OF SECTION S 6
SEWER NOT EXCAVATED
101·7
HOLLOW WAY 101·7
DITCH 101·6
SOIL 101 d
construction trench
CELLAR

10   0   10   50 FEET
10   0   10 METRES

LW 1980

Figure 34.

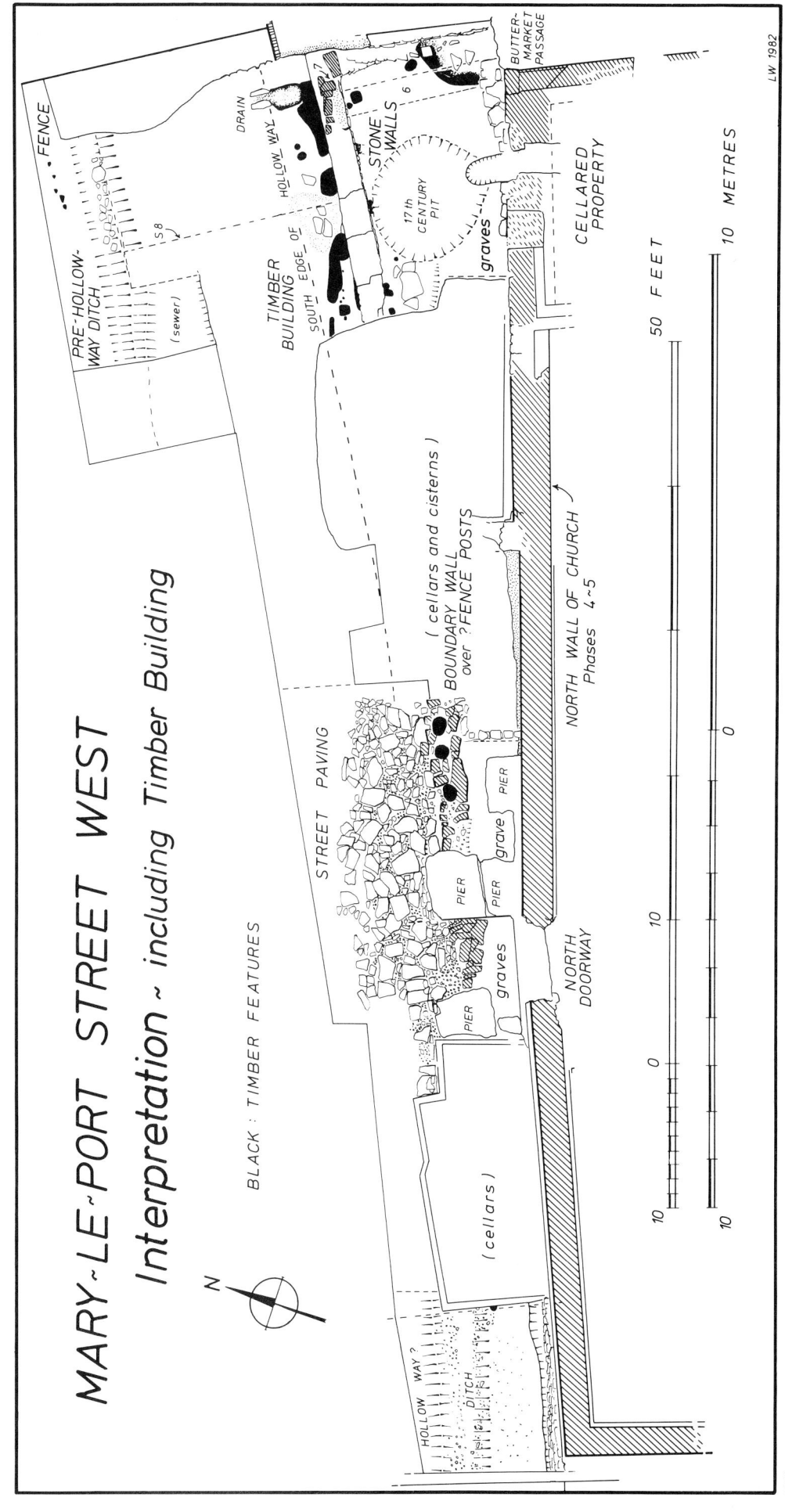

MARY~LE~PORT STREET WEST
Interpretation ~ including Timber Building

BLACK : TIMBER FEATURES

N

FENCE

PRE-HOLLOW-
WAY DITCH

(sewer)

S8

DRAIN

HOLLOW WAY

TIMBER
BUILDING

SOUTH EDGE OF

STONE WALLS

6

17th
CENTURY
PIT

graves

BUTTER-
MARKET
PASSAGE

CELLARED
PROPERTY

STREET PAVING

(cellars and cisterns)

BOUNDARY WALL
over ?FENCE POSTS

PIER

PIER

PIER

grave

PIER

graves

NORTH WALL OF CHURCH
Phases 4~5

NORTH
DOORWAY

HOLLOW WAY ?

DITCH

(cellars)

50 FEET

10 METRES

LW 1982

Figure 35.

73

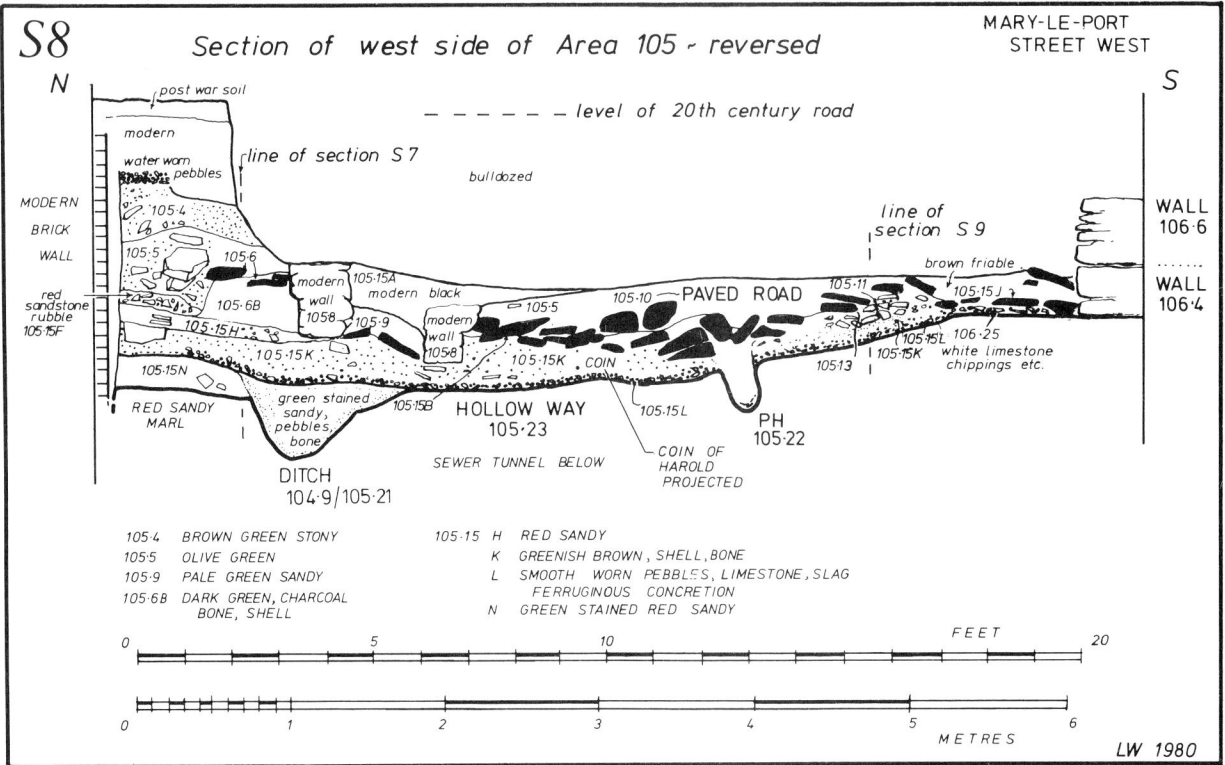

Figure 39.

with flint, ore, and animal bone. The natural at its base here is at a lower level than the base of the hollow way to the south (S8). While it is possible that 105.15N represents mud in a hollow way earlier than that defined further south, its lower base suggests that it is the fill of a pre-hollow-way ditch, or a lowered occupation area, itself cut by the ditch of Phase 2. Phase 1 could be pre-medieval.

9.3.2 PHASE 2

A ditch (104.9/105.21) was cut through 105.15N. It contained some finds (flint, metal-working residues, charcoal and animal bone) but nothing obviously medieval; it might, like Phase 1, be pre-medieval. It is more likely, however, that Phases 1 and 2 represent the earliest (?aceramic) occupation of this area in late Saxon times. Also probably of this phase were five stake-holes (105.16 – 20), on the north side of the ditch, interpreted as part of a fence of structure of this period. The ditch filled up, or was filled, with homogeneous material.

9.3.3 PHASE 3

A hollow way (105.23); see S8) developed, wearing away the sandy natural and the fill of earlier features to a depth of c.50 cm. (cf. level by walls on right of S8). Its surface, as finally lowered and stabilised, consisted of small pebbles and other material (105.15L in a ferruginous concretion) (cf. MLPS East, Phase 2a levels). It is argued, in relation to MLPS East (8.5.2a), that the formation of this surface, seen along the the entire length of the street excavated, was the result of use, rather than representing deliberate metalling. The ferruginous concretion, in Area 105, spread over the whole width of the hollow way, its southern edge formed by a cut or worn edge (S8, right). On the north side however the road surface died away gradually beyond the earlier filled-up ditch, in an area which may still have been part of a wider zone of movement or truncation (see Phases 1 and 2 above, and S8 left). It should be noted that 105.15L extended over the top of the covered drain 106.55 (figure 40 MF); this demonstrates that the primary phase of the Timber Building complex (see below, 9.6.2) was at least as early as the final surface of the hollow way, and provides the only direct stratigraphic link between the two areas. The layer of white limestone chippings (106.25) shown on the right of S8 was also found in a sparser form south of the wall (106.4, etc.) which breaks the stratification here; the extent of 106.25 suggests that the building complex was in use at the same time as the hollow way.

9.3.4 PHASE 4

A 'cessy' layer (105.15K) covered the bottom of the hollow way (S8). There had probably always been dirt on this surface. It has been suggested that similar material on the road further east was more likely to have resulted from mud continuously being churned, rather than from debris deliberately dumped or accumulating after disuse (cf. 8.5.2c). 105.15K, in contrast, is thought to represent the *final* dirt present—perhaps a dump, before the hollow way was abandoned. It contained much occupation debris, including animal bone, shell and an important group of pottery, some sherds being hand-sized. Also in this layer was the coin of Harold II (1066) (11.16), which is thus associated with the pottery. It provides a *terminus post quem* for the deposition of this layer and for those above; it also provides a hypothesis that some at least of the pottery, and the hollow way below, is of pre-Conquest date. It is an assumption on these lines, together with the assessment of the pottery (11.10) and potentially the parallels suggested for some copper-alloy objects (MF 11.15) which are the basis of a 'late Saxon' attribution for the earliest features in the Mary-le-Port area. The earliest activity may be of tenth-century date (cf. 11.10.4a).

9.3.5 PHASE 5
Above this dirt were layers of red sandy soil and red sandstone (105.15F, 105.15H, S8). Apart from a missing red clay component, these were similar to Phase 3a contexts in MLPS East, and are likewise interpreted as levelling-up material derived from major excavations (cf. 8.5.3a). If this equation is correct, this is an important link between the sequence in the two parts of the street. The very few pottery sherds from this material are of eleventh – thirteenth-century date.

9.3.6 PHASE 6
As with the sequence in MLPS East, this upcast was followed by a systematic paving of the road area, probably within a short time. Many areas of slabs were recorded (cf. S8), including (unlike MLPS East) repairs and replacements, though there was heavy disturbance by modern features.

To the south a limit at some time may be indicated by the post- or stone-hole 105.22 (S8), which cut through earlier levels, but as it was a long way into the road, it may instead be a single tethering-post or feature relating to a house structure such as an overhanging upper storey.

More definitely, some phases of slabbing (105.15J, S8 right) clearly extended further south right up to the wall 106.4; this appears to have been part of the road rather than a paved area by the house itself—the surface was continuous, at it was in Areas 102 – 3 further west.

9.3.7 PHASE 7
There were dirt layers above the cobbled road (105.2; 105.4 – .5 in S8 and cf. MLPS East, 8.5.5), but all these may have been re-deposited in modern time, rather than representing neglect of the paved road. There had been massive modern disturbances, though fortunately the main sewer was tunnelled in this area; a cross-section of the late Saxon and medieval roads thus survived, comparable with S2 further east.

9.3.8 PHASE 8
A later street surface is hinted at by a layer of water-worn pebbles at a high level on the left of section S8, seen in only a very small area (cf. R. Leech's evidence of rising street levels, MF 9.12.3). The final tarmac surface was eventually established at over a metre above the medieval cobbled road, and over 1.5 m. above the hollow way.

9.4 Area 101
(plans, figures 34 – 35)

The hard red marl substratum was here only 60 cm. below the paved medieval road surface of Phase 6. In the area adjacent to the church, it may have been truncated, as the level of its surface rose to the north, where a small area of the overlying orange sands also survived. Above it, 101d, a disturbed soil which contained pottery, is tentatively assigned to Phase 2.

101.7, a negative feature at the north end, is interpreted as the south edge of the Phase 3 hollow way. If this equation is correct, the hollow way here was of different character to the road as seen in S8, across Area 105. The bottom of 101.7 had only a slight ferruginous concretion, which may explain the profile and apparent depth of the hollow way, if such it is, at this point. The dirt, 101b, filling it, of Phase 4, was very dark and 'cessy' green. In contrast to 105.15K for example, it contained few finds. This may suggest Area 101 lay beyond the main sources of domestic and industrial debris. Was the street turning or ending here (cf. figure 25)? 101b merged with 101c, the lighter green fill of negative feature 101.6; 101b and 101c may have been contemporary. Both contained eleventh – twelfth-century pottery, as well as slag and furnace lining. 101.6 is interpreted as a ditch, perhaps alongside the road.

An alternative interpretation, however, is that the earliest hollow way did not extend this far west, and that both 101.7 and 101.6 may have been ditches with a different function. Whether ditches and/or hollow way, they were however clearly filled up before the area was paved in Phase 6.

Both in the upper dirt of 101c and at the interface of these with the stony layer 101a were cobbles and a few larger stones. These presumably represent metalling of the paved road at more than one level, laid over filled-up earlier features in a manner analogous to other areas observed further east. 101a had a greenish matrix, suggesting the presence of cess. There is no evidence in this part of the road for any massive levelling or sealing of earlier features and surfaces with sandstone or clay before the paving was laid.

At some stage in the life of the road, the north wall of the church's Phase 4 north aisle was built (cf. 10.3.4). Part at least of 101a sealed its construction trench.

101a also sealed the fill of a post-hole, 101.8, which was itself secondary to the features below, but of uncertain date; it may be part of a roadside fence or building (or churchyard boundary). It is in line with similar post-holes further east in Area 103 but its phasing could not be co-ordinated with them (9.5 below).

9.5 Areas 102,103

(plans, figures 34 and 35)

These comprise a small strip surviving between a cellar and the modern street and sewer, and the paved area outside the north door of the church. Here medieval stratification survived because the area outside the church door was not in secular use in the late medieval period. The hollow way of Phase 3 appeared to continue westwards as 102.7. This was named but not fully excavated. To its south was a layer of dark coal-studded ashy soil (103.9B). Three post-holes (103.12 – 14) were defined in this layer, filled with similar material, but not necessarily contemporary. They could be interpreted as part of a wooden fence (cf. 101.8 in 9.4 above), a churchyard or property boundary.

On the line of these holes and sealing the dirt layer was a wall foundation (103.9) on a similar but not identical alignment to that further east (106.4) to be described below in 9.6. 103.9 is more certainly interpreted as a churchyard boundary. It encloses a narrow area of graves to its south (cf. 9.6.3 and 9.10 below).

Graves in the area south of wall 103.9 included an articulated burial cut by buttress 103.5, associated with church Phase ?4 and by the porch masonry of 103.4 and of church Phase 5 – 6 (see below). There were also burials in the soil beneath the inner part of the porch. These did not appear to extend north under the paving or west under the porch foundations.

The proposed churchyard boundary must have originally extended right through this part of the road, but it may have ended before Area 101, turning south to abut on, or be cut by, the first north aisle wall of the Phase 3 church. In this case, the possible western boundary to burials under the inner part of the porch may mark the edge of the cemetery in this area before Phase 3 (cf. 9.10). Wall 103.9 is interpreted as having had a shorter life than 106.4 and its successors.

It is thus possible that burial in this area preceded both the present north wall of the church and also the original north aisle of church Phase 3. There was a clear northern edge to the grave-cut area apparent to the south of 103.9.

Most of the area was heavily paved with red sandstone, cobbles and worn Pennant flagstones (Phase 6), as elsewhere along the street. There was, along this part of the street, clearly more than one layer of paving. The paving north of the porch was not removed and has been retained as part of the conserved area.

The upper level of this paving (102.2) extended southwards towards the church, between two masonry foundations (102.1, 103.8). These were bonded with mortar similar to that in the Phase 5 modifications to the tower. They are interpreted as the foundations of a porch linked to the church wall on the west by a lighter foundation bonded with a soft pink mortar (102.4); and on the east side by another pier (103.4) with dark-red mortar which was also like that of the Phase 5 modifications to the tower and the south wall of the church. The inner area of the porch area was not paved. There may have been a wooden threshold here, or a no-longer-surviving stone slab north of the stone step F71 (cf. figure 45). This porch abutted the Phase 4 north church wall. The north doorway of the church was remodelled in church Phase 5 (or possibly 6), to which the later porch features are also assigned. With the subsequent levelling and covering of 103.9 with at least two levels of paving (so that the porch floor was continuous with the road surface outside), the church precinct was thus encroached upon by the street zone.

9.6 Area 106

(plans, figures 34, 35, 41, 43, section S8, figure 39)

9.6.1 INTRODUCTION

This comprises the area between the north-east corner of the church and the hollow way described above in Areas 102 – 105. It was bounded on the south by the north wall of the cellared property, possibly originally the parsonage, in the angle formed by the nave and chancel (cf. 10.6 – .7). On the west side all early levels had been destroyed; to the east there were successive north-south walls which continued the line of the north-east corner of a timber building (see below). These probably always formed a limit to the whole complex on the east side. There was always apparently a north-south lane here, to the east of both the church and the secular complex in its north-east corner. There was certainly such a lane here in modern times: Buttermarket Passage. Its line however must be slightly west of any former lane, as it lay directly above the successive north-south walls. The passage, with its paving, still (1983) exists east of the church, but was removed in the excavations in Area 106 under discussion (see figure 41).

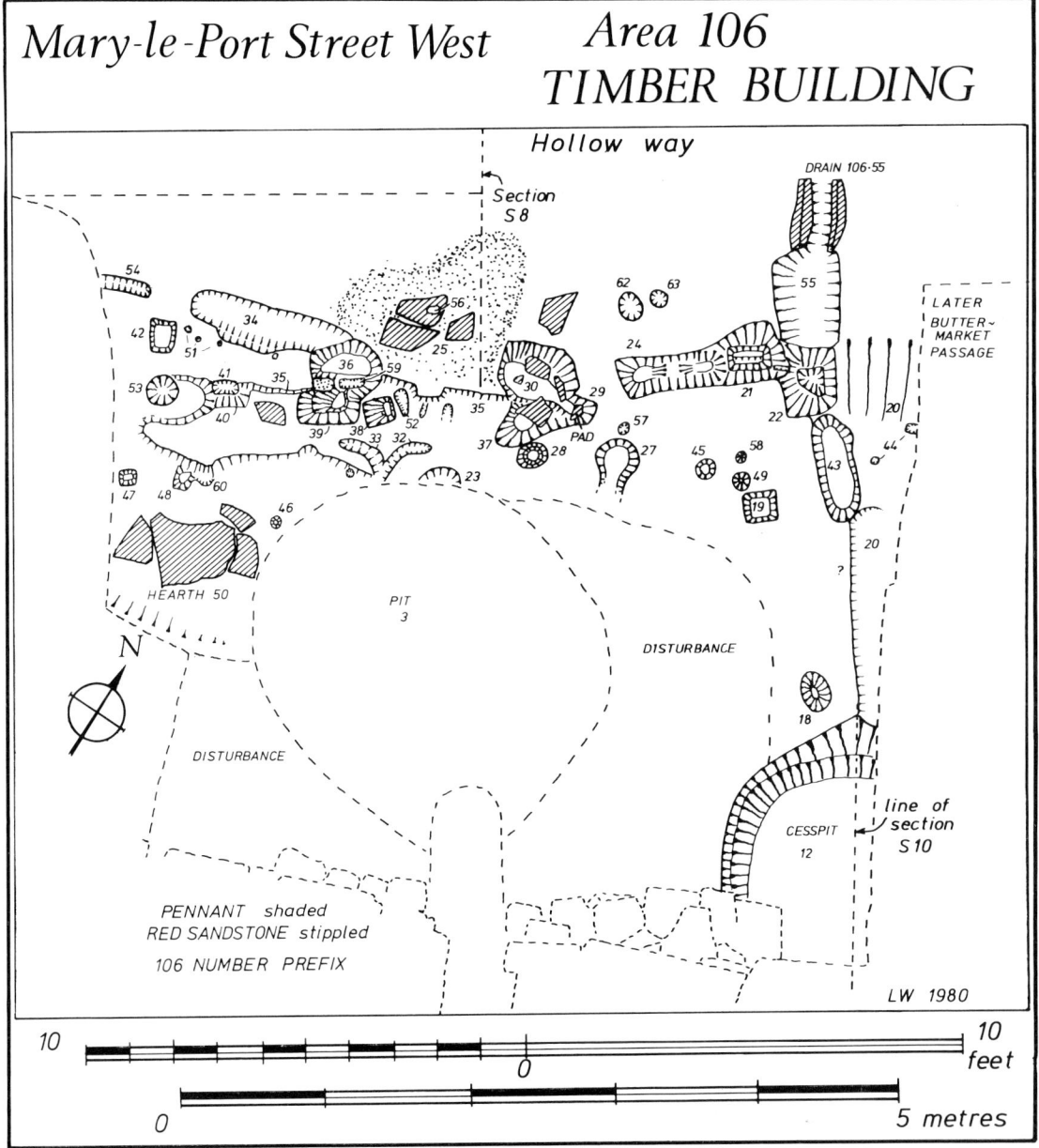

Figure 41.

There is evidence for two principal phases of activity in this area. The first consisted of parts of a timber building, possibly in two phases, and broadly contemporary with the hollow way to the north. The line of its north wall, parallel to the street, may have been continued to the west by a timber fence (9.5 above). The north and east walls of the Timber Building were overlaid by an L-shaped complex of walls in three phases. These enclosed an area north-east of the church, the east end of the northern churchyard, used for burial after c.1300. The north wall of this complex probably continued the line of 103.9 to the west (9.5 above). The life of the stone walls overlapped that of the stone-paved phases of Mary-le-Port Street. They could have been contemporary in origin.

By the post-medieval period, Area 106 had been divorced from the church and a five-storey building, built at least as early as 1648 (5.3.13a), was erected. It was eventually 38 Mary-le-Port Street. Fortunately, this part of the property, though rising to five storeys above, had no cellar so the buried features beneath its ground floor remained intact.

9.6.2 THE TIMBER BUILDING (plans, figures 35, 41, 43, plate 15)

The features shown in figure 41 were all defined in the lowest levels of the stratification in this area, cut into the natural sandy marl, and associated with the earliest types of pottery; they are assigned to Phase 3. The features comprised the eastern part of the north wall line which probably included the doorway to the street beyond; and probably the northern part of the eastern wall line, incorporating a cesspit. The original dimensions are uncertain, but if the proposed doorway was central the building was c.6 m. from east to west and less certainly c.4 m. north-south, assuming the cesspit to have been in the south-east corner. Other features include a hearth, probably near the north-west interior corner, and a drain into Mary-le-Port Street, possibly taking water into the hollow way from a gable end facing Buttermarket Passage.

The construction was substantial, based on post-holes, stake-holes, and possible timber slots (figures 41 and 43); the latter may have held short sill-beams, but there were also narrow and sharp basal impressions which may indicate the seatings for upright planks. The shape of the holes may in many other cases be those of the robbing holes rather than that of the timbers themselves. Several slabs of Pennant Sandstone were found set in the marl. Those named 106.50 were in a slight depression, and were covered with wood-ash and charcoal-studded soil; it is suggested that this was the hearth area. Other slabs around 106.30 may have been for packing the timber, and one at the base of 106.29 was certainly a padstone. Other slabs set on edge were used to form the drain exit. The composite pair of post-holes in the middle part of the north wall line (cf. figure 43) are interpreted as the jambs for a doorway, which may have been up to a metre wide. 106.35 may be the emplacement for a wooden threshold. Outside this possible doorway were several Pennant slabs (106.25) with blackened surfaces, covering deposits of slag, charcoal and white limestone (see below). One slab had fused slag on its surface. If there was a doorway here, this material cannot be in situ as an industrial feature, but should, in this interpretation, be material from such a feature spread here to raise the level outside the door. It also provided a consolidated surface in front of the house, forming a continuous surface with the south edge of the hollow way (cf. S8 and 9.3.3 above). The cesspit located in the south-east of the timber structure may have been set in its back corner and thus mark its limit. The pit stratification included characteristic green concretion around the edges, and laminated cess and soil levels which represent periodic 'sealing' of the cess layers. Post-hole 106.18 may have been part of an associated latrine structure.

Two features remain to be discussed. On the east side, the return wall to the south was indicated by 106.43. There was in addition also trench 106.20, which cut 106.43, and may therefore represent a later version of the east wall. It may however be only a trench for the later stone wall 106.13 since it was below this and on the same line.

The function of the Timber Building is presumed to be domestic and/or industrial; quantities of iron-ore, slag, crucible fragments, charcoal and white limestone chippings, possibly for iron-smelting flux, were found throughout this area, extending into the hollow way (cf. 9.7.3 – .4). Feature 106.23 (figure 41) may be the truncated edge of a furnace. It is not possible on the basis of the evidence available to argue whether the building was actually used for iron working or whether it was a domestic building associated with such a complex, or both; similarly, the scale of work is unknown. Together with the evidence from areas further west and east, and from the hollow way itself, it may be seen as one structure in a widespread complex of industrial activity on either side of Mary-le-Port Street in the early medieval period.

The building is among the earliest secular buildings for which there is evidence in Bristol. Table 5 compares its construction with broadly contemporary structures now known at Bristol Castle (Ponsford, 1979). It has already been suggested that the building was side-on to Mary-le-Port Street, and gable-end-on to the postulated lane or passage to the east. This, it should be noted, was not the arrangement of seventeenth-century and later buildings on the site which were gable-end-on to Mary-le-Port Street (cf. plate 3). There is a little evidence of daub (cf. 9.7.3 – .4) with wattle and ?lath impressions, but the building may have been principally of post and plank construction.

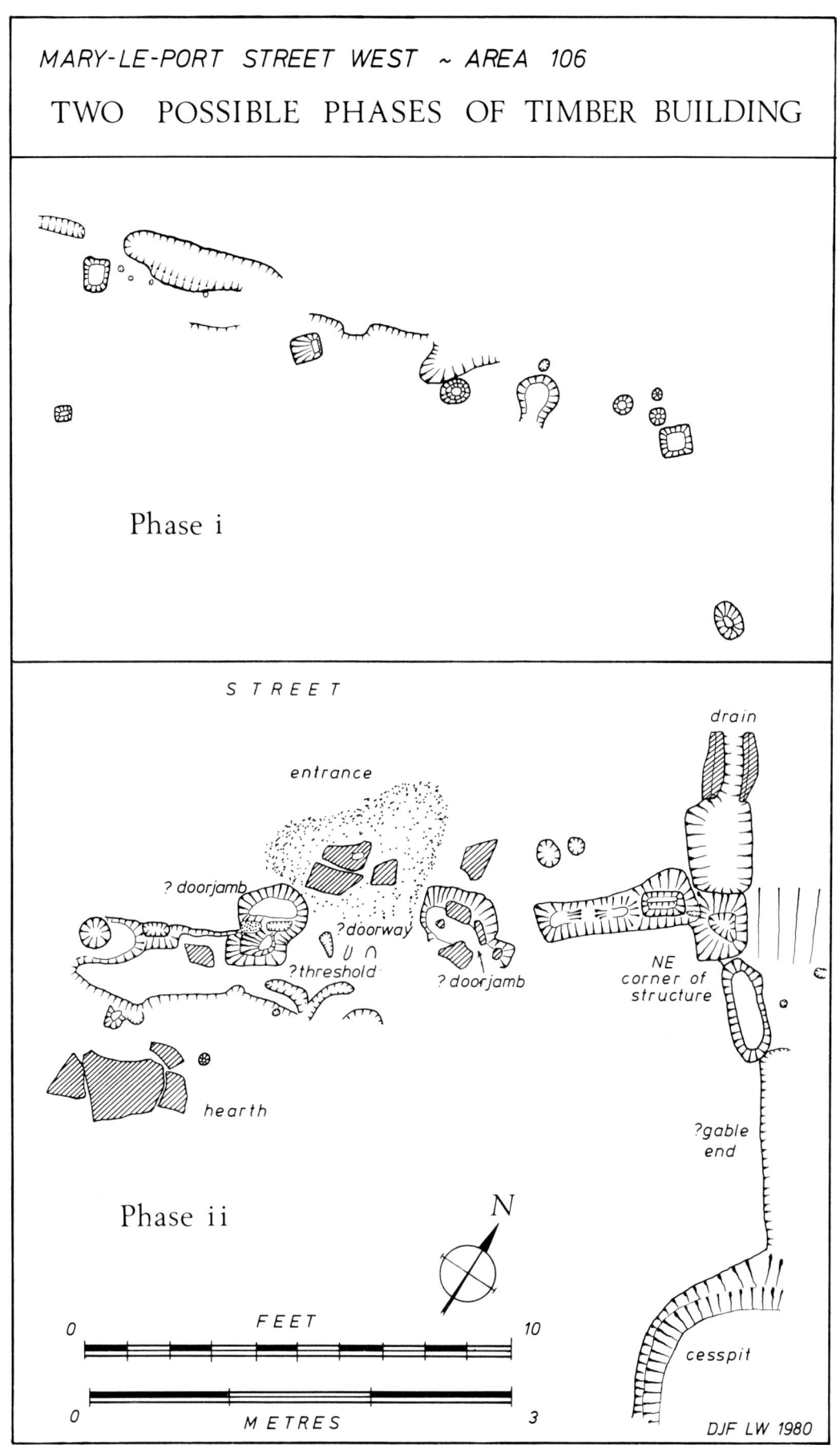

MARY-LE-PORT STREET WEST ~ AREA 106

TWO POSSIBLE PHASES OF TIMBER BUILDING

Phase i

STREET

entrance

drain

? doorjamb

? doorway

? threshold

? doorjamb

NE corner of structure

hearth

? gable end

Phase ii

N

cesspit

FEET

0   10

METRES

0   3

DJF LW 1980

Figure 43.

TABLE 5   COMPARISON OF MARY-LE-PORT, AREA 106, ?LATE SAXON-EARLY NORMAN TIMBER FEATURES, WITH THOSE OF BRISTOL CASTLE, SITE D

ASPECT	MLP, AREA 106	BC, SITE D (Ponsford, 1979)
Dating	MLPS West, Phase 3, eleventh – twelfth century.	Period I ii – iv, c.1000 – 1070 (p. 235).
Building elements	?Timber slots/trenches/planks. Post-holes, stake-holes, daub, wattle and ?lath impressions. Cesspit. Hearth. More dubious features.	Beams in trenches. Post-holes. Stake-holes. Post in trench. Sill beams.
Other elements	?Industrial activity—?furnace lining, iron ore, slag, charcoal, white limestone chippings, crucible fragments.	Iron working associated with forge stone *in situ*, also with clay, ash, sand (p. 241). (**NB** no direct stratigraphical relationship between this and timber features but both cut into natural) (p. 241).
Number of phases	?Two.	At least three.
Plan	Doubtful; two phases on different orientations very tentatively hypothesised.	None as not totally excavated.
Associated pottery	A, H, T ?Roman, u/c (Fabric A includes BPT 1 and BPT 115).	BPT 1, 2, 3, 176A, 251, 190 (Table 1, p. 417; cf. p. 395 also).
Function	Domestic and/or industrial.	Not suggested under Site D, but in conclusion described as 'late Saxon settlement' (p. 178).

In the part of the plan that survives, the features were complex, variable, and unsystematic (cf. figure 41). The 'superfluity' of post-holes and other features may be due to internal features and/or repeated alterations or patching; or they may represent two distinct periods, the later being a rebuild of the former. Daryl Fowler suggested the latter to be the case, and drew out a two-phase plan (figure 43), postulating a substantial change in orientation. There is no stratigraphical or other evidence to substantiate his hypothesis, except that he suggested that the fill of more features of the earlier phase were bluish and charcoal-flecked.

If Fowler was correct, the change of orientation would be important. The earlier phase would be closer to (but not on) that of the early church, and the second phase to that of the street; it was the latter alignment that was rebuilt in stone (see below). This might indicate that in the period of the first phase Timber Building, and of the early church, the street was not well-enough defined to influence the orientation of buildings to its south as it was later on. This may in turn suggest the possibility that buildings in this area preceded any well-defined street system.

9.6.3   THE STONE WALLS (plans, figures 34, 35, 44 and section S8, figure 39)
The features interpreted as the north wall of the Timber Building were directly overlaid by a series of stone walls in three definable phases (106.4 complex; 106.7; 106.6); their returns to the south were approximately on the same line as the suggested east wall of the Timber Building (figure 44, cf. figures 35, 43).

The earliest walls, the 106.4 complex, survived to a height of c.30 m. high on the line of section S8, but to over 60 cm. further east. Up to seven or eight courses, of angular limestone and Pennant Sandstone, packed with dirty red marl and sand, were extant.

106.4 returned southwards as wall 106.13, of similar construction, but surviving only as a footing. To the south this became fragmented as it crossed the filled-up earlier pit 106.12 (cf. figures 41 and 44); there is no evidence to indicate how far it may formerly have continued to the south, although it may have finished on the proposed south line of the earlier Timber Building; a southern limit is set by the chancel wall of Phase 2 and later churches (cf. figure 25).

Plate 15.   Area 106, Timber Building from south-west.

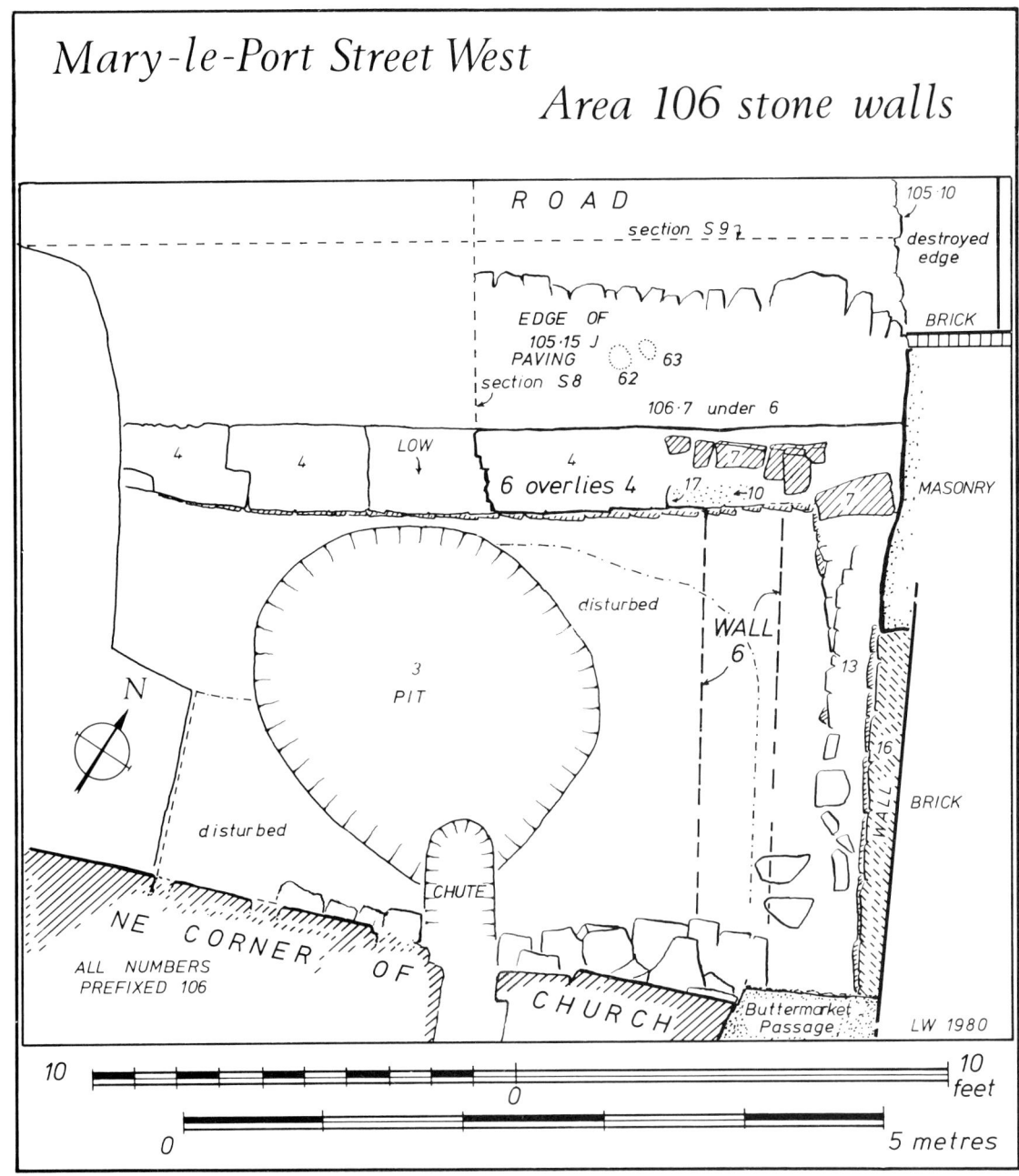

Figure 44.

In the surface of 106.4 towards its north-east corner at its highest part (= 106.10) was a worn stone, in which there was a well-defined groove (106.17 = ST 14) (figure 44). This stone may have been the west side of a door sill, the groove being caused by a door bolt opening inwards to the south. The evidence is hardly conclusive in view of the uncertainty about ground levels, but the suggestion is worth recording. It could be an entrance from the street into the churchyard.

The area of this possible entrance was covered by further stones, 106.7, the second phase of the walling, on a slightly different alignment, and packed with an earthy mortar. This may also have returned south on the line of 106.13, to judge by the lie of its easternmost stones.

The third phase of walling was represented by 106.6, similar stones packed with salmon-brown mortar. The north part of 106.6 (cf. S8) was built over 106.4, but its return south was west of its predecessor 106.7 and 106.13 (figure 34).

The external road or paved surfaces associated with the stone walls are shown in section S8. 106.25, the lowest layer on the Mary-le-Port Street side of 106.4, was overlain by the first road paving, 105.15J, of Phase 6, which is thought to have been contemporary with the earlier phases of the stone walls (106.4 and .7). There may have been higher surfaces, since destroyed.

Within the walls, where the ground was not destroyed by later features, the space was filled up with mixed brown mortary soil (106.2). This contained fourteenth – fifteenth-century sherds, including the greater part of a Minety-type pot, probably of the first half of the fourteenth century (cf. figure 80.107). Even if the burial soil was imported these sherds nevertheless provide a *terminus post quem* for burial in this area. This layer continued beneath the lightly-founded eastern member of the 106.6, extending as far as 106.13. So 106.6 is later than *c*.1300—possibly much later. At the base of the mortuary soil 106.2, but not beneath 106.6, were parts of articulated burials. These were not dug into the natural clay, but were in a compact level with fourteenth – fifteenth-century sherds similar to those in the dirt layer 106.2 above them.

It would appear therefore that 106.4, .7, .6 were built as churchyard walls to enclose an area of burial after *c*.1300—it is probably fortuitous that no graves were actually found beneath 106.6. The walls were presumably built high enough for soil to be piled inside them to provide depth for graves; 106.7 and .6 probably represent heightenings of the churchyard wall facing the street. 106.6 also marks the movement of its eastern arm a metre or so to the west. It is suggested that the occasion for this was the building of the cellared property in the angle of nave and chancel, 106.6 east returning to its north-east corner. Since this is dated to Church Phase 4 (later fifteenth century), the area for burial was quite large in the later life of the Phase 3 church (figure 25). Burial may have continued in the small space left by Church Phase 4, but this is perhaps unlikely; that there was no material later than the fifteenth century in the grave earth might suggest that burial ceased in this area with the construction of the cellared property. It certainly ended before 1648 (5.3.13).

9.6.4   LATER FEATURES IN AREA 106, AND BUTTERMARKET PASSAGE (plans, figures 34, 35)

These include a large pit (106.3), which had finds, including clay tobacco pipes, of the seventeenth century in its fill. Another north-south wall (106.16) was built over the east side of 106.13, packed with pink mortar. Above this was black soil with eighteenth-century finds (106.8) and this in turn was sealed by the paved alleyway known as Buttermarket Passage, which continued around the church on its south side. This was in Area 106, bounded on its east side by a brick wall.

Buttermarket Passage is thus, in this form, a relatively late feature. There must have been some access on the east side of the church to serve the doorway and window (of uncertain date) opening out from the cellared property (cf. 10.7). The eastern arm of Buttermarket Passage was shown dividing no. 38 Mary-le-Port Street from its neighbour to the east at least as early as the beginning of the nineteenth century (cf. plate 5), and had presumably done so since the erection of that building in the seventeenth century (cf. plate 3).

It may indeed have existed by the time of the Timber Building, which it is suggested was gable-end-on, not to Mary-le-Port Street, but to an earlier version of Buttermarket Passage. Subsequent changes to the latter's western edge can be traced at least in part. The Timber Building and churchyard walls 106.4/7 both had a more easterly boundary than the later cellared property; by the time this was built Buttermarket Passage had extended westwards to the east wall of its cellar, to wall 106.6 (east) and to the east wall of the chancel of Church Phase 2B and following (cf. figures 25, 43, and 45).

No. 38 Mary-le-Port Street (as it later became) was built on what was described as 'void ground' before *c*.1648 (5.3.13a). It was a five-storey building, including the attic (cf. 5.3.13b, no. 38). The roof plan of the 1875 restoration shows the properties along the north side of the church oversailing the north aisle (cf. plate 34 MF), and thus gaining a little more floor space in their upper storeys. This house must have covered the whole of Area 106; its east wall is shown on more recent maps to extend no further than 106.6 east, on which it may have been built. Its street frontage was about a metre north of the earlier churchyard wall, its north-east corner very close to that of the Timber Building.

This fine house may be seen in plate 5 as the premises of Plumleys the Poulterers in the earlier nineteenth century, and (with no. 39 next door to the west) as Jones' Brush Shop in more recent times (cf. plate 17). It was in this role that it was finally destroyed by fire in 1940, leaving after clearance no more than the slight remains uncovered in excavation.

9.6.5   DISCUSSION OF THE SEQUENCE IN AREA 106

The relationship between the south edge of the street and the church became increasingly awkward (figure 25). The Phase 1 church as reconstructed in figure 51 would have allowed considerable room at the east end of the church for any contemporary secular building, but by the time of the more certain reconstruction of the Phase 2B church, the area between the Timber Building, which certainly existed by or before this time, and the now-extended east end of the church had become restricted; this would finally result in the triangular piece of ground between Mary-le-Port Street and the latest north wall of the church, which was leased as one with the area of the cellared property in the seventeenth century (cf. 5.3.13).

9.7 Artefacts from MLPS West

9.7.0 INTRODUCTION

The volume of finds from MLPS West is less than from MLPS East. This may relate to the diverse character of the hollow way along its length, to different rubbish-disposal policies along the street, or to other, irrecoverable, factors.

9.7.1 PHASES 0–1

The earliest levels contained only flint scrapers, iron (haematite) ore and animal bone.

9.7.2 PHASE 2

Phase 2 contexts contained flint, utilised flakes and pebbles, charcoal, animal bone, furnace lining, and metal-working residues. The only pottery assigned to this phase are a few sherds from soil 101d, similar to sherds of Phase 3.

9.7.3–4 PHASES 3–4

Pottery from the timber features is consistent with their phasing with the hollow way, as already suggested on stratigraphical grounds. The few baked-clay fragments may provide some indication of the rendering of the superstructure of the timber features—daub with both wattle and ?lath impressions was found. The range of artefacts found in the cesspit 106.12 suggest that its fill included rubbish. In the hollow way, there was a single utilised flint and one ?Roman 'pie-dish' rim sherd. Stone objects include several domestic items, parts of two Old Red Sandstone quern stones and a limestone lamp. The only evidence of industry in this area is that of metal working, in the form of furnace lining, haematite ore, iron slag, ?flux, ?copper alloy and SL34, a ?bloom from the base of the hollow way; there is also a single sherd of crucible from the timber features.

Dating evidence for all phases of MLPS West before the heavy paving of the later road is based on the associated pottery and the single pre-Conquest coin of Harold II. Fabric A occurs throughout these contexts, in its early BPT 1 form, which had a currency before and around the Conquest (1000–1070). Fabric A also includes the later BPT 115 (current c.1070–1100). The fill of the hollow way included a single sherd of fabric J (Ham Green jug), current c.1225–1300.

9.7.5 PHASE 5

Much less levelling material prior to the paved road was present in MLPS West. It contained only four sherds of pottery of similar types to those in earlier levels.

9.7.6 PHASE 6

There were similarly few artefacts in the paving and associated levels. IR9 is part of a flesh-hook from the lower paving. Both the 'cessy' material and the upper paving have a wider range of fabrics than the lower paving, but included nothing clearly later than c.1300.

9.7.6a THE STONE WALLS AND 106.2

These walls were associated with only a few sherds, but these do extend later in time than Phase 6. The latest pottery associated with 106.7 were sherds current c.1250–1300; but there were also fourteenth-century green-glazed sherds and one current c.1250–1350 from 106.6. The presence of the greater part of a Minety-type pot (probably of the first half of the fourteenth century—cf. figure 80.107) in the lower fill of 106.2, which had partly accumulated before wall 106.6, shows that this fill was accumulating after c.1300.

9.7.7 PHASE 7

It is uncertain on stratigraphic grounds whether the levels above the paving had been disturbed; the pottery would suggest that they were intact as the latest sherds were of Fabric J, BPT 118 (current 1250–1350).

9.7.8 PHASE 8 (including unstratified)

Late and post-medieval levels were again disturbed in this part of the road. GL8 is a post-medieval bottle bearing a named seal, 'G Southcombe, Bristol'. CA5 and CA8 are part of a pair of tweezers and a pin for which early parallels can be made.

9.8   General summary of the sequence in MLPS West

9.8.1   PHASE 1
Above the natural substratum, the earliest context was 105.15.N, the fill of a ditch or a lowered area of ground. A similar truncation was also found in Area 101. The only finds were flint, ore and bone; Phase 1 represents occupation in late Saxon times, or possibly pre-medieval.

9.8.2   PHASE 2
Also aceramic was the fill of ditch 104.9/105.21, possibly a property boundary; there was in this phase flint, animal bone and metal-working residues. There were however sherds of early fabrics in one of the fence posts 105.16 − 20 and also in 101d, both assigned to Phase 2. All this could be pre-Conquest, but is more likely to be immediately prior to Phase 3.

9.8.3   PHASE 3
The hollow way and the Timber Building were broadly contemporary. The only stratigraphical links between these two sets of features are the drain 106.55 and the surface 106.25. Characteristic debris of metal working and animal bone does, however, link Phase 3 contexts.

It is suggested that fence 103.12 − .14 belongs to this phase. It could be a property boundary contemporary with the Timber Building, or (since its line is the same as wall 103.9 over it) the north boundary of an early phase of the north churchyard (figure 25, 1 − 2), west of the Timber Building, but in line with its north wall (in both cases the street frontage).

The hollow way at the east end was apparently similar to that in MLPS East, but not at the west end, where it may be ending or turning.

A predecessor of the later Buttermarket Passage must have existed by this time.

9.8.4 − 5   PHASES 4 − 5
The filling of the hollow way is equated with similar events in MLPS East, except that the early material in its base in Area 105 was clearly dumped rubbish, and the evidence for deliberate make-up in preparation for paving was restricted to the eastern end.

It is not clear at what stage the Timber Building became redundant. The later stone walls are thought to be broadly contemporary with the earliest paving of Phase 6; the Timber Building had therefore been removed by this time. There was no evidence of an intermediary phase between this and the building of the stone walls.

9.8.6   PHASE 6
The relationship of the paving of the road and the stone walls is not entirely clear (cf. figure 36 MF). At the east end, the earliest paving appeared to be broadly contemporary with the earliest phase of the stone walls; but under the church porch what appeared to be a continuation westwards of the earliest stone walls was sealed by paving and thus appears to predate the eastern churchyard wall. All the stone walls are interpreted as the boundaries of a churchyard in which there were graves; those at the east end were later than *c*.1300, but those further west appear to have been earlier, possibly even bounded by a timber fence in Phase 3 (cf. figure 25, 3) (cf. 9.10 below).

By the expansion of the church to the north in its Phases 4 and 5, the northern churchyard had shrunk considerably; the identity of its eastern end was retained by an L-shape of walls returning to the north-east corner of the cellared property in the angle of the church; but the western part was no longer in use, having been replaced by the north porch and the street paving having become one with the porch (figure 25, 4).

9.8.7   POST-PHASE 6
All features north of the church were ultimately absorbed into secular buildings, a tunnel entrance being the only link between the north door of the church and the street. These seventeenth-century buildings, with later additions or modifications, survived to modern times.

9.9   Evidence for secular occupation on the south side of the hollow way

The microfiche version draws together in this section the disparate and complex evidence from all parts of MLPS West south of the hollow way.

9.10 Burial evidence on the north side of the church

Evidence for burial on the north side of the church relates to three areas: the area to the immediate north of the first two aisleless churches; Area 102/103; and Area 106. Burials may not, however, have been confined to these areas alone—much of the north exterior beyond the extant north wall of the church was not excavated because of the extent of later destruction.

Within the area of the later north aisles of the church, burials had been much disturbed by later events and it was mostly impossible to phase such intact burials as were recognised (cf. 10.10). A number of potentially early cist burials could however be isolated, among which F76 is important because it was cut by F56 in Phase 3A at the latest and so it can tentatively be assigned to the Phase 2 (and ?1) church (cf. 10.10). It would have lain just outside the north wall of both of these. Its importance here is in providing some indication that burial occurred on the north side of the church from an early stage in its development. It should be noted that F76 lay south (by 5 m.) of wall 103.9 and of burial in Area 102/103 (figure 25, 2A – B).

The second area of burial was below the north porch of the Phase 5 + church. It is suggested that not only did burial in this area begin before Church Phase 5 but also possibly before the north aisle in any form, i.e. pre-Church Phase 3.

The phasing of the proposed boundary to the churchyard is uncertain. In its possible wooden form at the west end, 103.12 – .14, it has been seen as contemporary with the use of the hollow way and perhaps during the life of the timber features. It should be noted, however, that it runs, not on the orientation of the church, but on that of the timber features and the later stone walls. The phasing of 103.9, its stone replacement, is also uncertain and cannot be related directly to the structure of the church except that it precedes the north porch of Church Phases 5 – 6 (10.3.5a); it was however sealed by the lower paving in this area. It is suggested that 103.9 predates the 106.4 complex.

A definite north limit to burial was observed in front of wall 103.9, which is important in relationship to both the street frontage and to the function of 103.9. A possible north-west limit was also suggested (cf. 9.5).

A tentative sequence is that the wooden fence was roughly contemporary not only with the hollow way and timber features, but also with burials of Church Phase 2 and ?1; and the stone wall 103.9 with the church of Phase 3, but preceding burial within walls 106.4 (see below); and that burial in the western area of the churchyard ceased before that to the east.

The final area where burials were recognised was Area 106, from a date later than c.1300 on the basis of pottery evidence (9.6.3).

Neale suggests (5.3.12a) that a cemetery reference of 1394 may relate to the north side of the church. If the above arguments are correct, this could comprise both areas of MLPS West in which burials were made at that time. She also provides a *terminus ante quem* of 1648 for the cessation of burial in Area 106 (5.3.13) and the end of what had formerly been a 'void space', empty except for graves below the ground.

9.11 Alignments and orientations

Any discussion of alignments and orientations in relationship to MLPS West is beset by the limitations of the small areas observed and it may indeed be considered that major hypotheses, such as suggested by Neale (Chapter 5) are based, at best, on very slender evidence. Yet despite this, one important misalignment is indisputable—that of the church and Mary-le-Port Street, at least in its later form; and to this can be added the alignment represented by ditch 104.9/105.21 and the stone walls.

The orientations represented by the last two would appear to be, if not primary, then very early in the history of the road; if the southern edge of the hollow way can be taken as represented by 101.7 and as reflected in the later edge 105.15J, then it too is on the same general alignment. Buttermarket Passage appears to be at approximately right angles to this. Insufficient of the paved road was seen to be sure of its orientation, but the earlier orientation appears to be more at an angle to the church. Possible wider alignments that these may be related to are those of the parish boundary to the north and the river to the south.

If it is accepted that Buttermarket Passage is on this alignment and also that the Timber Building is gable-end-on to it, this may suggest that Buttermarket Passage had an early origin and an importance equal to Mary-le-Port Street at this stage.

The archaeological data have been unable to answer the question of which orientation, that of the church or street, had primacy, or even quite when the street became a tightly-defined route, rather than consisting of a zone of movement. Nor can it define clearly the extent of any possible early secular occupation on the south side of the road. Enough, however, was observed to suggest that the successive shifts and minor alignments were the results of trying to bring the two orientations closer together, resulting in an awkwardly-shaped piece of ground from the early history of the area. It may be that Neale's suggested route from the east already existed when the first church was built; certainly the Phase 2 church is not truly east-west but it was closer to it than is the road, as if canonical alignment was important. The subsequent changes in orientations were based on the interplay between the space required by secular properties and the expanding church (cf. figure 25).

9.12   The seventeenth-century and later houses to the north of the church

Roger Leech's appendix in MF derives from his wider studies on medieval and later buildings in Bristol, based on plans, watercolours, drawings and photographs. He has considered the construction, architectural details and plan form together with reconstructions of their former appearance. He concludes that nos. 38, 40, 41 and 42 Mary-le-Port Street were possibly built as separate dwellings. They were unusual amongst seventeenth-century houses in Bristol in being of one-room plan and yet built to four full storeys with attics above, because of space restrictions between church and street. The spaces between nos. 38 and 40 and between 41 and 42 were, he suggests, possibly not built on until the late eighteenth century at earliest, on the basis of certain architectural details and relative street levels. He suggests that until these later buildings were erected, there were spaces corresponding to the positions of windows lighting the north aisle.

Chapter 10: St. Mary-le-Port Church

10.1 Introduction

The church of St. Mary-le-Port was largely destroyed by fire in the blitz of 24 November 1940; the walls and tower survived in a damaged condition, and the former were largely dismantled in post-war years by Bristol Corporation for safety reasons (cf. plate 43). A further part of the south side was destroyed by the Norwich Union Insurance Company in 1962, the section of which was not available for examination. By 1962, when excavation began, the site was an overgrown ruin, with heavy rubble and bushes choking most areas. Resources did not allow for a proper excavation; the rubble and recent floor levels were removed by machine, except in the tower area where alone a complete sequence was recorded as shown in sections S11 and S12 (figures 46, 47).

It was soon apparent that most of the internal area had long since been destroyed to a great depth by brick burial vaults, which avoided only the standing walls and major structural elements such as the arcade piers. Nuclei of multi-period structures or columns of stratification survived between the burial vaults (plate 18). Each nucleus was therefore dug as a separate unit (Areas 1 – 12), resulting in a series of data-sets which can now to some extent be co-ordinated.

The excavation was further complicated by problems of spoil disposal; and also by the activities of a Bristol Corporation gang of workmen employed in parallel to empty all the burial vaults and to remove their contents for re-burial in out-of-town municipal cemeteries. Resources did not allow the recording of any of these burials, though some coffin fittings were rescued (11.15), nor could earlier non-vault burials receive proper attention. Available time and money was heavily problem-orientated towards the recovery of the details of the plans of successive churches and of the sparse associated stratification. The work did not include any recording or analysis of above-ground archaeology, i.e. the visible church architecture, which must be the subject of further research.

Under these circumstances recording was poor, even by 1962 standards, and many gaps in understanding remain. These could, however, largely be resolved by further extensive excavation under modern conditions, if ever circumstances and resources permitted. The present report must be regarded only as a provisional hypothesis.

All features were serially numbered in an F series 1 – 186, each referred to Areas 1 – 12. The phasing finally suggested is based on a variety of evidence, including structural relationships, stratigraphy, finds and, not least, inductive probability evaluation.

The evidence for the six phases of the church as a whole is first discussed, each illustrated by a plan of the new features relevant to that phase, and followed (for Phases 1 – 5) by a commentary on interpretation plans representing the church at successive points in time. These are followed by discussions of the particular problems relating to the tower, the south aisle, and the West and East Cellars; and a summary of the evidence for floors and floor-levels, wall surface rendering, and artefacts. All data are summarised by phase in table 11.

10.2 Summary of dating (figure 48, table 11)

Phase 1   Late Saxon or early post-Conquest; sherds of this general period; antecedent to Phase 2 dating.

Phase 2   Norman, later twelfth century; architectural detail of this date; possibly church built before 1170 and then given to Keynsham Abbey.

Phase 3   Early English, thirteenth century; ashlar detail and sherds in builders' levels.

Phase 4   Late Perpendicular, later fifteenth century prior to 1480; architectural detail, especially of tower; sherds in tower builders' levels; and *terminus ante quem* of 1480, when William of Worcester measured this church.

Phase 5   Late Perpendicular, early sixteenth century; *terminus ante quem* given by tomb-monument of this date; creation of chapel possibly that 'newly-built' in 1518; south aisle windows c.1520.

Phase 6   All later features to 1940.

PHASE	SUGGESTED DATING	STRUCTURES	LOOSE ARCHITECTURAL FRAGMENTS	FLOORS	WALL RENDERING
1	LATE SAXON OR EARLY POST-CONQUEST	Features: occupation layers; pit, P.H., or north-south linear features; ?hearth; ST features. Structures include ?church—cf. plan and possible orientation; ?aisleless, ??with ?tower; ?of stone or stone + timber or timber construction. Pennant Sandstone used, packed with orange clay and reddish sand; buff mortar; ?also Brandon H.G. + brown marl. ?Dead ground to west (cf. 10.3.1). Cf. figures 50 – 51		(Area 1—?hearth F11p + associated surface (S11)).	
2	NORMAN, LATER 12th	Features built mainly of Brandon H.G., with Pennant Sandstone; packed with red or brown sandy clay, sand or marl and/or with buff mortar. Of two phases, with secondary E'wards extension. ?Possible central tower. Function: ?church. (cf. plan, possible grave F76 (pre-Phase 3— ?re Phase 2 or 1), known purpose of successors, possible correlation with documentary reference and loose architectural fragments. Cf. figure 52	NB especially ST 8, decorated capital; also ST3 and ST4, frs. cable moulding.	Area 11, F84E—hard red sandy floor with ORG impressions. Above it, F84B—?organic or dirt floors represented by laminated brownish mortar and greyish-brown dust.	Buff stucco in F84F builders' level of Phase 2. ?re Phase 2 or Phase 1. Pale buff, white-painted stucco from F33 destruction layer of Phase 2A wall, ?re Phase 2 walls LBM7 + 15, also from F33, include stucco with cream and reddish washes.
	2A	?Aisleless nave, possibly with eastern apse. Dimensions, etc., see figures 52 – 53.			
	2B	Major alterations to east end of Phase 2A building—now definitely square; possibly incorporating central ?wooden tower (south aisle unlikely). Dimensions, etc., see figures 52, 54.			
3	EARLY ENGLISH, 13th	Major remodelling and enlargement, with minor secondary features.	These include details from the main structure and/or from freestanding elements and also gravecovers. ST 9, fr of stiff leafed foliate termination, and ST 1, a fr of fine angel relief from a ?tomb, deserve special note. F138 is one of the only features datable architecturally in the cellar complex but it appears to consist of re-used members. Gravecovers comprise an effigy fr and decorated and incribed slabs. The wide date range of these pieces reflects the long lifespan of Phase 3.	Area 5, F74—Pennant Sandstone bedded on soft brick-tempered mortar. DFT from Groups 1.2 – .4 and from Group III.7 + PFT, ?all late 13th – early 14th, are from F78, assigned to Phases ?1 – 4.	
	3A	Features isolated by structural relationships and by use of brown mortar. Church completely remodelled and enlarged by addition of north and ?south aisles and by lengthening of chancel; small north transept and ?mirroring south transept. Dimensions, etc., cf. figures 55 – 56.			Area 4—grey stucco from F38 destruction level re ?Phase 3A o Phase 4. Area 5 – white stucco edge to floor F74 on pier F56. Areas 11 – 12, cream stucco in F49 re Phase 3A or earlier.
	3A – 3B	Represented only by F179, cf. 10.3.3.		Area 11, F179—yellow mortar ?floor, but possibly make-up or base for superstructure.	
	3B	Minor features, post 3A—pre 4A, using distinctive pink-brown mortar. West wall rebuilt, alterations at east end. Dimensions, etc., cf. figures 55 – 56.		Area 11, F179A—dark fibrous material, ?remains of wooden or dirt floor.	

ROOFING	SIGNIFICANT SMALL FINDS	FLOATING CONTEXTS	MISC.
	Sherds of Fabric A are dated *c*.1000 – 1100.		
	BC 1 and BC 2, with wattle and ?ORG impressions, found in F121 post-hole fill of Phase 3, but cutting F84, may belong to Phase 2. Pottery consists only of Fabric A and 12th or earlier sherds.		
	Greater range of material, ?partly disturbed from earlier levels, e.g. BC. GLW7, greenish-tinted clear glass, from F78, is assigned to Phases 1 – 4 (cf. date suggested for DFT). GLW 8, of a similar colour, from F176A, is from a pre-Phase 4 context.		Phase 3 church had a long life; it is likely that there were many internal modifications not detectable archaeologically.
Pennant and slate RT frs from Area 3, F18 and 3A, and from Area 4, F38, could belong to pre-Phase 3A and/or Phase 4 contexts.	Pottery Fabric H occurs for first time in F84A, in Phase 3A builders' level (Fabric K, French imports, in robbing of F38 is relevant to dating of Phase 4, not Phase 3).		

Table 11:   Church Summary (continued)

PHASE	SUGGESTED DATING	STRUCTURES	LOOSE ARCHITECTURAL FRAGMENTS	FLOORS	WALL RENDERING
4 LATE PERPENDICULAR,	LATER 15th	Church at maximum size with west tower, north aisle widened (south unknown), chancel largely rebuilt, south doorway. North aisle windows apparently still functional, overlooking open ground. Characterised by hard reddish mortar. Internal features include two sedilia F52 + F53 and probably stucco-faced screen base. F99 + F176. Cellar complex built in angle between north-east church exterior and street ?late Phase 4. Cf. figures 57 – 58.	ST7 and ST17, in its re-used form, represent parts of free-standing structures, such as screens, shrines or tombs, of ?Phase 4. Both functions of ST 22, as a graveslab and its re-use as a column base, appear to belong to Phase 4.	Area 1, F11h—laminated ?floor levels + Area 1, F11c and above 1E/1F—Pennant floor + Pennant step F35 + Area 2, F5 floor, also of Pennant, with reddish mortar and lightly white plaster, associated with pier. Area 11, F182—Pennant floor (also see floating contexts).	
5 LATE PERPENDICULAR EARLY 16th		Last phase of medieval church, with major rebuilding of north arcade and ?separate north chapel achieved by encroaching on west cellar; ?south aisle demolished; new south wall built further out; rood stair added at south-west corner of chancel; cf. 59 – 60.	ST18, graveslab fr, and ST72, section of arcade pier.	Area 1, above 1E—Pennant floor. Area 11, F174 – DFT *in situ* near rood screen, presumably re-used (13th date suggested at time of excavation, not seen since). (If not of Phase 5, then ?of Phase 4 and contemporary with F182 Pennant floor.)	Pre-Phase 5—Area 3, F32, white-painted freestone. Area 11, in destruction level F177 of Phase 3 or 4, white plaster with red stripes = ?false jointing.
6 POST-PHASE 5—1940—		Major tomb, F186, of early 16th (?in 1518 chapel). 17th/18th—minor modifications, floor alterations, massive brick vaults, box pews, large pulpit over rood stair, Baroque reredos, strapwork design plaster roof vault, Dutch-style oak pews. Nineteenth—major changes including 1877 restoration. Burials continue until *c*.1877 (cf. 10.10). Cf. figure 61.		Area 1, above 1D, floor of mortared Pennant, associated with steps F35A, F3/4, F12 and F13. Area 2, F2 floor. Area 1, 1847 floor above vault. ?ORG dirt floors, 1C and 3C. 1877 tiled floor overall.	

ROOFING	SIGNIFICANT SMALL FINDS	FLOATING CONTEXTS	MISC.
Ceramic roof tiles (including ridge tiles) and Pennant roof tiles occur in 1G and 1H – ?from pre-Phase 4 roof.	Maximum size of church not obviously reflected in finds (but see following phase), except for greater range of pottery fabrics present, including J,K,L,N,R and S. The latter is probably the latest fabric from Phase 4 and comes only from 1G and 1H, tower builders' levels; these are the only Phase 4 contexts to contain Fabrics N, R, Tudor Green and south Netherlands maiolica. ST2 and LBM1—4, 8 and 16 are frs of rood screen (also cf. F99).	Area 9, floor of thick Pennant, over cellar, late ?Phase 4.	Area between north of church and MLP Street reduced. Ricart's map of 1479 should relate, if at all, to this phase (cf. 10.3.4b).
Slate frs, Pennant chippings and ceramic roof tiles found in Area 1, 1E, and in cellar fill, F175B, pre-Phase 5—from Phase ?4 roof.	Group of interest, including ST 7, crocket (see Phase 4) and glass vessel ?for ecclesiastical use, found in fill of west cellar—?of Phase 4 rather than 5.		This is structure which survives, with alterations, until 1940. Cf. pictorial illustrations, e.g. plates 28–29. Millerd's map of 1673 does not agree with archaeological record (cf. 10.3.5a).
Partly re-roofed; slate, Pennant and ceramic tile frs probably from earlier roofs (cf. 10.4.6).	Material disturbed from earlier, levels, e.g. ST 18 graveslab and DFT Group II.5. Window glass from Phase 6 contexts includes medieval pieces; some dated to fifteenth (cf. MF table 17.10 which should equate with Phase 4).		Space between north wall of church and MLP Street built up, also along entire length of church north wall—cf. plate 25. For church interior, cf. plate 29; Millerd's map of 1673 may be relevant to this phase, cf. plate 23.

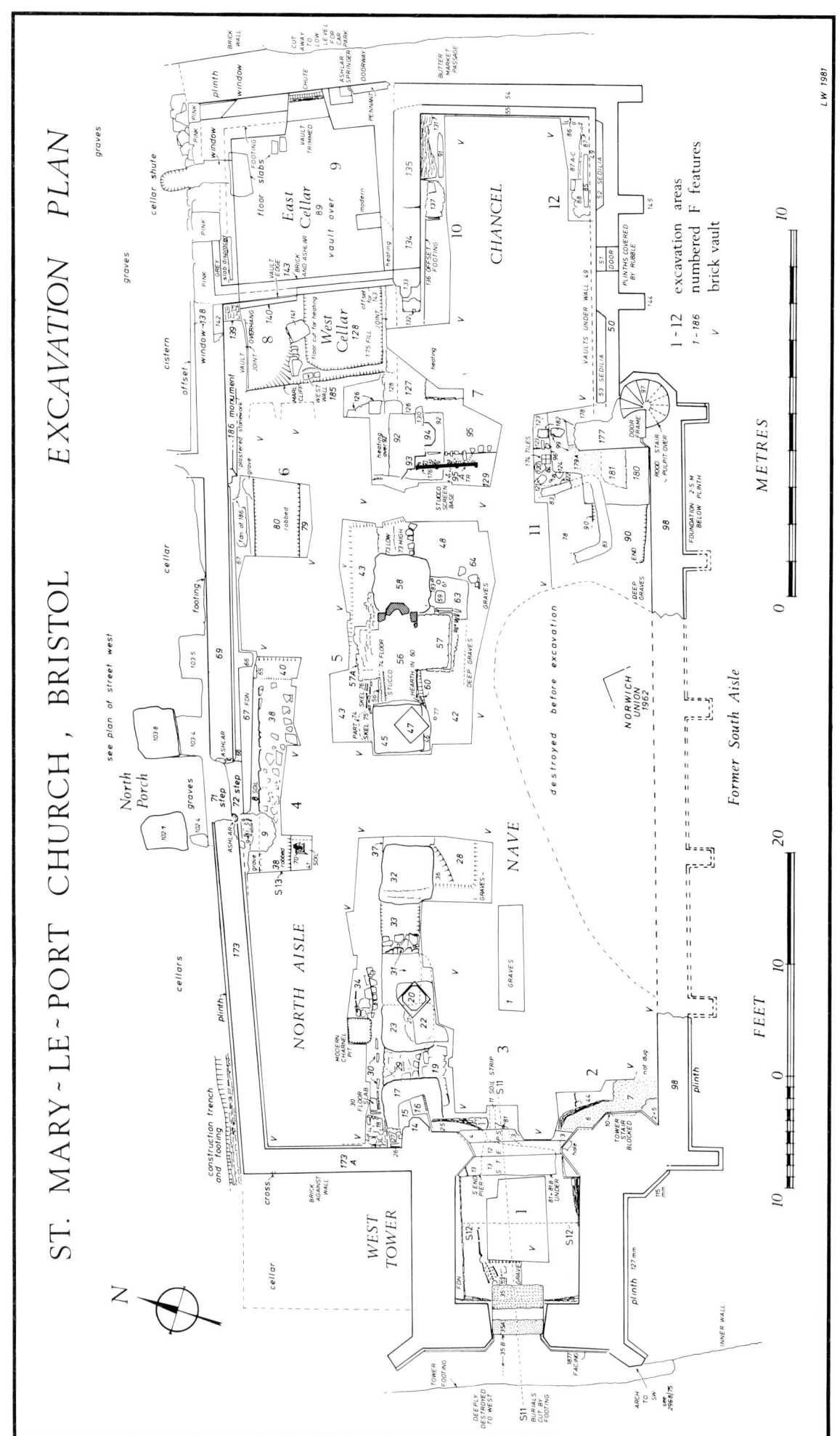

ST. MARY~LE~PORT CHURCH, BRISTOL   EXCAVATION PLAN

Figure 45.

94

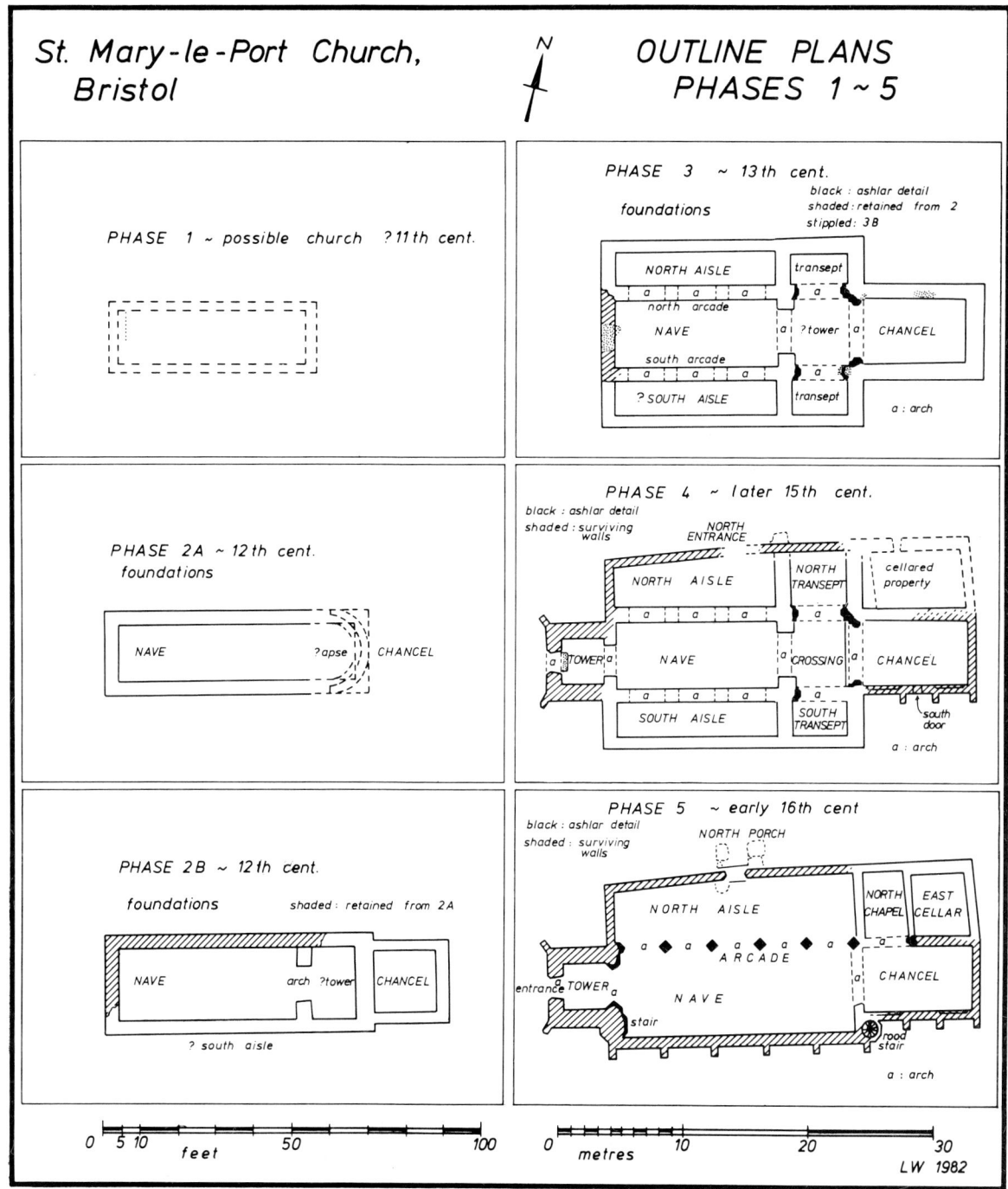

Figure 48.

10.3 Structural phases

10.3.1 PHASE 1

10.3.1a THE EVIDENCE FROM PHASE 1 (figure 50)

The earliest features in the area of the church interior are all of late Saxon or early post-Conquest date, though it is unlikely that they are all contemporary; they survived only in very small fragments. Some or all may be part of a church, of stone, timber, or mixed construction. There are a few elements of continuity, in plan or orientation, with later structures that are demonstrably churches.

At the west end, stratification survived in a strip only 15 cm. wide (F11—see projection onto section S11) (figure 46; see also 10.8.1). This strip includes not only 'occupation' layers, but also a cut-away edge at its eastern extremity; this may be the edge of a pit, a large post-hole, or a north-south linear feature such as a timber slot. Other soil features appear to pre-date later stone structures (e.g. F60, F77 and F84Z). This occupation on and in the original ground surface (see buried soil, F11r in section S11, figure 46) may be secular, since areas of burning, etc., are not normally found in churches. They may however be associated with church building, or with industrial (or even semi-domestic) activity inside or near a church—a feature known elsewhere (e.g. at Barton-on-Humber, *Medieval Archaeol.* 23 (1979), 239).

There are, in addition, three stone features which appear to be earlier than Phase 2. The most westerly (apart from F81B, discussed later in this section) is foundation F19. This is parallel to and south of what became the north wall and north arcade of later churches, and this might be part of the north wall of a first church. F19 was built of Pennant Sandstone, packed with orange clay and reddish sand. It was probably, but not conclusively, earlier than F29 but its depth was not ascertained. Further east was a robbed foundation trench (F36) cut only 15 cm. into the marl. Its fill was of hard orange sandy clay with some red and green Pennant Sandstone; it could be a further element of the north wall of a possible first church. Further east again, some Pennants (F64) were found, also set 15 cm. into the marl, at the base of a heavily medieval-grave-disturbed area, and cut by F63 of Phase 2. This could be part of an east wall of a first church.

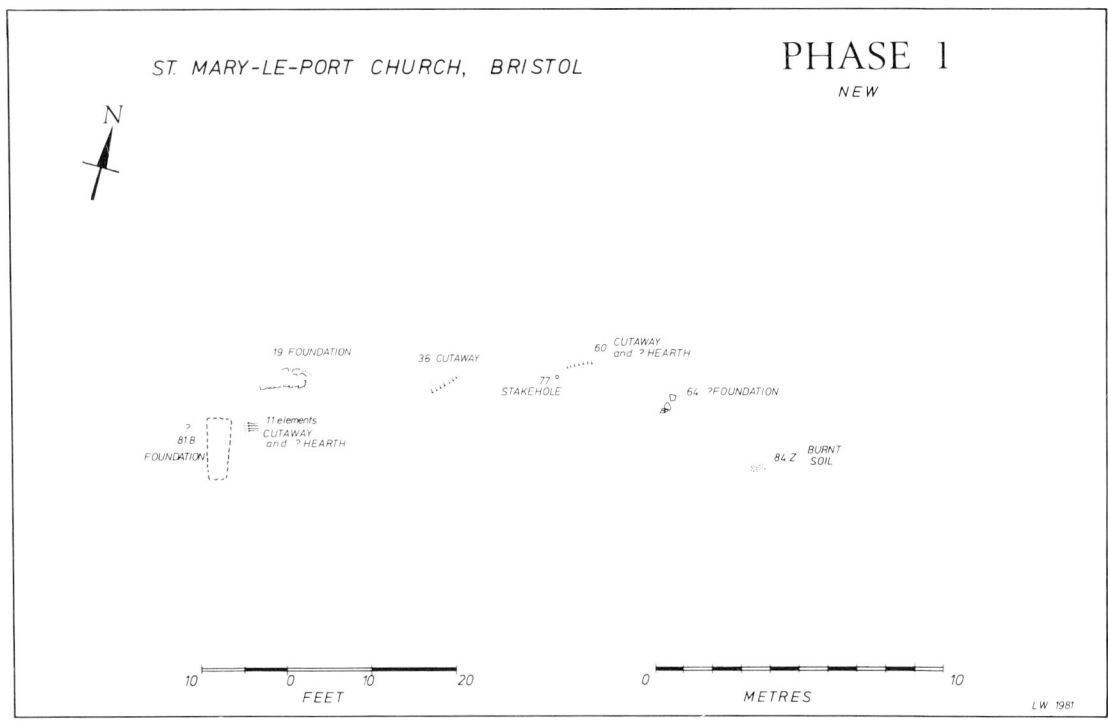

Figure 50.

The final feature that may be of Phase 1 is F81B. This is a substantial north-south foundation lying beneath the east tower face, and thus possibly defining the line of an earlier church's west end (but also cf. 10.3.4a below). The foundation (cf. S11) was of Brandon Hill Grit and Pennant Sandstone, packed with brown marl, the latter presumably derived from the foundation trench. This is structurally primary to other foundations in this area; the only reason for thinking that it may also be primary stratigraphically (i.e. that it was part of the earliest medieval occupation in the area) is that the packing did not include any dark soil or charcoal. This might have been expected if the foundation trench had been cut through the stratified deposits to the east (F11 sequence in S11, figure 46). It seems possible therefore that these layers (and the cut-away feature at their eastern extremity) developed after F81B was built. Whether or not these layers were secular or associated with a church, as discussed above, F81B could be associated with them, as a north-south wall. The relationship is not, however, decisive (the link being severed by F81) and F81B may be part of a later phase (cf. 10.3.2Aa).

If the features discussed are indeed part of the earliest church, little can be said about its date. A *terminus ante quem* is provided by the features of Phase 2. The seven sherds from Phase 1 contexts (from buried soil in Area 11, F84Z and from F11m, S11, right) include, amongst Fabric A, BPT 1 and BPT 115, for which periods of currency of *c*.1000−1070 and *c*.1070−1100 respectively are suggested.

Little can be said either about the plan or superstructure of this possible church. The only possible clue to the latter is that there was some buff mortar on some stone incorporated in walls of a later phase: in F81 (if F81B is of Phase 1), and wall F29 of Phase 2. This may suggest that any superstructure was of buff-mortared stone rather than timber. If the latter was contemporary with the lighter-founded possible north-wall elements, this may suggest a greater weight at the west end, possibly a tower, of stone, wood or mixed construction.

To summarise, the evidence for a church in Phase 1 is tenuous in the extreme; such features that can be defined as earlier than Phase 2 may not all be of the same date, and may include secular elements. Nevertheless there are some elements of continuity in plan and orientation between at least one of the structural features (F81B) and later church elements; there is also the possible north-south timber line at the west end. It is possible therefore that there was a church on the site in Phase 1 even if its plan and character cannot now be determined.

10.3.1b INTERPRETATION OF PHASE 1 (figure 51)

The restored plan of a rectangular building is hardly more than a guess, incorporating the above observations. It envisages a possible first church of $c.14-15+$ m. long internally, and a width of $c.4$ m., for which there is no evidence, apart from analogy drawn from the interpretative plan of the succeeding phase. It should be noted that F81B was substantial, perhaps to support a tower or other structure at the west end.

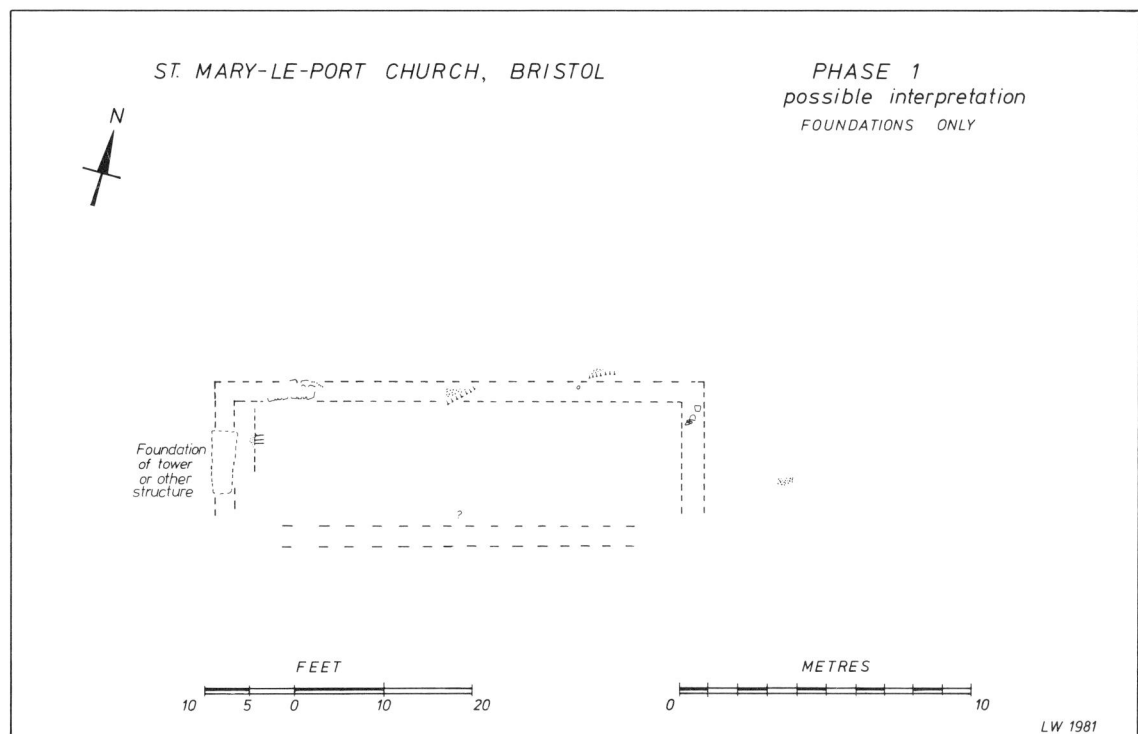

Figure 51.

10.3.2 PHASE 2—GENERAL (FIGURE 52)

The structural features of Phase 2 are built of Brandon Hill Grit, with smaller amounts of Pennant Sandstone. They are packed with red or brown sandy clay, sand or marl (derived from foundation trenches); with a mixture of these materials with some buff mortar; or wholly with buff mortar. The three kinds of packing are shown in figure 52. It is probable that the first two at least are contemporary, and these are designated 2A; those with buff mortar 2B. While all may be part of the same plan, it seems more likely that the 2B features represent a rebuild—a widening of the church to the south, and an extension to the east, with a chancel.

The building in one or two phases represented by Phase 2 features is assumed to be a church, not only because of numerous analogues to its plan(s), but also because of its direct antecedence to later phases which are historically the church of St. Mary-le-Port. There is also at least one burial which may be of this phase (or of Phase 1) (10.10). There are also architectural fragments which may belong to this church (11.2).

In view of the uncertainty as to whether 2A and 2B are separate phases, or parts of essentially the same church with modifications or variable construction, the evidence has been included in a single phase plan (figure 52) but divided into two reconstruction drawings (figures 53 – 54).

No direct dating evidence can be adduced for either or both phases, but on the basis of the plans both could be of eleventh or twelfth century date. If it were possible to equate either (but probably 2A) with the first church to be referred to in written sources of the late twelfth century (5.3.6) or to the similarly-dated architectural fragment (ST8, $c.1140-1170$, figure 67), then either could more confidently be dated to the second half of the twelfth century. The architectural fragment ST8 is also the only evidence which can be adduced for the construction, style and quality of the superstructure of the Phase 2 church or churches.

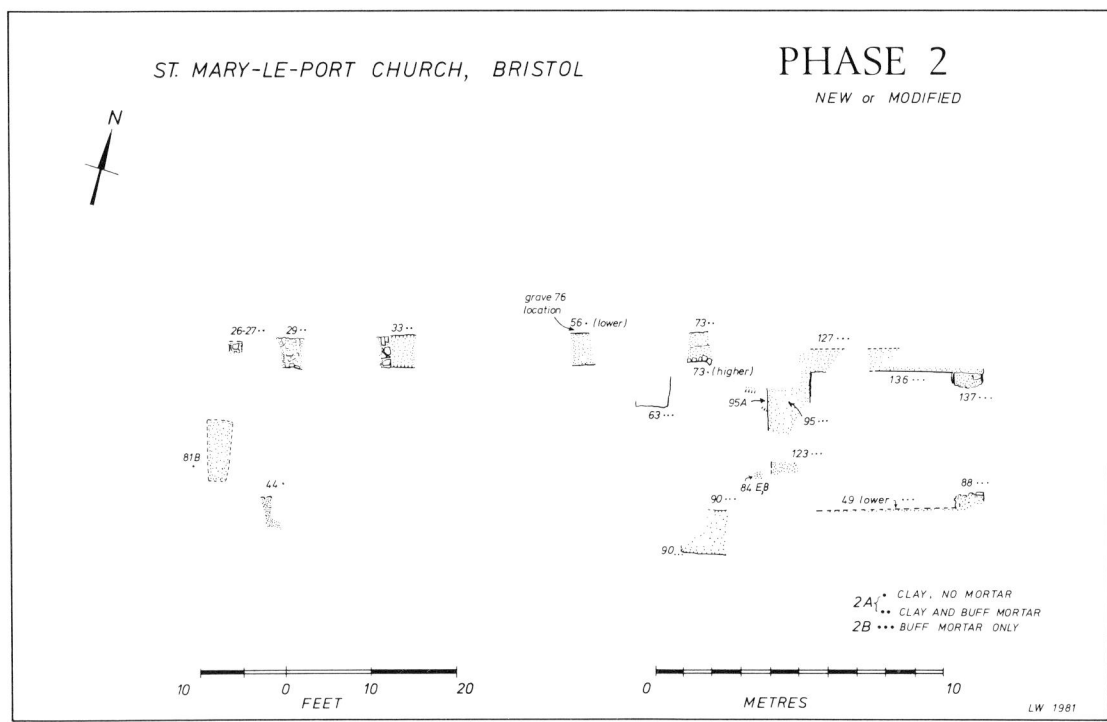

Figure 52.

10.3.2A   PHASE 2A

10.3.2Aa   The evidence from Phase 2A (figure 52)
The west wall is represented by the foundation (possibly re-used—see Phase 1, 10.3.1a above) under the eastern tower arch, F81B (see section S11, figure 46). It is presumed that this originally joined up at the south end with F44, and with F26, 27, 29, 33 and the lowest part of F56, to define the north and south walls of an aisleless church. The north wall can be extended to include the southern (higher) part of F73. If Phase 2A had a square east end, it may have been on the line of F95, wholly absorbed by or replaced by that foundation in Phase 2B; in this case the full width of F73 would be included. There is however a slight possibility that 2A ended in an eastern apse. The south-east stone of F73 appeared to be turning southwards, and F95A may be its robbed continuation. If this were the case (and the evidence is tenuous), then Phase 2B might more confidently be seen as a more drastic remodelling of the east end. The final possibility is that Phase 2A was of two (or even three) sub-phases, an apsidal east end being replaced by a square east end.

10.3.2Ab   Interpretation of Phase 2A (figure 53)
The reconstructed plan is of a rectangular church with a minimum length internally of *c*.18.7 m. and a width of *c*.4.3 m. Three alternative east ends are shown, any of which may have incorporated a separate chancel from a nave to the west. The squared east end ignores the possible turn inwards of foundation F73 south. The narrow inner apse wall width of *c*.50 cm. utilises only the southern part of F73, with its possible inwards turn; in this case the outer part of F73 would represent a slight 'shoulder' between the north-east corner of the nave and the north wall of the apse. The wider apse wall of *c*.1 m. utilises all of F73. The reconstructed plan also illustrates the possibility of the east end having undergone two (or even possibly three) alterations in plan within Phase 2A.

10.3.2B   PHASE 2B

10.3.2Ba   The evidence from Phase 2B (figure 52)
The major new element of the Phase 2B church is the east wall F95/F123 and the chancel represented by F127/F136/F88/F137/F49 (lower courses). As discussed above, there may in Phase 2A have been a square east end on the line of F95; but if there was instead an apse turning south-east from F73, then the northern part of F73 will represent (in its robbed superstructure) a new work, straightening out the north side of the apse to a new east end to the nave. The north wall of the chancel appears to have been set back *c*.50–60 cm. from that of the nave, to judge from the south faces of the re-used F73 and F127. If a similar width and set-back is assumed for the south wall of the chancel (of which only the north edge was

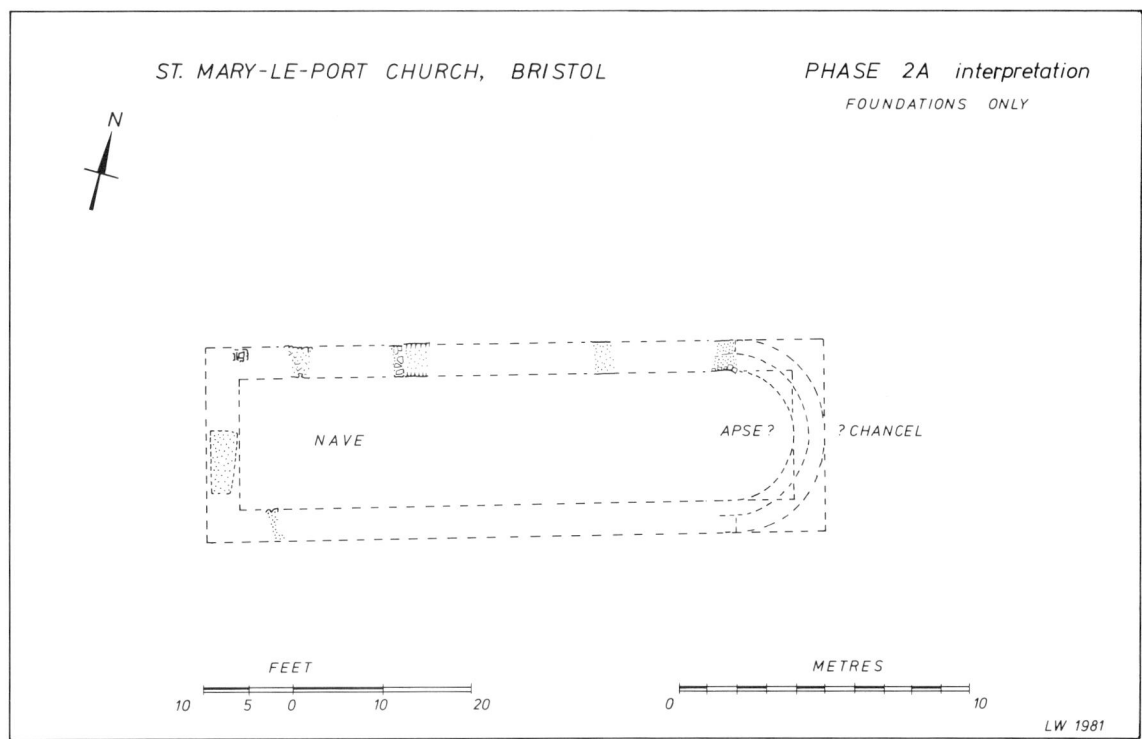

Figure 53.

found), then the postulated south-east corner of the nave is seen to be roughly in line with the south edge of the robber-trench F90. The south wall of the nave thus defined cannot be that of 2A (as represented by F44) and must represent a widening of the nave. The south edge of F90 appeared to turn north at its western limits and this raises the very slight possibility that F90 is the east pier of a south arcade, with a south aisle beyond. F90 is however only a robbing trench, so its south edge may in no way reflect the edge of the original foundation; its north edge seems too far north to indicate accurately the limits of the south wall.

Another factor makes a south aisle or arcade unlikely. F63 is of Phase 2B; it was probably a pier supporting the north side of an arch, dividing off a space (?below a tower) between the nave and the chancel arch proper based on F95/F123. Any presumed southern pier to match F63 would have to project from some masonry immediately to the west of F90 as defined.

10.3.2Bb   Interpretation of Phase 2B (figure 54)

The reconstructed plan in figure 54 assumes some symmetry between the north and south sides, notably the extent to which the south nave wall extends beyond the chancel. This puts the south nave wall on the southern part of the foundation trench F90, rather than centrally within it; if symmetry were to be ignored, then the nave would be c.40 cm. narrower, as would be the arch into the nave. The point is of some importance since the evidence for Phase 3 indicates a south wall or arcade rather more on this inner line than where it is shown in figure 54 (cf. below, 10.3.3).

The possibility of a south aisle (and therefore a south arcade) is hinted at in this plan, but the favoured interpretation is of a long and narrow rectangular nave, c.14 m. x 5.5 m. + internally, an arch c.2.5 m. + leading into a space possibly below a (?wooden) tower, of c.5.5 x 3.5 m. + and a narrower chancel to the east, entered through a chancel arch, of c.4.75 m. + square. Of this church of Phase 2B a large part of the north and west nave walls are assumed to have been retained from Phase 2A.

10.3.3   PHASE 3

10.3.3a   GENERAL (figure 55)

The structural features of Phase 3 have been isolated by their structural relationship to earlier or later features, and by the characteristic use of brown mortar in Phase 3A and pink-brown and reddish in Phase 3B.

The new church was a complete remodelling of that of Phase 2, and represents a considerable enlargement, achieved by the construction of one and possibly two aisles and the lengthening of the chancel. Two sub-phases are evident, 3A and 3B; the latter appears however to consist of no more than

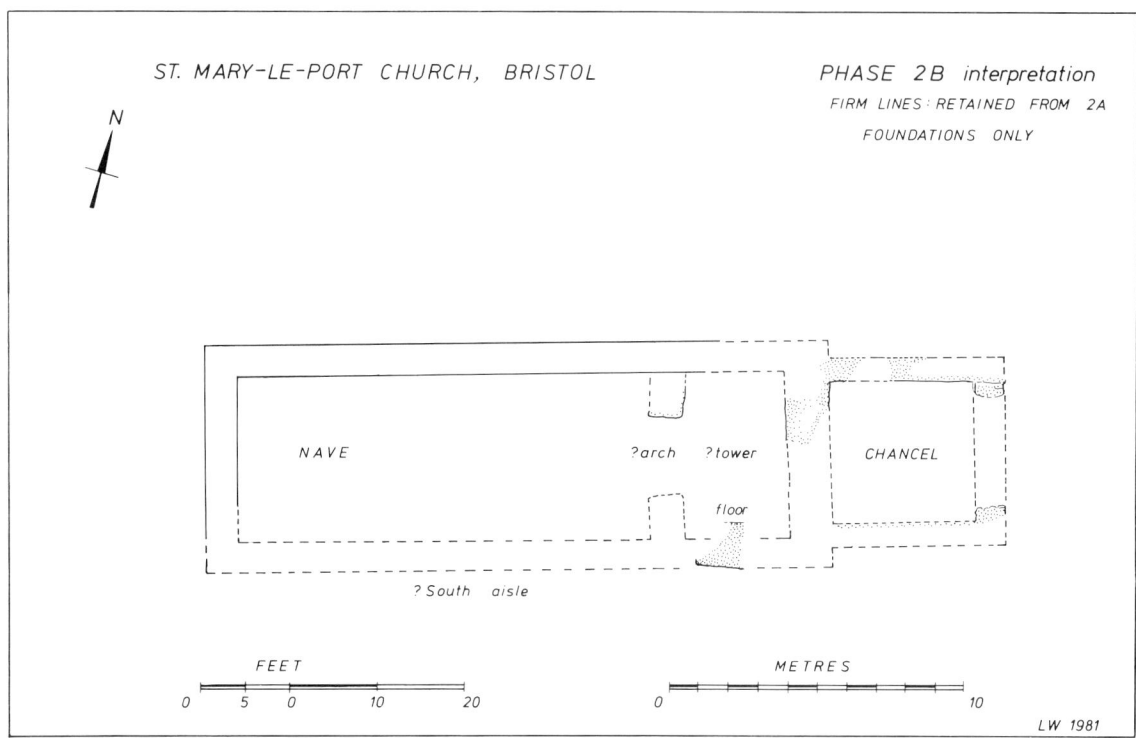

Figure 54.

minor modifications, although these may have been more substantial (especially at the west end) than the surviving evidence indicates.

10.3.3b THE EVIDENCE FROM PHASE 3A (figure 55)

The west wall of the new church was apparently still based on F81B. The west end of the new north arcade was destroyed by later features. The first definable feature of the arcade is therefore the pier F31. Further east there are three more piers, F37, F56 (upper) and F92. The north arcade was thus of four bays (including the north transept arch (see below) and assuming a bay to the west of F31).

On the south side only the easternmost pier survives, F180. This is of a different plan to its partner on the north side and there may be differences in the south arcade which make any assumptions of symmetry

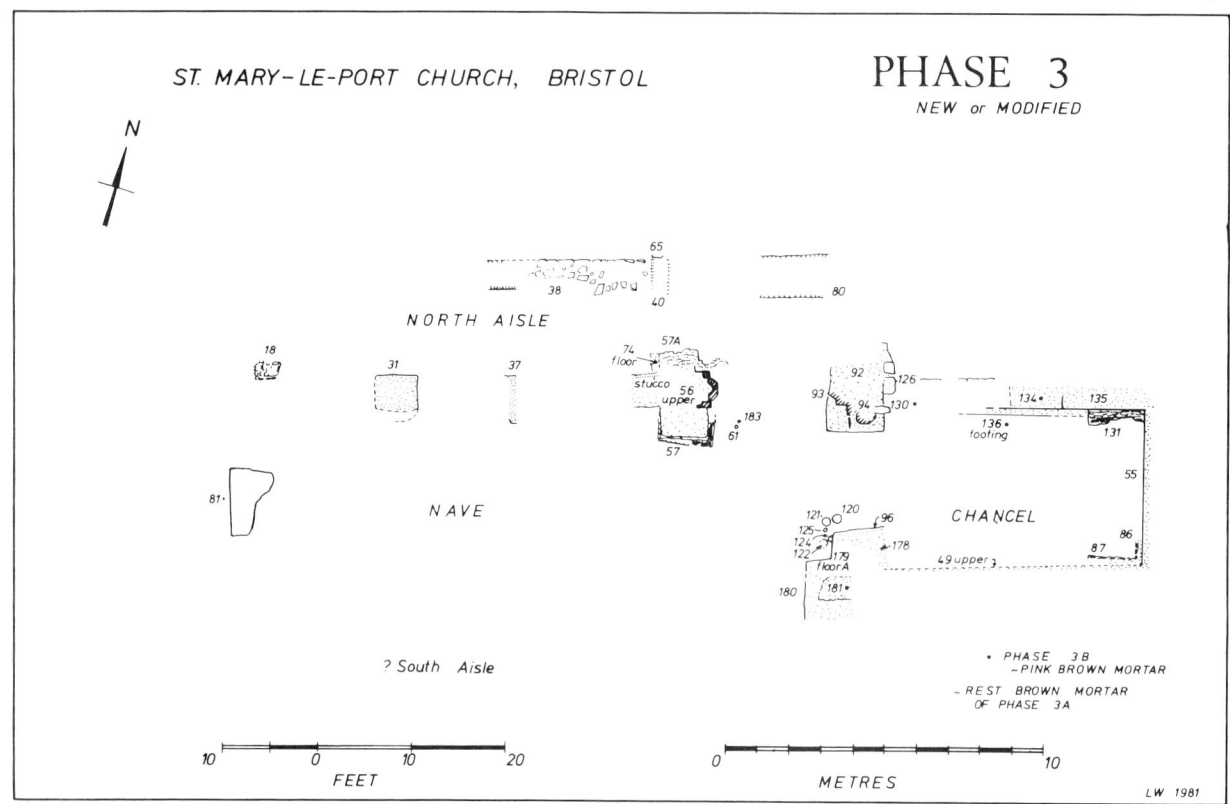

Figure 55.

Plate 18. Pier complex, features F45, F47, F56, F57, F58 and F63, from south-west.

unwarrantable. It is nevertheless assumed in the present hypothesis that the south arcade mirrored that of the north.

Detail survives for the east-facing respond of the north transept arch, and for the south-facing respond of the chancel arch; from these some idea of the size of all four crossing arches can be suggested, assuming that F180/F96 had a function similar to F92. It did however have a different history later. Its superstructure was replaced by F179, a continuous yellow mortar surface, possibly a make-up, or a floor and/or a base for a new superstructure. This mortar seems to represent a sub-phase between the 3A arrangements and the later wall F181 of Phase 3B (see below 10.3.3c). How this affected the south-east corner of the assumed crossing, if at all, is uncertain. It may have involved removing a superstructure built on F180, with consequent alterations to the associated west-facing arch, a rebuild for which no evidence survives; or the north-facing respond of the F180/F96 complex may have sprung from further to the east, closer to the position of the later F177 (cf. Phase 5 below), in which case it would not have been affected (cf. also F181 below).

The south end of the foundation of the west wall of the new north aisle survives as a small fragment (F18); the wall-line proper was presumably a little further east, in line with the west wall of the nave. The north wall of the aisle is well represented as a substantial length of partly-robbed foundation trench (F38). At the east end there was presumably an arch leading into the north transept; the north-facing respond for this is indicated by F57A, projecting from pier F56. Trench F40 may also be associated with this opening, with a possible buttress beyond (F65) (note in this connection the later buttress foundation 103.5 of Phase 4).

The north transept is further defined by F80, the robbing trench of its north wall; this is assumed to have returned south to F92.

The nave consists of the westernmost three bays of the arcade; the southward-projecting F57 indicates the north side of an arch separating the nave from the crossing.

The chancel was extended eastwards from that of Phase 2B by c.2 m., but was otherwise rebuilt on the earlier foundations (F49 (upper), F55, F86, F87, F126, F131 and F135) (plate 20).

Phase 3A is broadly dated to the thirteenth century or later by two sherds of Fabric H (Ham Green) in the builders' level F84A, and by the general form of the ashlar detail. This church appears to have survived for the greater part of two centuries.

10.3.3c THE EVIDENCE FROM PHASE 3B (figure 55)

There are a few features which appear to be later than those of Phase 3A, yet earlier than Phase 4, or different in their mortar; but none involved any radical alteration of the Phase 3A church.

The first is the rebuild of the west wall, F81. This was packed with a soft reddish mortar different from that of the tower foundation and also from any mortar of Phase 3A. The excavator was also very specific in asserting that the tower foundation was keyed into it at the north end, i.e. was secondary, as the mortar difference would imply and did not even touch it at the south end, which would be most unlikely if F81 was intended as a sleeper wall under the eastern tower arch and contemporary with it (cf. 10.8.1).

The other features of Phase 3B are all at the east end. F134 and F136 (upper) are characterised by a pink-brown mortar distinct from those of Phase 3A or of the tower. A piece of masonry, F130, protruding east from Phase 3A pier F92 may have originally been part of a rebuild of the west part of the north chancel wall.

The final complex of Phase 3B features to be considered are in the south-east corner of the crossing. The problems of F179 have been discussed above; on it was F181—a wall fragment, approximately on the assumed line of the south arcade, the function of which is obscure. It may have carried a respond to the next pier west on the south side, or have been a non-load-bearing wall, for example for a low screen. Associated with F181 was a dark fibrous layer, F179A, possibly representing a dirt or wooden floor. Unlike F179, which *underlay* foundation F181, F179A ended on a line short of the extant north edge of F181; this may indicate the original width of the latter.

10.3.3d INTERPRETATION OF PHASE 3 (figure 56)

The reconstructed plan embodies the discussion above. Foundation piers and ashlar detail have been reconstructed by mirror images; the approximate dimensions from north to south are given not only by the gap between the foundations of the north and south responds of the chancel arch, but also by the north edge of the foundation of the south wall of the chancel. It should be noted that there is no certain evidence for the south aisle: the defined western edge of the south-east crossing pier F180 suggests an arch to the south-west pier and thus a space to the south; but this may have been restricted to a south transept

*Plate 20.   North-east corner of chancel, from south-west; foundations
   F135, F137, F131 and F55; vault on right.*

or chapel, rather than, as it may be taken to imply, either a south arcade or aisle. If the general symmetry is accepted, it should be noted that the new south arcade is *c.*40 cm. north of that postulated for Phase 2 unless, as discussed above, the plan of that earlier church is not symmetrical (also see 10.5 *re* south aisle).

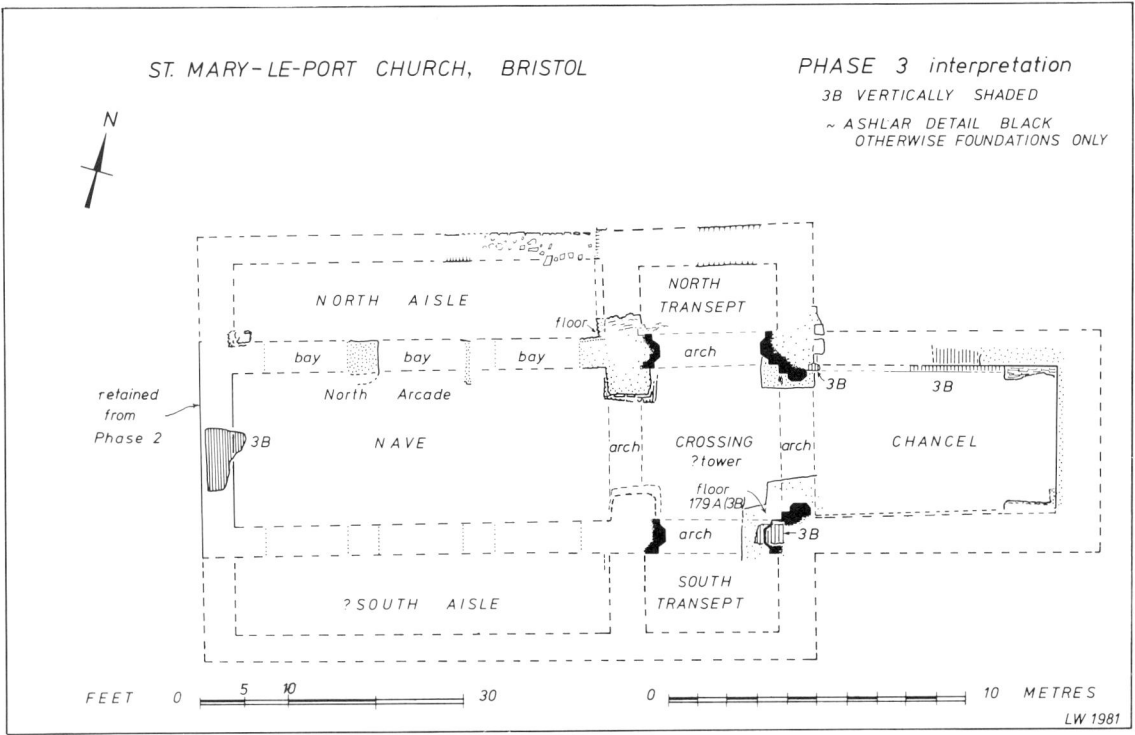

Figure 56.

The church as shown in figure 56 is of a familiar plan. The total internal length of the church is *c.*28 m., a nave of *c.*13 m. x 5+ m., a crossing *c.*5 m. square, and a chancel *c.*8 m. x 5 m. The nave arcades are of three bays of *c.*3 m. each, and the aisles *c.*13 m. x 2.5+ m.

The chapel of St. Katherine, known from 1411 (cf. 5.3.12 g.), should, whatever form it took, belong to this church.

In earlier drafts of this report, the cellared property was included in Phase 3, built in the angle now created between the north-east angle of the church and its chancel. Although it extended further than the north aisle, the dating of the window F138 (figure 63) to the late thirteenth century seemed indisputable evidence; it was assumed in this earlier hypothesis that the widening of the north aisle in Phase 4 corrected this anomaly, lining up the north sides of church and property. It now seems more probable that the cellared property utilised earlier window members, and was accommodated in the angle in Phase 4 or later (see 10.3.4a below); the point cannot however be taken as proven; the property could stratigraphically still be sometime within the lengthy span of Phase 3. For a discussion of the complex history of the ground north-east of the church, see Chapter 9.

10.3.4 PHASE 4

10.3.4a THE EVIDENCE FROM PHASE 4 (figure 57)

In Phase 4 the church reached its maximum size. A tower was added at the west end, and the north aisle was extended in width. The chancel was mostly rebuilt and the west ends of the north and south arcades were presumably rebuilt when the tower absorbed them.

The new work is characterised by a hard reddish mortar. The tower was built with both eastern and western arches (cf. F6 and F25), and this raises the possibility that there may have been a western entrance in earlier phases too, F81B and F81 being only a sleeper wall below a threshold rather than a west wall proper. The construction details of the tower are shown in sections S11 and S12, figure 46.

The tower appears to be of one build including the south-east stair turret (10.4.6); the latter must in some way have been accommodated to the west end of the south arcade of the Phase 3 church. No indication of such a join is now visible; it was for this reason that it was originally thought that the stair turret might be a secondary feature of the tower, built in Phase 5, when the south arcade and south aisle of the Phase 3 church were demolished and a new wall built just south of the line of the old arcade. It seems more likely, however, in view of the apparent structural unity of at least the lower part of the stair turret with the tower, that any trace of the former joins have been obliterated by successive refacings of the stair turret in Phase 5 or later.

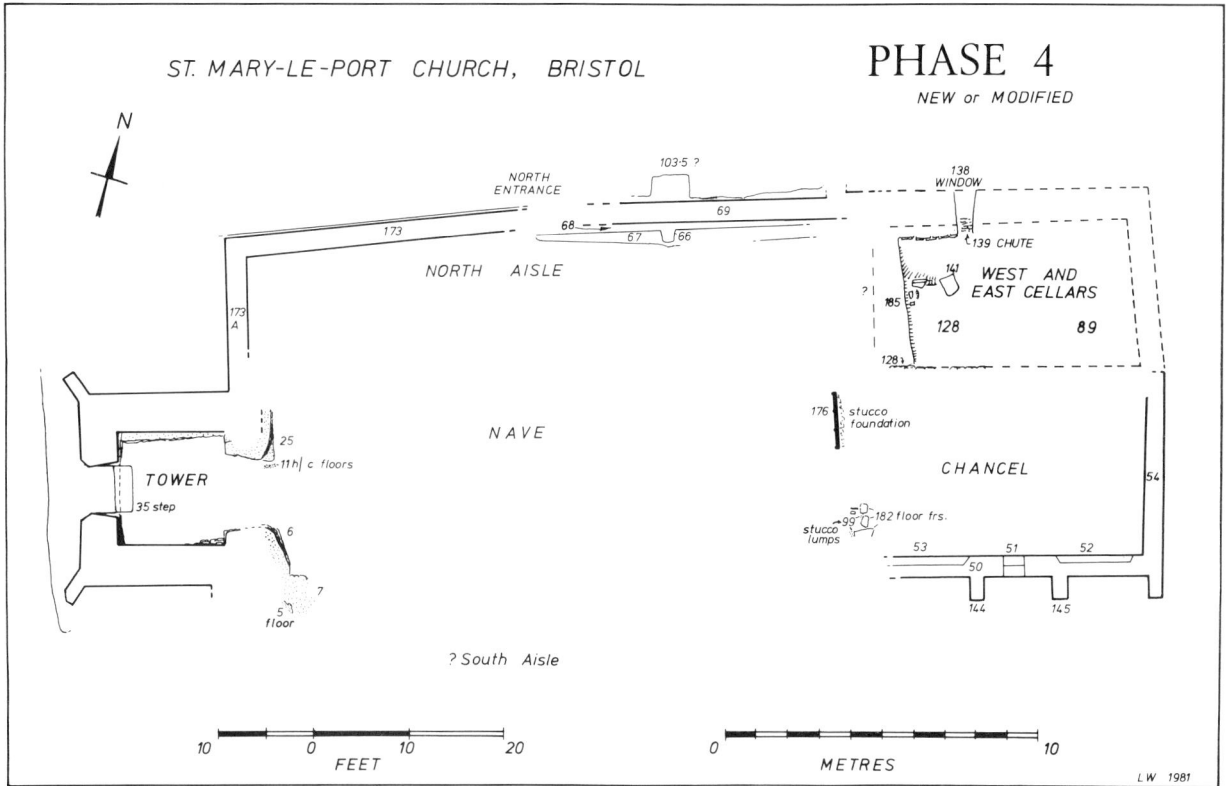

Figure 57.

The erection of the tower involved the rebuilding of the west end of the north aisle. F173A and F173 represent the new line. The north wall elements, F173 and F68 + F69 were in two orientations. These lie on either side of a northern entrance to the street, defined more clearly in Phases 5 – 6, but probably on the basis of this disorientation originating in Phase 4.

Although the inner face of the new north wall is shown as continuous on the plan, this being its recent form, there may still have been a north transept, continuing to utilise pier F92 in its south-east corner, as on figure 58; 103.5 externally may represent buttressing for this in Phase 4; or the aisle may have been extended east to absorb the old transept.

The chancel rebuild was principally on the old foundations; the north wall was however retained from Phase 3; the reason for this is unknown. The east wall (F54) was built on F55; the south wall (F50) now included two sedilia (F52 – 3), and, inserted later, a south doorway (F51). Buttresses on the south exterior, F144 – 5, were added at this time. The stucco-faced screen base (F176, originally extending further south, cf. F99, plate 21) also seems to have originated in Phase 4, as fragments of similar material were sealed by the foundation F177 of Phase 5.

No evidence survives for the chancel arch of Phase 4. The south side was replaced in Phase 5; this and the north side may well have retained their Phase 3 form, only a slight rebuilding being needed for the west end of the new south wall.

The north aisle presumably had windows which looked out on to a still open space (5.3.13); they may have been those which survived to later phases and were discovered just before 1881 (Nicholls and Taylor, 1881, II, 229), or these may have been of Phase 5; they were presumably blocked only when properties were built against them, in the seventeenth century or later (9.12).

The cellared property is assigned, in two phases, to Phase 4 (cf. 10.6 and 10.7) and appears to have been fitted into the angle between the eastern end of the north aisle and the chancel. Its north wall extends that of the eastern section of the north aisle; its east wall is at a slight angle inwards from the chancel. This alignment (and that of its west wall) is tenuously related to features to the north and to Mary-le-Port Street itself (cf. figure 34). The cellared property is described in 10.6 – 7; the window F138 is assumed to have been inserted, from existing members, in this phase. A *terminus post quem* for its construction is

Plate 21. Stucco screen base F176, from north-west.

given by the date assigned to Phase 4 (see below) and a *terminus ante quem* (for the cellar) by its subdivision in Phase 5. It thus appears to be dated to the later fifteenth century, and to have had a relatively short life, of only a few decades at most in its original form.

The dating evidence for Phase 4 is of several kinds. The architectural evidence of the tower, of late Perpendicular style, suggests a date in the later fifteenth century. A mid-fifteenth century date is given to the style of the south door arch F51, inserted into the south chancel wall. A *TPQ* is also given by sherds of red earthenware, 'Tudor Green', and south Netherlands maiolica in the tower construction trenches (cf. MF 10.4.4). The maiolica is conventionally later than *c*.1475, but could be earlier. A *TAQ* is given by the tomb monument F186 of the early sixteenth century built into the north wall. The most important *TAQ* is however given by the fact that William of Worcester (5.3.12g) described the church with a tower in *c*.1480, with a 'length' of '60 steps' (32 m.), remarkably close to the internal length of the Phase 4 church of 32.50 m. The dating for Phase 4 would therefore appear to be in the later fifteenth century, prior to 1480, the Phase 3 church having survived for some two centuries.

10.3.4b   INTERPRETATION OF PHASE 4 (figure 58)

The shaded areas in the reconstructed plan show the new work, which also was part of the church surviving to modern times. Apart from these alterations, the rest of the church is assumed to be that of Phase 3B; if there had been a central tower over the crossing in Phase 3, this may have been dismantled in Phase 4, together with the wall dividing the north aisle from the north transept. There must be considerable uncertainty not only about the retention of the north aisle/transept wall but also about the extent and angle of the eastern wall of the north transept, in view of the orientation of the cellar, and especially of its west wall; an uncertainty which obscures the relationship of the cellar entrance to the

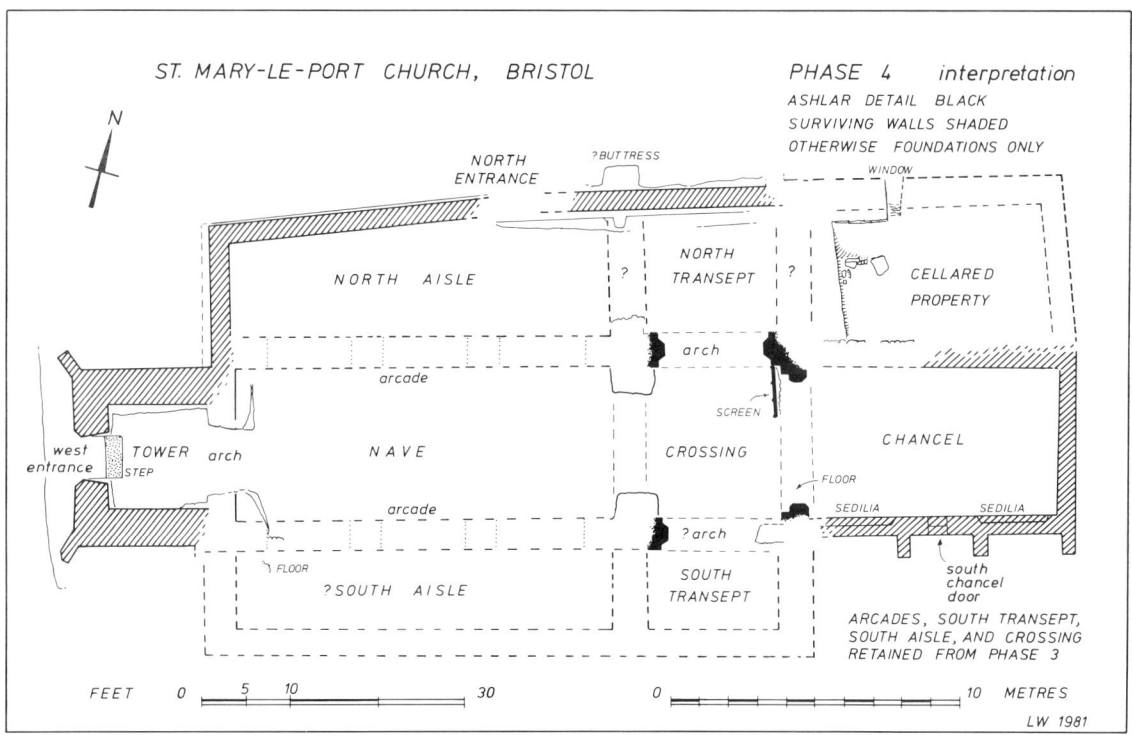

Figure 58.

church (cf. 10.6.2). The dimensions of the Phase 4 church are assumed to be the same as those listed above for Phase 3, except for the new tower, internally *c*.3.5 m. square, the north aisle and transept now widened to a maximum of *c*.4 m., and the chancel lengthened very slightly to 8.5 m.

Ricart's map of 1479 should be relevant to this phase of the church if it was based on accurate observation. He shows three towered buildings in Mary-le-Port ward. The one marked C on plate 2 may represent St. Mary-le-Port church (cf. 5.3.12b). This has a south porch (in an area not excavated) and a low central tower structure, but this does not correlate with the archaeological interpretation of this phase—the lack of a substantial western tower in Ricart is an obvious omission—and, unless Ricart's drawing has archaic details (cf. suggested central tower of Phase 3, figure 56), it appears to be schematic, at least in relation to St. Mary-le-Port.

10.3.5 PHASE 5

10.3.5a THE EVIDENCE FROM PHASE 5 (figure 59)

The final phase of the medieval church is represented by a major rebuild of the north arcade, the demolition of any south aisle, and by modifications to the tower. The latter remained the same in plan, but its eastern arch responds (and probably also the junction with the west wall of the north aisle) were altered as part of the major reconstruction of the body of the church, and some work was done on the roof and floor (10.4.5).

The north arcade was rebuilt in five bays (F15 – F17, F20 – F23, F32, F45 – F47, F58). New piers were made for all but the most easterly one (F92). This appears to have been left in its Phase 3/4 form, but its superstructure must have been altered to accommodate not only the west end of the nave arcade and the new chancel arch, but also the new eastern arch into the north chapel (see below).

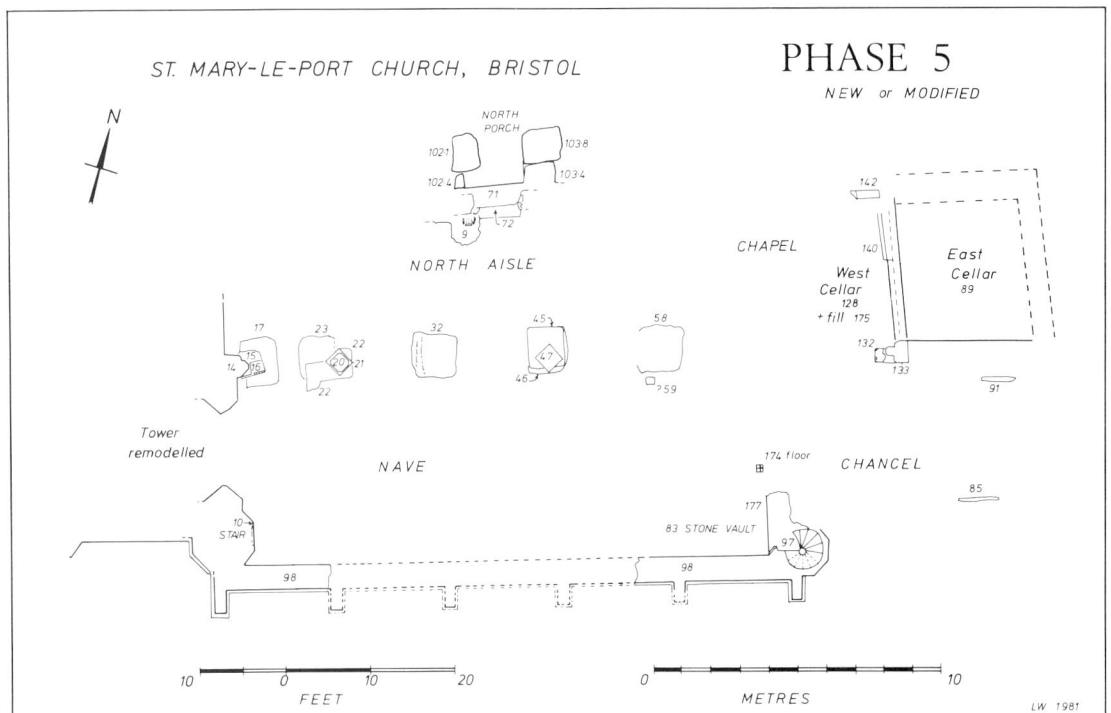

Figure 59.

The north entrance was rebuilt at this time (or possibly later) with new responds (F71 – 2, 102.1, 102.4, 103.4 and 103.8). The mortar of the north porch is similar to that of the Phase 5 tower alterations.

The cellar in the north-east corner was divided by the insertion of a cross wall (F140 and F142) and the blocking of the cellar window F138. The west element was filled up, but the eastern one was left as a smaller cellar, with a floor above. The fill of the West Cellar included a large quantity of charnel in the lower fill, F175B, which also included sherds of Fabric FF, current 1275 – 1400. None of the pottery could be dated with certainty to later than 1400, but fourteenth-century forms and fabrics may have continued. Fifteenth-century pottery is at present notoriously difficult to recognise. The pottery is probably as residual as the charnel.

If the north aisle had not absorbed the Phase 3 north transept in its Phase 4 reconstruction (see above, 10.3.4a), it presumably did so now. The new floor space, it is suggested, was not an extension of the north transept, but a separate area, entered only from a new arch created by the demolition of the western half of the north chancel wall. This arrangement is explicit in a representation of 1828 (plate 29). This was in fact a chapel, perhaps that of St. Uncumber, newly-built in 1518 (5.3.12g). The west-facing respond of this arch (F133) survived, still exhibiting much detail.

A further drastic change was the demolition of the assumed south arcade and south aisle and the building of a new south wall (F98) to the church just to the south of the old arcade line. The mortar of the new south wall was similar to that used in the Phase 5 alterations on the north side. The loss of the aisle gave less room to the living in the church, but more to the dead, and this was perhaps the reason for this change (cf. 10.5 *re* the south aisle).

The new work also involved a remodelling of the south-west corner of the chancel. Here a new block of masonry (F177) was built, incorporating a spiral staircase, interpreted as a rood stair (F97). F177

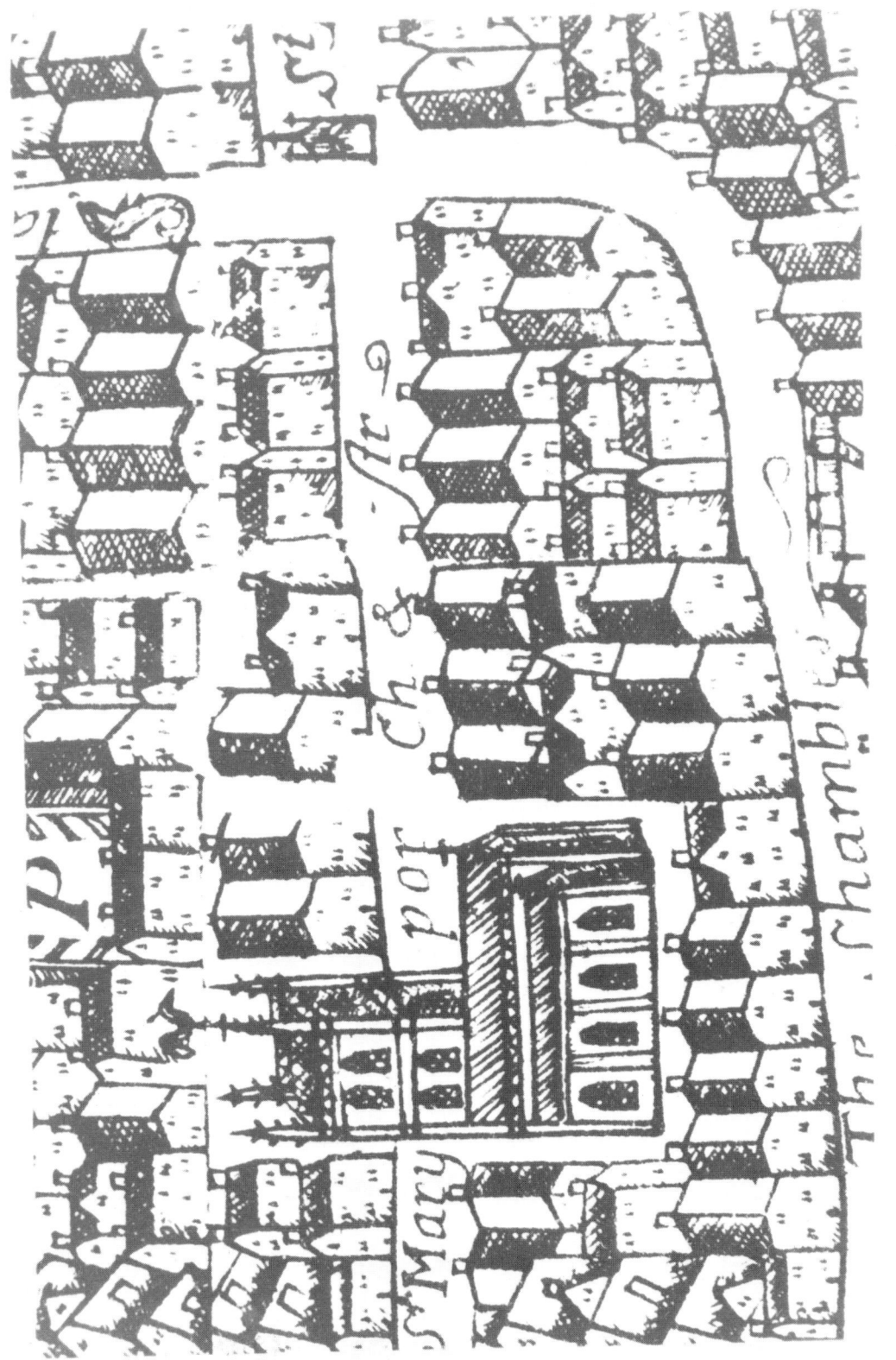

Plate 23.   Detail of Millerd's Plan of Bristol, 1673—St. Mary-le-Port church.

presumably carried the south side of a new chancel arch, replacing that of Phase 4. On the north side, the Phase 3 pier foundation still survived (with some ashlar detail); but its superstructure was presumably modified to accommodate the responds to the three new arches.

These alterations on the south side were assigned at the time of excavation to Phase 5 on the basis of mortar similarities between the new south wall and the modifications to the tower, also on the medieval character of the work, including a rood-stair loft.

There is however a conflict here with one of the earliest pictorial sources—Millerd's map of 1673, which shows Mary-le-Port with a south aisle (plate 23). Millerd has been shown to be, in general, a reliable artist (cf. 5.3.13c) so this evidence cannot be dismissed without further consideration. There are nevertheless various suspicious details in relation to St. Mary-le-Port church. The nave and chancel are shown as a continuous cell, contrary to all known arrangements, which involve a narrower chancel. The south tower windows are paired at each stage, instead of the single lights of today; there is no stair turret, assigned archaeologically to pre-1673; the tower pinnacles are exaggerated; the relationship of the tower to the body of the church is incorrect: all the churches in this part of Bristol are drawn on the same convention. Similarly, all roofing is represented by a uniform hatching. Turning to the south aisle, Millerd has only four windows, although the surviving Phase 5 wall has five. F. Neale suggests that this may have been dictated by the practicalities of the number that could be engraved in the given length allowed on the map. In contrast, although details of the south window tracery are not visible, the general shape of the window heads, the window-to-wall ratio and the buttresses are broadly similar to the south aspect of the church as known from pre-war photographs.

These differences between Millerd's church and the structure known in the early twentieth century could be explained as belonging to separate remodellings. The weight of the evidence, however, is against Millerd illustrating a *contemporary* building. The archaeological link between the south wall and the Perpendicular work is sound. To this can be added the architectural dating of the south windows, for which Lawrence Butler suggests a broad time span of *c.*1480 – 1540. Unless it could be demonstrated that these were a later insertion from another wall, this south wall must, on this evidence, have existed before Millerd's drawing. If Millerd was not merely using imaginative licence (by, for example, transposing the south wall windows to a non-existent south aisle), it nevertheless remains possible that he was utilising earlier illustrations, and that he may actually be representing not the Phase 5, but the Phase 4 church.

David Dawson, who has made extensive study of the Millerd map, comments as follows:
'To be fair to Millerd it should be remembered that he was working within a tradition of town plan making which derives from the sixteenth century. Although his publications bear very favourable comparison with, for example, Nicholas Berey's plan of Paris (1645) or Wencelaus Hollar's plan of London for Blome (1673), they cannot be compared with or used in the same way as the latter's prospects of the cities of London and Westminster which indicate that Hollar took particular pains to portray individual buildings with great accuracy. Millerd has been proved time after time to have been remarkably perceptive in depicting the spatial layout of his own city, especially in his plan of 1673, but, true to his tradition, he shows his buildings in conventional not realistic form. Tantalisingly he often does include tiny pieces of detail, a clock-face for instance, to suggest the individual personality of different buildings. The evidence is in his publications:
(1) *An exact delineation of the famous cittie of Bristoll and suburbes thereof,* dated 1671, scale seven inches to one mile.

(2) *The famous citie of Bristoll with its suburbes,* undated but probably done after (1) and it appears to be a prototype for (3), scale 14 inches to one mile.

(3) *An exact delineation of the famous citty of Bristoll and suburbs,* dated 1673, scale 24½ inches to one mile. The plates for this plan were re-engraved at least four times within the next sixty years.

(4) *The Citty of Bristoll,* undated but probably 1673, a prospect from the south.'

'His conventions change from publication to publication and so does the detail he shows. The first plan (1) is a small-scale work and only the Cathedral and St. Mary Redcliffe receive particular attention apart from the spires of St. John Baptist, Christ Church and St. Nicholas. It is in the larger-scale works (2, 3 and 4) in which one is tempted to look for detail. Here, however, his churches are still conventionalised.'

'He understandably contracts the length of his churches so that their height and therefore their prominence can be exaggerated. The cruciform St. Mary Redcliffe which has a nave of six bays and a quire of four is shown in (2) and (3) as having five and three bays respectively, in (4) as seven and four, but in a vignette on the border of (3) as having five and five bays. Indeed a comparison between the map (3) and the three churches shown in greater detail in the border reveals startling discrepancies. Further, these three drawings also differ in detail of plan, fenestration and overall design from the buildings which survive substantially in the form in which Millerd must have seen them.'

'So what conventions did Millerd use in his plans of 1673? Comparison with surviving building evidence suggests the following: the length was normally reduced by showing fewer bays, but low east ends are shown if the height difference was marked. All churches appear (with the exception of St. Philip's) to have a single aisle on the south side although most of them are known to have had north aisles as well (unfortunately, St. Mary-le-Port is the only church which may not have had a south aisle). With the exceptions of the Cathedral, St. Stephen's, St. Philip's and St. John's, towers are shown standing behind the body of the church. All the belfry stages, except for the Cathedral, St. Leonard and St. Mary Redcliffe, are lit by two windows in the south face although only two churches are known to have been designed this way and nine others are known to have had single lights. This convention may have developed from plan (2) where every belfry is lit by two windows. Care has been taken to depict spires and rood-clerestories but none of the distinctive "Bristol type" towers are shown with the prominent stair turret rising up above one corner.'

'If therefore one poses the question, "If Millerd saw St. Mary-le-Port in the form we know it had in 1939, would he have drawn it as it appears in his 1673 plan?", the answer would be, "yes, very possibly".'

Phase 5 is assigned to the early sixteenth century, on the basis of architectural dating. Detail on the eastern respond of the north chapel arch is not closely datable beyond being late Perpendicular; this dating is however consistent with that assigned by Dr Butler to the south windows of the nave, as seen in their modern form, of *c*.1480–1540 with a preference for *c*.1520. This is not inconsistent with a *terminus ante quem* given by an early sixteenth-century monument, F186 (plate 24 MF), erected against the north aisle wall. Closer dating, and indeed other evidence, may be adduced from later representations of the church (e.g. plate 29) which clearly depict much detail attributed to Phase 5—notably that of the arcade bases, shafts, capitals and arches. Dr Butler suggests that ST72, part of the Phase 5 arcade, belongs closer to 1450 than to 1500, but as Phase 5 seems to represent, archaeologically, a single building operation, the later dating for this phase must be accepted. Finally, if the new north chapel is indeed that of St. Uncumber, newly-built in 1518, this could confirm a date in the second decade of the sixteenth century for Phase 5, consistent with that suggested above.

10.3.5b INTERPRETATION OF PHASE 5 (figure 60)
The shaded walls in figure 60 survived to the modern church, some surviving from Phase 4. The new north arcade is reconstructed from the surviving square plinths F21 and F47, and the hexagonal upper

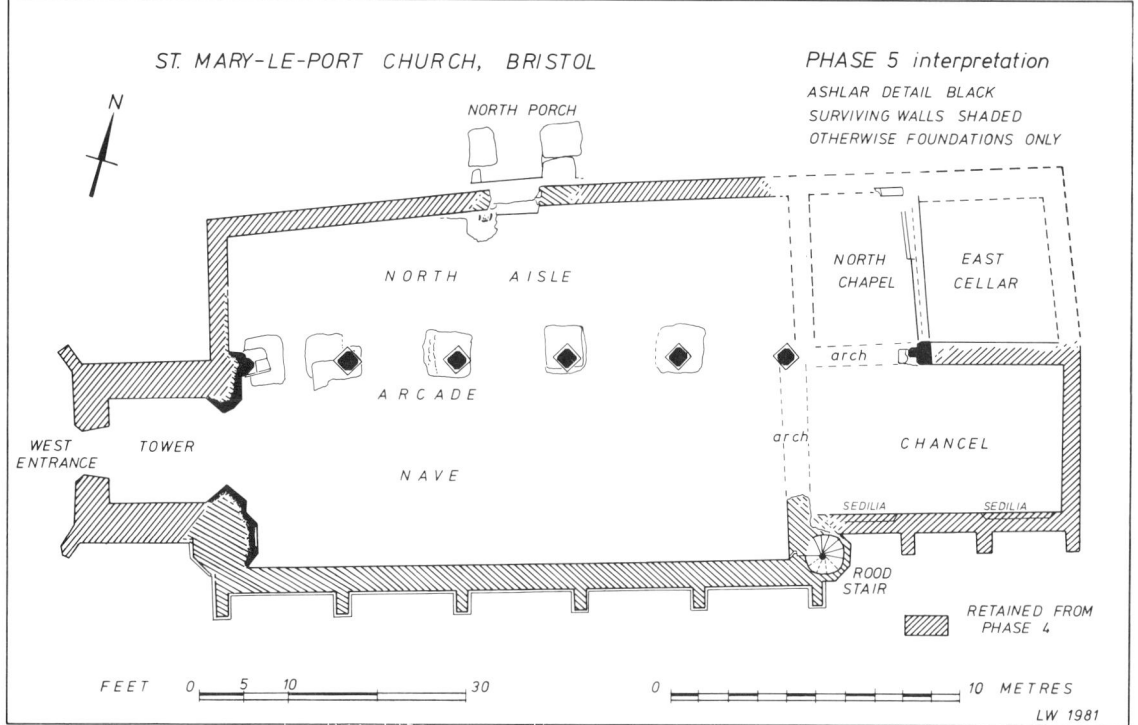

Figure 60.

plinth F20, lying on F21 (for upper structure, see ST72). From these are extrapolated five plinth bases at 3.7 m. centre to centre, or an intercolumniation at this level of 3.1 m. This gives a five-bay arcade, terminating in the north respond of the chancel arch, whose foundation was retained from Phase 4. The plinth base of this easterly pier may also have retained earlier elements, and not have been of the square and hexagon shown in the reconstructed plan. If there were something more complex here, it would reduce the size of the arch to the north chapel to something less than the 3.9 m. indicated.

The final north aisle was c.19 m. long x c.4.5 m. wide; the nave 18 m. + long and c.6.5 m. wide, and the north chapel c.5 × 3 m. The surviving East Cellar was c.4.5 m. square. Since part of the cellared property had now been incorporated into the church, it must be assumed that in Phase 5, if not from its inception, the cellared property belonged to the church, and may indeed have been its parsonage (cf. 5.3.13a). The East Cellar, and the room above it, continued in church use until 1940 (cf. 10.7).

It was the Phase 5 church which survived with modifications until 1940, and which is shown in the pictorial sources of the nineteenth and twentieth centuries. Detail shown on these is discussed in the next section on Phase 6, but much of what was depicted must have had its origins in Phase 5.

10.3.6   PHASE 6 (figure 61)
This phase includes all post-Phase 5 features, and those which cannot be assigned securely to 5 rather than to 6. It includes, archaeologically, the early sixteenth-century tomb monument (F186, plate 24 MF) built against the north wall of the north aisle at its east end.

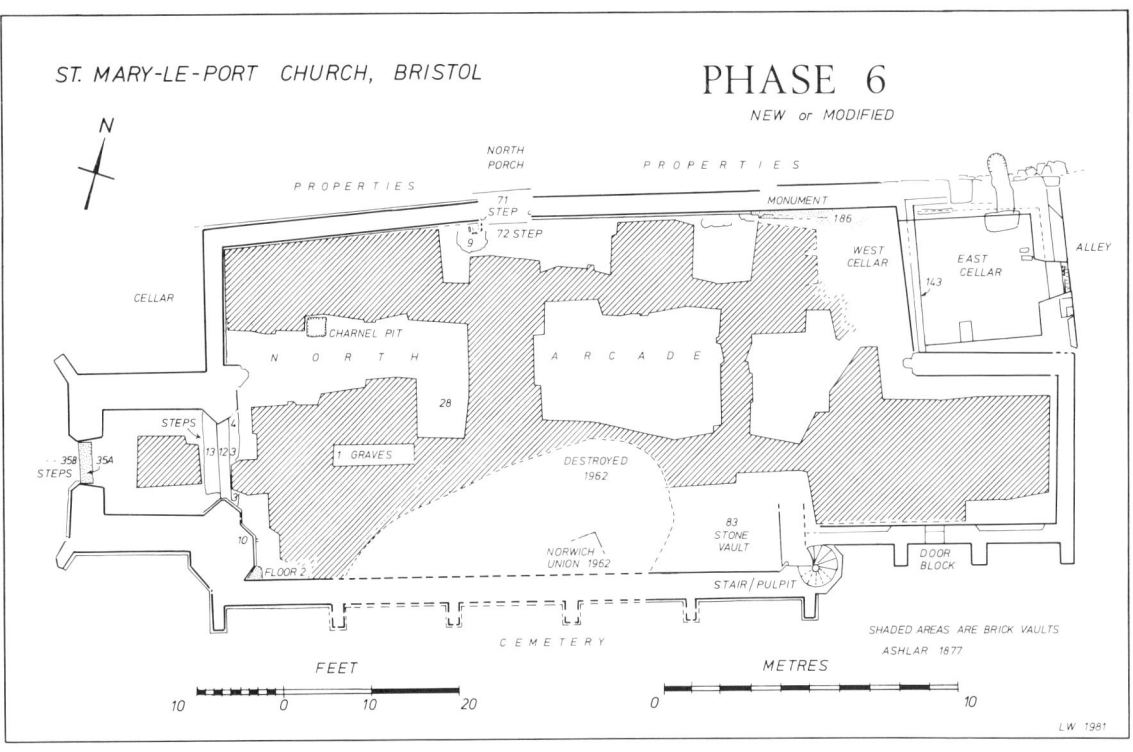

Figure 61.

In the seventeenth to nineteenth centuries there were minor modifications and floor alterations, and massive interment in brick tombs. During this period, too, the space between the north wall and Mary-le-Port Street had been built up. Any former northern churchyard bounded by a wall (Chapter 9) had been sacrificed to commerce, together with the northern aspect of the church, which was hidden by buildings of up to five storeys high; any windows on this side would thus have become redundant, only the top of the tower being visible (plate 7). The north entrance which had in the fifteenth – sixteenth century presumably been a free-standing porch was eventually a tunnel entered from Mary-le-Port Street through the ground floor of properties above (plate 25).

Apart from the 1479 Ricart map (cf. 10.3.4b), Millerd's map of 1673 is the first pictorial illustration of a building which may be securely identified as the church of St. Mary-le-Port; the problems of its accuracy as a depiction of 1673 have been discussed above (10.3.5a), notably in relation to the south aisle.

The next pictorial source is the painting of the church of Jackson in 1825 (plate 28). His view from the south-east of the exterior shows the upper part of the tower of Phase 5, with its stair turret; the five windows of the south side of the nave, with the six buttresses flanking them; the rood-stair turret on the south-east corner of the nave; and the set-back chancel with its two windows and two of the three

Plate 25. Mary-le-Port Street, south side; church north porch right of centre; drawing ?early twentieth century.

Plate 28. St. Mary-le-Port Church from south-east, Buttermarket Passage in foreground; painting by S. Jackson 1825; monochrome photo.

Plate 29. St. Mary-le-Port Church interior, from west; painting by I. Johnson 1828; monochrome photo.

buttresses. It illustrates the relatively extensive space of the south graveyard, with a high stone wall to the south, and railings of a low stone wall to the east. The roof material is shown only schematically, but the painting does show that the nave roof was higher than and separate from that over the chancel. This is obviously a reliable depiction of the church in the early nineteenth century.

Johnson's painting of 1828 (plate 29) is another very useful source. This shows the shafting, capitals and arches of the two most westerly bays of the arcade of Phase 5 and the eastern shaft, capital and arch of the arch into the north chapel (apparently identical to those of the nave arcade). Through the open bays of the arcade can be seen a substantial wall separating the north aisle from the north chapel. The nave itself is full of box pews, and a pulpit has been superimposed on the Phase 5 rood-stair, utilising its lower treads. The roof is of plaster with a strapwork design, and there is a Baroque reredos at the east end of the chancel, screened off by a low communion rail.

The next source is an incomplete architect's plan of 1842 showing proposed alterations at that time. Neither this, nor the later architects' plans of 1861 and 1875 are reliable for the overall plan; they agree neither with each other nor with that of the present day. By 1842, it is nevertheless clear that the wall between the north aisle and north chapel of Phase 5 had since 1828 been demolished or that this was planned; the north aisle now extends in this plan well beyond the line of the chancel arch. The east cellar, or rather the room above it, is to be the 'new vestry room'. The monument F186 is shown set into the north wall, and the form of the north porch is shown, going out to Mary-le-Port Street between two blocks of 'dwelling-houses'. A western gallery is named. The four westerly piers of the arcade of Phase 5 are depicted as simple square shapes, but the pier of the north side of the chancel is shown as much more massive, the arch to the east by the north chapel being the same width as those of the nave, not wider as

115

shown in the archaeological plan (figure 60) of the remains of Phase 5. The south respond F177 of the chancel arch is shown much as found in excavation. Most of the plan is concerned with new pews. The fact that some of these are against the 'new vestry room' may suggest that the absorption of the north chapel into the north aisle was not a *fait accompli,* but was part of the new proposal of 1842.

There is a Faculty for 1861 (Bristol Record Office EP/V/6/2/66) which includes details of alterations and improvements, the removal of the reading desk, the need for more pews, and of 'reading from the Brass Eagle'. The accompanying architect's plan shows both present and proposed plans which differ only in minor internal arrangements. The room above the East Cellar is now confirmed as the vestry, and the eastward lengthening of the north aisle is now a fact, even if it had not been in 1842. More detail is shown in this plan of the precise form of the arcade and other pier bases.

The most complete set of architects' drawings is that of 1875, for work done in 1877. There is no significant difference in the overall plan, but it does show the precise detail of the plan of the pier bases, according with the depictions of the 1828 painting. Close detail is shown of parts of the tower in plan and elevation; a plan of the roofs shows four roof-lights illuminating the north aisle, and one for the vestry. Some curious arrangements are shown here on the north side, the implications of which are that properties (including a 'basket-shed') are not just built *against* the church, but overhang it, at least at roof level, perhaps at a first-floor or higher level. Details are also shown of heating systems (using the East Cellar as stoke room), pew, window, and arch detail, and roof pitches. The work involved the re-facing of many wall surfaces with sawn freestone, tiled flooring, and the blocking of the tower staircase. This was evidently in response to a petition of 1875 from the rector and churchwardens to the bishop (Bristol Record Office EP/V/6/2/66). The condition of the church at this time is illustrated by the following quotation: 'said church is from age and natural decay . . . in a bad state of repair . . . stonework . . . iron', 'pews of painted deal . . . incommodious and unsightly . . . stoves in church insufficient to warm . . . that in consequence of the interments which have taken place in former times in the church it is advisable for the health of the congregation that the vaults throughout the church should be properly sealed with a layer of concrete and the church newly paved . . .', 'plastered ceiling unsightly . . . entrance to Church under Tower dark and incommodious . . . Encaustic or tesselated tiles . . . To take down pews etc . . . and to reseat with stained pitch pine . . . remove flooring and paving and cover entire surface with 3″ concrete + wood floor over—to remove plaster and paint from walls, . . . replaster . . . paint and point to match ashlar . . . remove ceiling . . . put in new windows of 'Cathedral Tinted Glass' . . . replace gas fittings . . . take away and remove present stoves . . . and to erect and fix under present vestry a proper apparatus for heating . . . with hot air with all necessary pipes and flues in and through the said Church communicating with such apparatus . . . alter floor levels of Tower . . . move Eagle and new plinth . . . platform enclosed at front and sides by a neat Brass or Iron railing.' Further work was done in 1908. Another petition (Bristol Record Office EP/V/6/2/66) speaks of the need for: 'stripping roofs, making good defective timbers, . . . felting, tiling . . . gutters . . . downpipes . . . repairing internal ashlar on North wall and shake in west pier of Arcade . . . turret repairs, weather vane . . . grouting, new w.c. to Vestry . . . relaying drain in Heating Chamber, repairing floor and cleansing Heating Chamber, . . . glazing . . . lightning conductor'.

It was however the church as restored in 1877 which was familiar to Bristolians before 1940.

Few photographs survive of this church interior. A postcard of the ?1930s is a view looking east, showing the altar area, the north arch of the chancel, and two of the chancel windows. The eagle lectern is shown on the north side of the nave. Another postcard shows this from the south by the north side of the chancel arch; beyond it through the opening of the east bay of the nave arcade can be seen the F186 tomb.

Many other photographs show the church exterior. Plate 41 shows the south exterior as seen from the south-east. Another shows the tower and south side very similar to the painting of 1825. Plate 41 has identical detail, but shows the whole of the four westerly windows on the south side, the best evidence for their form. Plate 43 shows the inside after the bombing of 1940. Other views of surrounding street aspects are more topographical and give no more information on the architecture. Photographs taken in 1950–1 and 1974 give further detail of the church in decay; a further set was taken in 1981 by the authors.

Many of the burial vaults were put in during the nineteenth century. The latest archaeologically-dated burial is 1847 (a coffin plate cf. 10.10) but burial probably continued later into the century when all city burial ceased in favour of out-of-town cemeteries. The Faculty of 1875 includes provision to seal down the floors of the church where interments had recently been made. The more recent fate of the church is described in Chapter 3.

Plate 41.   St. Mary-le-Port Church from south-east with south churchyard.

Plate 43. St. Mary-le-Port Church interior from east after blitz, 1940.

This report does not include any detailed consideration of the architectural features of the church (e.g. the two roof lines now visible on the north tower face—see 10.4 and 10.5 below) other than those directly related to the below-ground archaeology. This is a task beyond present resources, which will have to take into account all extant elevations, written sources, and in particular the considerable pictorial data. Summary accounts will be found in, for example, Nicholls and Taylor, 1881, II, and in Shipley and Rankin, 1945; David Dawson contributes a preliminary statement on the tower, in 10.4 below.

10.4   The tower (S11, S12, figures 46 and 47)

10.4.0   GENERAL

No survey or architectural study of the tower, or of other standing parts of the structure, were done at the time of excavation. Casual observations were hindered at that time by the Victorian cladding which obscured the tower structure. Since then, much of this has weathered off and recent photographs show details not previously visible, which should be recorded. A preliminary account by David Dawson of the present appearance is appended to 10.4.6 below.

The below-floor sequence in the tower may be summarised as follows, related to the church phases (also see main discussion under phases).

10.4.1 – 2   PHASE 1 AND/OR 2

The earliest wall appears to be F81B, under the east face of the standing tower. This is interpreted as the west wall of a pre-tower church or building (of stone, timber or mixed superstructure). It does not cut any burials, and there are no loose human bones in associated levels. It may or may not be contemporary with the hearth under F11 (F11p in section S11) which itself lies on what appears an undisturbed buried soil (F11r in S11).

10.4.3B   PHASE 3B

F81B may have been partly lowered; its surviving surface was covered with dirty soil, possibly derived

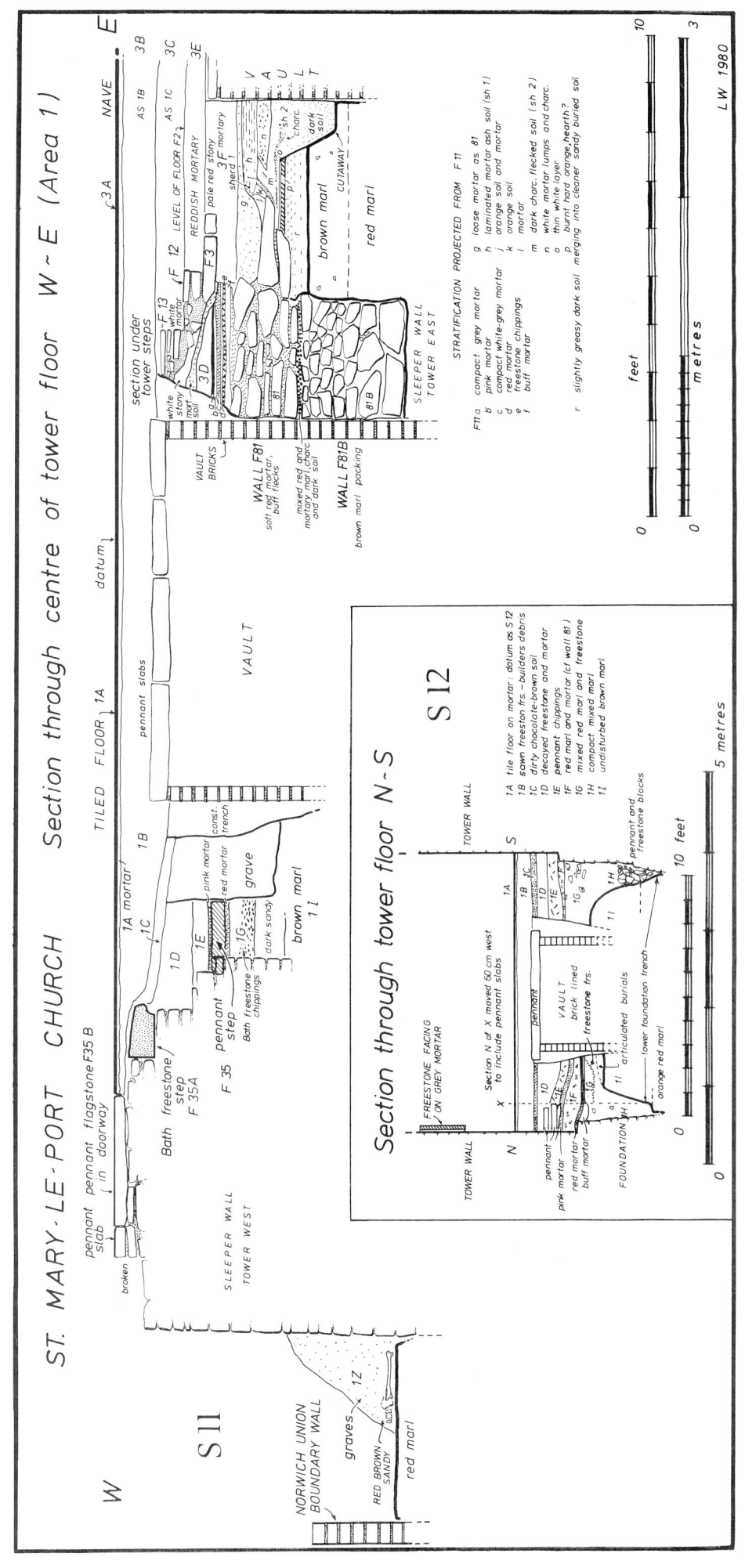

ST. MARY·LE·PORT CHURCH   Section through centre of tower floor W ~ E (Area 1)

Section through tower floor N ~ S

S 12

Section N of X moved 60 cm west
to include pennant slabs

STRATIFICATION PROJECTED FROM F 11

F11 a compact grey mortar
     b pink mortar
     c compact white-grey mortar
     d red mortar
     e freestone chippings
     f buff mortar
     g loose mortar grey mortar
     h laminated mortar ash soil (sh 1)
     j orange soil and mortar
     k orange soil
     l mortar
     m dark charc. flecked soil (sh 2)
     n white mortar lumps and charc.
     o thin white layer
     p burnt hard orange, hearth?
     r slightly greasy dark soil merging into cleaner sandy buried soil

S 11

LW 1980

Figure 46.

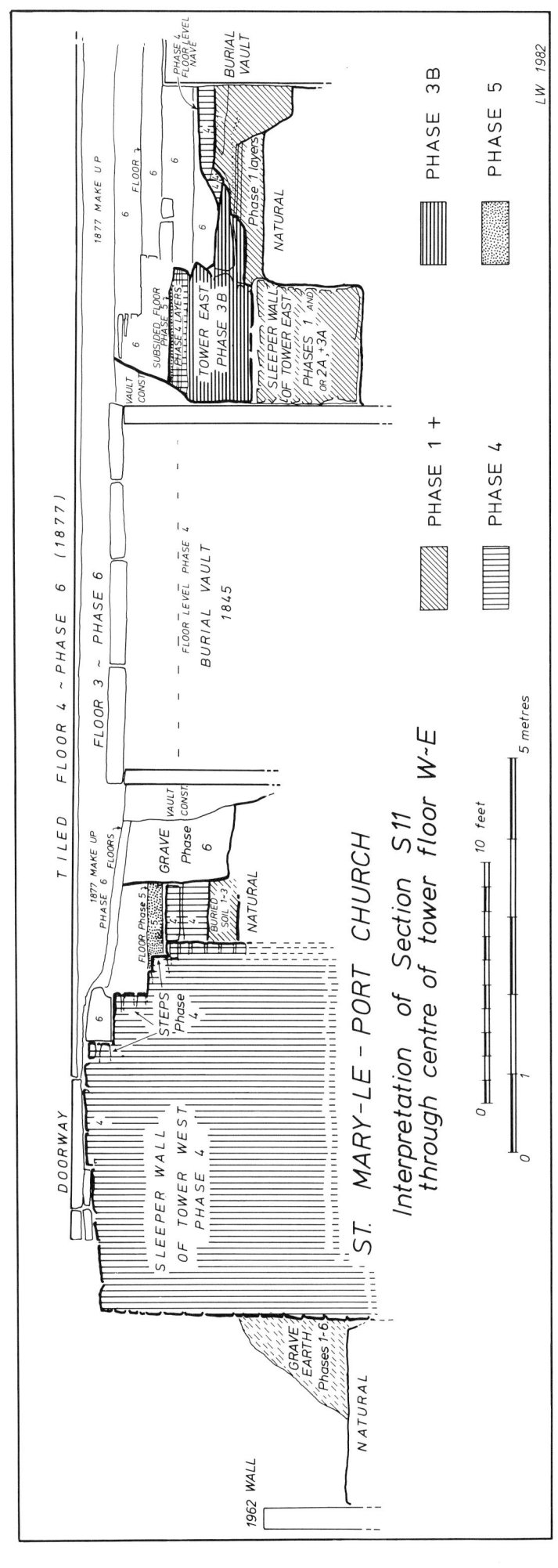

ST. MARY-LE-PORT CHURCH

Interpretation of Section S11
through centre of tower floor W~E

LW 1982

Figure 47.

from builders' disturbance of adjacent layers. On this was built wall F81, of better construction, though of similar stone and now certainly the west wall (or possibly a sleeper wall for a western arch) (cf. 10.3.1 – 3) of a pre-tower church.

10.4.4 PHASE 4
The present tower was built, on the evidence of architectural and other detail, in the later fifteenth century prior to 1480 (10.3.4). The foundation of its north wall was keyed into the remains of F81 at the north end of the latter, but not at its south end. F81 was presumably left as a rough sleeper wall under the doorway beneath the western tower arch, although the failure to bond at the south end would reduce its usefulness for this purpose.

10.4.5 PHASE 5
The floor level was further raised by 1E, a layer of Pennant chippings and off-white mortar. Slate in this layer suggests that the new work included some re-roofing, the previous roof having been of Pennant, ridged with green-glazed tiles. The new floor-level was indicated by a further Pennant slab (S12 left).

10.4.6 PHASE 6
The floor level was again raised by a layer mainly of decayed freestone (1D). This suggests repairs to freestone parts of the tower. Further slate and broken Pennant roof tile suggest improvements to roofing.

A further levelling of the floor is indicated by a dark-brown soil 1C, perhaps the remains of a wooden floor. This sealed graves and also the Bath stone step (F35A) (S11 left). In this stage the large central vault was built, destroying a large area within the tower. The middle coffin in this had an inscribed plate: 'Charles Smith. Died 22 December 1847. Aged 83 Years', which should date the use of the vault (cf. 10.3.6).

Finally in 1877, the tower was re-faced with 5 cm. of sawn Bath stone. The builders' debris—bits of sawn stone, slate, brick and mortar—were used to raise the floor level to accommodate pipes of the heating system, and a tiled floor was laid on top.

David Dawson examined the tower in 1982, and contributed a summary of his preliminary observations.

'The following notes are based on a visual inspection of the structure as it existed in 1982. Those parts beyond the reach of a 4 m. ladder were examined with binoculars but would repay full study and measurement with the aid of scaffolding.'

'The remains of the church are in the care of, and have been consolidated by, the City of Bristol. During these works, the tower was re-roofed, a reinforced-concrete wall was built into the tower arch and much of the external limestone detailing and facing was restored. The internal faces of the tower are still exposed though they were seriously damaged by fire in 1940.'

'The tower (Phase 4) consists of three diminishing stages and stands at the west end of the nave. It is built of Pennant Sandstone ashlar with limestone buttresses, stair turret and other architectural detail. The diagonal buttresses are divided into six weathered stages, except on the south-east corner where the octagonal stair turret rises an additional stage above the tower and finishes in a crocketted spire. Each storey is marked by a string course which continues round the buttresses and the stair turret, uninterrupted except by the tower arch. The lowest string course has been cut flush to the wall surface on the north and east faces save for one fragment on the north. The original plinth and its weathering survives on the south face, but has been cut back on the north side (presumably where a secular building once abutted the tower) and has been obscured on the west by the re-facing of the lowest storey in limestone ashlar. The west doorway has a two-centred arch under a label with two apparently nineteenth-century stops but much of it is more recent restoration. The west window has four trefoil-headed lights under subarcuated reticulated tracery in a two-centred head but is again a post-war restoration. The tower arch is unrestored but was damaged by the fire. It is two-centred and rises from the plinth uninterrupted by caps. There is a blocked door opening in the stair turret here which may have once given on to a west gallery.'

'The second stage of the tower is lit in each face by a window of two trefoil-headed lights under a reticulated quatrefoil in a two-centred head and each face of the belfry by one of two trefoil-headed lights under panelled tracery in a two-centred head. Although all the windows in the second stage are post-war restorations, those of the belfry stage seem to be earlier. The tower is crowned by a battlemented and blind-panelled parapet with a niche in the centre of each face and a battlemented and crocketted pinnacle above each buttress. Similar blind panelling but in two bands decorates the uppermost stage of the turret.'

'Judging by the masonry inside the tower as well as the design of the structure and its external wall faces, the tower is of one build with subsequent restorations and re-facing, particularly the lowest stage of the west front and much of the lower parts of the stair turret. The possible exception is the east face which seems to incorporate an earlier gabled west wall of the nave. There is a clear straight joint here, and the string course between the first and second stages of the tower butts this joint. Unfortunately its lower ends are obscured on the one side by the re-facing of the stair turret and on the other by the later heightening of the wall above the north arcade. The appearance of the masonry above the tower arch also suggests that this arch is an insertion into an earlier wall.'

'The south wall of the nave (Phase 5) has been reduced to about a metre in height and it is clearly separated from the stair turret by a straight joint. The plinth and its weathering is identical to that surviving on the south side of the tower, though they are attributed to different building phases. The roof line on the east face of the tower, which cuts across the turret and the north-east buttress, indicates that this wall was built further south than the original south side of the nave and that the north wall was raised at the same time.'

'In sum, available evidence suggested that the church was extended in the late fifteenth century by the addition of a typical 'Bristol-type' tower (Smith, 1970), the nave being subsequently enlarged by pushing out the south wall and raising the roof.'

10.5   The south aisle

Because of the extent of later destruction, evidence for arrangements on the south side of the church in all periods is sparse (cf. figure 45). For the north wall, long stretches of robber trenches survived; on the south, however, only two lengths of possible wall were found—F44, a fragment of W-E foundation at the west end of the nave; and F90, also a small area of west – east foundation, at the east end of the nave; the south end of the latter appears to end on a well-defined west edge. F44 and F90 do not obviously line up and are assigned separately to Phases 2A and 2B on the basis of different packings (figure 52). It remains uncertain whether there was a solid wall or an arcade on the proposed lines of these Phase 2 features. Although F90 could be interpreted as part of a discrete feature rather than as part of a continuous foundation, too little was observed either to assess the nature and extent of its robbing or of its original form (cf. also 10.3.2A – B).

Consideration must turn to less-direct information. The possibilities of a central crossing area and the consequences of reconstructing a symmetrical church are discussed under Phase 3 (10.3.3).

The relevance of roofing arrangements may also be considered. Recent photographs of the east face of the tower show two nave roof-lines. The higher, which uneasily cuts across the stair turret, belonged to the latest roof, illustrated, for example, in prints and photographs of the early twentieth century. The lower part of the turret facing, up to the level cut away by this roof-line, appears to be part of nineteenth-century restoration, which provides a *terminus post quem* for this roof-line in its latest form. The awkward junctions of the nave south wall with the turret and the tower are visible in photographs.

The lower roof-line must belong to an arrangement between that considered above and the building of the tower, i.e. it belongs to Phase 4 or later. It appears, from the angle of pitch, only to roof the nave. Plate 29, which shows the interior of the church *c.*1828, suggests that the north aisle was roofed separately, without a clerestory (the north aisle was, by this time, entirely without windows, cf. 10.3.6). There is no direct information about any putative south aisle roof-line; any suggestions can be made only by analogy. There is thus no data here to substantiate independently the existence of a south aisle.

Another source to consider is the 1673 Millerd drawing. The difficulties of using Millerd are discussed under Phase 5 (10.3.5a).

To summarise, there is no direct evidence for a south aisle at any period, nor of the south wall until Phase 5 though a south arcade for both the Phase 3 and Phase 4 churches is favoured in the foregoing sections. All discussions are based on indirect evidence and interpretations.

10.6 The West Cellar (F128) (Phases 4–6) (plan figure 45, isometric elevation figure 63)

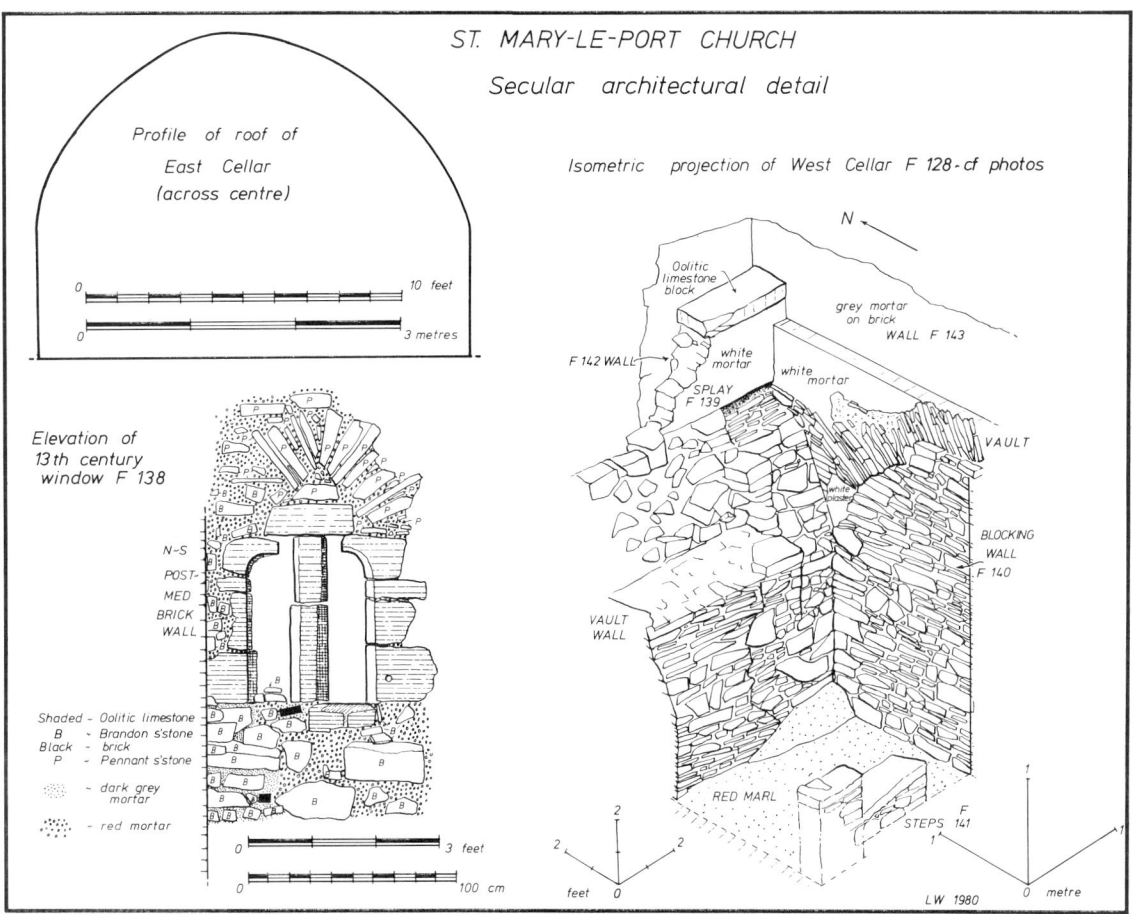

Figure 63.

10.6.1 METHOD

The East and West Cellars were originally part of a single substructure, but, because of their divergent later history, they are discussed separately. They were also excavated independently.

The West Cellar was first defined during the excavation of the north-east corner of the church. The internal elements of the north part of the cellar were exposed by removing both modern debris and less-recent material, F175A and B (see below). Massive modern masonry still blocked the south part of the cellar. This was later removed and shown to be part of the heating system for which the East Cellar became the stoking area (10.7) The south wall of the cellar was revealed only at this stage. The north exterior, including window F138, was seen when post-medieval structures were removed in Mary-le-Port Street.

10.6.2 CONSTRUCTION

The original West Cellar of Phase 4 did not extend as far west as the later F185, but was closer to F141 (see below and cf. figure 57).

The lower parts of the cellar side walls were vertical for 1.5 m. or more, and were then corbelled inwards to a roof profile which was probably part of and identical with the profile shown of the East Cellar in figure 63.

As part of the original scheme of construction, the main part of the floor was excavated to a maximum depth of 46 cm. into the sandstone bedrock, 3 m. deep in all. An unexcavated tongue of hard marl was however left at the west end, in the centre of which was built a series of steps down from the west, of which the lowest survived as F141. The west wall of this original phase must have been roughly in the region of these steps. The latter must therefore originally have descended through the thickness of the west wall, but it is not known if the approach was from the church or from the street exterior or whether access was through a conventional doorway or via a trapdoor for example (cf. figure 58 for suggested arrangement of the east end of the church in Phase 4).

Later, but still within Phase 4, the cellar was extended westwards, with a slight change in alignment of the north wall. The west wall, F185, was built against a newly-excavated marl cliff, but extended over its upper edge so that the upper part of the surviving corbelling extended slightly to the west of the marl cliff (cf. also westerly extent of south wall of F128 as far as F126, figure 45). F185 was butted against the north and south walls of the cellar—straight joints were visible against both—and must therefore have been built as a secondary operation. There is no means of assessing whether this was done as part of the same building operation as the cellar extension or whether there was an intermediary stage, when the west end of the cellar merely ended against the marl cliff for example. In this extended form the upper part of the vaulted roof, as reflected by the East Cellar vault, was higher than the church floor. The oolitic limestone block remaining on the later wall F142 (figure 63) may reflect the floor level above the cellar at this phase.

F185 was later robbed away. The robber trench for its eastern edge was defined; only two stones from F185 remained *in situ* at its base (figure 45).

Window F138, in the north wall, lit the West Cellar by way of a splayed opening, F139. F138 is dated to the late thirteenth century on the basis of architectural style but it is thought to be a later insertion into the West Cellar, utilising a re-used window frame (cf. 10.3.3d). It is thought to have been inserted in Phase 4 as it was blocked in Phase 5 (cf. 10.3.4a – 5a).

There was buff stucco on the south wall on both the original part and traces extended over part of the west extension.

The relationship of the cellar to the church in this form remains unclear. It was integrated with the north wall of the chancel—its south wall built into the chancel wall of Phase 3—and must have obscured the chancel if indeed it was associated with an above-ground structure (there is no evidence about windows in the north chancel wall at any phase). There is still no evidence about how access was gained, whether from the church or street. The cellar is assumed to be the basement of a property above (=cellared property) which Neale suggests (5.3.13a) was the medieval parsonage. She also has details (5.3.12e) about cellared properties recorded from the fifteenth century in this part of Bristol.

In Phase 5, the whole cellar was subdivided, to form the West and East Cellars. A blocking wall, F140, was built into the vault (cf. figure 63; cf. also F142), the roof was removed from the western part and, at this time or later, the west wall was also removed (cf. F185 above). It is assumed that this stage marks the incorporation of the cellared property into the church and the use of the area above the West Cellar as a north chapel (cf. figure 60). In the space beneath this north chapel, charnel and rubbish (F175A and B) were subsequently dumped. The lower part, F175B, contained a mass of human bones (cf. 10.3.5a). Meanwhile, the East Cellar remained in use.

In Phase 6, the dividing wall between the cellars was continued up by F143 (figure 63). Also in Phase 6, the whole of the south part of the West Cellar was eventually cut away to insert the heating system of 1877 (cf. 10.7).

10.7   The East Cellar (F89) (Phases 4 – 6)

Excavation of the East Cellar was confined to clearing away bomb rubble and other debris and exposing what was left of the pre-1940 structure. Much of this was patently of modern origin; resources and time did not allow for its proper recording. The main outline was planned and some photographs taken. The cellar still survives and could at some future time be dissected to reveal its medieval history. What follows is therefore only a very limited record of its relationship to the West Cellar and to the church.

It is assumed that the East Cellar was originally in Phase 4 of one build with the West Cellar (10.6), the whole cellar being initially *c.*5.5 x 4.0 + m. internally, extended to 6.5 x 4.0 + m., also in Phase 4. Its south wall was secondary to the chancel walls F134 and F135, being built into them and inserted slightly to overlap the upper courses of F135. The south side bends slightly towards the later Phase 5 chancel wall, here faced with hard pink mortar. The peaked barrel vault (cf. figure 63) was built by corbelling inwards from the side walls with pitched Pennant Sandstone slabs packed with red clayey sand and some lime. It was finished off on top with coarse pebbly mortar and levelled off with large stone slabs on either side, which formed a foundation for a stone floor above.

The thick Pennant floor which survives in places over the East Cellar may be contemporary with the original construction of the cellar or it may be later. The provision of a floor at all, however, indicates the presence of a structure above the vault (part of the assumed cellared property or the later north chapel). This continued in use as the floor of the modern vestry. The door and windows in the East

Cellar may likewise be original features or later additions—they survived only in modified forms (cf. 9.6.4 for possible relationship to external features).

When the western part of the cellar was absorbed into the church and partly filled in church Phase 5, the East Cellar remained in use, although its function at this time is uncertain. Later, at ground-floor level, the area was used as a vestry (10.3.6). Plans for the proposed restoration of 1842 include a 'new vestry room' in this area.

The East Cellar remained in use until the Second World War as a stoke hole beneath the vestry for the church heating system. Before the war there were windows giving light into the East Cellar from the north and east, and chutes into both north and east walls, the latter used for coal (cf. figure 45). There was a doorway in the south-east corner to the floor above, giving access to Buttermarket Passage. There was also a flight of steps leading down into it from the floor of the vestry above. The dating of all these features is uncertain.

It was destroyed in 1940 and subsequently filled with rubble.

10.8   Floors and floor levels (figures 45 – 47; S11 – 12) (including occupation layers and features of Phase 1)

10.8.0   GENERAL
Floor surfaces survived only in very small areas, and are difficult to correlate from one area to another. Such as can be discussed here are described from west to east. The only datum used, since no surveyors' level was available, was the tiled floor of 1877; this was reasonably level and can be used crudely to define relative levels where possible. Depths from this are described in this section as 'cm. below TF'.

10.8.1   TOWER AREA (S11 and S12, figure 46)
Activity to the west of foundation F81B was slight before Phase 4; it seems that it was only with the construction of the tower that this area became part of the main church complex. Floor levels, both within the tower and also leading into the west end of the nave via a series of steps, can be reconstructed for Phase 4. There is less information surviving about the arrangements of Phase 5, as these had been removed by later activities. At least four floors can be traced in Phase 6.

Above the natural marl, the buried soil, F11r survived to the east of F81B, 90 – 100 cm. below TF. On the line of S11, there was no evidence of activity on the buried soil before Phase 4. If the ground has not been truncated here, this suggests fairly 'dead' ground to the west of F81, which may be primary in this area, but which may in any case mark the western end of any structure in Phase 1 (cf. 10.3.1). The clean soil under 1G ('dark sandy' in S11) may indicate that the tower area was also unused in Phases 2 and 3; the tower construction trenches, however, appear to have disturbed burials—disarticulated bones occurred in their fill.

To the east of F81, within the west end of the postulated Phase 1 and later churches (cf. figure 51), a series of activities were represented. The surface of F11r was burnt hard orange, suggesting a hearth, F11p. This was covered by a thin white layer, F11o, perhaps a lime screed. These are either contemporary with or cut by the negative feature on the right (cf. 10.3.1 *re* structural details of Phase 1).

The next event in this area was the rebuilding in Phase 3B of the west wall in its F81 form. The height to which F81B originally stood is unknown. The top of F11n (S11, right, figures 46 – 47) may suggest a minimum level. F81B may itself have been the basis for a superstructure in a different material (cf. 10.3.1a).

The level from which the construction work for F81 was carried out is marked by an irregular line dropping down from the top of F11n to the top of F11r (S11, right) (figures 46 – 47). The two stones protruding on the right of F81 may be filling up soft ground or an earlier negative feature (caused for example by removing an earlier step) and/or they may be the foundation for a step of Phase 3B.

No other activities can be associated with this phase in the area of the later tower.

The building of the tower in Phase 4 is marked by construction trenches, filled with 1H – 1F in S12. Above this fill in S12, the mortar slick between 1F/1E marks the contemporary floor level on which Pennant slabs were laid (at a level similar to the later F3 – 4). This is the level represented by F11c on S12, which is a little below the level of the basal tower mouldings inside the eastern tower arch.

The tower itself was entered from the exterior in Phase 4 and later through a western arch at some level on or just above the extant top of the west wall foundation, at only a few centimetres below TF (S12) and this may equate with the former contemporary exterior level. If so, then the church interior must have risen considerably (nearly 1 m.) above the buried soil ground surface as defined inside the tower. It suggested in general that rising street/church levels were broadly similar (did the latter reflect the former?).

Access through the tower to the nave was by a series of steps. Moving from the west, in Phase 4 there was a step down to the level of the later F35A (S11). This involved a drop of c.20 cm., another of a further c.20 cm. to the next step, marked by the next offset of the tower footing (S11), and a further c.10 cm. down to the pink mortar-coated Pennant step F35, which is bonded into the tower footing and projects to the east of it at 60 cm. below TF (S11). The floor level through the tower was at the level of the Pennant above 1F/1E and F11c (cf. above), from which there must have been another step to the east of F81, in the gap occupied by F11g of Phase 6 (cf. 10.4.4). To the east of this, F11h consists of clearly laminated floors at the west end of the nave, at a slightly lower level than the contemporary tower floor which correlates with floor F5, of mortared Pennant (10.8.2).

In Phase 5, the floor level in the tower is marked by the Pennant above 1E on the left of S12, which was laid above a make-up of Pennant chippings (1E). On S12, a floor above 1E would be at about the level of the top of the later step, F12, of which F11a may be the compacted, subsided remnant.

Above this, layer 1D (S11), of Phase 6, represents either a long period of neglect or a further make-up. Sporadically above 1D (but not on section lines) was the first floor of Phase 6, a hard white mortar bonding another Pennant floor. This was contemporary with the freestone step F35A to the west, and with the three steps to the east of the later central vault, F3/4, F12 and F13. From the west exterior, there was apparently a slight step down onto F35A. Step F13, at the east end, was level with the new Pennant floor inside the tower. The contemporary nave floor to the east had been removed by a later vault (S11, right).

Later still, F2, a floor at the west end of the nave (S11; cf. 10.8.2), level with step F12, was laid above a make-up of reddish mortary soil, 3E, which contained eighteenth-century combed slipwares.

Above both 1D and F2 were 1C and 3C, a thick dirt layer, which may be partly or wholly derived from organic floors. 1C partly covered and should be later than step F35A. Its surface was presumably originally flush with the surface of F35A (itself by then already worn), but it subsided into layers below, resulting ultimately in a slight slope down to the east, as in S11.

By 1847, the date of the central vault, an absolute floor level is given by the surface of the slabs covering this vault, which probably stood slightly proud of the surrounding dirt, as in S11.

It was above this, and 1C and 3C, that the builders' layer of 1877 was dumped, to bring the level finally up to the tiled floor, 1A and 3A, which survived throughout the church until it was bombed, with a Pennant flagged entrance, F35B, at the west entrance to the tower, flush with the floor.

10.8.2   AREA 2

Two fragments of Pennant floors, F2 and F5, survived in the south-west corner of the Phase 6 nave (figure 45). F5, the lower, is contemporary with the foundations of Phase 4, and should thus be in the south aisle, if this is correctly inferred for Phase 4 (figures 57 – 58). It is recorded as 80 cm. below TF and level with the basal stops of the tower eastern mouldings. This is 20 cm. lower than that recorded inside the tower (level of step F3). The level of F5 is confirmed as being lower than the level of F3 as it was covered with layer 3F (cf. S11).

F2 in Area 2, of Phase 6, is recorded as lying on 3E and 3F, thus equating stratigraphically with the junction 3C/3E in S11, but slightly lower, at 46 cm. below TF compared with the 42 cm. seen in S11—an acceptable variation.

10.8.3   AREA 3

The only area here not disturbed by graves was F28, but even this soil was disturbed to natural in Phase 6 and no floors were seen.

10.8.4   AREA 4

Similarly here no floors were defined between that of 1877 and the buried soil F41; a further strip F8 was not totally excavated, but no floors were defined in its upper part. Step F71 marks the level of the porch floor of 1877. There was a step down (to F72) of *c.*25 cm. to the inside of the church; the presumed level of the medieval floor, given by the base stops of Phase 5 mouldings, is that perpetuated in 1877.

10.8.5 AREA 5

A small area of undisturbed soil (F60) survived in the south-west angle of the aisle pier-complex (F56, etc.) here. A dark-brown soil (F60A) was apparently an 'occupation layer' of Phase 1, lying on buried soil; there was a dip in the north-west corner with a hard-baked base, interpreted as a hearth.

On the north-west side of this pier-complex were fragments of Pennant Sandstone floor (F74), bedded on a brick-tempered mortar rather like *opus signinum*. This floor is assigned to Phase 3A; it covers the edge of pier F56 of this phase, but ends on a stucco edge set into a slight rebate on F56; this should indicate the limit of the superstructure on pier F56. The floor was probably cut away by F45 in Phase 5.

10.8.6 AREA 6

F79 here apparently included only a buried soil.

10.8.7 AREA 7

The only undisturbed area here was F129, where there was some ashy soil on the natural marl, probably of Phase 1.

10.8.8 AREAS 8, 10, 12

No floor levels survived in these areas.

10.8.9 AREA 11

Here survived the best preserved stratification apart from the tower area. At the base, above the natural marl, there were remnants of a buried soil of Phase 1 with sherds (F84Z). This is sealed by a builders' level of Phase 2 (F84F), and above this a floor-level, F84E, of Phase 2, a hard red sandy surface with impressions of straw or reeds. Further builders' layers and ?make-up (F84C – D) are covered by layers of laminated brownish mortar and grey-brown dust F84B, interpreted as organic or dirt floors, also apparently of Phase 2. A further builders' level of Phase 3A, F84A, is capped by a yellow mortar ?make-up/surface/floor, F179, which also spread over pier F96 and F180 (cf. discussion 10.3.3b *re* function).

A more certain floor is a coating of dark fibrous material, F179A, possibly the remains of a wooden or dirt floor of Phase 3B, which stopped short of the remains of F181 on a straight line, indicating the limit of its north edge and presumably contemporary with it.

A further floor of Pennant Sandstone, F182, of Phase 4, survived in places, sealed by F177 of Phase 5 and its destruction layer. A few tiles, F174, from a further floor of ceramic tile remained *in situ* (rather burnt and apparently re-used), which may be contemporary with F182; or they may be later, as they are not sealed by F177, and may instead be contemporary with this—they have been assigned to Phase 5. Later floors here were destroyed.

10.8.10 AREA 9

The only other floor which may be mentioned is a thick Pennant slab floor which covered the vault of the East Cellar and which survived in places. It may be as early as the cellar itself, i.e. of Phase 4, or may be of later date (cf. 10.7). It was also the floor of the modern vestry.

10.8.11 CONCLUSION

To summarise, the earliest surfaces which survived of Phase 1 were of the buried soil or an 'occupation layer' of similar texture developing on it; in one case there was a coating of a thin lime wash or screed. Later floors were, in several places, of Pennant Sandstone, sometimes bedded on mortar. Major steps were also of this material or in one case of Bath oolite (freestone). But many floor areas were only of dirt or organic material. In one place there were impressions of straw or reeds, and there were laminated layers which may have been organic. Other dark soil layers, in one case of a fibrous texture, may be the remains or imprints of wooden floors. By Phase 4 or 5 definitely, but probably from Phase 3, glazed ceramic floor tiles were in use; there were further dirt or organic floors in the post-medieval period, but the medieval tiled floor was finally perpetuated in the 'encaustic' tiled floor of 1877.

10.9   Wall surface rendering

The greater part of all wall surfaces were re-faced in 1877 with sawn freestone (cf. 10.3.6); this operation probably removed all earlier plaster or paint. The only evidence for former wall rendering therefore comes from below-ground stratification.

The destruction layer of F33, a Phase 2A wall, also in Area 3, yielded pieces of pale buff stucco, white-painted, which was presumably on the walls of the Phase 2 church, though not necessarily in its primary state. Further buff stucco was found in F84F from Area 2, in a context of Phase 2. A destruction layer of Phase 3A foundation F38 in Area 4 contained grey stucco on some large stones. Also of Phase 3A was the upper part of F49 in Area 11 – 12, with which some cream stucco was associated. White stucco also formed an edge on the ?Phase 3A part of pier F56 to the floor F74 in Area 5.

The best evidence for wall decoration came from a Phase ?4 destruction level F177A sealed by the Phase 5 foundation F177 (Area 11). This included white plaster with red stripes; the latter may have been false jointing. F32 pier foundation in Area 3 incorporated some white-painted freestone, which presumably survived from some structure earlier than Phase 5.

Other painting is described in association with stone objects in 11.1. Painting of vault walls is described with the graves in 10.10, and with these are perhaps to be grouped the fragments of stone found in association with F186 tomb-monument, plastered and painted successively white, purple and red.

To summarise, several contexts from various parts of churches belonging to Phase 2 and later yielded buff, grey, and white stucco, presumably as a basic wall-rendering. In some cases this was painted white, and in one context with red stripes, possibly false jointing. There was no evidence of wall paintings.

10.10   Graves

Scant attention was paid to graves. This was principally due to lack of time and resources, and the decisions made that the structural and stratigraphic sequence was the principal aim of the excavation; but also because in the early 1960s the importance of the investigation of medieval Christian cemeteries had hardly been realised (cf. 3.1). The general impression, including the 'official' view of central government and local museum sponsorship, was that we knew all we needed to know about Christian burial, that in any case they had no finds, and that there was an element of impropriety in disturbing or even looking scientifically at interments of a community whose religious beliefs and mortuary practice were at least nominally those of our own day. There had in the 1950s been some scandal in Bristol about the destruction of cemeteries (notably one in Horsefair), when the skeletons were taken away unceremoniously in lorries. This was stopped only when some fell off a lorry, were picked up by children and taken to show their schoolteachers. By 1960 the Corporation of Bristol had issued strict orders that all disinterments should be done behind screens and all remains packed in wooden boxes for decent re-interment in municipal cemeteries. Accordingly, as referred to above (10.1), the Mary-le-Port vaults were emptied by unskilled workmen, any coffins being smashed in the process. In one case a lead coffin was put to one side and attacked by vandals for dubious reasons.

These vaults appear to belong to Phase 6, principally of the eighteenth and earlier nineteenth centuries. They had cut through many earlier graves; the resulting charnel had been backfilled in the construction trenches, and in one case was buried in a pit in Area 3 (figure 45).

Earlier excavations, for construction of foundations of various phases of the church, had also destroyed many earlier graves. This too generated charnel, which was found in the backfill of, for example, the construction trench of the tower. A major deposition of charnel (F175B) was made in Phase 5 in the subdivided western part of the cellared property (cf. 10.3.5 and 10.6.2). This was also apparently the purpose of the medieval stone-lined vaults of Phases 5 and 6 (F83, F85, F91) in the east end of the nave and chancel (figure 45).

Some earlier graves were defined in excavation and several areas of 'grave-earth' were identified, the graves at their base being largely undisturbed where they penetrated below archaeologically-significant levels. All intact burials observed were of supine adults, all had heads to west and extended arms. No other body position was recorded. A few were drawn in diagrammatic form (figure 45).

Only in a few cases was it possible to date any burials by their relationship to phased structures or layers, and these are discussed below.

Most burials were in earth graves; no evidence was recorded of shrouds or wooden coffins other than one with brass studs presumably of relatively recent date. The most interesting graves are those in cists. These consisted of end, side and floor slabs of Pennant Sandstone. Four are shown in figure 45, F30 and F34 in the north of Area 3, F76 in the north of Area 5, and F70 in the south-west corner of Area 4. F76 is cut by F56 pier of Phase 3, and should thus be of Phase 2 (or of Phase 1, if this does represent a church). This phasing could apply to all, and suggests that cist-burials were among the earliest in the church, perhaps reflecting the relative abundance of space. Later burials were clearly heavily superimposed. F75 for example had three superimposed skeletons.

The monument, F186, at the east end of the north aisle, is dated to the early sixteenth century on art-historical grounds. It is archaeologically secondary to the demolition of the West Cellar roof (assigned to Phase 5, 10.6.2). Some of the stones of the east side were plastered and painted successively white, purple and red. The monument was drawn in the early nineteenth century (plate 24 MF) and is again depicted in the background of the painting of an exhumation of 1814. This exhumation was of a burial of the seventeenth century, and was attended by very curious circumstances recorded at the time, which are detailed in 11.24.2. It is clear that this burial was not contemporary with the monument and was below a brick vault which had been built adjacent to the monument.

The vaults which had destroyed so much of the church's interior (cf. figure 61) were lined with bricks, internally painted white or purple, and capped with Pennant Sandstone slabs, presumably at contemporary floor level. The only one observed was that in the tower (S11 and S12, figure 46). This was whitewashed internally and contained three coffins. The top one was of wood encased in zinc; a middle one was of wood, with an inscribed brass plate. This was of Charles Smith who died on 22 December 1847, aged 83, the latest dated burial found. These two coffins were removed by workmen. Below them was a decayed lead coffin, in which a child's skull was observed. This was left *in situ*.

Apart from burials within the church, there was an extensive cemetery to the south, now largely destroyed by the Norwich Union. In Phases 1 and 2 any cemetery may have covered a similar area as immediately pre-1940 (but cf. 10.3.2 concerning a possible south aisle in Phase 2), to be reduced in size in Phases 3 and 4 by the assumed south aisle and expanded again with its demolition in Phase 5. There were also burials of pre-Phase 4 in the tower area and destroyed by it (cf. 10.8.1) (i.e. west of earlier churches), and also west of the tower in Phase 4 and later. The cist and other burials of Phase 2 were to the north of the expanded church, in the area later built up (cf. 9.10). Those in the north porch area and in the area north of the East Cellar are referred to in the street text (chapter 9). The latter appear to have been of a limited period only, later than *c*.1300, secondary to the definition of the stone walls here, and ceasing by 1648 when there was a secular property in this area.

Other medieval and post-medieval burials are related to the graveslabs, some with inscriptions, and one with an effigy, discussed with stone and metal finds in 11.2.2. and 11.15.

In the later nineteenth century, attention was drawn in many quarters to the perils to public health caused by dense burial in city churchyards and churches. The same concern which led to the cessation of city interment and the creation of out-of-town cemeteries is reflected in the 1875 Petition from the rector and churchwardens of St. Mary-le-Port to seal the church vaults with a layer of concrete and newly pave the church—work which was done in 1877 (cf. 10.3.6).

10.11   Artefacts from the church

Apart from architectural fragments, there were relatively few artefacts from the church. This may reflect its function rather than the conditions of excavation. Most of the architectural fragments were found unstratified in later rubble. It is only pottery and copper-alloy fittings which have contributed directly to the discussion of dating and these details have been integrated into the text. CA7, a pin with Viking-period parallels, is especially important, although it was found in a secondary context; it is one of several possible pre-Conquest artefacts which may provide the earliest evidence of activity from the excavation. Some of the artefacts do reflect the function of the building, especially the funerary monuments; others, such as the architectural fragments, the window glass, roofing and flooring materials, could be either from a secular or ecclesiastical context.

The earliest artefacts from the area of the church are from Phase 1. There are very few and they do not clarify the function of these features. LBM9, from wall F19, is not necessarily a mortar in a technical sense. Further analysis is needed to clarify this.

There are seven sherds of pottery from Phase 1 contexts. The buried soil in Area 11, F84Z, included Fabrics A and C; the latter represent distinctive cuplike vessels which do not occur widely at Mary-le-Port (cf. 11.10.4c). Fabric A equates with BPT 1 and BPT 115, for which periods of currency of 1000 – 1070 and c.1070 – 1100 respectively are suggested. There was also a sherd of BPT 115 in F11m (S11, right). There is too little pottery to rely on it alone to date Phase 1; there is also insufficient from the immediately succeeding phases to assess whether the Phase 1 pottery is part of a consistent chronological sequence; it is not inconsistent, however, with the suggested dating of Phase 1 (cf. 10.2).

From Phase 2, there are more definite mortar samples, together with stucco.

The burnt clay from Phase 3 was from F121, a post-hole which cut a Phase 2 context and may thus be derived from an earlier structure (cf. 11.5). The pottery from both Phase 3A and 3B still contains apparently residual Fabric A, but also later sherds of Fabric H, Ham Green cooking pot (= BPT 32, current 1250 – 1300), from F84A builders' level. Phase 3 has the first occurrence of potential roofing material, both slate and Pennant.

By Phase 4, pottery is more plentiful and broadly supports the dating suggested in 10.2, from contexts associated with the building of the tower (cf. 10.3.4a).

Pottery from Phase 5 does not clearly extend later than that of Phase 4, and the dating of Phase 5 is dependent on other forms of evidence. CA7, referred to above, was found in a Phase 5 context in the fill of the West Cellar.

The pottery from Phase 6 reflects the several centuries of this phase.

10.12   The medieval priests' houses at All Saints' and Mary-le-Port Churches

Roger Leech's section in MF describes the fifteenth-century priest's house built into All Saints' Church in some detail; it was one of several structures built within or against the walls of that church. It is compared with the evidence for the ?parsonage at St. Mary-le-Port Church (the 'cellared property'). The two are of identical length (6.71 m.) but that at St. Mary-le-Port was wider (4.27 m. compared with 2.74 m.). There was a third priest's house in medieval Bristol, at St. Stephen's Church.

Chapter 11: Artefacts and Samples

11.1 Introduction

Numbered objects and samples are described by material, in the order mineral, vegetable and animal. Within each category there is a numerical sequence ST1, FL2, etc. Each category is tabulated on a standard format in the tables 17.1—20 in MF, which, together with the figures and plates, form the basic record of this aspect of the excavated data. Relevant data from the artefacts, etc., have been integrated with the stratigraphical discussions of the three separate units of the excavation, both directly with the excavated sequence and separately in the commentaries on artefacts by phase. This section is concerned with types of objects and classes of material.

Some of this data is from unstratified contexts, but there are also considerable difficulties in dating stratified material. Art-historical criteria can be applied to some categories, such as sculptural fragments; in general however, there is no direct means of distinguishing date of manufacture or period of currency from the general dating assigned to the context in which an object was found. In most cases, it is the latter that is recorded in the 'phase' columns in brackets on tables 17.1 – 20 in MF; material dated by external means and assigned to phases are not bracketed; 'dates' are those suggested by various specialists. External parallels, themselves established by a variety of considerations, have been utilised, especially in relation to architectural fragments, pottery and copper-alloy objects, which provide the backbone of the chronological sequence of this report. Clearly much depends on the validity of these methods of dating and also on basic identifications; these caveats must be borne in mind in relation to the following section, where uncertain data must not be made more definite than the archaeological record warrants.

Much further work remains to be done on placing this material against the background of the range of contemporary artefacts and in delineating their environmental and economic implications. Here the raw data is presented, which will enable this to be done at a future date.

11.1.1 CATEGORIES OF MATERIAL AND ABBREVIATIONS

Stone	ST	Window glass	GLW
Flint	FL	Iron	IR
Soil samples	SO	Copper alloy	CA
Burnt clay	BC	Coins and tokens	CO
Fired clay	FC	Other metals	OM
Brick	BR	Slags	SL
Clay tobacco pipes	CP	Charcoal	CHAR
Decorated floor tiles	DFT	Other botanical	OB
Plain floor tiles	PFT	Animal and bird bones	AB
Ceramics	POT	Bone objects	BO
Lime-based materials	LBM	Other animal	OA
Vessel glass	GL	Human bones	HB

It will be useful here to summarise the dating of the various street and church phases which are referred to in this chapter as the authority for the dating of the contexts in which material was found, although this is not of course necessarily the date when the objects were made. This summary is taken directly from figure 24 in Chapter 7.

PHASES

MLPS East	MLPS West	Date	Church	Date
0 – 1	0 – 1	geological and pre-Saxon	0 – 1	geological, Saxon and earlier
1	2	late Saxon or earlier		
2a – f	3 – 4	late Saxon to c1300	1	late Saxon or early post-Conquest
			2	twelfth century
3a – b	5	late thirteenth – fourteenth century	3	thirteenth – later fifteenth century
4a	6	later thirteenth century plus		
4b	7	later thirteenth century plus	4	later fifteenth century
			5	early sixteenth century
5 – 6	8	late and post-medieval	6	early sixteenth century to 1940 +

11.2 Stone (figures 65 MF, 66 – 73; tables 17.1 and 18 MF)

11.2.1 INTRODUCTION

Stone forms an important class of material at Mary-le-Port. It reflects the rich variety available locally, suitable both for building and for tools and utensils. Most of the stone was available in the immediate vicinity (table 18 MF) (Ponsford 1979, 14 – 17 has already summarised the local geology in relation to archaeological contexts). At Mary-le-Port it was used in connection with both the secular and ecclesiastical aspects of the site.

11.2.2 STONE RELATING TO THE CHURCH (figures 65MF, 66 – 71)

Stone fragments from the church are derived from the fabric of the successive buildings, from both the main structure and from decorative details; from internal fittings; and from funerary monuments. These are described in detail in table 17.1 MF under the headings 'architectural and church fittings and frs' and 'graveslabs and effigies'; 'structural fittings' are also relevant.

Pennant Sandstone and Brandon Hill Grit are used from the eleventh century onwards, but there are insufficient data to reconstruct the proportions of different stones in the successive phases of the church. Much of the stone is local; apart from the two major sources already named, Carboniferous and other limestones, sandstones, and the Old Red Sandstone conglomerates are available in the Bristol locality, while the Jurassic limestones are found only a few kilometres away in the Dundry and Cotswold areas; chalk, flint and Lias limestones are rather more distant (c.20 – 30 km.), but still within a 'local' marketing radius.

Long-distance trade is evidenced by the pieces of Purbeck marble (a notable traveller) and slate, from Wales or Cornwall. The only definite 'foreign' stone perhaps associated with the church is ST12, a fragment of *porfido verde antico* rock, found in the excavation of MLPS East, but which may be part of a monument.

Stone was used for architectural details as well as foundations, walls and roofs (cf. ST15). The architectural fragments contribute to the general understanding of the character of the buildings; they include the massive and impressive capital, ST8 (figure 67; assigned to Church Phase 2; dated c.1140 – 1170). Such unstratified architectural fragments complement discussion, based on the character of the foundations and material associated with them, about the construction and fabric of the superstructure.

These fragments are thus important in reconstructing the architectural history of the successive churches and are fundamental, in conjunction with the series of plans reconstructed through excavation, to the phasing and dating of these buildings.

Few stone fittings from the church were found; only a meagre portion of what must have once been present, if compared to the potential range utilised in medieval and later churches. The one certain item is part of the rood screen of the Phase 4 church, which was constructed in a combination of stone (ST2, a creamy limestone and probably of local Jurassic origin) and of lime-based material (cf. 11.11 and figure 84). ST7, a small pinnacle or crocket, also of a ?local Jurassic limestone, possibly from a shrine, tomb or screen, has coloured detail surviving (gold leaf, red and gold ground and ochre detail) and is a reminder that colour was prominent in medieval internal church decoration.

Parts of six medieval funerary monuments were recovered, as well as post-medieval gravestones. The former were all probably from the interior of the church and certainly their condition would not argue for extended exposure outside. Each is different in form and detail and several different types of stone were used. They probably include freestanding structures as well as flat slabs. Especially notable amongst the possible former group is ST1, a very fine ?flying angel in high relief (figure 66, plate 56), which is suggested to be from a spandrel on a mid-fourteenth-century tomb canopy. ST16 (figure 70, plate 58) is part of a full-scale civilian effigy, again with colour surviving. Its form is linked to other effigies found both locally and at Westminster Abbey. ST18 (figure 69) and ST20 (figure 71) both bear inscriptions, the latter in Norman French; ST18 is said to be a common local form.

Dr L. A. S. Butler has contributed the following notes on the civilian effigy ST16 and the graveslabs ST18 and 20;

> 'The effigy is full scale, of a civilian; only the head survives. The carving of the face is similar to that of Eleanor of Castile in Westminster Abbey (1291 – 1293), with a finely-drawn mouth, bulbous eyes, short curling hair with exposed neck and upper collar of close-fitting gown. The head rests on two pillows, with evidence of paint as shown on figure 70. The shape and arrangement of the pillows suggests the Bristol school of sculpture as in the diminutive effigies at Berkeley (Fryer, 1925, 46 and plate XI).'

'ST18 has a border inscription in black-letter Gothic: of bryd . . . . . ?tva.'

'ST20 consists of three pieces; the edge with the hollow chamfer carries a Norman-French inscription; the upper surface has a geometric cross, probably from a three-step base. The Lombardic inscription commences from the foot with the name . . . MAN : GIS (T:) ICI (SOUS : CET : PIERRE : DIE) V DE SA AL (ME : EYT : MERCI . . .) (cf. Rodger, 1911, 35 and plate VI); last quarter of thirteenth century.'

Plate 56. Angel sculpture ST1; cf. figure 66.

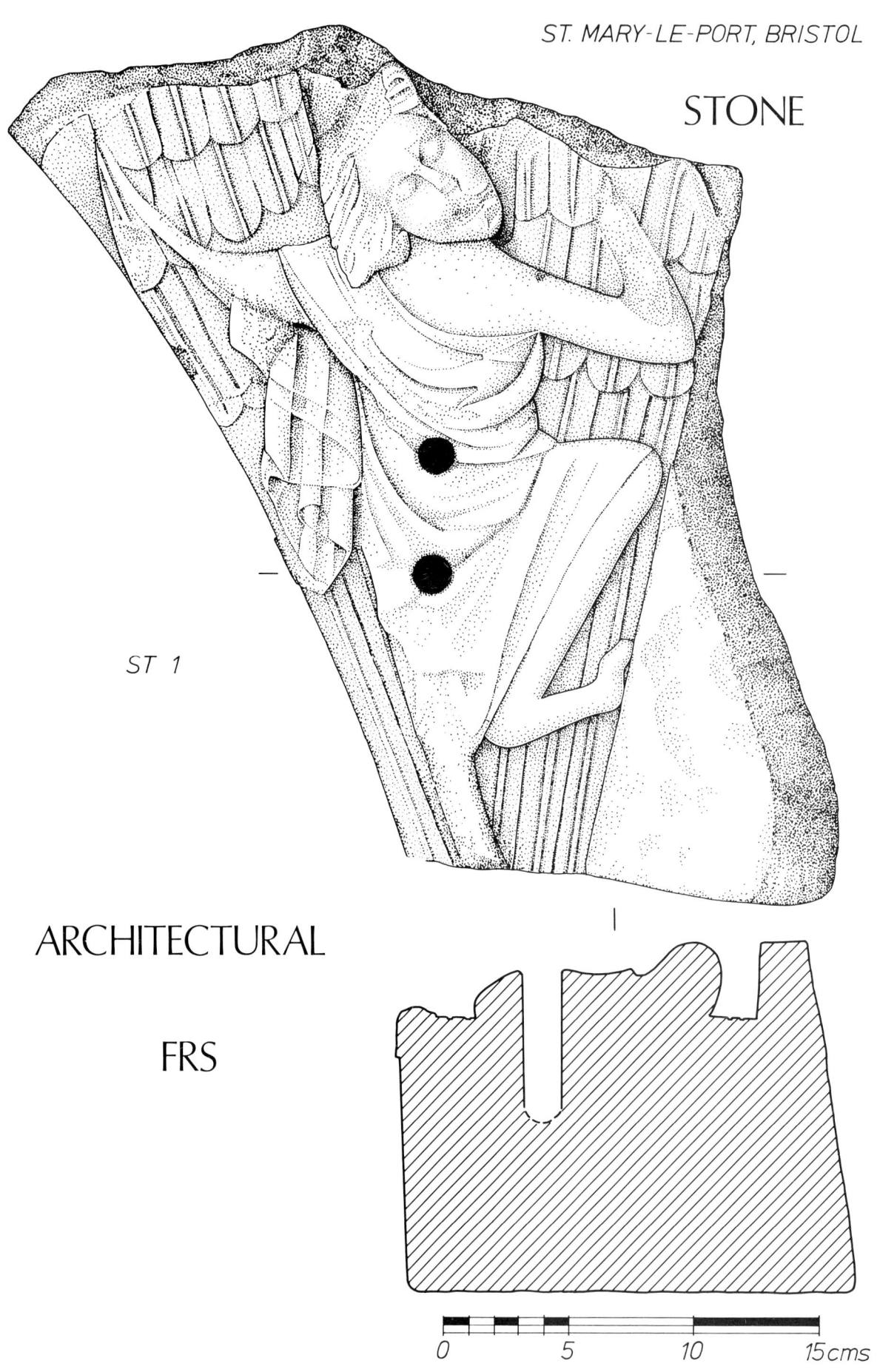

ST. MARY-LE-PORT, BRISTOL

STONE

ST 1

ARCHITECTURAL

FRS

0   5   10   15cms

Figure 66.

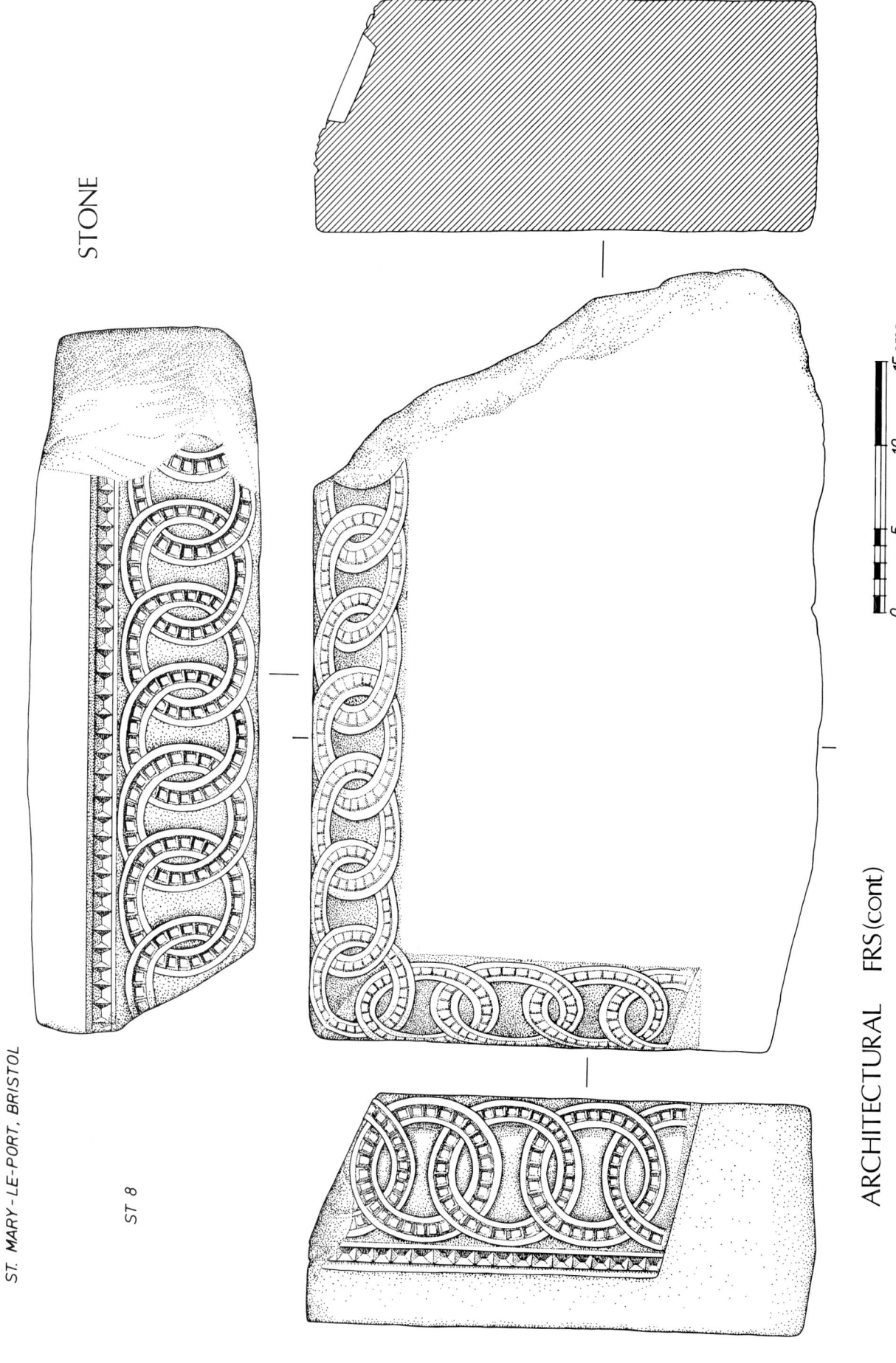

ST. MARY-LE-PORT, BRISTOL

STONE

ST 8

ARCHITECTURAL   FRS (cont)

Figure 67.

STONE

ARCHITECTURAL

FRS(cont)

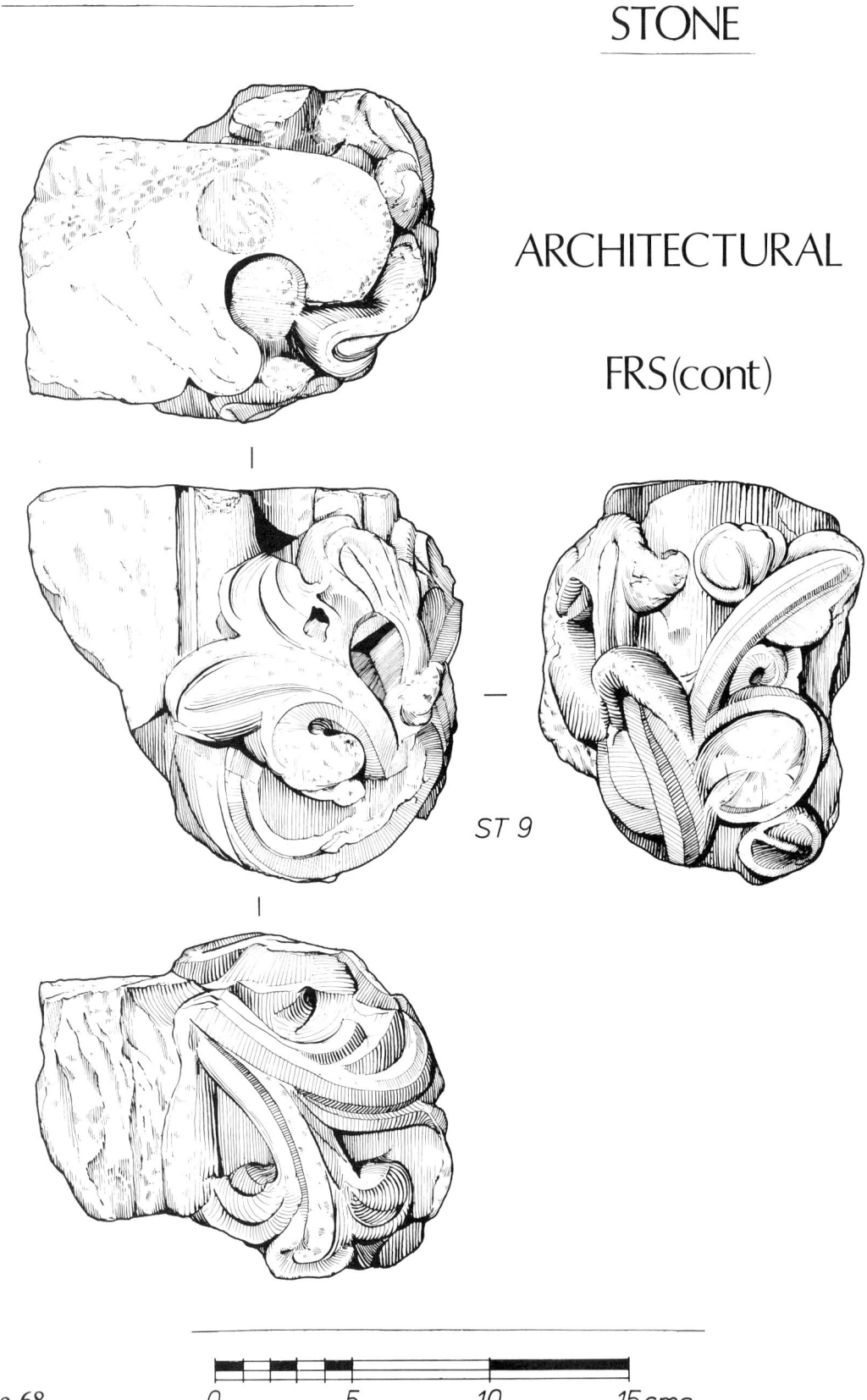

ST 9

Figure 68.

0   5   10   15 cms

The funerary monuments can contribute to two main aspects of analysis, to sociological considerations and to establishing the function of the site.

Their sociological implications are wide-ranging. Like the architectural pieces, they belong to the mainstream of art-historical data and through such studies could yield information about patronage, wealth, fashion and conspicuous display in death, thus offering multifaceted reflections of contemporary attitudes and values. Analysis of their post-depositional history also reflects attitudes about the propriety

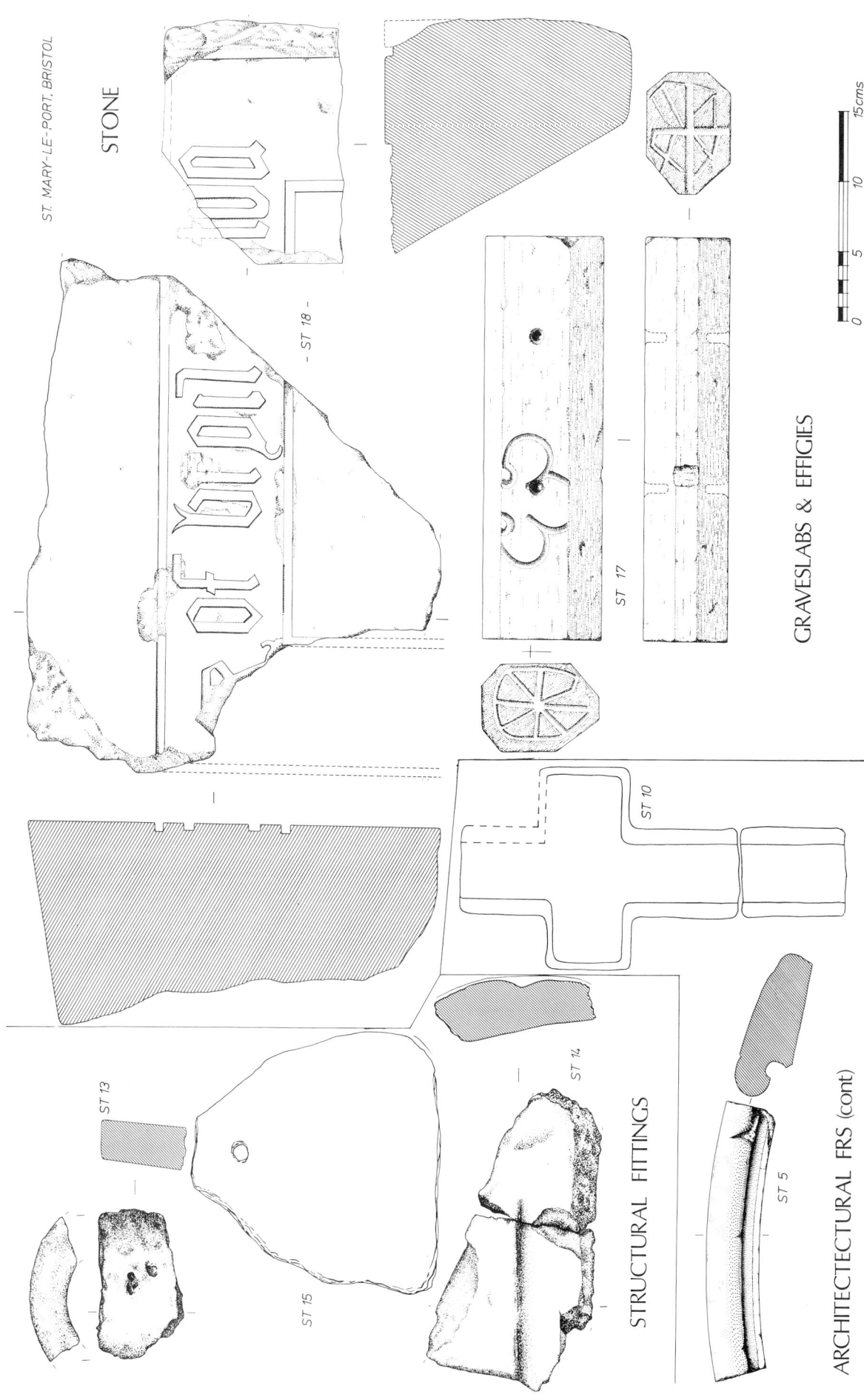

ST. MARY-LE-PORT, BRISTOL

STONE

- ST 18 -

ST 17

ST 10

ST 13

ST 15

ST 14

ST 5

GRAVESLABS & EFFIGIES

STRUCTURAL FITTINGS

ARCHITECTECTURAL FRS (cont)

Figure 69.

137

of both disturbing and dispossessing the dead. None of the medieval grave monuments survived *in situ*—this applies even to the late example, F186, where, although the architectural frame remained, the associated burial had been disturbed (cf. 10.10). They had been variously re-located and covered up (ST16, ST18, ST19); the stone re-used for a different purpose (ST17, ST22); or broken up and/or scattered, displaced from the immediate church environment (ST20, ST21). The chronological gap between their original function as gravemarkers and their re-use can be gauged in some cases. Disturbance was certainly occurring by Church Phase 4 in the late fifteenth century—ST16 and ST17, both originally dating from the end of the thirteenth century to the beginning of the fourteenth century, were found in Phase 5 contexts.

Plate 58. Graveslab effigy ST16; cf. figure 70.

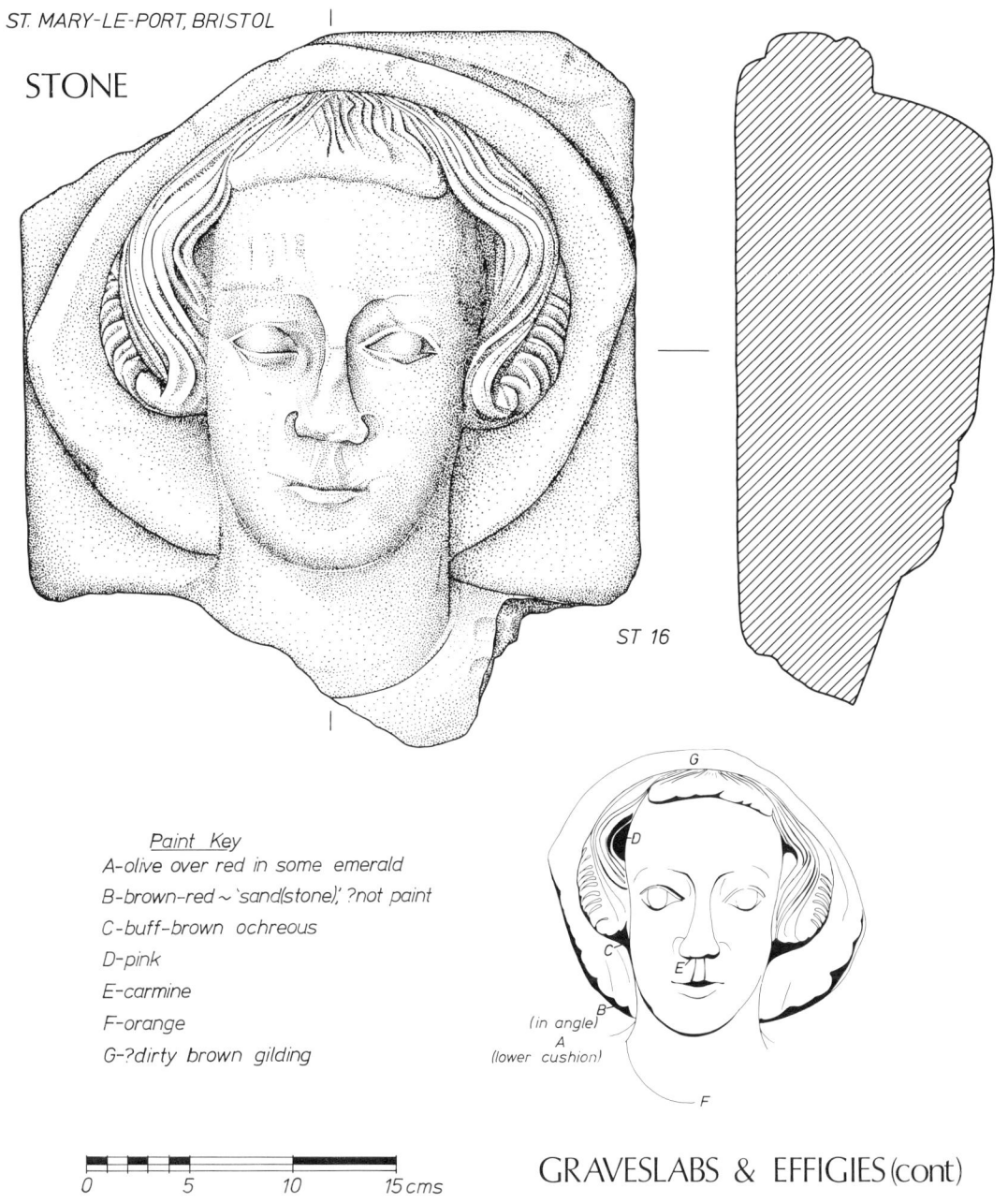

ST. MARY-LE-PORT, BRISTOL

STONE

ST 16

Paint Key
A-olive over red in some emerald
B-brown-red ~ `sand(stone)', ?not paint
C-buff-brown ochreous
D-pink
E-carmine
F-orange
G-?dirty brown gilding

(in angle)
A
(lower cushion)

0   5   10   15 cms

GRAVESLABS & EFFIGIES (cont)

Figure 70.

It is the funerary monuments, together with a single consecration cross, ST10 (figure 69), and the human bones, which allow an archaeological (as distinct from a historical) identification of the function of the main structure and its immediate surroundings, although they cannot define its specific status within the Christian hierarchy, beyond its possession of burial rights.

Stone from the church is thus especially significant in relation to dating, reconstructing the superstructure of the buildings and in establishing function. Potentially it could provide an important bridge between archaeologically-derived data and documentary evidence, in relation to such topics discussed above.

One occupation is recorded on a post-medieval graveslab (ST23), to the wife of Robert Bush, 'pewterer of this parish', who died in 1794, aged 42 (cf. CA22, 11.15).

11.2.3   TOOLS AND UTENSILS
The tools and utensils from Mary-le-Port were found (except for ST37) in the excavations of the two street areas. Their range and forms are now familiar from other sites in Bristol (cf. Ponsford, 1979) and from cities such as Norwich and Northampton where large-scale excavation has taken place (cf. Clarke and Carter, 1977; Williams, 1979).

11.2.3a QUERNSTONES (figure 73)
Parts of four rotary querns were found, all of conglomerate and all probably from the Old Red Standstone conglomerates, which were available locally. Three are upper stones, the fourth probably part

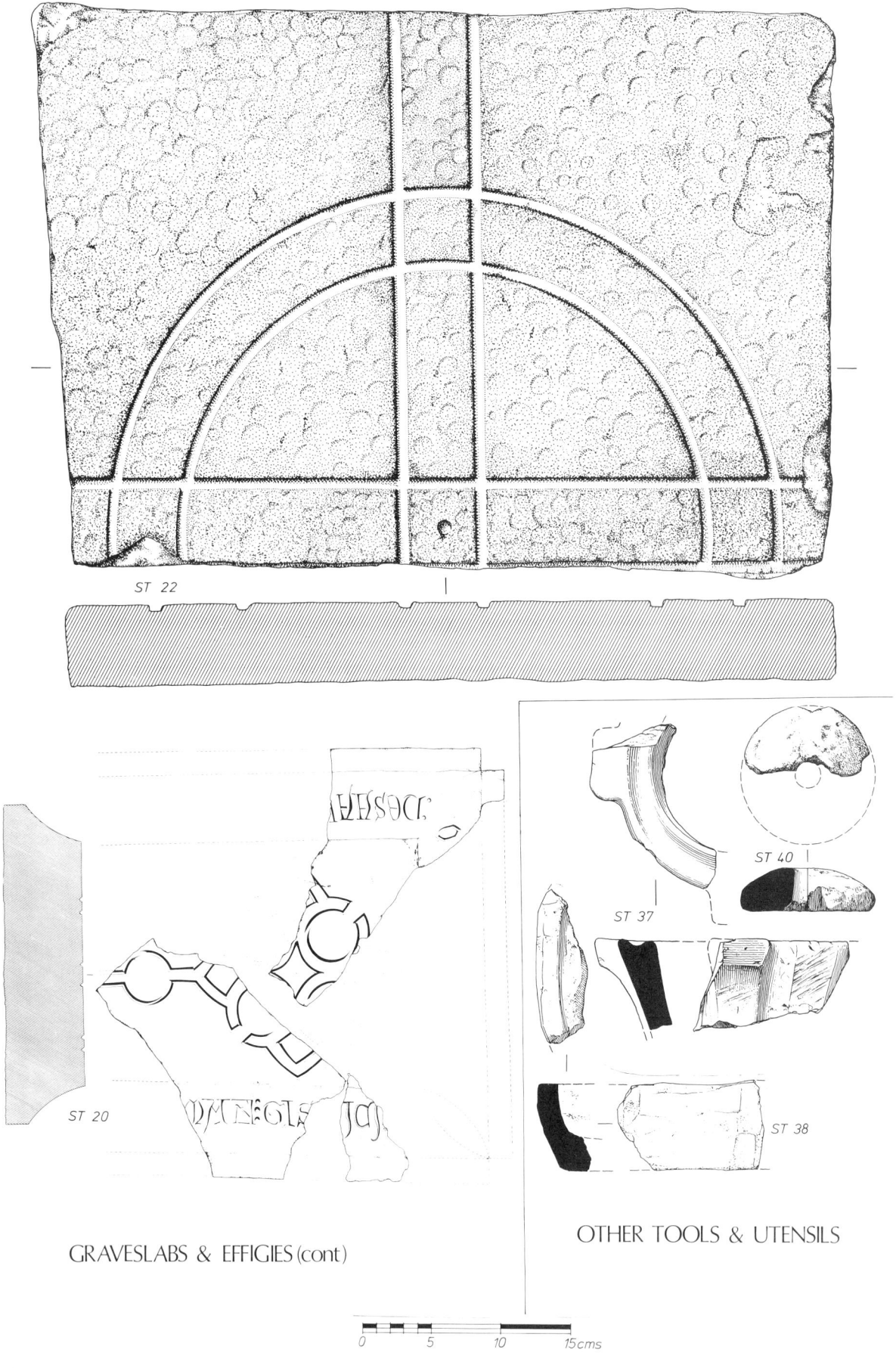

ST 22

ST 20

GRAVESLABS & EFFIGIES (cont)

ST 40

ST 37

ST 38

OTHER TOOLS & UTENSILS

0   5   10   15cms

Figure 71.

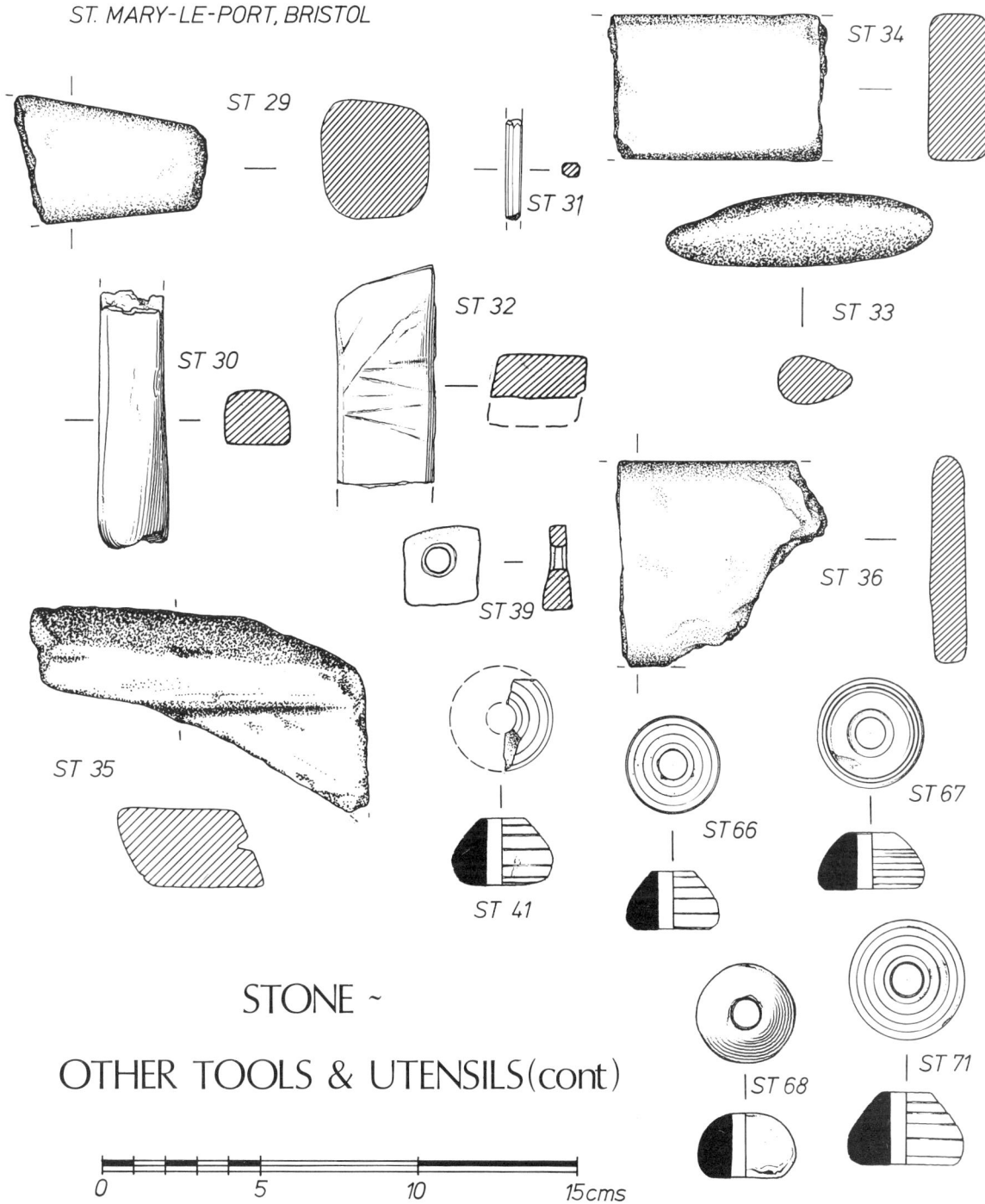

ST. MARY-LE-PORT, BRISTOL

ST 29

ST 31

ST 34

ST 33

ST 30

ST 32

ST 39

ST 36

ST 35

ST 41

ST 66

ST 67

ST 68

ST 71

STONE ~

OTHER TOOLS & UTENSILS(cont)

0   5   10   15cms

Figure 72.

of a lower, all from handmills. The reconstructed diameters of ST24 and ST26, both upper stones, are 70 and 73 cm. respectively. ST26 and ST27 are from unstratified contexts, but ST24 and ST25 are from the fill of the hollow way in MLPS West, Phase 4.

11.2.3b   HONES (figure 72)
The eight hones are all of different size and shape, being designed for use in conjunction with different blades (although the latter are not reflected in the IR record, cf. table 17.11 MF). They also exhibit different degrees of wear, but the number of incomplete hones must reflect breakage during use.
D. Moore comments that ST29, of Devonshire Batt, ST30 and probably ST31, of Norwegian Ragstone, and ST34 and ST36, both Pennant Grit, are common hone types; he suggests the remainder, ST33 of phyllite and ST32 and ST35 of variously composed wackes, may be makeshift hones. Other hones of Norwegian Ragstone have been found in Bristol; it was commonly used in medieval England (cf. Moore, 1978). Hones occur from MLPS East, Phase 2e (*re* ST32), in dirt above the hollow way (cf. tables 17.1 – 18MF).

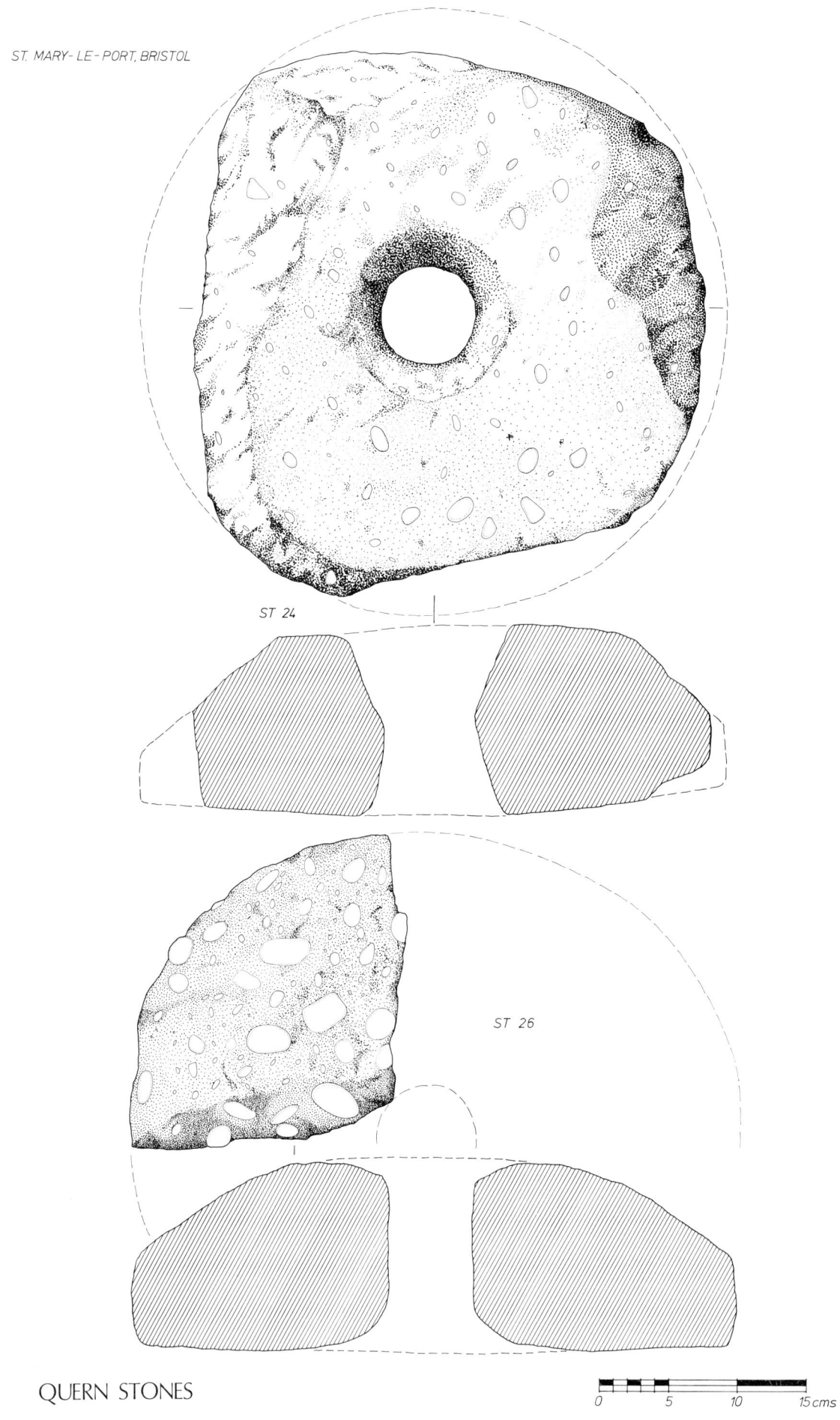

ST. MARY- LE- PORT, BRISTOL

ST 24

ST 26

QUERN STONES

0   5   10   15 cms

Figure 73.

11.2.3c SPINDLE WHORLS (figure 72)

Seven spindle whorls are recorded, although two were not available for examination. The five described are all of similar manufacture, lathe-turned with concentric rings around the body, and of similar size, with diameters between 30 and 34 mm. and heights between 18 and 33 mm. ST40, whose function is uncertain, falls well outside this range at 95 mm. diameter. ST41 has been examined petrologically by Dr A. Vince and identified as calcite mudstone, which was available around Bristol. Dr Vince adds that he '. . . believes that many of the whorls come from one source. . . . The production of spindle whorls could be a sideline of a large quarry production . . .' (cf. table 17.1 MF). The earliest context in which a spindle whorl is found is MLPS East, Phase 2c, dirt on the hollow way (ST69, ST70); others occur later in the 'fill' of the hollow way (cf. tables 17.1 and 18 MF).

11.2.4 OTHER STONE OBJECTS

ST28 is identified as a ?hammerstone of red sandstone, found in an early context, MLPS West, Phase 2; it may have been utilised before the medieval period.

The function of ST36 (figure 72) is suggested to be related to leather dressing.

ST37 (figure 71) is part of a mortar (or stoup?) of Purbeck marble. Its lugged rim and reconstructed diameter is compatible with known mortar forms (cf. Dunning in Clarke and Carter, 1977, 320 – 347). Mortars of Purbeck marble have a wide distribution in England and are also found on the Continent. Dunning considers their main period of production to have been the thirteenth and fourteenth centuries, although they are known from the twelfth century and continued for an undetermined period afterwards (ibid., 324). ST37 was found built into repairs of the East Cellar vault, a structure of Church Phase 4 or later. Dunning notes, even when broken, mortars are 'almost indestructible' and have been re-used elsewhere as building material (ibid., 321).

ST38 (figure 71) is identified as a lamp, probably of local Jurassic limestone, from a MLPS West Phase 4 context (also cf. ST13, of uncertain function). ST39 (figure 72), a small piece of perforated chalk, may be a small weight.

11.2.5 MISCELLANEOUS STONE

Two fossils of sea-urchins were recovered, ST42 unstratified, but ST43 from dirt in the hollow way, MLPS East, Phase 2c. They may have been obtained locally and kept merely as curios or have had a more potent influence as votives (cf. Oakley, 1965), although the latter is not apparent from the archaeological context.

The remaining stone consists of samples. ST46 and ST48, both probably local sandstones, for example from the hollow way and paved road.

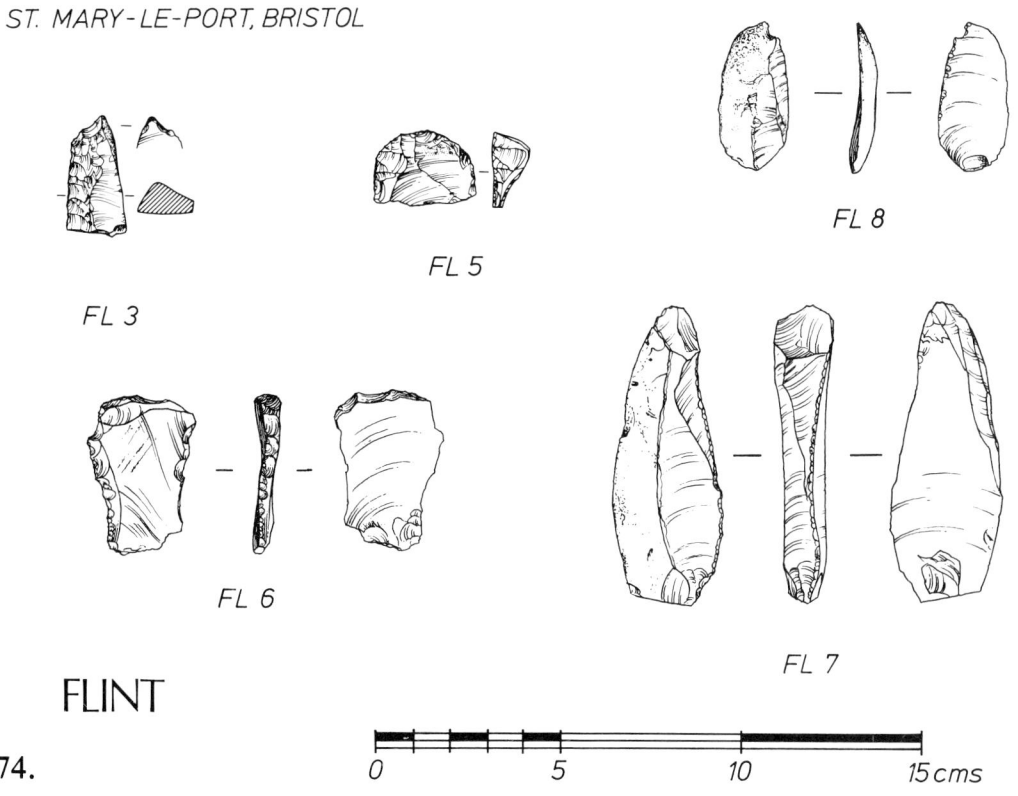

ST. MARY-LE-PORT, BRISTOL

FL 3

FL 5

FL 8

FL 6

FL 7

FLINT

Figure 74.

0   5   10   15 cms

Table 18 MF summarises the geological identities of the stone from Mary-le-Port, but clearly greater refinements would be required to enable its economic and trade route implications, for example, to be assessed fully.

11.3   Flint (figure 74)

Under thirty pieces of flint were found scattered through the areas of MLPS East and West. Within MLPS East, the majority was found in the west end, in Area A, with pieces from single contexts in Areas B and C; from MLPS West, most came from the east end, in Area 106, with single pieces from Areas 103, 104 and 105.

FL2, 13 and 15 were found in an occupation surface on the surface of the natural. They are not closely datable, which also applies to FL18, again from an early context. Flints occurred in the following phase, in contexts associated with the hollow way and the Timber Building. They include an implement (FL3), but most are only retouched or unretouched flakes. There was a relative concentration of flint through the fill of cesspit 106.12, consisting of natural, unretouched and retouched flakes; it is suggested that some of this may be waste from strike-a-lights. Four of the more diagnostic pieces (FL5, 6, 7 and 8) were found in recent or disturbed contexts.

Distinctive typological features are mainly absent in the small quantity of flint from Mary-le-Port although some are considered by A. Saville to be prehistoric. Indistinctive worked flint has sometimes been claimed as contemporary in primary contexts on medieval sites; such an interpretation should be considered in the case of Mary-le-Port, as well as the more obvious possible reflection of sparse prehistoric frequentation of the area.

The nearest major source of flint to the site is the chalk of Wiltshire, but local quaternary deposits, including the gravels of the Bristol Avon (Lacaille, 1954), contain re-deposited flint suitable for knapping (information: A. Saville).

11.4   Soil samples

None of the soil samples from Mary-le-Port has been analysed. The Environmental Archaeology Unit at York estimates that such soils have a post-excavation life of only about five years, so no further work will be possible.

11.5   Burnt clay

BC1 – 17 comprise daub samples. BC1 and BC2, with wattle and organic impressions, were found in a Church Phase 3 context, but may have been derived from the superstructure of an earlier building (cf. table 11). The remaining samples, BC3 – 17, are all from MLPS West. There are samples from both suggested phases of the timber features and from the fill of the associated cesspit, and one, BC5, from the surface of the hollow way, also of MLPS West Phase 3. Wattle impressions are present in both timber phases; BC4, from the second phase, also has a ?lath impression. These are important details to consider in reconstructing the superstructures of buildings known only at foundation level. BC7 and BC8 come from the uppermost fill of the MLPS West Phase 3 cesspit and include smoothed, shaped surfaces and wattle impressions. These may be from rubbish thrown in from elsewhere, rather than part of the cesspit lining or covering (cf. 9.7.3 – 4). BC10 and BC12 are both from the stone walls and BC3 is from a later soil.

11.6   Fired clay

Materials of fired clay are described separately, except for a Roman *tegula* fragment found in MLPS East (cf. 8.6.2). They are listed under BR, CP, DFT, PFT and POT; furnace lining is included with SL, with which it was associated. Spindle whorls included with fired clay at earlier stages of classification are, with one exception, actually of stone and now described under ST, in 11.2.3c.

11.7   Brick

Brick was used extensively in the post-medieval burial vaults in the church (cf. 10.10), but only one type has been catalogued, from a MLPS West, Phase ?6 context. There were also a few fragments of Roman brick (8.6.2).

11.8 Clay tobacco pipes

The pipes are mainly from two contexts in MLPS East and MLPS West. CP9 is from the church, in a disturbed area.

CP10 – 12 are all from MLPS East, from modern levels. CP12 is probably of North French manufacture. They are dated to between the late seventeenth and late nineteenth centuries.

CP2 – 8 are from ?garden soil in MLPS West. They include pipes made in Bristol and others common in the West Country. They are all dated to the seventeenth century.

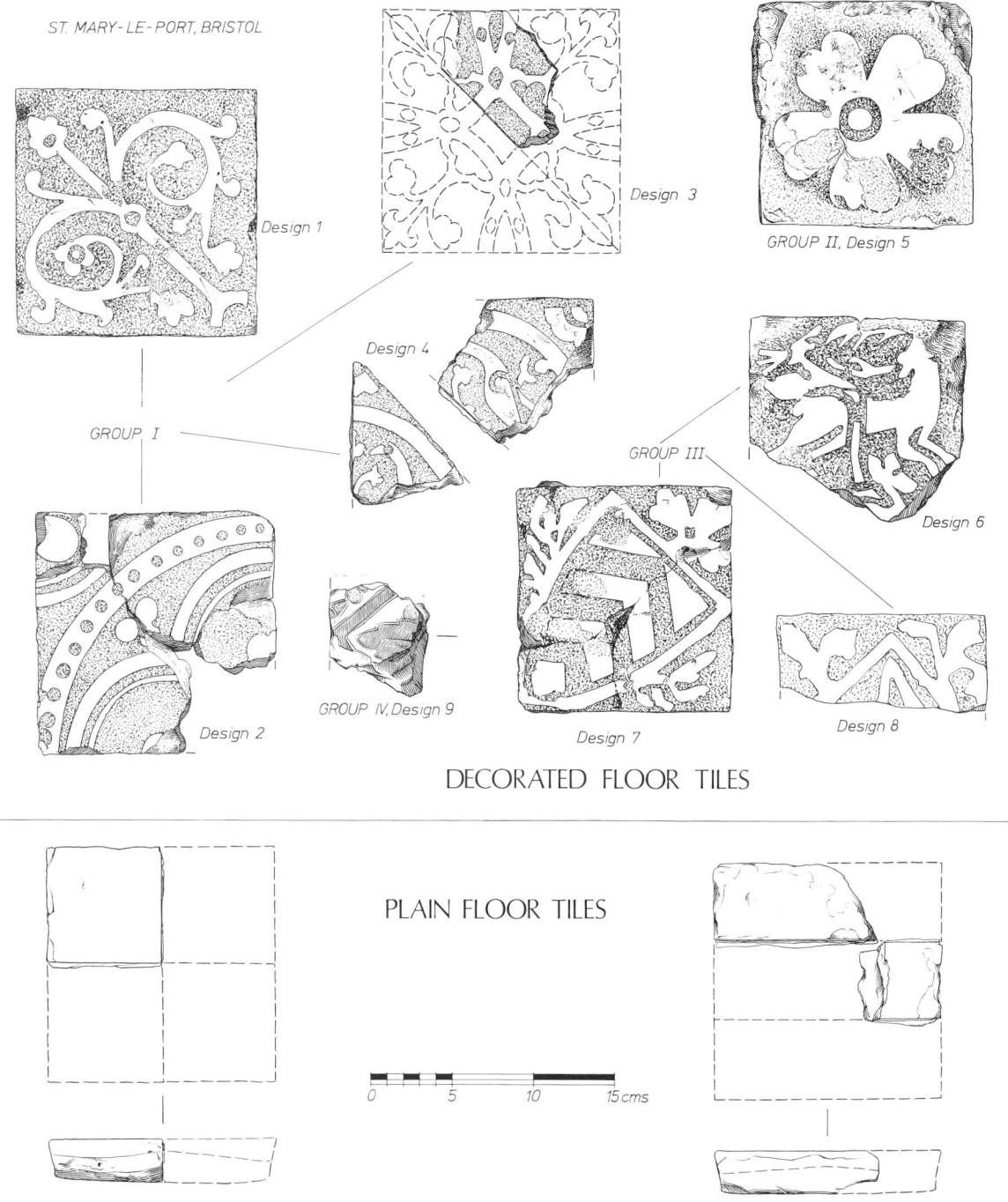

ST. MARY-LE-PORT, BRISTOL

Design 1

Design 3

GROUP II, Design 5

Design 4

GROUP I

GROUP III

Design 6

Design 2

GROUP IV, Design 9

Design 7

Design 8

DECORATED FLOOR TILES

PLAIN FLOOR TILES

0   5   10   15 cms

Figure 76.

11.9 Decorated and plain floor tiles (figure 76)

11.9.1 INTRODUCTION
Ceramic tiles formed only one material used in flooring the churches of Mary-le-Port. Stone, earth and organic material were all probably used as well (cf. 10.8). The 1877 floor throughout the church which lasted until its destruction was of tiles.

The number of tiles recovered was small, with even fewer remaining *in situ,* so little can be said about which areas were tiled and how this related to their functional status. Art-historical dating suggests the tiles recovered were all of a similar date, of the ?late thirteenth – early fourteenth century, which would place their original use in the Phase 3 church. ?Thirteenth-century tiles were found *in situ* (F174), near the rood screen, but in a Phase 5 context, so they must have been re-used, as one of a series of floors in different materials (cf. 10.8.9). The tiles from F78 are from a disturbed context, which can only be given a general phasing, Church Phases 1 – ?4.

One tile, III.6, is recorded from a non-church context, from an early level in MLPS East (cf. 8.6.3 – 4).

In MF 11.9.2 Bruce Williams gives a full report on the tiles. They include a Spanish tile of the early sixteenth century (figure 69, Design 9).

11.10 Ceramics (figures 77 – 81, 83)

11.10.1 INTRODUCTION
The Mary-le-Port site yielded a large quantity of pottery, much of it of the eleventh and twelfth centuries. Little of this was from the church; most came from layers associated with the hollow way to the east (=MLPS East).

A much more comprehensive series has recently been worked out for Bristol by Ponsford, notably on the basis of his Bristol Castle excavations, where he was aided by a stratified sequence, which, in the absence of coin data, was correlated with documentary references (Ponsford, 1979). The Mary-le-Port series has been closely linked to that although the present Mary-le-Port classifications are much coarser. Most Bristol fabrics have been analysed by Vince, by thin sectioning and by microscopic examination, the results of which have been incorporated into Ponsford's type series (= BPT numbers) (see also Vince below, 11.10.5). The systematic ordering of Bristol pottery has been given its essential foundations by Vince and by Ponsford (1979).

Little statistical work has been done on the pottery (not all was retained), though some data for this will be found in tables 4, 9, 10 and 16 MF. The published series is related to layers and features. Where these are dated by pottery, the period suggested is based on that outlined in the following pages, which is based partly on internal stratigraphy and associated finds (e.g. the coin of Harold II gives a *TPQ* of deposition for a large group) or on links with the better-dated series worked out by Ponsford, to whom this report owes a great deal. Comments by him are prefaced MP, and those of Vince by AV.

For comparison the reader is referred to the minor reports on local sites already published and especially to that by Ponsford on Bristol Castle and other city centre sites (cf. Ponsford, 1972 and various Bristol City Museum and Art Gallery Monographs). Two other major series from the area south of Bristol, which have recently been published, may be compared with the MLP series. They are from the Chew Valley (Rahtz and Greenfield, 1977) and Cheddar (Rahtz, 1979). The latter especially includes some of the earlier Saxon pottery of the area, earlier than any from Bristol. The whole post-Roman series in Somerset up to the eleventh century is discussed in Rahtz, 1974. A further important series from Ilchester and Taunton is in preparation for publication by Peter Leach and others (e.g. now Leach, 1982). Vince has also discussed production and distribution of medieval pottery in the region (cf. Vince, 1981).

11.10.2 THE FABRICS AT MARY-LE-PORT
Vince comments (see below 11.10.5) that the majority of the fabrics are locally produced. Notable omissions, compared with series from other sites in the Upper Severn region, include shell- and chaff-tempered wares, Stafford-type wares, Malvernian wares, and any of South Wales origin.

The earliest fabrics are coarse-gritted with calcareous inclusions. Most were made on a slow wheel with much hand-finishing. In the later eleventh and twelfth centuries some development can be seen within Fabric A; the fabric tends to become more oxidised. In the later twelfth and earlier thirteenth century the fabrics are harder-fired but continue to exhibit evidence of hand-working and the use of a slow wheel. The temper continues to be basically calcareous but is less obvious on the surface of the vessel. There is more variation and glazing becomes more frequent.

11.10.3 FORMS IN LATE SAXON AND EARLY MEDIEVAL FABRICS
In the late Saxon fabrics there appear to be three main types of vessels: 1. a full-bodied profile with an upright flat-topped rim with beaded exterior; there is normally a pronounced angle between the neck and the body; 2. a slack profile with a strongly everted rounded section to the rim; there is no angle at the shoulder and neck; 3. a slack profile with an everted rim between types 1 and 2 with a slight concavity on the inside of the neck. The bases of all three types are sagging, occasionally with a basal angle. Decoration occurs with stamped rouletted strips, stamped dimples, stamped spouts and some combing.

There are also three main types in the early medieval fabrics, but there is of course much overlap between the groups. The forms include: 1. a sharp profile with rim rounded on everted neck with no neck-shoulder angle, sometimes with a slight bead externally; 2. a sharp profile with an everted neck and more of a neck-shoulder angle than 1; 3. a full-bodied profile with a strongly-everted neck and internal moulding; this type tends to be grittier but represents a direct link with the earlier period. The bases are all sagging with a pronounced basal angle. The decoration used is combing in wavy lines, often profuse.

In the late twelfth and early thirteenth century the rim forms vary from a roundish everted to upright flat topped. Decoration also exhibits more variety on the inside and outside of rims and there is scribed line decoration.

11.10.4 DETAILS OF FABRICS AND THE ILLUSTRATED FORM SERIES (figures 77 – 81, 83, Nos. 1 – 162)

Details of the illustrated figures are given in the following order: description, references, comments by M. Ponsford (including equivalent BPT numbers) (MP) and then by A. Vince (AV) (both in the main made 1981 and earlier); context; stratigraphic phase.

BPT = Ponsford's Bristol pottery types (cf. Ponsford, 1979); with other fabrics lettered.
BC = Bristol Castle and Ponsford's excavations there.
Bristol A, B, C = Vince categories, 11.10.5 below.
Vince references to 'M Sherds' are in MF 11.10.5. The pie-diagram on the pottery figures represents the portion of the rim surviving.

11.10.4a FABRIC A (figures 77 – 79, 1 – 77)

Early medieval medium hard gritty wares, mainly cooking pots.

Most have grey core; a few have dark-grey surfaces; most have buff to brown surfaces; a few are oxidised to reddish-brown; surfaces are sometimes smoke-blackened. Within Fabric A there are minor variations of fabric for which scientific analysis may ultimately indicate distinct sources—Vince's analysis (below) indicates that this group includes both local and non-local wares. MP: Fabric A is *not* the same as BC motte ditch types (e.g. BPT 6 – 11). Fabric A is mainly different in its emphatic limestone content, frequent *red* inclusions (haematite?) and buff coloration. Excavations at both Westbury College and Peter Street, Bristol, both appear to have produced sherds of Fabric A, although it does not occur at Bristol Castle except for one certain sherd in a much later context. The Castle types, however, do occur at Mary-le-Port; it is therefore suggested that Fabric A and relatives are *earlier* than BC groups, with perhaps a starting date in tenth rather than eleventh century. Nos. 1 and 2 are very roughly made and would, on basis of general appearance, be considered earlier than rest, i.e. later tenth or earlier eleventh century.

Figure 77
1   Squat cooking pot with simple rim, no beading or decoration; MP: BPT 2/3; AV: Bristol A; B4 (MLPS East, Phase 2e).

2   Squat cooking pot with simple rim, very slight internal beading; thrown on slow wheel and hand-finished; exterior and interior of rim decorated with rather crude combing approximating to cruciform pattern; MP: fabric not at BC: AV: Bristol A; 104.4 (MLPS West, Phase 8).

3 – 39 are mainly undecorated cooking pots, grouped under minor variations of fabric.

3 – 17 all have sagging bases and are thrown on a slow wheel and then hand-finished; similar sherds were recently found in excavation in Peter Street, in thirteenth-century features, probably derived from disturbed earlier layers. BPT 2 is present at BC; all are of AV Bristol C.

3   Simple slightly everted rim with very small bead on outer face; C2 (MLPS East, Phase 5).

4   Simple everted rim; unusual in being reduced on both surfaces; F2 – 3 (MLPS East, Phase 2c).

5   Simple beaded rim; F2 – 3 (MLPS East, Phase 2c).

6   Vertical neck and simple beaded rim; E2 (MLPS East, Phase 3a).

7   Everted rim decorated by fingernail impressions on outer face of rim; D4 (MLPS East, Phase 2e).

8   Sharply everted rim and simple external bead; B3 (MLPS East, Phase 3b).

9   Near-vertical neck and simple beaded rim; MP: pre-Conquest form at BC; Z1 + 2 (MLPS East, Phase 5).

10   Vertical neck and small bead on outer face of rim; A2 (MLPS East, Phase 5).

11   Vertical neck and simple beaded rim; evidence of hand-finishing by brush or coarse cloth on body of vessel; MP: probably pre-Conquest; F2 – 3 (MLPS East, Phase 2c).

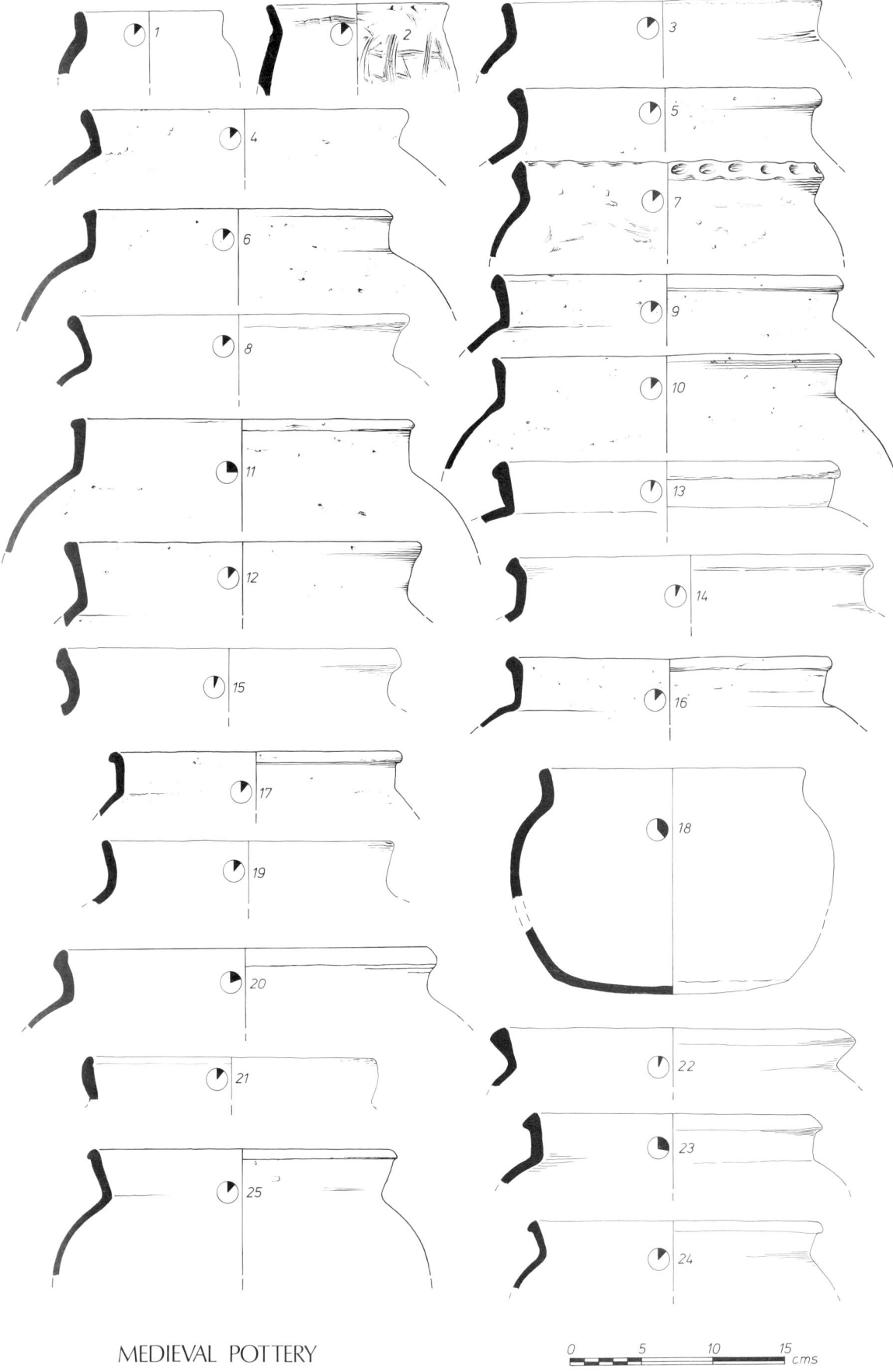

MEDIEVAL POTTERY

0   5   10   15
cms

Figure 77.

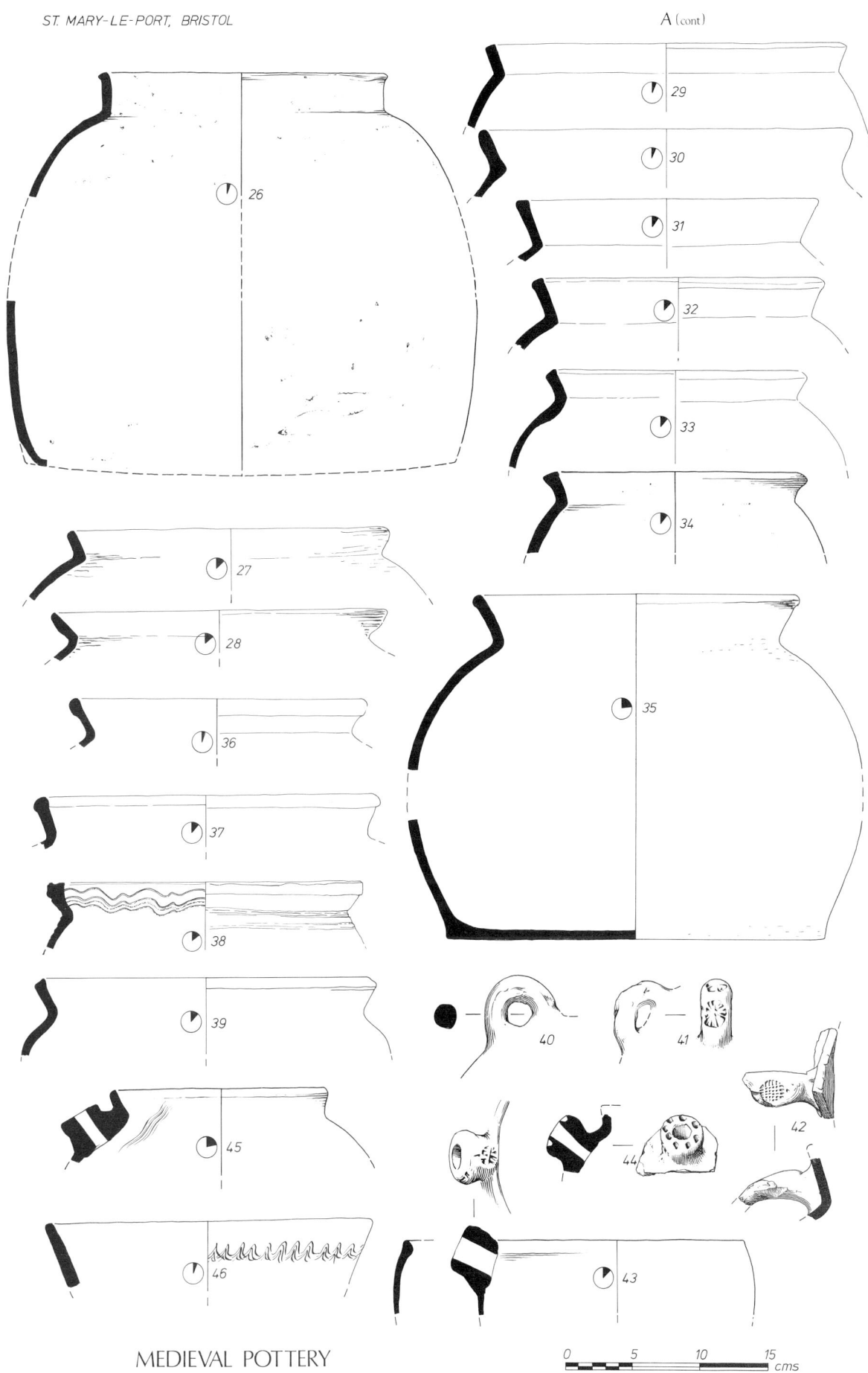

MEDIEVAL POTTERY

0   5   10   15
cms

Figure 78.

12   Vertical neck and thickening at rim; F2 – 3 (MLPS East, Phase 2c).

13   Sharply everted rim with pronounced simple bead; F2 – 3 (MLPS East, Phase 2c).

14   Vertical neck with pronounced external bead giving internal groove to rim; F2 – 3 (MLPS East, Phase 2c).

15   Neck coming from body of vessel in gentle curve with beaded rim and slight hollowing of inner face of rim; F2 – 3 (MLPS East, Phase 2c).

16   Vertical neck and beaded rim; distinct shoulder to vessel just before neck rises; E2 (MLPS East, Phase 3a).

17   Vertical neck and beaded rim; MP: probably BPT 2; F2 – 3 (MLPS East, Phase 2c).

Nos. 18 – 26; MP: no direct parallels to 18 can be found among rim forms from BC Site D and I suspect MLP ones are earlier. At BC pottery was well-stratified below ring-work rampart; as there were three periods of structures some at least must be pre-Conquest (see Dunning, 1952, figure 9.5—and parallels from elsewhere). There are no direct parallels for 19 – 26 and only one sherd is known from BC Site A, Sherd 42, from the motte ditch, dating pre-1147.

18   Simple everted rim, wide base slightly sagging; AV: Bristol C; A3 (MLPS East, Phase 2e); B4; (MLPS East, Phase 2e); E4 (MLPS East, Phase 2d).

19   Simple rim rising from body of pot in gentle curve; AV: Bristol C; C2 (MLPS East, Phase 5).

20   Straight neck, external bead and internal groove at top of rim; AV: Bristol C; D4 (MLPS East, Phase 2e).

21   Incurving rim and internal bead; MP: BPT 3, pre-Conquest; AV: Bristol A; C2 (MLPS East, Phase 5).

22   Everted rim; AV: Bristol C; D4 (MLPS East, Phase 2e).

23   Vertical neck and pronounced external bead; AV: Bristol C; E2 (MLPS East, Phase 3a).

24   Everted rim and external bead; AV: Bristol C; C2 (MLPS East, Phase 5).

25   Everted rim and external bead; AV: Bristol C, variant; C2 (MLPS East, Phase 5).

Figure 78

26   Wide-based, slightly sagging with vertical neck and small external bead; AV: Bristol C; A3 (MLPS East, Phase 2e).

27 – 37—surface decoration is restricted to vessels with oxidised surfaces, but without distinction in fabric; rims are grouped by form; 27 – 28—simple everted rims without internal or external beads in reduced fabrics; 29 – 35—nearer to vertical rims, with cut top surfaces gradually developing external and internal bead; 36 – 38—everted rims with pronounced beads.

MP: oxidised and decorated sherds with limestone temper are paralleled from Pithay collection in Bristol City Museum and also in levels of 1040s from Dublin; they do not however occur at BC and should therefore be earlier than the 1060s at least; decorated sherds rare at BC; BPT 3 = pre-Conquest version of BPT 115.

27   Simple everted rim; MP: BPT 3; AV: Bristol A; B11 (MPLS East, Phase 2e).

28   Simple everted rim, slight swelling of outer face of rim; MP: BPT 3; AV: Bristol B; C4 (MLPS East, Phase 2e).

29   Everted rim, cut at top with sharp angle; MP: BPT 3; AV: Bristol B; B4 (MLPS East, Phase 2e).

30   Everted rim, inside junction of rim to shoulder splayed and reinforced; MP: probably BPT 3; AV: Bristol B; C2 (MLPS East, Phase 5).

31   Everted rim with slight bead to outer and inner face; MP: ?BPT 3; AV: Bristol B; B14 (MLPS East, Phase 2e).

32   Everted rim and external and internal bead; MP: probably BPT 3; AV: Bristol B; B4 (MLPS East, Phase 2e).

33   Everted rim and internal bead; MP: BPT 3; AV: Bristol B; A3 (MLPS East, Phase 2e).

34   Everted rim, pronounced external and slight internal bead; MP: BPT 3; AV: Bristol B; F2 – 3 (MLPS East, Phase 2c).

35   Everted rim and simple bead; vessel reconstructed from several sherds; MP: BPT 2; AV: Bristol A; 101c (MLPS West, Phase 4); 101d (MLPS West, Phase 2).

36   Sharply everted rim and distinct bead to exterior face; MP: BPT 3; AV: Bristol B; D4 (MLPS East, Phase 2e).

37   Everted rim and bead to both internal and external face; MP: BPT 3; AV: Bristol B; A9 (MLPS East, Phase 2e).

38 – 39—distinguished by being entirely reduced.

MP: possibly from Long Ashton kilns; at BC Site D appear to be later twelfth century, from floor of Building A; for internal combing cf. Davison, 1972, figure 24.6; ?BPT 48.

38   Rim, external surface decorated with crudely-scored lines; inner face of rim decorated with multiple-toothed combing; 104.1 (MLPS West, Phase 8).

39   Everted rim: MP: resembles Cheddar Fabric CC (Rahtz, 1979, 310—suggests late tenth – early eleventh-century currency); Vince Sherd M417—Bristol A; C4 (MLPS East, Phase 2e).

40 – 42—handles from spouted tripod pitchers.

MP: handles of similar shape to 42 but placed lower on shoulder are known on fabric BPT 114, sherds from BC, Site D, Building A (floor); none of these are decorated with stamped rosettes; also common at Peter Street.

40   Simple looped handle from shoulder of spouted pitcher; diameter of loop 55 mm.; AV: Bristol C; B3 (MLPS East, Phase 3b).

41   Simple looped handle decorated on upper surface with two stamped rosettes; diameter of loop 58 mm.; AV: Bristol C; F2 – 3 (MLPS West, Phase 2c).

42   Handle from neck of vessel; upper surface decorated with rectilinear stamp; AV: Bristol C variant; u/s.

43 – 45—spouts, ?from tripod pitchers.

MP: there are direct parallels for spouted and combed wares at Taunton in pre-Conquest contexts but in coarser local fabric. See also examples from St. Neots (Dunning *et al.*, 1959, figure 15.4), Somerset (Rahtz, 1974, 95 – 126, figure 6, 66 – 69), Group 8 from Taunton no. 66, dated by 1042 coin hoard, and Cheddar (Rahtz, 1979). Other examples have come recently from the Peter Street excavations in Bristol in 1970 and 1975 – 6 by Bristol City Museum but these are all out of context in much later features. Upright rims may well be an early dating feature as some late Saxon material from BC Site D (BPT 1 fabric) has this type of rim (Ponsford, Appendix in Rahtz 1974, 75, 77 – 79 and Dunning *et al.*, 1959, figure 9.7).

43   Spout of bowl, decorated on upper surface with single rosette stamp; rim form is simple internal bead; AV: Bristol C; F2 – 3 (MLPS East, Phase 2c).

44   Spout decorated on its pouring face with stabbed indentations; AV: Bristol C; E2 (MLPS East, Phase 3a).

45   Small spout, oxidised surfaces; area of combed decoration beside spout; cf. Rahtz, 1974, figure 6.70; AV: Bristol B; D1 (MLPS East, Phase 6).

46 – 58—sherds with rough-comb decoration. 47 – 51 are tooled vessels with pouring holes; reduced to even state with outer surface finished with light-brown slip; tooling does not go through slip to expose core. Paralleled from Castle Neroche (Davison, 1972, figure 25).

MP: no parallels for these at BC, but some from Taunton in pre-Conquest context, though in much coarser fabric. All pre-Conquest, except for BPT 20, 1080 – 1100, a very short-lived post-Conquest type.

52 – 54—?from tripod pitchers. Similar sherds found in Bath (information Patrick Greene).

46   Possibly a large lamp; combed wavy line decoration; fabric oxidised; MP: fabric as BPT 3; form not at BC; AV: Bristol B; A2 (MLPS East, Phase 5).

Figure 79

47   Simple curved rim; thrown on slow wheel with much hand-working; shoulder decorated with heavy scoring done while clay still in plastic state; exterior surface heavily oxidised with many grits showing through outer surface; simple pouring hole just below rim of pot; MP: fabric as BPT 1, but form not at BC; AV: Bristol A; C11 (MLPS East, Phase 3a).

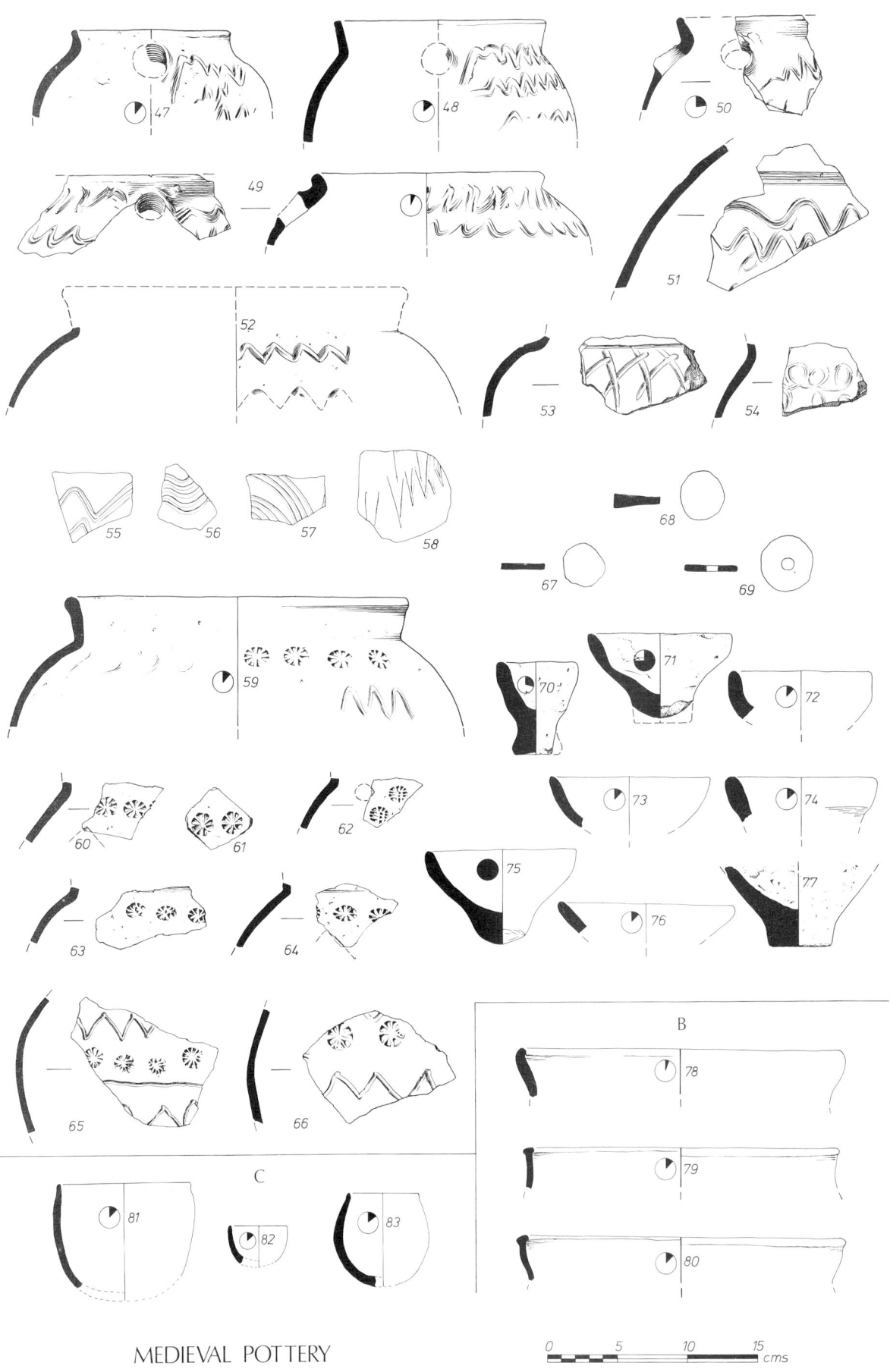

MEDIEVAL POTTERY

Figure 79.

48   Spouted pitcher with slightly everted rim, shoulder and body decorated with heavy scoring while clay still in plastic state; simple pouring hole at top of shoulder; external surface oxidised light-brown slip; inner surface heavily pitted possibly by vessel's contents; AV: Sherd M294—Bristol B; A3 (MLPS East, Phase 2e).

49   Vessel with simple rim, shoulder decorated with multipoint tooling while clay still plastic; simple pouring hole just below rim; exterior coated with light-brown slip, inner surface heavily pitted; AV: Bristol B; A3 (MLPS East, Phase 2e).

50   Cooking pot with slightly everted rim and simple pouring hole; shoulder decorated with scoring while clay still plastic; AV: Bristol B; D4 (MLPS East, Phase 2e).

51   Body sherd of larger vessel, scored decoration; MP: BPT 20, 1080 – 1100 (very short-lived); AV: Bristol B; A3 (MLPS East, Phase 2e).

52   Two lines of chevron scribing; AV: Bristol C; C4 (MLPS East, Phase 2e).

53   Shoulder of vessel with scribed interlace decoration; AV: Bristol C; C2 (MLPS East, Phase 5).

54   Scribed spiral decoration; AV: Bristol C; C2 (MLPS East, Phase 5).

55   Oxidised fabric with two sets of chevron combing; MP: BPT 20; AV: Bristol B; B14 (MLPS East, Phase 2e).

56   Oxidised fabric with wide wavy-line combings; MP: ?BPT 20; AV: Bristol B; B14 (MLPS East, Phase 2e).

57   Oxidised fabric with circular combing; AV: Bristol B; B11 (MLPS East, Phase 2e).

58   Oxidised fabric with chevron scoring, not done with comb; MP: lots of quartz; *not* BPT 3; AV: Bristol B; A3 (MLPS East, Phase 2e).

59 – 66—stamped sherds (also see 41 – 43).

MP: *re* 59; see Dunning *et al.,* 1959, figure 11; rosettes are fairly rare in Bristol but occur as late as twelfth century on pottery of fabric BPT 114 (BC, Site D, floor of Building A).
60 – 66—cf. general description 52 – 54. All pre-Conquest, except for BPT 20.

59   Bead on outer face more distinct than inner; shoulder of vessel decorated with stamped rosettes and wavy line scratched with single prong; AV: Bristol C variant; C2 (MLPS East, Phase 5).

60   Two rosette stamps and corner of chevron scribing; MP: similar to BPT 20; AV: Bristol C; E4 (MLPS East, Phase 2d).

61   Two rosette stamps; AV: Bristol C; B3 (MLPS East, Phase 3b).

62   Two rectilinear stamps probably from spouted pitcher; AV: Sherd M295—Bath A; D4 (MLPS East, Phase 2e).

63   Three rosette stamps; AV: Bristol C; F2 – 3 (MLPS East, Phase 2c).

64   Two rosette stamps; AV: Bristol C; D4 (MLPS East, Phase 2e).

65   Four rosette stamps and chevron scribing above and below; AV: Bristol C; D1 (MLPS East, Phase 6).

66   Two large rosette stamps and chevron scribing above and below; AV: Bristol C; C16 (MLPS East, Phase 2f).

67 – 68—counters.

67   Unfinished; AV: Bristol C; B3 (MLPS East, Phase 3b).

68   Unfinished; AV: Bristol C; F2 – 3 (MLPS East, Phase 2c).

69 –   ?spindle-whorl.

69   Complete; AV: Bristol C; F2 – 3 (MLPS East, Phase 2c).

70 – 77—lamps; all pre-Conquest.

70   Small lamp; MP: cf. BPT 3; AV: Sherd M299—Bristol B; A9 (MLPS East, Phase 2e).

71   Complete, with smoothed exterior surface; MP: cf. BPT 3; AV: Bristol B; B4 (MLPS East, Phase 2e).

72   Rim, with pimply exterior surface; MP: probably cf. BPT 2; AV: Bristol C; B3 (MLPS East, Phase 3b).

73   Rim, with smoothed exterior; MP: ?BPT 1 – 2; AV: Bristol A; D4 (MLPS East, Phase 2e).

74   Rim, with smoothed exterior and thinning of vessel below rim; AV: Bristol C; B4 (MLPS East, Phase 2e).

75   Small lamp; B4 (MLPS East, Phase 2e).

76   Rim of small lamp; MP: BPT 3; AV: Bristol B; C2 (MLPS East, Phase 5).

77   Base of lamp; MP: BPT 3; AV: Bristol B; C2 (MLPS East, Phase 5).

11.10.4b   FABRIC B (figure 79.78 – 80)
Hard, gritty.

MP: rare at BC but there is one rim in this fabric in motte ditch (pre-1147). Forms of 79 – 80 may be compared with BC Site A, Sherd 29 (BPT 13).

78   Simple rim, incurving profile; MP: probably overfired BPT 3; AV: Bristol C; A19 (MLPS East, Phase 5).

79   Vertical neck which leans out near top, with pronounced internal bead; MP: BPT 3/115B—could be c.1100; AV: Bristol A; E1 (MLPS East, Phase 6).

80   Everted rim with internal and external bead; AV: Bristol C (very sandy); D4 (MLPS East, Phase 2e).

11.10.4c   FABRIC C (figure 79.81 – 83)
Hard, sandy. Cup-like vessels of various sizes. Fabric used exclusively for this form. They are not considered to be crucibles because they do not contain any residues.

MP: no Bristol parallels.

81   Cup, dia. 86 mm.; F2 – 3; (MLPS East, Phase 2c).

82   Small cup, dia. 42 mm.; report; D1 (MLPS East, Phase 6).

83   Cup, dia. 52 mm.; A3 (MLPS East, Phase 2e).

11.10.4d   FABRIC D (figure 80.84)
Medium hard, flint-gritted—only sherd of this fabric from excavation; heavy scouring to both surfaces and fingernail stabbing to rim done while clay in wet state.

MP: parallels to type of decoration in the twelfth century on lamps from BC Site A, Sherd 86; and from Westbury College.

Figure 80

84   Rim sherd of large lamp; AV: Bristol C; D2 (MLPS East, Phase 3b).

11.10.4e   FABRIC E (figure 80.85 – 93)
Early medieval glazed wares, including tripod pitchers.

85 – 91—all pieces have dull green-glaze, some with brown tinge; all from tripod-pitchers or related vessels.

MP: fabric common in Bristol in twelfth – thirteenth contexts; at least one vessel can be shown to be contemporary with Ham Green B Ware (Barton, 1969); handles typical of many examples from Bristol and Gloucestershire; base of combed vessel from BC Site A is datable to c.1250. In general type is twelfth rather than eleventh century but there is range of types and few fragments from motte ditch at BC Site A.

85   Rim of large vessel with light-green glaze externally and round top of rim internally; AV: south-east Wilts. ware; Z1 + 2 (MLPS East, Phase 5 – 6).

86   Rim of large vessel, glazed externally and internally in light green; inner surface and top of rim decorated with knife cuts; AV: south-east Wilts. ware; B3 (MLPS East, Phase 3b).

87   Handle and rim of large green/brown-glazed pitcher, glazed patchily externally and for depth of rim internally, handle decorated with applied clay strip down centre; thumb-pinched into crest; AV: south-east Wilts. ware; Z1 + 2 (MLPS East, Phase 5 – 6).

88   Handle of pitcher decorated by thumbed clay strip down centre, knife slashing and stabbing; glazed in light olive-green on outside and patchily on inside; C2 (MLPS East, Phase 5).

89   Spout and rim of pitcher; olive-green glaze externally and internally; cf. Gloucester (Hassall and Rhodes, 1974, figure 37); AV: south-east Wilts. ware; F2 – 3 (MLPS East, Phase 2c).

90   Spout of pitcher, with olive-green glaze round most of it; spout leans forward from body of vessel and is restrained by applied strip of clay; cf. Wareham Castle (Renn, 1960, figure 19, D4); AV: south-east Wilts. ware; C4 (MLPS East, Phase 2e).

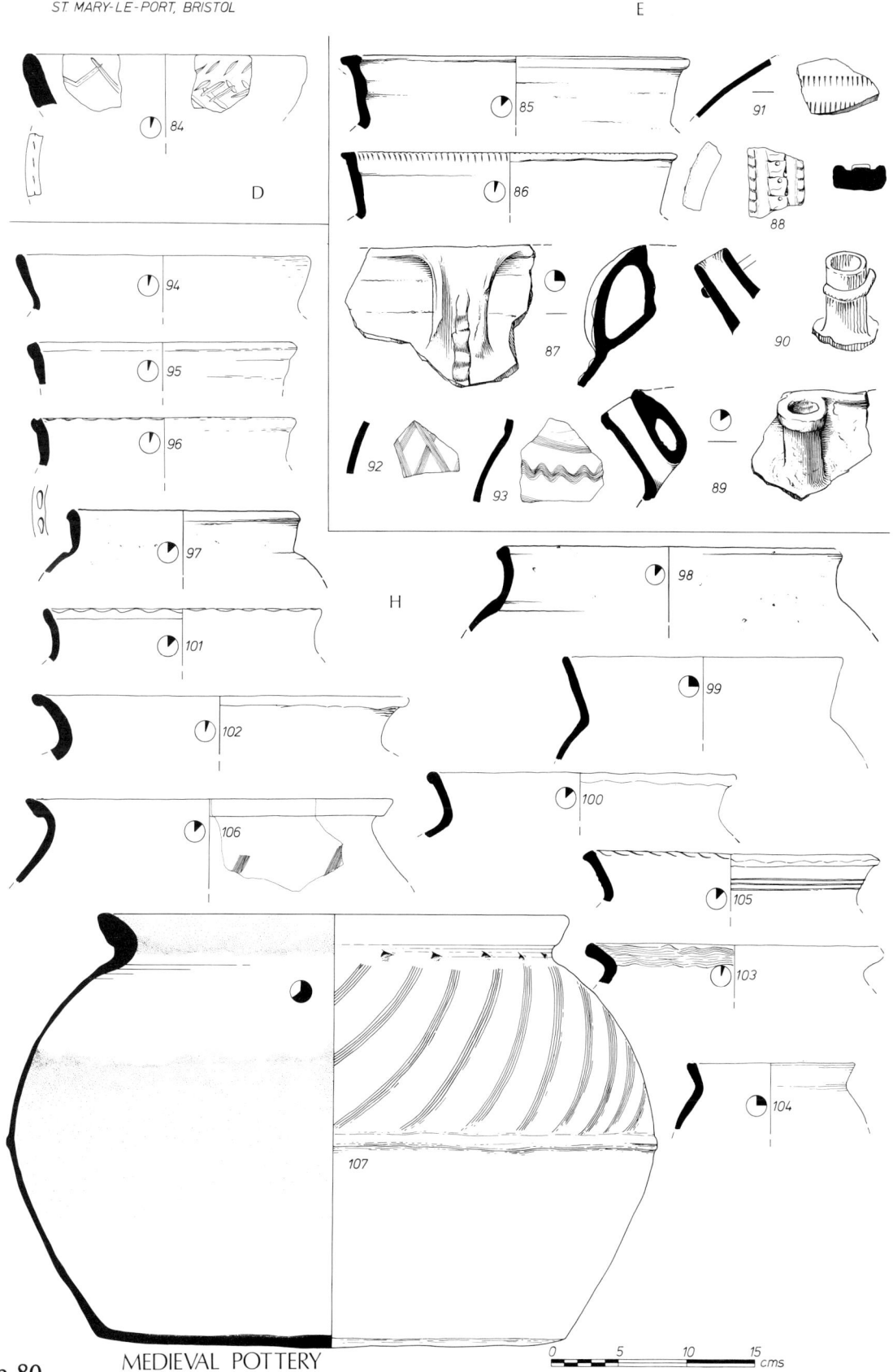

ST. MARY-LE-PORT, BRISTOL

Figure 80.   MEDIEVAL POTTERY

91   Sherd from tripod pitcher with olive-green glaze externally and incised decoration probably roller-applied; AV: Sherd M297—Bath M, = south-east Wilts. ware; E1 (MLPS East, Phase 6).

92 – 93—cf. general descriptions, etc., of 85 – 88, except that inclusions leached out.

92   Pale-olive-green-glazed body sherd decorated with diagonal seven-tooth combing. MP: BPT 18; AV: Minety-type ware; B3 (MLPS East, Phase 3b).

93   Pale-olive-green-glazed body sherd decorated with eight-tooth combing; MP: BPT 18; AV: Minety-type ware; B3 (MLPS East, Phase 3b).

11.10.4f   FABRIC F (not illustrated)
Stamford ware (late).
Three small body sherds from A3 (MLPS East, Phase 2e), A19 (MLPS East, Phase 5) and B4 (MLPS East, Phase 2e); also sherd from 103.3B (MLPS West, Phase 4).

11.10.4g   FABRIC G (not illustrated)
?Winchester-type ware (cf. Biddle and Barclay, 1974)

Characterised by having very glossy, iridescent glaze which is finely crackled.

Two body sherds from B16 (MLPS East, Phase 2c) and from C4 (MLPS East, Phase 2e).

11.10.4h   FABRIC H (figure 80.94 – 107)
Medium-hard, smooth, gritty cooking pots.

94 – 98—MP: this fabric commonest in motte ditch of BC Site A (BPT 6 – 11) (pre-1147). Infolding feature characteristic of Gloucestershire, Avon and South Wales (for recent survey see Fowler and Bennett (eds.), 1973, 36 – 7 and figures 5 and 6; see also Davison, 1972, figures 24 and 25).

94   Simple everted rim; MP: probably paralleled in BC motte ditch; AV: Bristol C; C2 (MLPS East, Phase 5).

95   Everted neck with an internal and external bead; MP: ?BPT 4 (motte ditch type); A3 (MLPS East, Phase 2e).

96   Vertical neck and external bead to rim decorated by fingernail crimping on top surface; MP: BPT 6 – 11, Fabric AA; AV: Bristol C; D2 (MLPS East, Phase 3b).

97   Vertical neck and simple external bead; MP: cf. Sherd 34, motte ditch; AV: Bristol C; C2 (MLPS East, Phase 5).

98   Wide, slightly-sagging base; rim slightly everted with simple bead on external face; MP: BPT 6 – 11 from two pots, Fabrics AA and AC; AV: Bristol C; rim C2 (MLPS East, Phase 5), base C15 (MLPS East, Phase 2f).

99   Everted tall rim; surface heavily reduced and shows signs of working with cloth or brush; MP: BPT 6 – 11, Fabric AA; B3 (MLPS East, Phase 3b).

100   Everted rim and simple external bead; underside bead folded with fingers to give crimped appearance; MP: BPT 17; parallel from BC motte ditch; fabric similar to that used in tripod pitchers; AV: south-east Wilts. ware; C4 (MLPS East, Phase 2e).

101   Slightly everted rim; finger crimping on top surface and internal ledge; MP: BPT 6 – 11, Fabric AA; AV: see thin-section report; F2 – 3 (MLPS East, Phase 2c).

102 – cf. general description 89 – 91.

102   Slightly everted rim and very shallow external bead; AV: south-east Wilts. ware; C2 (MLPS East, Phase 5).

103   Sharply everted rim, inner surface decorated with multi-toothed combing (cf. Davison, 1972, figure 24.10); MP: ?BPT 32; AV: Ham Green ware cooking pot fabric; C2 (MLPS East, Phase 5).

104 – 105 Ham Green B (Barton, 1963).

104   Small cooking pot, simple everted rim; upper flat surface of rim has been cut by knife; MP: early Ham Green—contains lime; BPT 114; 106.1 (MLPS West, Phase 8).

105   Sharply everted rim with pronounced external bead; neck of vessel decorated with multiple scoring; MP: Ham Green, BPT 32; 105.1 (MLPS West, Phase 8).

Plate 59.   Pot of Minety-type ware; cf. figure 80.107.

106 – 107—Minety-type ware (ex-Selsley Common; Dunning, 1949).

MP: this fabric is so common in Bristol that source close by (probably Minety) must be postulated. AV suggests north Wiltshire. Rim-glazed cooking pots probably late thirteenth century at earliest; still common in the fifteenth century when forms include bung-hole cisterns (Dunning, 1949, figure 2 and Jope, 1952, figure 2 for distribution of fabric and type with rim glaze with high (five per cent) tin content; see also Fowler and Bennett (eds.), 1973, 38 – 41).

106   Cooking pot with sharply everted rim with close diagonal combing on shoulder; internal surface has had limestone grits leached out, possibly by contents of vessel during use; splashes of green glaze on interior of vessel; MP: BPT 84, *c*.1300 ff.; AV: Sherd M296—Minety-type ware; F175B (Church Phase 5).

107   Almost complete cooking pot with everted rim (not seen by PAR/LW); plate 59; MP: Minety-type ware, BPT 84A; probably first half fourteenth century; cf. Ponsford, 1979, figure 78.148 where decoration similar—shortly after 1300; 106.2 (MLPS West, Phase ?6).

11.10.4i   FABRIC H/J (not illustrated)
Ham Green jug sherds which cannot be defined as Fabric H rather than Fabric J.

11.10.4j   FABRIC J (figure 81.108 – 124)
Medieval glazed jugs.
108 – 110—Ham Green A (glazed) (Barton, 1963).

MP: there is no reason to doubt that Ham Green A is earlier than Ham Green B—recent work is corroborating this initial idea.

Figure 81

108   Rim of jug, pale yellow and green glaze; decorated with roller stamp and neck ornamented with applied strip, finger pinched into crests (cf. Barton, 1963, figure 1.1 – 13); MP: Ham Green A, BPT 26; Z1 + 2 (MLPS East, Phase 5 – 6).

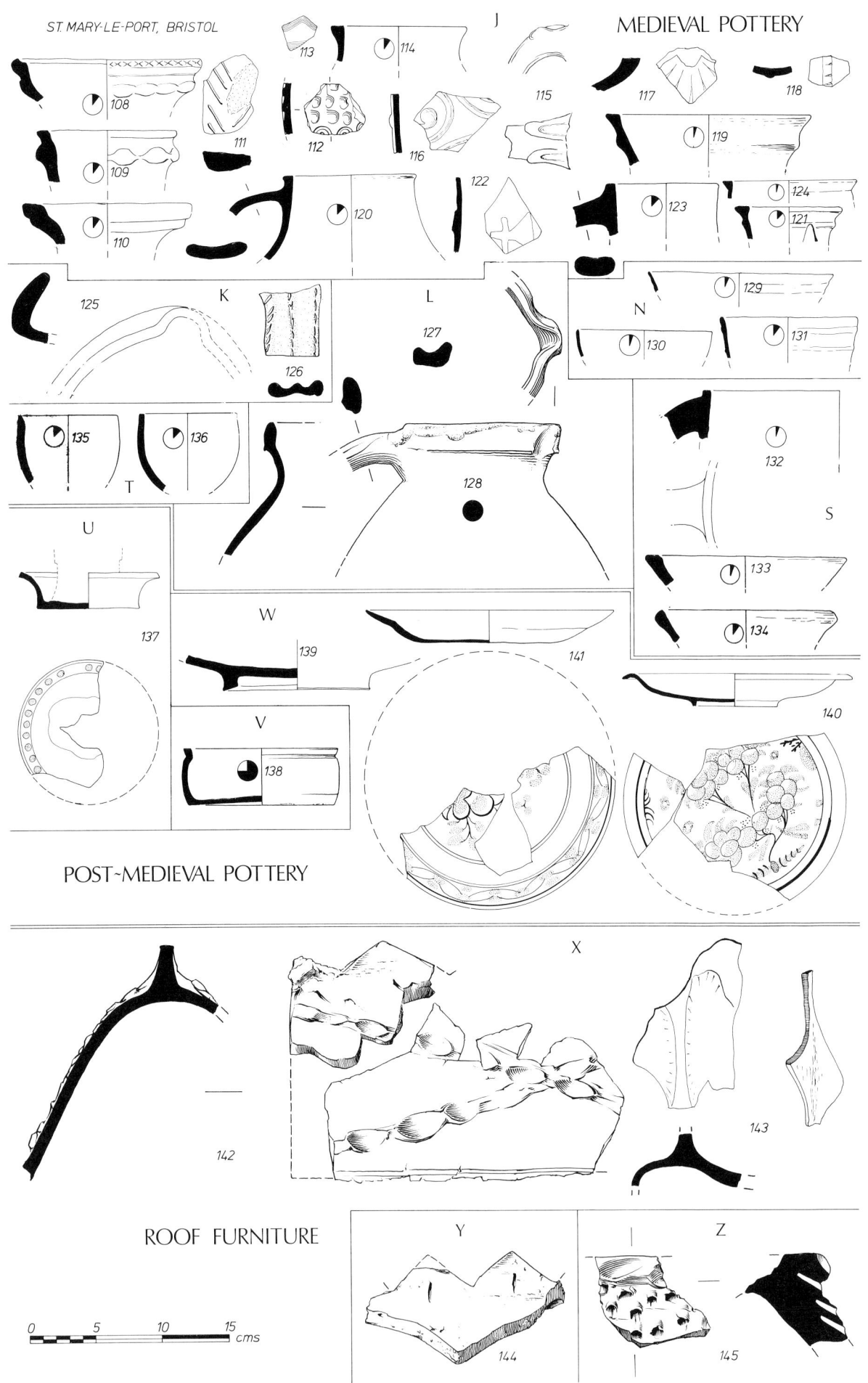

ST.MARY-LE-PORT, BRISTOL

MEDIEVAL POTTERY

POST~MEDIEVAL POTTERY

ROOF FURNITURE

0   5   10   15 cms

Figure 81.

109   Rim of jug with dark green/brown glaze; simple bead rim with broad applied clay strip on neck finger pinched into crest (cf. Barton, 1963, figure 1.18); MP: BPT 26; F89A (Church, Phase 4 – 6).

110   Sharply splayed moulded rim of jug, glazed dark bottle green; MP: ?handleless bottle; BPT 26; D1 (MLPS East, Phase 6).

111 – 112—Ham Green B (Barton, 1963).

111   Green/brown glazed handle decorated with knife slashes; MP: Ham Green B, BPT 27; C2 (MLPS East, Phase 5).

112   Body sherd from brown glazed jug, decorated with thumbnail pinching and circles; MP: BPT 26/27; A19 (MLPS East, Phase 5).

113—MP: grooving suggests date in the fourteenth century; cf. BC Site F of the fourteenth century.

113   Sherd of ?jug; exterior glazed green, decorated with combing; F175B (Church, Phase 5).

114—MP: probably Bristol imitation of French import.

114   Rim of jug; pale-green glaze with dark-green specks; AV: Bristol jug; 106.2 (MLPS West, Phase ?6).

115 – 124—Redcliffe ware (figure 81.115 – 124).

MP: cf. sherds found in waster pits in Redcliff Hill, Bristol, in 1970 (Ponsford in preparation).

115   Handle of jug, rod type, thumbed into upper portion of vessel: glaze dark olive-green with darker-green speckles; 105.1 (MLPS West, Phase 8).

116   Body sherd of glazed jug, raised modelling of spirals; MP: Redcliffe, BPT 118; B1 (MLPS East, Phase 6).

117   Portion of 'beard' from bottom of bridgespout; green/brown mottled glaze; MP: common Bristol decoration; BPT 118; A7 (MLPS East, Phase 4b).

118   Body sherd decorated with applied clay strip cut at 10 mm. intervals with knife; E1 (MLPS East, Phase 6).

119   Rim of jug with raised band in centre, glazed with green and brown dappled glaze; MP: standard Redcliffe and Bristol rim form late thirteenth – fourteenth centuries. A19 (MLPS East, Phase 5).

120   Top of jug with simple bead rim; handle: plain strap; glazed with green speckles; MP: Redcliffe, BPT 117; very fine, copying French, 1300 – 1325; F175B (Church, Phase 5).

121   Rim of jug decorated with ridge and applied clay strip, glazed deep green; MP: standard Bristol form; BPT 118; 106.2 (MLPS West, Phase ?6).

122   Body sherd of glazed jug, decorated with raised clay model of halberd. Glazed jug body in dappled green, glaze of halberd in dark brown almost vitrified; A4 disturbed (MPLS East, Phase 0 disturbed).

123   Rim of green glazed jug with thick strap handle; 1H (Church, Phase 4).

124   Rim of small ?jug; surfaces coated white slip and interior green-glazed; MP: BPT 118; F175B (Church, Phase 5).

11.10.4k   FABRIC K (figure 81.125 – 126)
French imports.

125   Rim of shallow bowl, possibly oval in shape with lip; inside glazed reddish-brown becoming greener as lip approached; AV: ?south-western French baking dish; A1 (MLPS East, Phase 6).

126   Light-green glazed handle, flecked with darker green; centre of strap raised and edges rolled, three crests decorated with knife cuts; 106.2 (MLPS West, Phase ?6).

Not illustrated. Sherd fine salmon-pink sandy, cream core, lustrous green glaze on cross-combing, glaze darker in combing; ?western French import, cf. Gloucester H 53/69; Criccieth Castle and Castell-y-Bere Group B2 (Butler, 1974, 86 and figure 3.8 and 9).

11.10.4l   FABRIC L (figure 81.127 – 128)
Late medieval or later glazed jugs.

127   Jug handle; MP: Wanstrow, late sixteenth – seventeenth; u/s Church.

128   Rim of large jug, simple pinched lip for pouring; very coarse interior green glaze and brown slip

on exterior; cf. Miles and Saunders, 1970; MP: Devon gravel-tempered ware, late sixteenth – early seventeenth; u/s.

11.10.4m   FABRIC M (not illustrated)
Post-medieval glazed jugs.

All sherds fragments of strap handles with simple folded edges, with lustrous green glazes.

MP: not certainly Donyatt (near Taunton, Somerset), but types are similar. Similar pottery also made at Falfield (Gloucs.) but more brown glazed (Fowler and Bennett, 1974, 123 – 6).
Two sherds, Church, u/s; and F87A (Church, phase uncertain).

11.10.4n   FABRIC N (figure 81.129 – 131)
'Tudor Green' (cf. Hurst, 1964).

MP: vessels illustrated not typical 'Tudor Green' forms; may be similar ware being produced in Bristol area, rather earlier than general dating of these wares, especially narrow cup form. From BC Site F, layer 23 (section 1) is similar cup with slightly less glossy glaze, but not Tudor Green; this context not later than 1350 (cf. Hurst, 1964). In Bristol generally, true 'Tudor Green' is pre-1455 at Westbury College and possibly as early there as 1420s.

129   Thin-walled cup; u/s Church.

130   Ibid; F83 (Church, Phase 5 – 6).

131   Ibid.; two external decorative ridges; MP: cf. BC 1970 Site F, *c*.1350; A19 (MLPS East, Phase 5).

11.10.4o   FABRIC O (not illustrated)
Devon gravel-tempered.
Single sherds from F1 (Church, Phase 6), 1D (Church, Phase 6), F87A (Church, phase uncertain), D1 (MLPS East, Phase 6); see also figure 81.128.

11.10.4p   FABRIC P (not illustrated)
Stoneware imports.
Base sherds of Siegburg-type jug; late fourteenth – fifteenth; 104.2 (MLPS West, Phase 8); 106.2 (MLPS West, Phase ?6).
Body sherd of Westerwald tankard; 1B (Church, Phase 6).
Base sherd Raeren plain jug with frilled base, late fifteenth – early sixteenth (Hurst, 1964); F175 (Church, Phase 5).

11.10.4r   FABRIC R (not illustrated)
South Netherlands Maiolica.
Two body sherds, blue on white decoration; 105.1 (MLPS West, Phase 8).

11.10.4s   FABRIC S (figure 81.132 – 134).
Red earthenware.
132   Rim of large pitcher-type vessel with simple rod handle; glaze dappled light brown and light green; AV: sand-tempered jug; source possibly Nash Hill, Wilts.; 1Z (Church Phase 1 – 6).

133   Rim of small bowl; simple cut rim with no glaze; AV: Malvern Chase jug rim, late or post-medieval; 1H (Church, Phase 4).

134   Rim of small bowl; body covered with white slip inside and out, inner surface green glazed; AV: slipped bowl with abundant very fine quartz and white mica sand; source unknown; 105.14 (MLPS West, Phase 8).

11.10.4t   FABRIC T (figure 81.135 – 136)
Crucibles.
Small cup-shaped vessels with external glaze, of dull yellow, light moss green, dark green, nearly black; maximum thickness of fabric 7 mm., minimum 3 mm.; fused residues on outside, associated with crucible processes.

135   Rim sherd with external dappled moss-green glaze; AV: quartz sand tempered; A3 (MLPS East, Phase 2e).

136   Rim sherd with patchy moss-green glaze and traces of slaggy residues; AV: quartz sand tempered; A3 (MLPS East, Phase 2e).

11.10.4u FABRIC U (figure 81.137)
Fine yellow, lead-glazed (cf. Barton 1964, 201).

137   Base of small candlestick holder, centre portion missing; yellow dots with brown (possibly manganese) slip dots on upper surface of rim; MP: probably Bristol, early eighteenth; 106.2 (MLPS West, Phase ?6).

11.10.4v FABRIC V (figure 81.138)
Plain white, lead-glazed.

138   Small dish, tin glaze over white slip; MP: ?Bristol-made; u/s.

11.10.4w FABRIC W (figure 81.139 – 141)
Tin-glazed earthenware, blue and white decoration.

139   Base of plate; interior face tin glazed and rear face lead glazed; MP: made at Brislington, Bristol, late eighteenth; 1B (Church, Phase 6).

140   Shallow bowl or plate; interior decorated with blue painted flowers and leaves on white background; foot ring has groove in lower surface; MP: Bristol-made; A1 (MLPS East, Phase 6).

141   Plate with no foot ring; top surface painted in blue on white background with flowers and leaves; edge of plate has interleaved motif between blue lines; MP: made at Temple Back, Bristol; u/s.

11.10.4x FABRIC X (figure 81.142 – 143)
Roof furniture, hard black core; triangular crests decorated with knife stabbing and punched holes, both on one face of crest only.

MP: probably products of Redcliffe kilns and produced from the late thirteenth century.

142   9 mm. thick with green/brown glaze on exterior surfaces; flat surface decorated with applied clay strip, width 10 mm., thumb pressed crossing down the length of sides; crest knife cut to give series of triangular projections; estimated height 170 mm., estimated length 400 mm.; F175B (Church, Phase 5).

143   Fragment of chimney louver, centre surface finished with green glaze; F175B (Church, Phase 5).

11.10.4y FABRIC Y (figure 81.144)
Roof furniture, cream core; triangular crests decorated with knife stabbing on one side only.

MP: products of Redcliffe kilns, dating from fourteenth to late fifteenth century.

144   12 mm. thick with dark-brown/yellow glaze crest cut by knife, and face of triangles decorated with knife stab; MP: overfired Redcliffe Fabric 1 tile, fourteenth: 1H (Church, Phase 4).

11.10.4z FABRIC Z (figure 81.145)
Roof furniture, red sandy.
145   32 mm. thick; general character of crest very heavy, top ridge decorated with thumb pressing and sloping face has deep stabbing; yellow/brown glaze on part of external surface; possibly part of a louver; 106.3 (MLPS West, Phase 8).

Not illustrated. Traces on external surface of brown glaze with green speckles; only piece is fragment of curved ridge tile with no decoration, not drawn; MP; cf. Westbury College, late medieval; 1G (Church, Phase 4).

11.10.4aa FABRIC AA (figure 83.146 – 162)
Post-medieval crucibles, all from one, ?secondary, deposit.

MP: the crucibles are characterised by cuprous deposits on interior surfaces and cuprous dribbles on exterior surfaces and base and were presumably used for smelting or melting of copper alloys. All pots are vitrified to an extremely porous crystalline material and were probably used only once, as by then they were already cracked and impregnated with gangue. Dribbles of cuprous material on base of pots suggest that they were already cool before being put down. Tong marks can be seen at the base of crucible BRSMG: Q 2296. Tongs would have been used to pour molten material out of spout of crucibles, but in many cases the crucible spout seems to have been missed in the process! Fabric suggests seventeenth-century date.

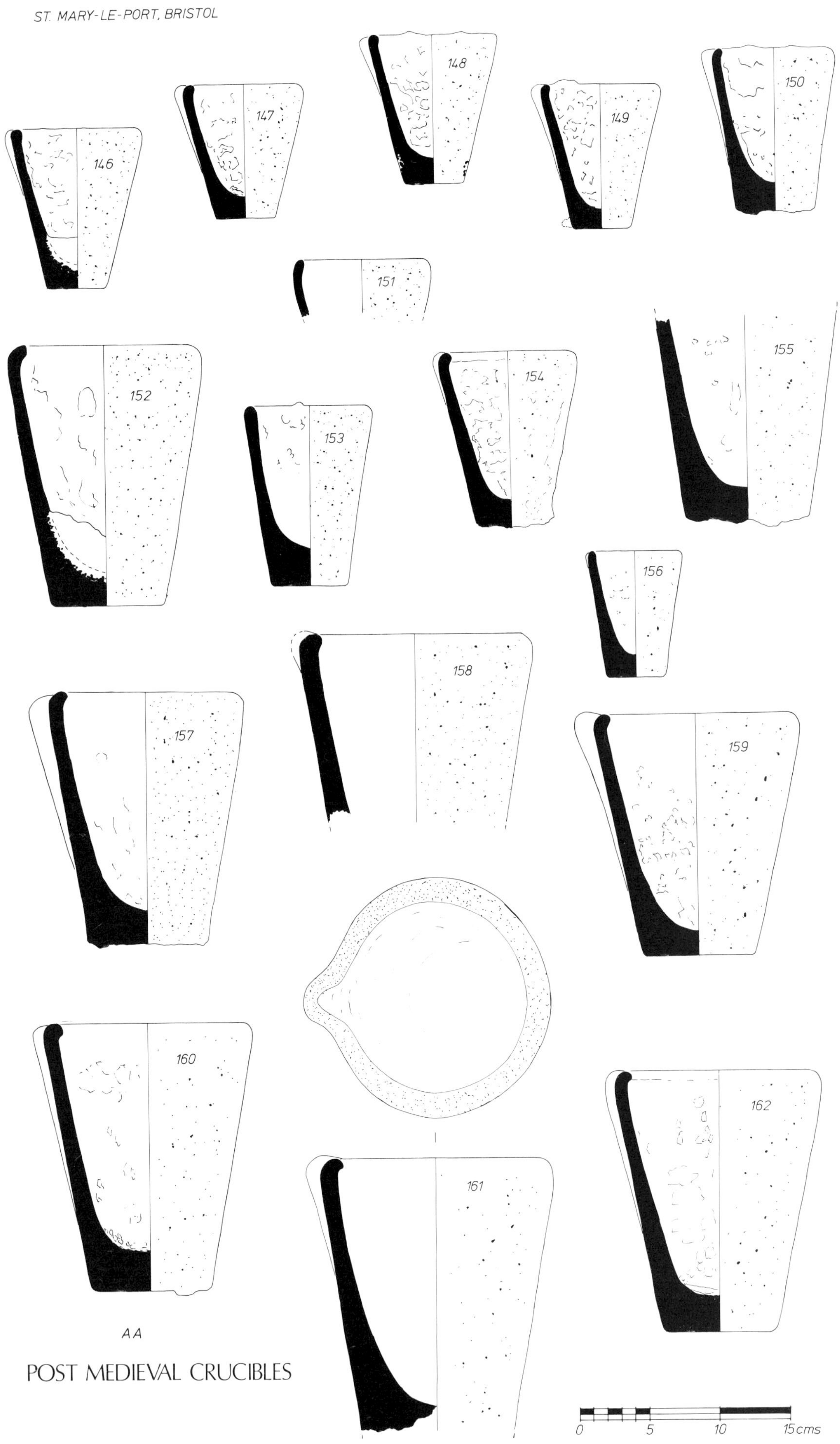

AA

POST MEDIEVAL CRUCIBLES

Figure 83.

11.10.5 THE PETROLOGY OF SOME EARLY MEDIEVAL POTTERY FROM MARY-LE-PORT, BRISTOL, by Dr A. G. Vince, then of Department of Archaeology, University of Southampton.

11.10.5a INTRODUCTION

Samples of medieval cooking pots and jugs were examined in thin section to compare with fabric groups identified by Fowler and Ponsford among the pottery from Mary-le-Port. Fourteen sherds were thin-sectioned and in addition a number of sherds were examined using a binocular microscope on a polished section. In ten of the thin-sectioned sherds, and most of the sherds examined on polished sections, the inclusions present were similar and varied only in the size and proportions of different minerals. The sherds were also compared with others from sites in Avon and the surrounding counties. It was shown that the pottery falls broadly into two goups—local (defined as Bristol A, B and C) and non-local wares (from the areas of Bath, Gloucestershire and Wiltshire).

(11.10.5b – c   are in MF)

11.10.5d DISCUSSION

The recognition of a group of fabrics distinctive to Bristol in the period before the existence of the well-known Ham Green and Bristol Redcliffe industries provides an opportunity to compare the role of Bristol as a port and market in the eleventh and twelfth centuries with that in the thirteenth century and later.

Only two sites outside Bristol—Dublin and Chepstow—have produced sherds of my Bristol A, B or C groups in any quantity. In both ports recent excavations have produced Bristol wares stratified in association with locally-produced and imported wares. Neither site has yet been published but a study of material from one site in Dublin—Christchurch Place—excavated by B. O'Riordain, suggests that Bristol A is earlier than either Bristol B or C. It was not possible to calculate the proportion of Bristol wares to others since processing of the excavation was incomplete. At Chepstow late eleventh- or early twelfth-century contexts produced Bristol A, B and C sherds with a few sherds of Gloucester TF41b and Bath A.

As stated above, probable contemporary collections from sites inland contain no, or very few, sherds of Bristol wares. This is similar to the distribution of Ham Green cooking pots, with the exception that more findspots of the latter are known along the coast of South Wales. Ham Green and Bristol Redcliffe glazed jugs, however, have a wider coastal distribution and are found inland, along the Avon Valley and at sites in the Severn Valley as far north as Worcester.

11.11 Lime-based materials (figure 84)

The MF version of 11.11 discusses the range of mortars and other materials, and their relationship to structural contexts. The pieces illustrated in figure 84 are from the rood-screen; this was constructed partly of stone (cf. 11.2.2).

11.12 Vessel glass (figure 85)

Vessel glass was found in small quantities in all three units of the excavation. GL9, from the cellar fill of Church Phase 5, may be part of a glass vessel, perhaps for ecclesiastical use, as a container for example for holy oil. GL1 and 2 are fragments of two bluish beads from early contexts, the filling of the hollow way in MLPS East. Because there is Roman material in these levels (cf. 8.6), the beads may also be Roman rather than later. The other vessel glass from MLPS East is a group, GL3 – 7, from a Phase 5 filling and consists of three apothecary-type phials, and two wine bottles, including an 'onion' type, all of late seventeenth – early eighteenth-century date. GL8, from MLPS West, is a wine bottle with a name medallion, for which a late seventeenth—early eighteenth-century date is suggested. The named person, 'G Southcombe, Bristol' has not yet been identified.

11.13 Window glass (figure 85)

GLW9, a clear greenish fragment of window glass from the road surface in MLPS East, Phase 2a (cf. 8.6), could be Roman or later. The remainder is derived from the glazing of the church. As far as is known, no medieval window glass survived in the pre-1940s church; the Faculty of 1875 refers to putting in new windows of 'Cathedral Tinted Glass' (cf. 10.3.6).

GLW7 and 8, greenish tinted clear glass, are from the earliest archaeological contexts in the church

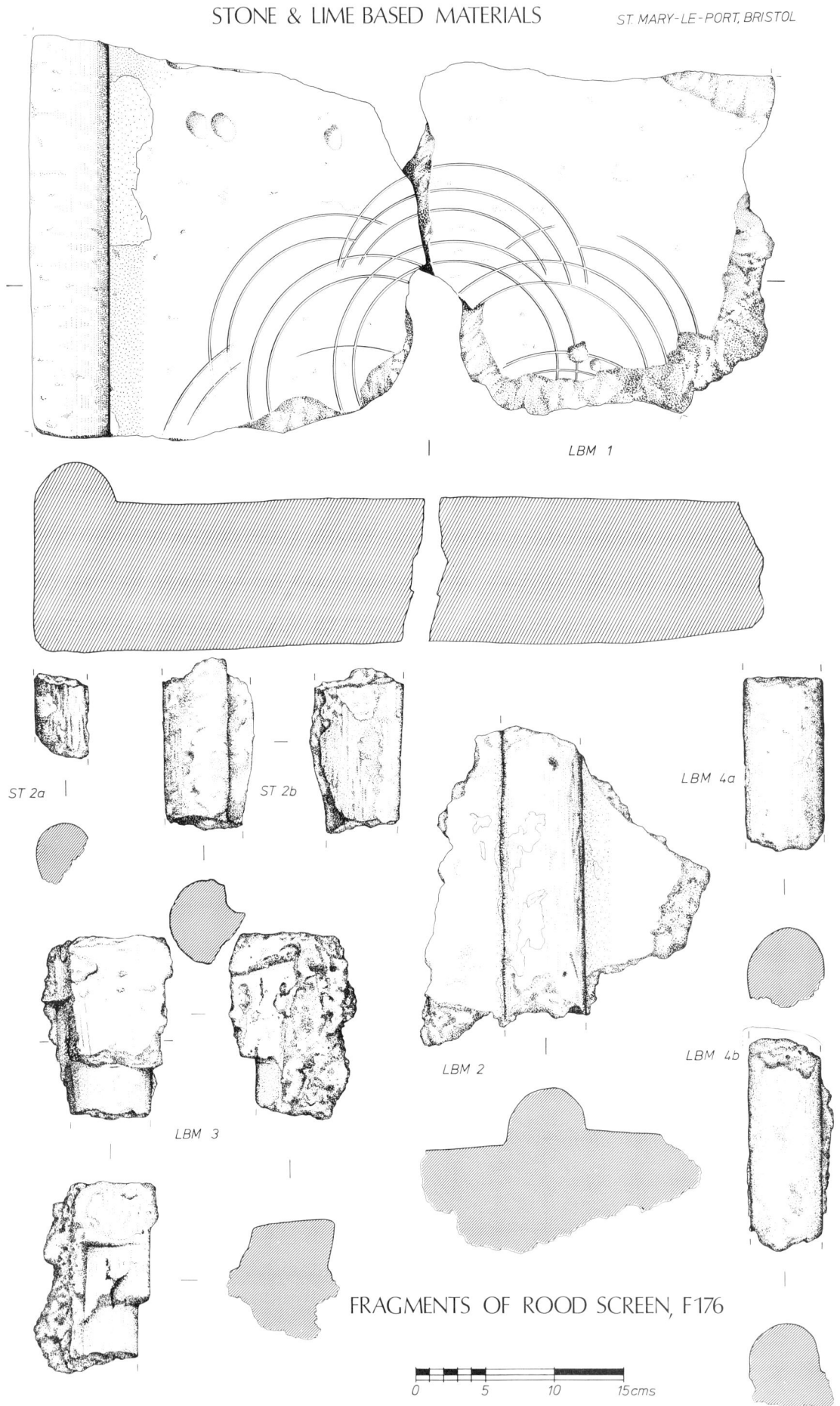

LBM 1

ST 2a

ST 2b

LBM 4a

LBM 2

LBM 3

LBM 4b

FRAGMENTS OF ROOD SCREEN, F.176

0   5   10   15cms

Figure 84.

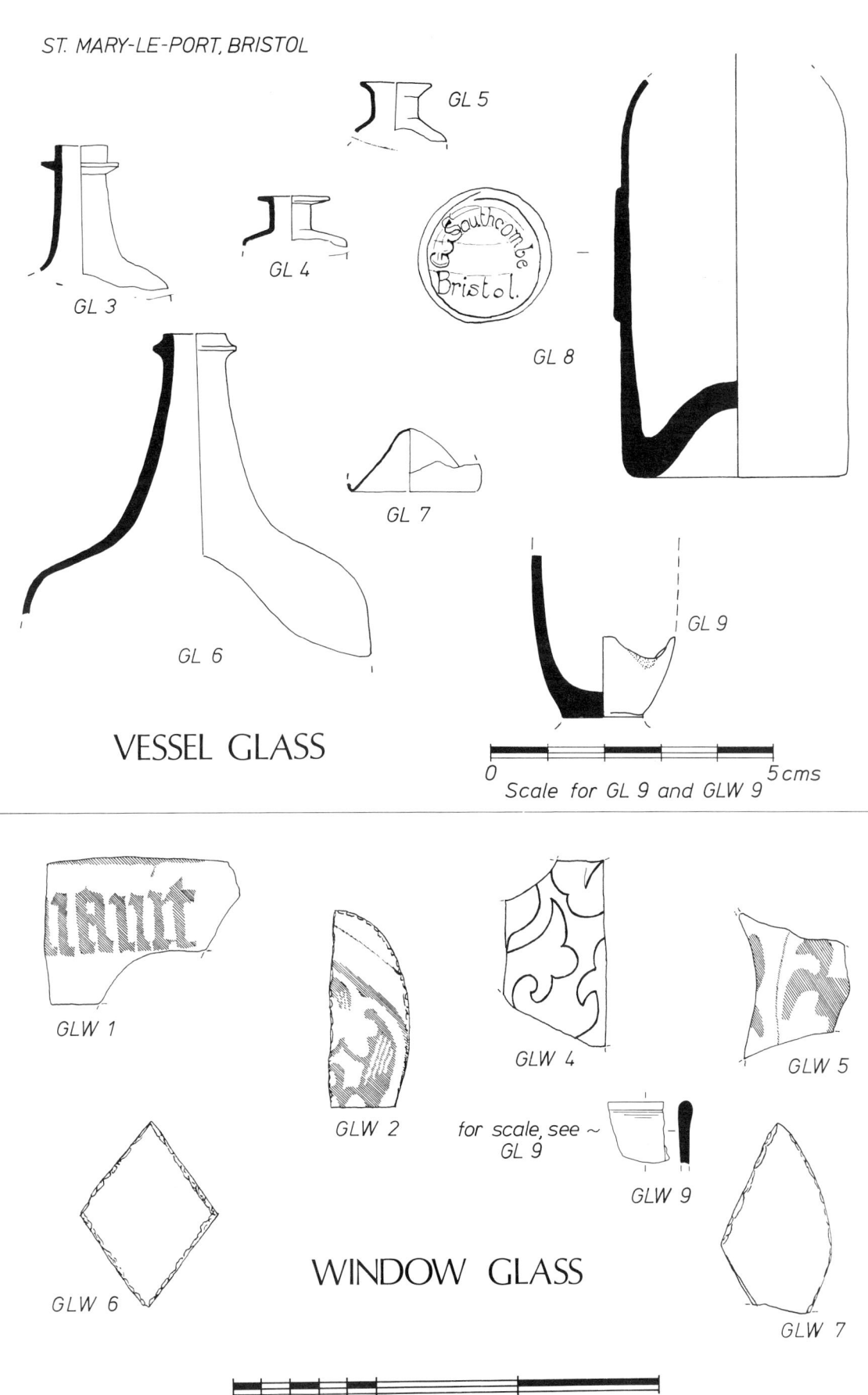

GL 5

GL 3

GL 4

Southcombe
Bristol.

GL 8

GL 7

GL 6

GL 9

VESSEL GLASS

0   5 cms
Scale for GL 9 and GLW 9

GLW 1

GLW 2

GLW 4

GLW 5

for scale, see ~
GL 9

GLW 9

GLW 6

WINDOW GLASS

GLW 7

0   5   10   15 cms

Scale for all except GL 9 and GLW 9

Figure 85.

containing window glass, both from Phase 4 or earlier. GLW6, a piece of ruby glass, was found in the cellar fill of Church Phase 5. GLW1–4 were incorporated within the make-up for the 1877 floor and so may have survived *in situ* until then since the fifteenth century, the suggested date of their manufacture, perhaps in the nave south windows. All are greenish in tint and include parts of a Latin inscription and painted designs, with a possible architectural or figurative detail.

M. Ponsford comments that glass was inserted in the chapels of the Castle in the 1220s, possibly the earliest glass in Bristol (cf. Ponsford, 1979, 169).

11.14   Iron (figure 86)

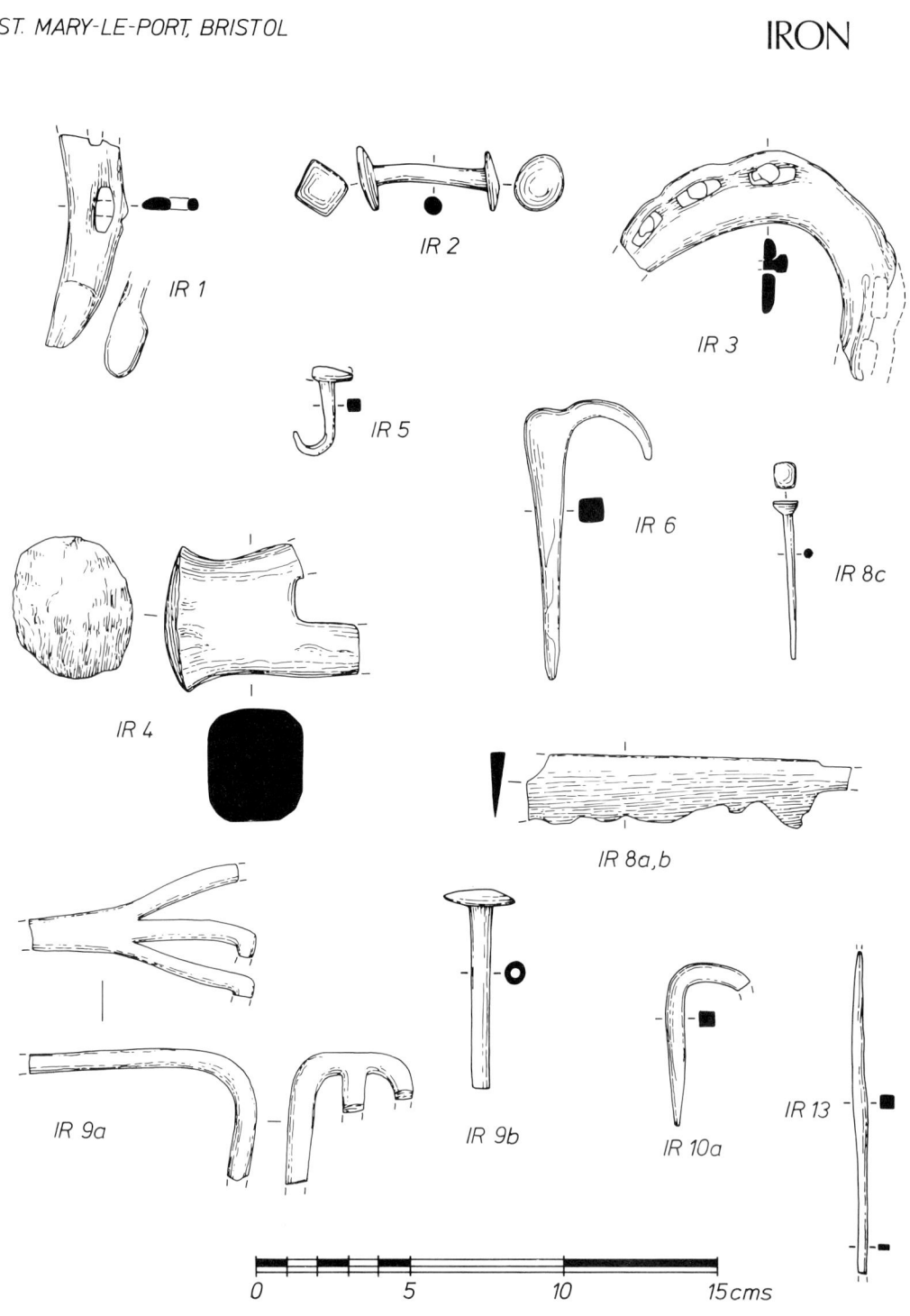

Figure 86.

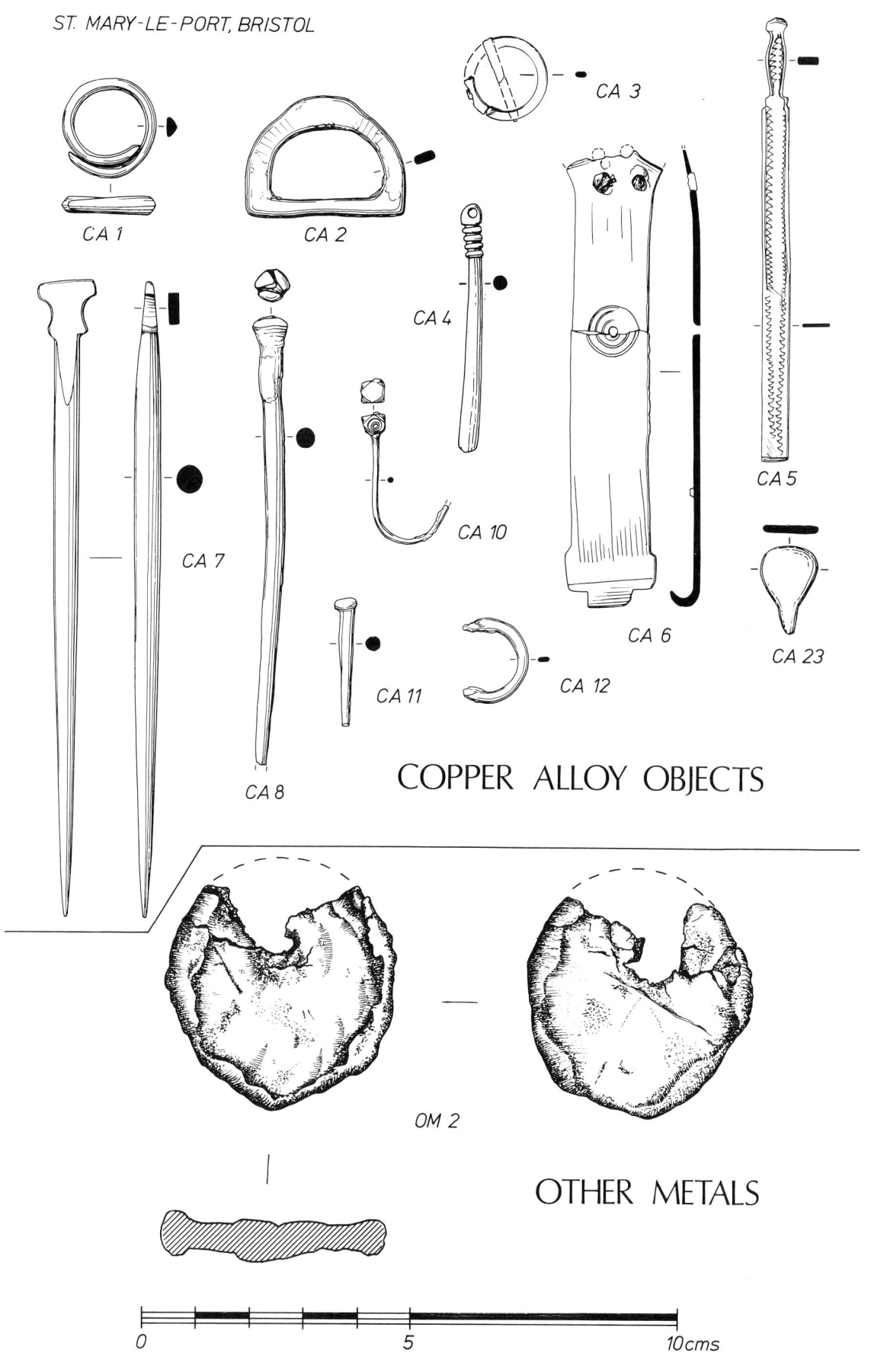

ST. MARY-LE-PORT, BRISTOL

CA 1

CA 2

CA 3

CA 4

CA 5

CA 7

CA 10

CA 6

CA 23

CA 8

CA 11

CA 12

COPPER ALLOY OBJECTS

OM 2

OTHER METALS

0   5   10cms

Figure 87.

Iron objects were found in all three areas of the excavation. Those from the church are from Phase 3 and comprise only a nail and a wallhook (IR5 and IR6). Iron objects from both areas of the street include items from levels also associated with ?iron working. There are small fittings—nails, bolts, a staple—and also tools—a hammerhead and an awl, the latter of which may be associated with leather working (cf. IR13; 8.6.2). IR10 – 12 all came from the fill of the cesspit associated with the Timber Building of MLPS West, Phase 3. The presence of animal traffic along the hollow way is reflected by IR3, part of a horseshoe. From later contexts are part of a knife, IR8, from MLPS West, Phase 5 and from MLPS West, Phase 6, IR9, a flesh-hook.

Plate 60.   Breastplate 1786, CA13; see figure 88.

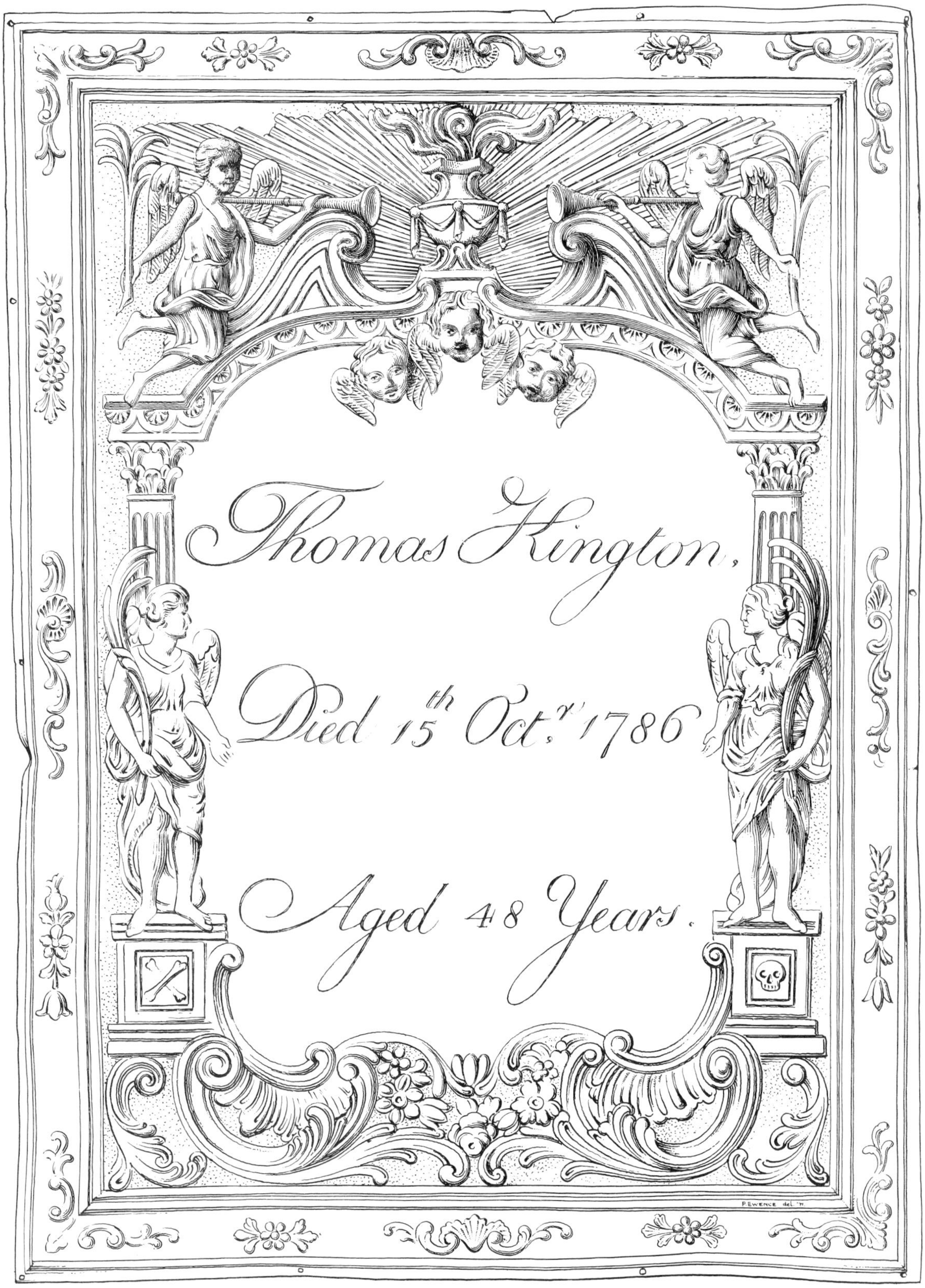

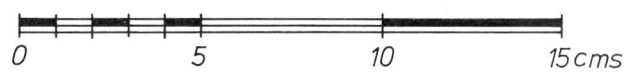

COPPER ALLOY COFFIN FITTINGS ~ CA 13

0   5   10   15 cms

Figure 88.

11.15   Copper alloy (figures 87 – 91)

The group of copper-alloy objects is both more interesting and informative than most classes of artefacts from Mary-le-Port. There are important items from all three areas of the excavation. CA7, from the cellar fill of Church Phase 5, is a pin which can be paralleled in Viking-period contexts. CA6, again from a secondary context, is part of a book-clasp, possibly of sixteenth-century date; its width suggests it was derived from a massive book, such as a Bible. CA22 (figure 89) is possibly a commemorative plaque or a

Plate 61.   Motif from coffin-lid, eighteenth century, CA14, length 28 cm.

Plate 62. Grip plate, eighteenth century, CA17; cf. figure 89.

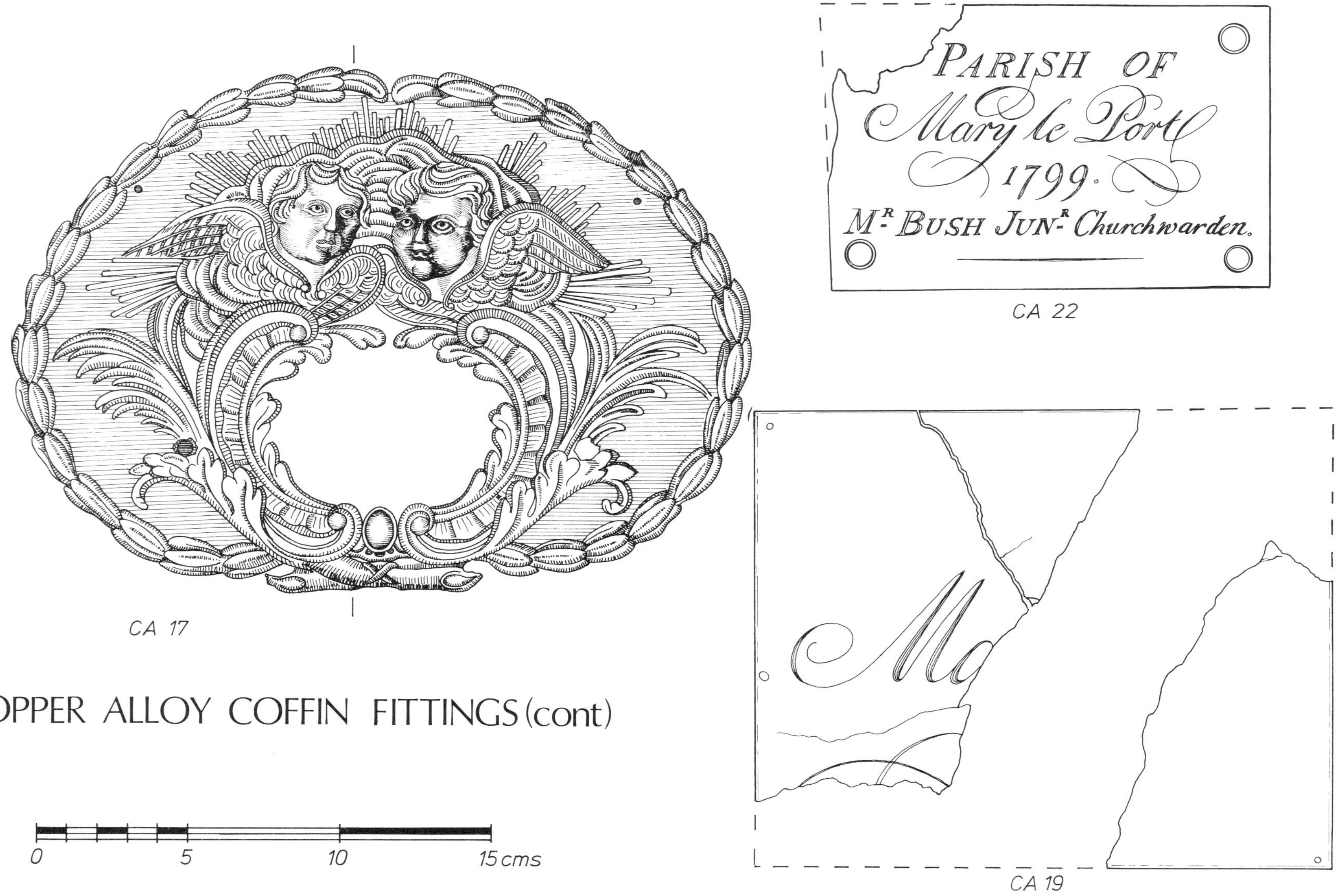

PARISH OF
Mary le Port
1799.
Mʀ. BUSH JUNʀ. Churchwarden.

CA 22

CA 19

CA 17

COPPER ALLOY COFFIN FITTINGS (cont)

0   5   10   15 cms

Figure 89.

pew plate of 1799, certainly associated with a churchwarden, Mr Bush (cf. Robert Bush, who is recorded on the graveslab of his wife of 1794—ST 23, 11.2.2). The remaining copper alloy from the church is derived from eighteenth – nineteenth-century coffin furniture. This, like the burials it accompanied, was undervalued at the time of excavation. CA13 – 17 and CA19 – 21 (figures 88 – 91, plates 60 – 62, 66) represent the finest pieces of those rescued during the hasty removal of recent interments (cf. 10.10). Copper-alloy objects from the prolific dirt levels associated with the hollow way include CA4, part of a set of balances. CA25 may have preserved the impression of an associated textile weave. Viking period and Saxon parallels can be cited for items from both areas of the street. All such objects from Mary-le-Port may be pre-Conquest, but until more accurate periods of origin and currency can be established from well-stratified archaeological contexts, caution should be exercised over the use of such material as chronological indicators (information D. Tweddle).

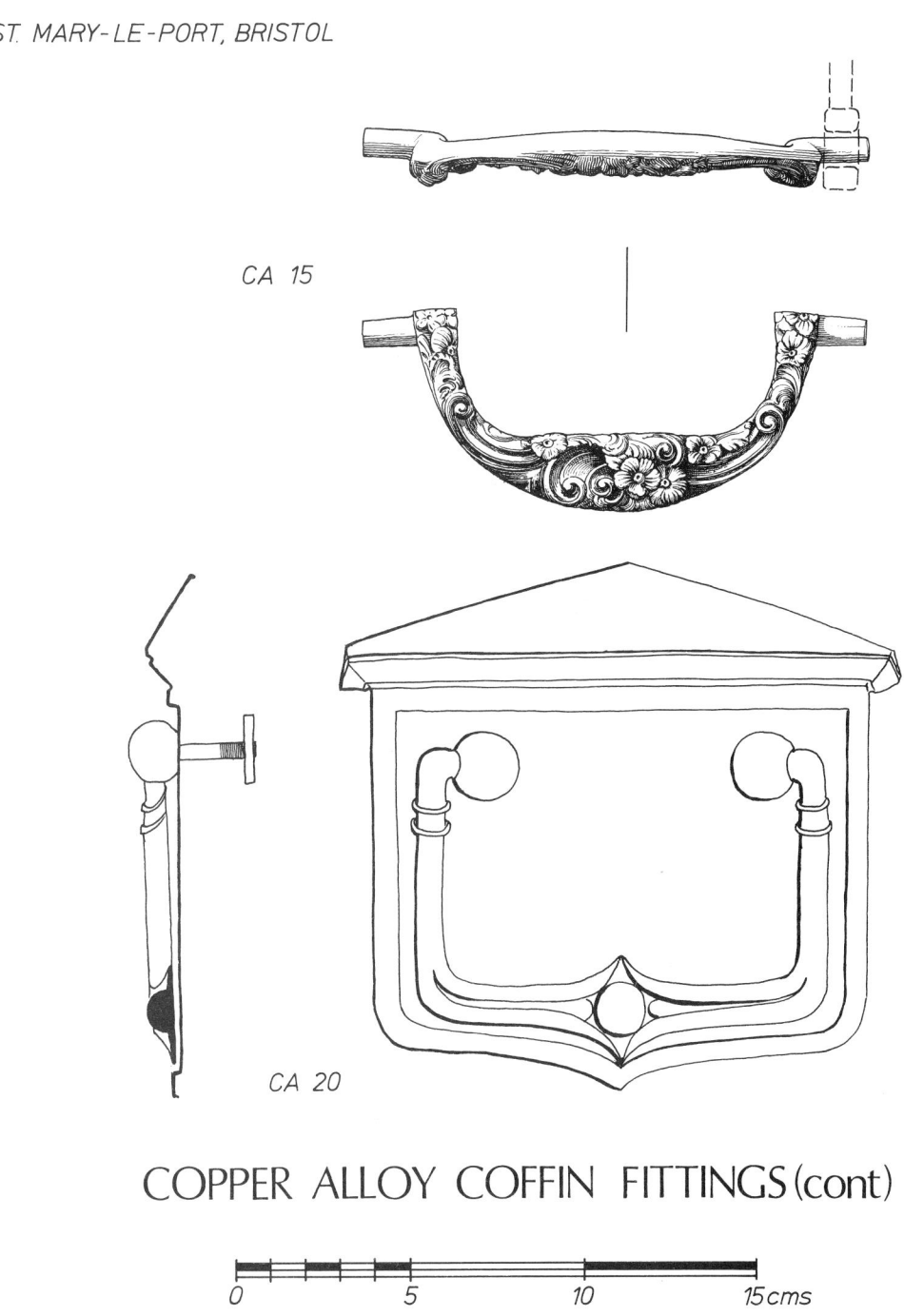

ST. MARY-LE-PORT, BRISTOL

CA 15

CA 20

COPPER ALLOY COFFIN FITTINGS (cont)

0   5   10   15cms

Figure 90.

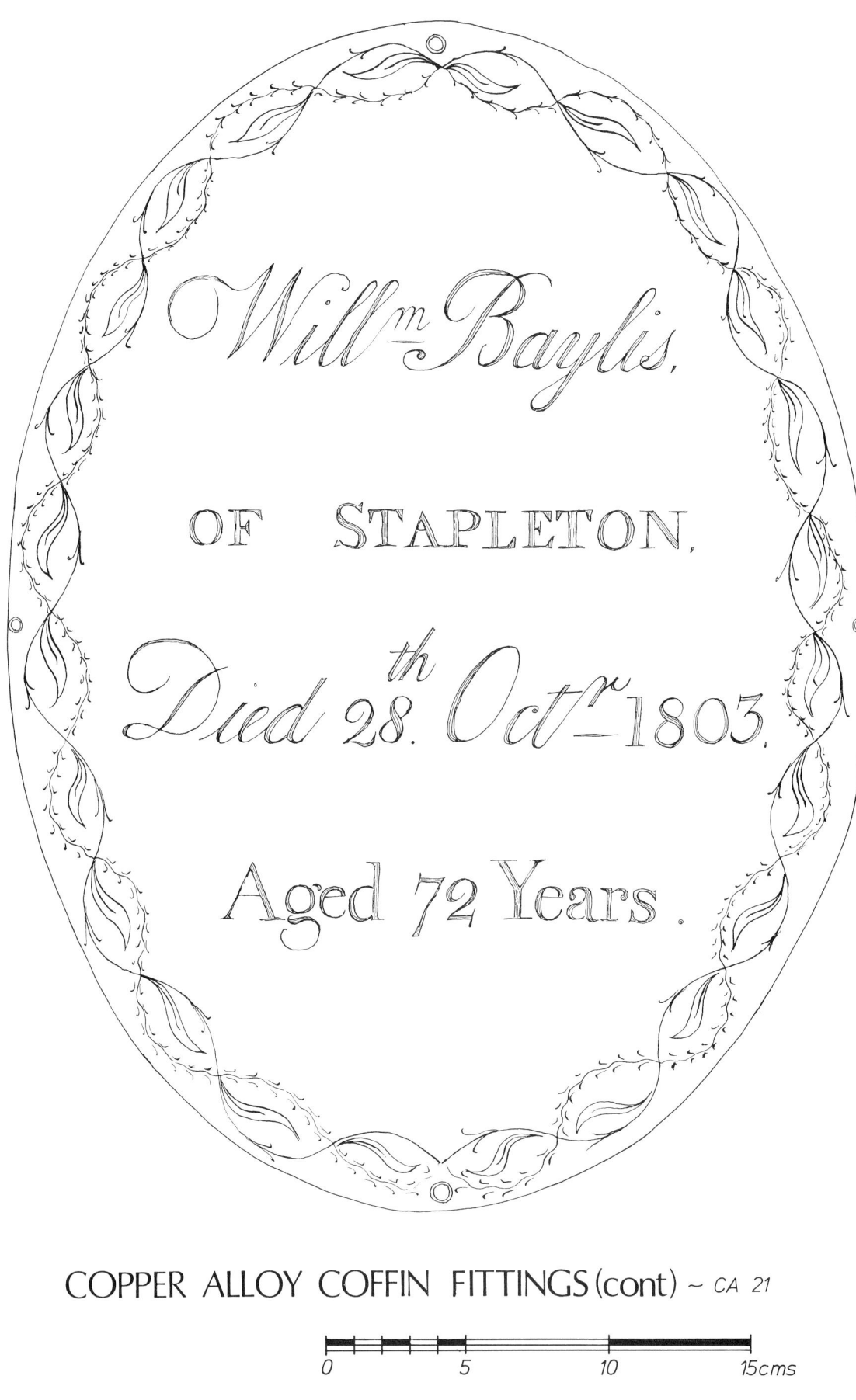

COPPER ALLOY COFFIN FITTINGS (cont) ~ CA 21

Figure 91.

11.16 Coins and tokens

A total of eight coins and tokens were recorded during excavation, but not all have survived; they include the single coin (CO6) from the church (cf. Rodwell 1981, 120), from F178A, phase uncertain. From MLPS East, there were two late third-century Roman coins (CO4 and 7) (Claudius II and Gallienus) (cf. 8.6.2), and a 'long cross' type of token in base metal (CO8) (from E1, MLPS East, Phase 6). From MLPS West there were a lead/pewter token of the thirteenth century or earlier (CO2) (104.2); a ½d. of George V (CO5) (from 105.15); a jetton of 'Nuremberg' style (CO9) (?104.2); and the most important coin, a silver penny of Harold II (1066), from 105.15K, MLPS West, Phase 4 (CO1); this identification was made by L.V. Grinsell and confirmed by R. H. M. Dolley. The reverse inscription is enclosed within

Plate 66.   Breastplate, 1803, CA21; cf. figure 91.

two concentric circles, between which are the remains of the legend, CEORL ON (BRUCI), Ceorl (Moneyer) at Bristol.

11.17   Other metals (figure 87)

Few objects of this category were found. From the church, OM2, a lead disc, may be a weight. OM3, from a late church context, is a bell fragment. There were eight bells in the tower at the time of the blitz (Shipley and Rankin, 1945). Also until the bombing, the church housed a massive seventeenth-century brass eagle lectern which had been transferred from Bristol Cathedral to Mary-le-Port in the early nineteenth century. OM1, a small circular lead disc, was found in dirt above the hollow way, of MLPS East, Phase 2e. Two runnels of lead waste, OM5, occur in the fill of the early ditch of MLPS East, Phase ?1/2a, a fill which may be associated with activities of Phase 2 (cf. 8.6.1). Another piece of lead waste, OM4, comes from modern bulldozed levels in MLPS East.

11.18   Slags

11.18.1   INTRODUCTION

Slag is the most prolific indicator of industrial activity associated with the hollow way. A little of this material has been scientifically analysed but in the main this is a preliminary note upon which, it is hoped, future work will expand (for other early iron slag from Bristol, see Ponsford, 1979, 497–500).

Table 21 MF sets out the occurrence by phase of different materials associated with the working of iron-ore, partly-worked ore, slag, ?furnace lining and ?flux; it also lists the slight presence of cuprous slag. All these identifications are based on visual inspection and may be subject to future refinement.

Concentrations of slag, apparently associated with the phase in which they occur, as distinct from residual material, occur in MLPS East, Phase 2 and MLPS West, Phases 3 and 4, all of which are subsumed within the master street phase, III. All stages of processing, from ore to residues, which may represent smithing and even a possible object, are present, but mostly not *in situ*. Much of the slag and associated materials occurs in dirt deposits in the hollow way and may be derived from adjacent properties (cf. Chapters 8–9). The apparently displaced material associated with 106.25, of MLPS West, Phase 3, includes a ?hearth and ?flux. There are, however, two features which may be *in situ:* B24, of MLPS East, Phase 2d, may be an area of iron slag and furnace material; and 106.23, from MLPS West, Phase 3, is suggested to be part of a furnace edge (the feature has been truncated). Haematite ore occurs in the Winford area.

The few pottery crucibles may have been used for small-scale work, possibly with copper alloys.

11.19   Charcoal

None of the six charcoal samples have been examined scientifically or identified. CHAR1 is from a post-hole of Church Phase 3, which also contained evidence of other organic material, viz. wattle and hazelnut shells. CHAR5 is from the fill of the cesspit of MLPS West Phase 3 and CHAR6 from the early ditch of MLPS West, Phase 2.

11.20   Other botanical

The one OB sample was found on analysis to be of mixed organic and animal origin, containing both wood and leather. It is from a dump of debris on the road of MLPS East, Phase 2d. SO3 and OA1 also came from this context.

11.21   Animal and bird bones

11.21.1   INTRODUCTION

The bulk of the animal bones from Mary-le-Port was derived from a single context, associated with the hollow way in MLPS East, which Ms B. Noddle reports on below. Other animal bone from MLPS East which should be noted are horn-cores (AB36 and 35), from Phases 2a and 2d respectively (cf. 8.6.2). Over five dozen pieces of animal bone (and some oyster shells) were found in the fill of cesspit 106.12, also of this phase.

Mary-le-Port has been included in a more general survey of animal bone from seven British sites and some continental ones (Noddle, 1975).

11.21.2 *SOME OF THE FAUNAL REMAINS FROM MARY-LE-PORT, BRISTOL (AB 1, 2 and 4) by Ms B. Noddle, Department of Anatomy, University College, Cardiff (written 1970, revised 1980)*

The majority of the conclusions in an archaeologically-derived faunal report are based on numerical analyses of the identified material. The excavated material is, however, likely to represent only a small proportion of that originally deposited (cf. Noddle, 1977); only the vaguest of guidelines for assessing what proportion survives can be deduced from modern conditions and recent studies. A study of a semi-slum area of Glasgow in the autumn of 1967 did suggest however (assuming that each dead animal produced 75 bones) an upper limit of 25,000 bones accumulating per acre per year (Noddle, unpublished). Even with the far lower levels of past consumption, a wealthy household could consume a number of animals in a week (Curle, 1908) and it was recorded that 100 head of cattle were slaughtered daily in Renaissance Florence (Rubinstein, 1968). Obviously even this amount of waste bone could not be allowed to accumulate in the streets; in addition to the depredations of scavengers, including wild rodents and birds, and domestic carnivores, periodic clearances probably occurred. Bearing this in mind, an account is now given of the excavated material.

The animal bone from Mary-le-Port was well preserved but, in common with most urban material, it was very fragmentary. Allowing for the exclusion of ribs, which are difficult to assign to the different genera, about 80 per cent of the fragments were nevertheless identified. AB1, 2 and 4 all came from F2–3, 'dirt' in the hollow way in MLPS East, Phase 2c. AB2 formed the bulk of the material, c.1500 fragments weighing c.127 kg.

The greatest number of recognisable fragments originated from cattle, followed by sheep, with far fewer numbers of goat and pig. There were also a few fragments from horse, dog and cat. When, however, the minimum number of individuals from which these fragments could have been obtained is deduced, the order changes—on this criterion, there are nearly twice as many sheep as cattle, and twice as many goats as pigs. The value of both these statistics has been discussed by Chaplin (1971), but they must both be considered in relationship to the assumed rate of accumulation of the deposit.

Teeth are more durable than other bones, and a high number of loose teeth suggests that a deposit accumulated slowly, being subjected to both weathering and trampling. The number of loose teeth at Mary-le-Port is fairly high; hence the minimum number of individuals is probably too low, but one cannot be dogmatic. When discussing sheep and goats, it must be borne in mind that it is very difficult to distinguish between some of their bones, and rather than create a third 'capra/ovis' category, which makes subsequent analysis difficult, the dubious bones have been included with sheep; in this case the minimum number of goat individuals is more reliable than the identified fragments, but it makes little difference to the more numerous sheep (cf. tables 24–25 MF).

Whatever method of analysis is employed, however, from the point of view of the consumer, there can be little doubt that the bulk of meat eaten was beef, and pig the least. In the writer's experience, this has always been the case with other urban material of this period, but this proportion of pig is the lowest yet found. Hence there may be some additional reason for it, such as religious dietary restrictions, support for which should be sought from the excavated artefacts.

Again from the consumers' point of view, not all of the bones of the animal come from joints of equal value; economic deductions can therefore be made from anatomical analysis of the fragments—this is set out in table 24 MF. Only 11 of the 28 bovine individuals are represented by first-class bones, or 38 per cent of the total, and the difference is even more marked in sheep, only 19 per cent of the total being good joint bones. A reasonable explanation for this is the practice of retail butchery; in modern butchers' shops the bulk of sheep meat is sold on the bone but beef is boned out. If this was the case in the past, bones going to the consumer would then end up on small local middens or go to scavengers and so would not be incorporated with the excavated material.

This analysis provides some indication of the derivation of the material, i.e. that it contains more slaughterhouse and butchers' waste than consumers' waste. This absence of small bones suggests that the midden was a secondary deposit, the result of clearing material from elsewhere, when the small bones were left behind. On the other hand, the number of loose teeth suggests that the heads were deposited once only. This is not to say that the head meat was not used, but that it was removed from the heavy skull at the slaughter site.

Besides containing butchers' and consumers' rubbish, an urban midden may well contain industrial waste. The possible 'candidates' for this are the horn-cores (horn working), metapodial bones (bone working) and phalanges (tanning), assuming that the medieval German practice of selling the hide with the hoofs still on was practised (E. Arnold, pers. comm.). There were a large number of horn-cores from all the possible genera, and it seems possible that some of these were indeed industrial waste; on the other hand many of the bovine horns were from very young animals and those of goats, supplying the biggest horns, were frequently still attached to a half-skull. The largest number of loose adult horn-cores were from sheep, so the matter must remain open; perhaps the horny parts were abstracted alone for working elsewhere.

A fairly high proportion of the bones were metapodials, the favourite bone workers' material, but as none of them showed any signs of cutting, working of these seems unlikely. There were also a fair number of phalanges from cattle but not sheep. Both beef metapodials and phalanges can be used for human consumption; the writer has seen metapodials on sale in butchers' shops in the poorer parts of Sicily and the consumption of calves' foot jelly is not unknown in this country. Sheep's feet are not used in this way, and there are few phalanges in this deposit. They were presumably removed by skin and leather workers, not using this midden. Bones can also be used for the preparation of glue. The heavy boiling which this necessitates, however, considerably reduces the keeping powers of bones, and again there is no positive evidence of this being carried on.

This concludes the information derived from the deposit as a whole from the point of view of the townsman. It remains to consider the type of animals involved and the type of agriculture of which they were a by-product. The chief clue to this second aspect is given by the age range of the individuals. The criteria used in ageing animals are the state of the dentition and the fusion of the epiphyses of the bones. Though precise ages are frequently given for these events it seems to be a very dubious practice to project these back into the past. The information can, however, be very conveniently used to deduce stages of maturity without any chronological implications. At the neo-natal stage, the bones are very small and none of the post-natal epiphyseal fusions have taken place; unworn temporary teeth only are present. In the juvenile situation, the condition is much the same, but the first permanent molar may be present but unworn, and the bones are much nearer the adult size; the individual is probably less than $1 - 1\frac{1}{2}$ years old. In the immature stage, the second permanent molar is present and the third may be appearing but unworn. One to three permanent incisors may be present. The early fusing epiphyses, of the incisors may be present. The early fusing epiphyses, of the phalanges, distal humerus, distal tibia and metapodials have fused, but not the later maturing bones. In modern terms the animal is between $1\frac{1}{2}$ and 4 years old. In the mature animal the dentition is complete and all the bones have fused.

In economic terms, the most extravagant use of an animal is deliberately to slaughter it before it is mature; the only returns from it are the carcass and the hide; although it has taken less to keep it than an older beast, there remains the parents' keep to be offset against this. The older animal will have also produced young, wool, milk or its labour in addition to the flesh and hide. The livestock of the past was much slower maturing than the modern; even in the nineteenth century when early maturity was being deliberately sought after and winter nutrition was adequate, it was only about half-way through the century that three-year-old animals appeared among the Smithfield Show entrants, and five years at least was considered to be needed to produce prime meat, making it a very expensive commodity. It therefore seems reasonable to assume that neo-natal and juvenile animals were casualties or killed in the face of winter dearth in the medieval period. The immature animal demands careful evaluation; it might have produced one off-spring (or failed in the attempt) and have given at least one wool slip. The meat is unlikely to have been prime, but possibly met a demand for cheaper meat. It would also have produced a hide, which might have been the primary reason for raising the animal. The Midland graziers' industry of the eighteenth century for example was set up not by butchers but by tanners. Certainly the large proportion of immature animals in this deposit suggests deliberate slaughter at a chosen age for both cattle and sheep. Pigs, having no other economic function than meat or breeding, are mostly killed at the immature stage in all periods.

11.21.2a CATTLE
Because so many of the bones were immature, few measurements could be obtained for cattle.

This information has been compared with most published data on British sites of this period (see below) and with unpublished data in the hands of the writer; it is invariably within the same range. Apart from animals on exposed northern island sites, livestock seems to be at its smallest consistently viable limit, and no increase of size is found even where rich pasture is present today and might seem to offer improved conditions. This is in contrast with Roman data in the writer's possession where size can be related to the expected fertility of the site. These animals are smaller than those found at roughly the same period in Lund, Holland, and some southern German sites.

The number of horn-cores found allows some discussion of the type of animal (breed is rather too precise a term to use at this period). It must be borne in mind that the animals need not necessarily be local, since the Welsh droving trade was already in operation at this date (Skeel, 1926), reaching much further afield than Bristol. The majority of the cores were, however, of one type, medium length and bent upwards to give an appearance not unlike the modern Ayrshire (no direct relationship is implied). One specimen was strongly curved forward in the manner of either the Celtic shorthorn or of Dutch cattle of the period (Clason, 1968). One specimen was backward turned, and one had strong spiral grooves in it.

11.21.2b SHEEP
The sheep from Mary-le-Port were small, with slender bones comparable with the primitive Soay type. Their dimensions are again typical of the medieval period. Horn-cores of male and female type were found, and no polled skulls or frontal fragments. It thus seems likely that the animals were horned in both sexes, but polled frontal bones are extremely fragile and liable to be lost. The animals were not, however, all of one type, and amongst the horn-cores, two specimens could be attributed to the primitive short-tailed heath type. Another seems likely to be of the duplex variety, that is the horns in the male make at least one complete circle. A third type was observed exhibiting grooves on the medial surface in the male and a notch at the posterior base in the female; these characteristics have been observed in eighth-century specimens from Norfolk (Noddle, 1971) and also in the present-day Norfolk horn and Scottish blackface.

11.21.2c GOATS
The goats were of the usual large-horned type which has been observed in many parts of England at this period. This type of goat probably still occurs in Scotland in the feral condition. The majority of horn-cores found were male (or male castrate). The number of such animals found here and also at King's Lynn (Noddle, 1977) suggests that quantities of male goats were kept.

11.21.2d PIGS
It is difficult to give much account of pigs from sites prior to the eighteenth century when pigs began to assume the modern type and adequate comparative material is consequently available. From Mary-le-Port there are also few measurements which could be taken as so few of the bones were mature. The animals were probably like miniature wild pigs in appearance, like those illustrated in many medieval manuscripts.

11.21.3 BIRD BONES
There is a small collection of bird bones, AB38, also from F2 – 3, which produced the bulk of the mammal bones. D. Bramwell reports that they include goosander and wigeon. These imply the taking of waterfowl, probably in the autumn and winter.

11.22 Bone objects (figure 92)

Bone objects from the church comprise BO10, a small polished, burnt flake; it is from a post-hole of Church Phase 1 and could therefore be derived from an earlier, pre-medieval, context. BO5 and BO8 are both from unstratified contexts and may belong to post-medieval internal church fittings.

The three bone-comb fragments from Mary-le-Port are all from dirt above the hollow way in MLPS East. BO3, from Phase 2c, is a single-sided composite comb and BO1 and BO2, both from Phase 2e appear to be of single-sided simple type; none has decorative details. Also from MLPS East, Phase 2c is BO9, a piece of worked ?antler, possibly waste. All these items may be part of tentatively proposed bone-working activity in this area during the life of the hollow way. The bone-comb fragments may represent objects broken during manufacture rather than during use.

BO4, part of a modern nailbrush, should be associated with the disturbed top of B3, rather than with MLPS East, Phase 3b. BO7, a toggle, is from modern bulldozed levels. BO6, of uncertain function, is also from a late context, MLPS West, Phase 7.

11.23 Other animal

OA samples are derived from two contexts and, on analysis, overlap with SO and OB samples. OA2, ?excreta, is from the cesspit of MLPS West, Phase 3. OA1a – g are samples from debris on the hollow way of MLPS East, Phase 2d and contain worked leather of goat and/or sheep. They should be considered with SO3 and OB1, all of which may be derived from industrial working associated with the hollow way (cf. 8.6.2).

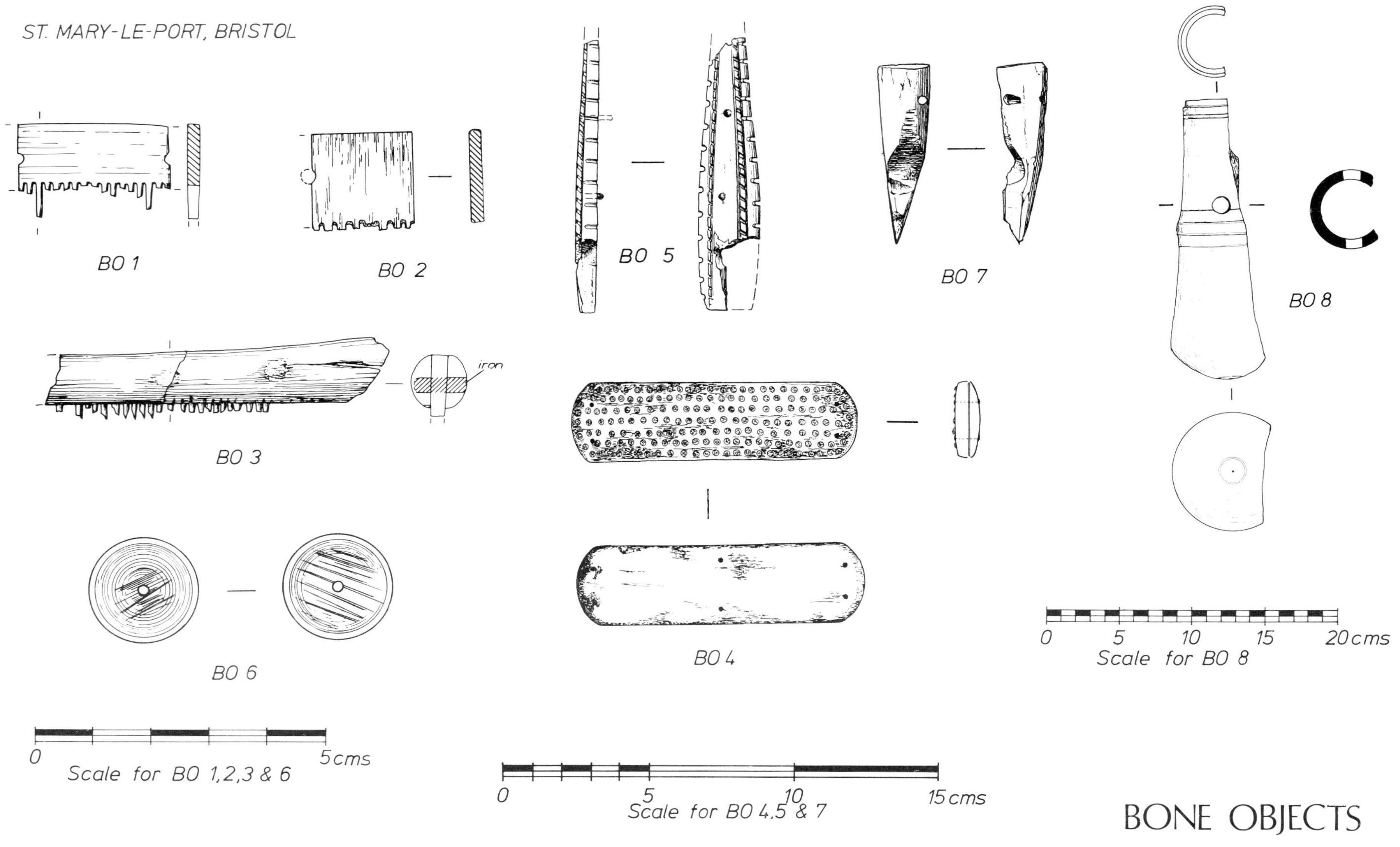

ST. MARY-LE-PORT, BRISTOL

BO 8

Scale for BO 8

BO 7

BO 5

BO 4

Scale for BO 4, 5 & 7

BO 2

iron

BO 3

BO 1

BO 6

Scale for BO 1, 2, 3 & 6

BONE OBJECTS

Figure 92.

11.24 Human bones (slides 8112, 8187)

11.24.1 INTRODUCTION

No human bones were retained for future study—instead they were speedily re-interred elsewhere (cf. 10.1 and 10.10). A description of a preserved body in a lead coffin exhumed in the nineteenth century is given below. L. Biek, then of the Ancient Monuments Laboratory, also noted, at the time of excavation, cases of partial organic preservation in nineteenth-century burials—for example a skull with ginger hair and some remaining tissue.

11.24.2 AN EXHUMATION OF 1814 IN ST. MARY-LE-PORT CHURCH
(plates 67MF, 68, slides 12673, 12676, 12678)

The *Bristol Mirror* of 19 March 1814, contains an account headed: 'Curious Exhumation of a Corpse—excavated at Mary-le-Port church'; extracts from this account are here reproduced:

> 'The oldest of the four removed coffins had been in the vault only 16 years; but all of them were quite decayed, and their inhabitants nearly mingled with their kindred dust'.

Below the bottom brickwork they discovered a 'Coffin of Lead'—without inscription.

> 'The lead was of considerable thickness, and contained a thick shell, of red deal, with the interstice stuffed closely with straw. When the lid was lifted up, some gas, of soapy odour, escaped, and the whole became perfectly inoffensive. There lay, in a most perfect state of preservation, the body of a robust man, measuring six feet two inches. The flesh, in some parts resembled supple brown leather—in others it was quite white, and bore a natural appearance—in others again, it appeared fatty. The features were perfectly distinct, the teeth regular, the nose projecting; the eyes so little injured that the transparent part was still pellucid, like horn. The hands, in admirable preservation, rested upon the upper part of each thigh; and scarcely a bone of the toes was wanting. The throat was swollen very much under the lower jaw, giving the idea of strangulation . . . from the chin to the top of the head passed a blue and white linen handkerchief . . . probably to retain the lower jaw in its place' . . . 'The lungs were somewhat shrivelled and black; but the heart was in such a perfect state, that its vessel, cavities and valves, would have admitted of an anatomical demonstration, as easily as a recent one. It was quite white, felt like soft chamois leather and was evidently converted into that substance which the chemists call "adipocere", being an inferior sort of spermaceti. The midriff was completely so changed. The liver had a yellow crust of this substance, the eighth of an inch thick; deeper down it was but imperfectly formed; and towards the centre, this organ appeared quite fresh and natural. The bowels were shrivelled, and an entire curiously coiled up mass of spermaceti, appearing quite covered with crystals. The muscles in front, between the ribs, upon the loins, in the thighs, and, in fact, everywhere, were, more or less, converted into a brown, dirty-looking fatty substance. The gristles were elastic; and the bones quite firm, fresh, and sound. The weight of the body had been apparently a good deal diminished, although the limbs had yet considerable plumpness . . .' 'Were any means used to preserve the body? . . . it can be boldly asserted, that no searcloth, wax, gums, varnish, spices, or any gross enbalming materials were used—at least they could not be detected. There is, however, one curious circumstance now to be mentioned, which is, that there was an oblong hole, of about 10 inches by 4, in the wooden shell, closed by a piece of wood, which was easily removable. This led to a conjecture, that rum, brandy, or ardent spirit in some shape, or another, had been, through that aperture poured upon the corpse; and this opinion was strengthened by its flexibility, as, when raised forwards, it easily retained the sitting posture. The lower part of the shell, too, was damp'.

A painting of the occasion is preserved in the Braikenridge Collection. and is reproduced here as plate 68 (also plate 67 MF).

During the excavation a visitor brought for the excavators' attention a scrapbook found in the Bristol Royal Infirmary, which contained further details of this exhumation, a further watercolour sketch (colour-slide 12676), and also fragments of blue and white material fixed to a page (colour-slide 12678) which was probably from the handkerchief referred to in the above account. Part of the notebook account was transcribed by R. J. Lampert, and is here reproduced. It is entitled 'More last words', is handwritten and signed 'W. H. Goldwyer, Surgeon':

> '. . . the numerous Chrystals and Mouldy furr enveloping the whole gave it a most beautifull appearance . . .'

> At 'eleven o Clock the following morning . . . the above mentioned appearances were gone, but the peculiar soapy feel of the corpse, proves what must have been its appearance on first being open'd . . .'. '. . . the Mouth . . . covered with a white mold or damp . . .'. 'The feet were

retracked at the heels and the toes bent backward, giving the idea of the Personage using high heel'd shoes—The face was of a dark brown color, the breast less so and the back perfectly natural for a Corpse,—the belly flattened and pressed as would be in a body the day after being laid out—nor did any break issue from raising the Corpse to a sitting posture, rotating on the thighs as the living'.

'Lastly I am fully satisfied the body was buried in a liquor, which had preserved it so well, the face being longest out of the liquor was the darkest, and the linen must have long since perished had it not been preserved by the aid of spirits that on the back as might yet be serviceable'.

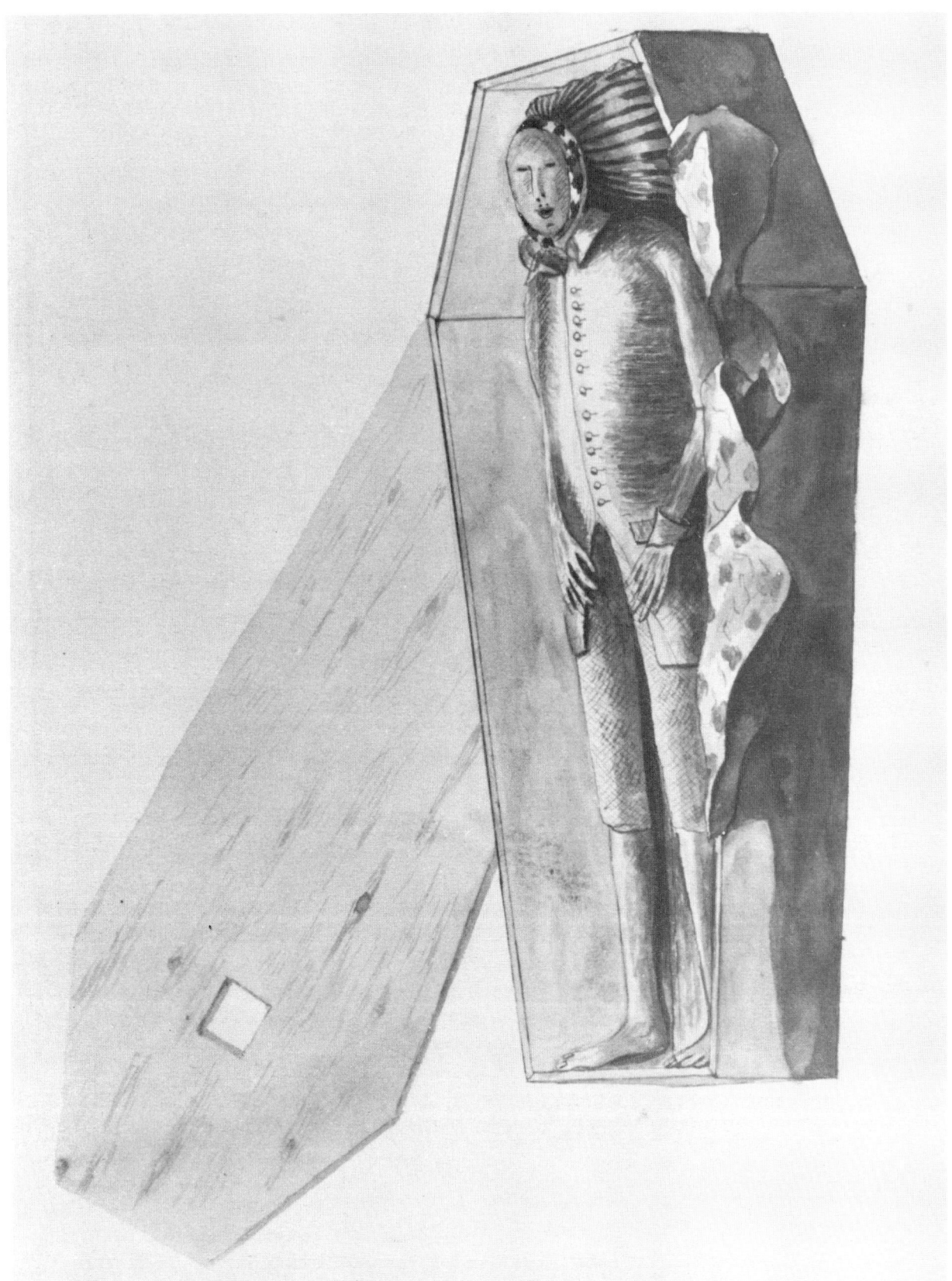

Plate 68. Corpse and coffin of 1814; monochrome photo from painting.

The watercolour sketch has a handwritten addendum 'drawn by my brother Henry Smith'. This suggests that the drawing was associated with the Richard Smith of the newspaper account as much as with W. H. Goldwyer.

Among the excavation records is a Xerox of a newspaper cutting of uncertain date and origin. It was probably from a local Bristol paper of 1962, reporting the excavations, perhaps the *Western Daily Press* or *Evening Post* or *Evening World*. It is evidently from a series of local history articles. It is here reproduced:

'But this probing after long lost secrets is nothing new as far as this church is concerned. Back in 1814 a discovery sent local antiquarians hurrying to St. Mary-le-Port. They had high hopes of what they were about to find. Hopes that were, in due time, to be brushed away.

'Workmen digging a new vault near the vestry of the church felt their spades grate on a coffin. Under a wall monument of the early Tudor style they had come upon a lead coffin.

'It had obviously been buried for many decades. The church authorities agreed that it was worthy of the attention of local antiquarians. A party of amateur historians gravely inspected the coffin and reached a remarkable conclusion. They announced that it contained the remains of Robert Yeomans.

'Yeomans was an ill-starred former Sheriff of Bristol. He ended his life kicking his heels from a gibbet erected in Wine Street near the High Cross. With him to the scaffold went George Bouchier, a wealthy merchant.

'They had been accused of laying a plot against the Parliamentary forces during a Civil War siege of Bristol. They were both staunch King's men and planned to let Prince Rupert into the city and hand Bristol over to the Royalist forces.

'But the plan misfired and the two ring leaders paid the penalty with their lives. Yeomans had the added humiliation of being hung outside his own house.

'He died in 1643—at least a century after the old lead coffin was interred in St. Mary-le-Port church. Moreover there was substantial proof that Bouchier was buried in St. Werburgh's Church, then in Wine Street. Yeomans was laid to rest in Christ Church, City.

'But quite undaunted, the amateur antiquarians claimed that the body in the old coffin must be that of Robert Yeomans. The discovery created considerable interest and it was decided to open the coffin and inspect the body of the man who had gone down in Bristol's history as the "Royal Martyr, victim of Puritan vengeance".

'News that the coffin was to be opened quickly whetted the interest of a well-known Bristol surgeon.

'Mr Richard Smith was always on the alert for a chance to display his skill as an anatomist. Here was a golden opportunity to add a few specimens to his own private museum.

'The coffin was duly opened and Mr Smith, surgeon, took charge. He took out the body and conducted an extensive post mortem. Finally he removed the heart as one of the exhibits in his museum.

'Then it was the turn of the audience of gentlemen who had been watching. They cut off part of the garments in which the body had been wrapped and part of the handkerchief bound around the head. These were taken away to be kept as relics.

'The coffin was then re-interred and Surgeon Smith published an account of the gruesome proceedings. All the time the real body of Yeomans was safely buried in Christ Church.'

The writer of this article seems to assume that the coffin must be associated with the tomb monument of the early sixteenth century (F186). The illustrations make it clear that the corpse was of seventeenth-century date, and could not therefore be that of the monument. Whether it is that of Yeomans is another matter—the writer does not give his authority for the burial in Christ Church. It may be noted that the surgeon mentioned here—Richard Smith—is not the one who signed the account in the notebook. There is also a discrepancy between this account and that of 1814. The latter implies that the lead coffin was below a brick vault of 1798, which had been used for four interments in the intervening 16 years; whereas the latter implies that a new vault was being made. Perhaps the latter involved the destruction of an older vault.

12. Synthesis—Church and Street at Mary-le-Port, Bristol

12.1 Mary-le-Port and the topography and origins of Bristol (figures 1 – 4)

The origins and development of the Bristol landscape (3.2, 5.2) are heavily determined by the topography of the slightly elevated promontory in the angle of confluence of the Rivers Frome and Avon (figure 1). The location was appropriate for defence, and it is surprising that the potential was not realised in the Iron Age and earlier Anglo-Saxon periods. The rivers, in deep silted gorges, provide water and communications; the latter were the principal factor in Bristol's medieval prosperity.

The land route to the sea must always have been from the east, down the 'spine' of the promontory, to any settlement area, or beyond to any ford or bridge across either river.

In the area of the excavations, and in the area around St. Peter's explored by boreholes (4.1, figure 4), some original levels survived, enough to indicate the general profile to the original land surface, but the greater part of the natural marl has either been truncated or totally cut away to a depth of several metres.

From the Mary-le-Port excavations, there are sparse prehistoric finds (flints, 11.3) and a few of Roman date (8.6.2) (tile, brick, pottery (11.6 – .7, 8.6.2); fragments of ?Roman glass beads and window glass (11.12 – .13); and two coins of the third century A.D. (11.16)). These may only be part of a general scatter over the whole of the promontory, but they could be part of a more linear distribution broadly on the line of the spinal route, which in this case might be the determinant for the later Mary-le-Port Street. While the general area of Bristol is relatively dense in both prehistoric and Roman occupation (allowing for survival factors in urban archaeology), there is as yet no evidence of any *sites* on the promontory (but see Boore, 1982). Specifically at Mary-le-Port, there are no pre-Saxon finds stratified in the minute areas of surviving buried soil; a few are in areas of 'disturbed surface of natural' (marl), which could originally have been in such a soil, but most are in later levels. All indeed could have been re-used, as raw material (e.g. Roman tile), 'souvenirs' (e.g. coins), or as chance finds; some of the flints, moreover, may be waste flakes from medieval strike-a-lights (cf. 11.3).

Under these circumstances, the data are too sparse to allow any clear picture to be formed of the landscape in which Bristol developed. There is no evidence that there was not (say in the ninth century) a relatively open landscape on the promontory, in which (allowing for potential constraints of field and other properties) any through route need not have been closely channelled.

Bristol's origins as an urban settlement must be at least as early as the later tenth century. Coin-minting, a prime urban attribute, is attested in the early eleventh century; coinage also provides the earliest reference to a bridge (5.2). It can hardly be doubted that neither coin-minting nor a bridge important enough to give Bristol its first recorded name were *ab initio*. Clearly the origins of urbanism must lie a few decades before this, perhaps developing from scattered, dispersed, settlement in the area, such as has been suggested for *Hamwih* (Saxon Southampton) and Haithabu, Denmark (cf. Hodges, 1977, 193,n22). It would be unsafe to speculate on *urban* origins much earlier than this, as the town or *burh* is so notably absent in the otherwise relatively comprehensive list of *Burghal Hidage* (conveniently in Hill, 1981). It could however belong to the period of the secondary *burhs* in Athelstan's reign, before *c.*940.

Frances Neale suggests (cf. 3.2) that the origins of Bristol could be associated with a royal estate in the Barton area, at the east end of the spinal route referred to above; in this case, a settlement at the west end would be an integral part of its economic activities and would also provide access to wider waters and communications.

This model still leaves open the debate on the location of earliest Bristol. Much of the discussion about this has previously centred on analysis of the more-recently-mapped layout, notably the line of parish boundaries (figure 2) and the orientations of streets and churches (Mary-le-Port is a classic case of this last problem), lines in general defined in the documentary sources only as late as 1295 (5.2 and 5.3.9iii). Domesday Book does not clarify the picture.

The archaeological evidence has as yet done little to settle this argument. Although there are from Mary-le-Port a few objects of iron and copper alloy for which parallels may be cited in Anglo-Saxon and Viking contexts (8.6, 9.7, 10.11) (pins CA7, 10, etc.), none is certainly dated to pre-A.D. 1000, and the same is true, *a fortiori,* of the pottery. The Bristol area is virtually aceramic before the eleventh century, and while we can now identify some forms and fabrics as being current in (or more characteristic of) pre-Conquest times, greater precision is not at present possible.

Ponsford's work has located substantial pre-Conquest levels, of more than one phase, sealed beneath the Castle (Ponsford, 1979, 25 and *passim*), which has persuaded him to claim primacy for this area. Mary-le-Port may have been on the western edge of such an early nucleus (cf. 3.2); alternatively, the layout around Mary-le-Port and St. Peter's might be even earlier than that in the Castle area, existing perhaps by the later tenth century. No material that can be certainly dated as early as this has so far been found there, or anywhere else, except for the sherd of a late tenth-century imported pitcher from the area north of Peter Street (Boore, 1982).

The excavations have nevertheless indicated that the area of Mary-le-Port was very probably subject to substantial development before the Conquest, at a date earlier than that suggested by written sources. This applies to both street and church areas.

The street, as defined archaeologically, was initially a hollow way, in which there were early finds. It must be realised however that, in archaeological terms, the hollow way was a 'negative feature'; any finds or other evidence in this can only offer a *terminus post quem* for its disuse and filling-up. Whatever the date of any material in the hollow way, one must allow for a preceding term of unknown duration for the wearing down of the hollow way once it had become a defined route at the level of the surrounding ground surface; and possibly also for repeated cleaning out, before 'archaeological finds' became part of its fill, to be displaced only by archaeologists. We can therefore know little of the origins of the street (except that it did not 'cut' earlier occupation levels), nor of its initial role in local communications. The 'double ditch', sealed beneath early road metalling close to Dolphin Street (8.5.1), however, hints that at an early stage of the archaeological sequence, Mary-le-Port Street did not in fact exist, or that it ended short of this boundary, or crossed it by a bridge.

The evidence from the church is even less positive. The earliest levels survive so sparsely that there are no more than tantalising hints of occupation at the level of the original soil; what must in archaeological terms be telescoped into a hazy 'Church Phase 1' includes not only possible secular evidence of unknown duration, but also some more substantial features tenuously put forward as the earliest church.

Further evidence about the origins and early development of Bristol will only accrue through more archaeological work and by further documentary analysis. Both church and street at Mary-le-Port can nevertheless be regarded as major features of the urban landscape from an early stage. With notable exceptions, neither is likely to have been moved or transformed as readily as secular properties. In a changing townscape, described in detail by Neale (Chapter 5), in which relatively open spaces between buildings rapidly disappeared, Mary-le-Port Church and Street survived as static elements, and still survive, but now without any function.

12.2   Streets, frontages, boundaries and orientations (figures 1 – 4)

In 12.1, the Mary-le-Port area was considered in relation to the origins and early routes of Bristol. This section concentrates on more specific relationships in this area and the evidence afforded about them by the excavations (cf. Chapter 5). They can however only be more fully understood within the wider context of the surrounding street pattern; the observations below are interim notes towards this.

The area comprises an east-west strip of land, defined in recent times by Mary-le-Port Street on its north side, High Street to the west, Dolphin Street to the east, and Bridge Street to the south (figures 1, 3). Buttermarket Passage enclosed the churchyard of St. Mary-le-Port and linked it, down some steps, to Bridge Street. Figure 3 also shows the relationship of this area to the oddly-carved-out parish boundary.

The eastern part of Mary-le-Port Street (MLPS East) had a 'double ditch' (a ditch in two phases) at its east end, referred to in 12.1 above, with reference to its relationship to the hollow way. If it was a property boundary or defensive feature, was it private or corporate? In either case, it represents the earliest potential alignment in this part of the street, apparently at approximately right angles to the later road.

At the western end of the street (MLPS West), the alignment of the hollow way appeared to be shared by the ditch 104.9/105.21, by the Timber Building and by the succeeding stone walls, and also by Buttermarket Passage, at least in its early phases (cf. figures 25, 34). The latter's eastern member, adjoining the church's east end, appears to have been in existence since the late eleventh – early twelfth century (cf. 9.6.2 and 9.6.11); the Timber Building was built into the angle it made with the hollow way, and was gable-end onto it. Buttermarket Passage may thus have both an early origin and an importance equal to Mary-le-Port Street at this stage.

The reason for the orientation of the hollow way, in this later phase of its development and possibly as a defined routeway before that, is not clear. It could have been roughly parallel to the Avon, originating from a point mid-way between the two rivers to the east; since it does not seem to be heading for the area of Bristol Bridge, it must be assumed that either it was heading for some other crossing or location, or that it met a north-south route on the line of High Street and Broad Street. Alternatively, it may have originally ended in the area of St. Mary-le-Port Church, only later being extended to High Street, as it certainly had been by 1673 (plate 3), but perhaps not by 1479 (plate 2). Ricart's map, though schematic (5.3.12b), shows no exit from Mary-le-Port Street to High Street, and one can imagine a street ending by the church; too much cannot however be built on these pictorial sources. Yet was 'the way of the Blessed Mary' (5.3.9ii) so named because it led *to* the church from the east?

Whatever the factors determining the orientation of the street they clearly were not those influencing the church. Which orientation had primacy, or whether they co-existed from the beginning has not been resolved. The church is orientated neither with the street plan (at any stage of its life), nor with any known natural or other feature, nor on an approximate canonical east-west line. Whatever the reasons, the diverse orientations of church and street left a wedge-shaped piece of land between them. In the eleventh – twelfth centuries, when the church was apparently relatively narrow, this may not have caused problems; there was still space for secular activity along the south side of the road, if not set out in regularly sized tenements (cf. Chapter 9). With the expansion of the church in the thirteenth and later centuries, however, the wedge became narrower and more awkward, presumably resulting in problems about boundaries and space. Once Mary-le-Port Street was paved and the church expanded to its northern limits, all other developments were adaptations to the two conflicting orientations of church and street (9.11), and the rival claims of the churchyard and its burial space with those of secular and commercial properties. The orientation of the east wall of the cellared property, built in the north-east angle of the church by the late fifteenth century, and with it the eastern arm of Buttermarket Passage in its later phases, may fossilise the compromise between the different orientations (cf. figure 25).

The church and the cellared property, the latter probably originally the parsonage, kept their northern frontage onto Mary-le-Port Street until 1648, with burial in the northern churchyard probably at least as late as the fourteenth – fifteenth centuries (9.10 and 12.8 below). But by c.1648, the 'void place' which had been the churchyard in front of the cellared property was densely built upon. The erection of four- or five-storey buildings on such an awkward narrow plot well illustrates the value of inner-city space in seventeenth-century Bristol. The buildings effectively separated the church from the street, leaving only a 'tunnel' entrance through properties to its northern doorway. Thenceforth the church retained only its southern aspect, Mary-le-Port Street becoming the busy commercial thoroughfare of modern times.

One of the most impressive aspects of the area, as revealed by archaeology, is the essential continuity of certain key points in the landscape. There was originally a church separated from the street by secular occupation; the church expanded and acquired a churchyard fronting the street; and then in turn was forced to relinquish this to secular encroachment. In all this, one point remained the same: the north-east corner of the eleventh – twelfth-century Timber Building was very close to the north-east corner of Jones' Brush Shop, where Buttermarket Passage came out to Mary-le-Port Street (plate 7).

12.3   Mary-le-Port Street

Two stretches of the street were excavated—part of the east end extending to Dolphin Street (MLPS East, Chapter 8) and a shorter length near the church (MLPS West, chapter 9) (figure 23). Although separated by a 16 m. gap, their stratification could be linked (Chapter 7).

The street's history may be summarised as: unmetalled route way/erosion/hollow way/fill/ paving(s)/tarmac. This outline sequence is complicated by phases of destruction and replacement. In general the filling of the hollow way was a prelude to paving, but not necessarily that found in surviving areas of stratification, where the paving was itself at more than one level.

The street is first defined archaeologically as a hollow way, c.3.5 m. wide (8.5.2b), whose morphology must by its nature be secondary to both its primary use as a route way (12.1 above), and also to other pre-hollow way features, such as ditches, stake-holes and occupation areas (8.5.1, 9.3.1 – .2). The few possibly pre-eleventh-century finds could be derived from the earliest use of this route, finding their way ultimately into later levels.

The base of the hollow way was in places clearly rutted by wheeled traffic and had a surface (probably not a deliberate metalling) of compressed 'dirt' and stone, concreted with iron-ore or industrial ferrous residues (8.5.2a and 9.3.3). Traffic included not only carts (on the evidence of the width of ruts (8.5.2b)), but also perhaps sleds, animals (cf. horseshoes such as IR3) and humans. Traces of associated features (kerb stones, fences, etc.) survived in places (8.5.2b, 8.5.2e).

'Dirt' in the hollow way was of two kinds: that which became embedded in the mud base or sides (= cess and mire) and that which was the result of dumping rubbish in it. The latter really marks the end of the hollow way as such. While this rubbish includes finds of pre-Conquest and probable pre-Conquest date (e.g. the coin of Harold II) it may not have been deposited in the street as early as that; it could be derived from redundant neighbouring middens used to fill up the street in the twelfth or thirteenth centuries. Indeed the dirt dumped in the road did not appear to be homogeneous or all contemporary (cf. 8.5.2, 8.6.2). It was sufficiently different at the west end of the area excavated in MLPS West to suggest that the hollow way here may have been distinct from the rest of the street investigated (cf. 9.4. and 12.2 above). In general, however, the finds in both dumped dirt and the make-up above it extended to the thirteenth century (cf. 8.5.3a and 9.3.5).

The make-up of tons of clean sand and clay plus stone is seen as remarkable evidence of communal town-planning, organised by the men of the locality or by the burgesses of Bristol (8.5.3a). The source of this material is clearly excavation into the substrata of the promontory, and cellar-digging is suggested as a likely activity which would produce it (8.5.3a, 9.3.5). The thirteenth century was, from other evidence, a time when such prosperity and communal effort might be expected (cf. the roughly contemporary diversion of the river Frome (Lobel and Carus-Wilson, 1975, 7)).

The paving itself was of large cobbles and slabs, substantial and systematically laid; in its final form at least it appears to have extended beyond the roadway proper to the houses on either side (cf. 9.3.6 and figure 39), up to 6 m. wide, similar to the tarmac and steel-edged sidewalk of its modern successor.

The paving could be in some form as early as 1245, when the street appears in written sources together with shops (5.3.9ii). Or it could be in part as late as the later fifteenth century, the street being described as 'newly-paved' in 1491 (5.3.12f). This is as likely however to mean 're-paved', the interpretation favoured here.

The thirteenth century and later history of the street is well documented by Neale (Chapter 5 and cf. 12.3 below) and realised in graphic form in figures 5 – 22, from its first-known mention in written sources in 1245 (5.3.9ii), through fuller documentation in the fourteenth – fifteenth centuries detailing a mixed community and a street of shops, to the first informative map of 1673 and the small artisans of the seventeenth century; and finally to the precise layout in modern times, to 1940. Its appearance at c.1800 is shown in plates 4 – 5, where there is a cobbled unrutted road c.3 – 4 m. wide, with paved sidewalks a metre or so in width extending into the doorways of shops. By the twentieth century, the sidewalks are slightly more raised (plates 7 and 9), and wider in relation to the road width, as they were in the 1940s, with a total width of 8.5 m. and a surface 1.75 m. above the base of the hollow way of nine centuries earlier.

12.4   Materials and resources

Structures and loose finds indicate the wide range of materials available locally or imported from more or less distant areas to meet the needs of building, street surfaces and boundaries, art materials, mortuary practice, craft and industry and everyday life. They reflect economic availability or the purchasing power and status to command more exotic material. Chapter 11 discusses them by category, but here they are considered by *function*, broadly under the somewhat overlapping labels above.

Building accounts for the bulk of the material. In the absence of organic preservation, wood is represented only by soil transforms (post-holes, stake-holes, timber slots, etc.), notably the complex defined as the Timber Building (9.6.2). The kind of timber used and the sources of its supply must remain unknown, as must the extent to which such buildings were principally of wood or other composite materials, as were the seventeenth-century buildings subsequently built on the site—small amounts of daub with wattle and lath impressions provide the only indications archaeologically (9.7.3 – .4). Photographs and paintings, such as those in Chapter 5, give some idea of the range of materials used on the exteriors of the fine post-medieval buildings in Mary-le-Port Street.

The principal buildings excavated (church and ?parsonage, lower storey) were of stone; the commonest used (Chapter 10 and cf. table 17.1 MF) were the local Brandon Hill Grit and Pennant Sandstones, the latter used for roofing as well as for walls. There are smaller amounts of the less tractable Carboniferous

Limestone, Dolomitic limestones and conglomerates, Old Red Sandstones and conglomerates, and Lias limestones. Local freestones of Jurassic origin (oolitic limestones from Bath and Dundry) were used for steps and, in the nineteenth century, for facing the older wall fabrics. In the thirteenth century and later, slate was used for roofing (table 11 MF) (source not identified). Stone was used also for flooring and steps; and of course for mortuary memorials.

Lime-based materials, derived from any of the local limestones, played a major part in the church; oyster shells were also used in mortars. Several different mortars have been identified, though not analysed—some of the phasing is based on these visual differences and groupings (Chapter 10 and MF 11.11). Lime was used too for rendering (stucco) and lime washing (some of it coloured); stucco was used for the elaborate screen base of the Phase 4 church. Glass and lead fittings were of course also used.

A proper survey of the standing structure and a more thorough examination and dissection of its foundations (including those rather superficially recorded in excavation) would enable a much fuller account to be given to the stone and other materials used. Further details are again available in the pictorial sources and in the surviving building and architects' schedules for the nineteenth century and modern church (Chapters 5 and 10).

When Mary-le-Port Street was metalled in the thirteenth century or later, it was paved with large stones, slabs and cobbles which proved very durable and lasted (although with some replacement) until the modern tarmac and steel edging.

Boundaries began as timber fences (defining road edges and churchyard) and later, probably when the street was paved, became stone walls (Chapters 8 and 9). In 1825, there was a substantial stone wall around the south side of the south churchyard (plate 28). In the late nineteenth century the west boundary of the south churchyard was a low wall with iron railings; iron railings are also visible in modern photographs of the south wall (plate 41).

Art objects are represented in the excavated material almost entirely by finds from the church, related to the architecture of the fabric itself and to mortuary structures. The carved capitals, effigy, grave covers and fragment from a ?shrine, tomb or screen are of high quality and many use local limestones (table 17.1 MF). They include exceptional pieces such as the angel of plate 56, and the civilian effigy head in plate 58, the latter displaying a range of several pigments (not analysed). Lime coating on stones may hint at the existence of other decorative schemes within the church (cf. MF 11.11). Other materials used in mortuary practice are discussed in 12.9 below.

Decorated floor tiles were used in both the medieval church and in the 1877 refurbishment. The former are of a number of different designs and fabrics with local and regional affinities, with the exception of one from Spain, of which examples are known elsewhere in Bristol (MF 11.9).

Craft and industry are represented by raw materials (iron-ore, limestones for smithing or smelting flux, animal bone and leather, a very little surviving wood, coal and (?wood) ash for fuel, tools (including flints and hones from in al. Norway (11.2.3b)), crucibles of ceramic, and residues (slags, melted metal) (Chapters 8 and 9). Of these animal bone is the only material of which sufficient bulk was recovered to result in a worthwhile analysis (11.21). The few coins (11.16) and part of a copper-alloy set of balances (8.6.2) may be related to the marketing end of such processes (see also 12.5 below).

The daily life, habits and tastes of the inhabitants of Mary-le-Port Street are, as so often from excavations, represented principally by animal and bird bones, a few bone, glass and metal objects, and by pottery and clay tobacco pipes. Fragments of quernstones, lamps, flint strike-a-lights and a ?mortar were also found, the latter of the much-travelled Purbeck limestone, as well as spindle whorls of stone and fired clay.

Barbara Noddle points out (11.21 and 12.5 below) that there is no reason to think that the animal bones are wholly derived from food debris. Insofar, however, as slaughterers and butchers were providing for meat-consuming Bristolians beef was probably the dominant meat consumed, with pork the least. There were also small quantities of bird bones, likely to have been caught locally. The few horse, dog and cat bones reflect other possible inhabitants of the area. The animal remains are the main reminder of the important relationship of Bristol to its hinterland. The only other possible food residues are a few hazelnut shells from a post-hole in the church, and oyster shells, presumably marine.

Pottery forms one of the most difficult materials to assess (11.10). The series from Mary-le-Port is an important one, especially for the eleventh and twelfth centuries. Sources of manufacture are still ill-defined. Most of the early fabrics may be relatively local, but by the twelfth – thirteenth century there are imports from the Gloucester area, North Wiltshire and the Bath area (with rare sherds from Stamford). In the thirteen – fourteenth centuries there are examples of the products of local kilns at Redcliffe, Long Ashton and Ham Green (with a few imports from France: Normandy, Rouen, Saintonge). In the later medieval and post-medieval periods, there are imports from the South Netherlands (maiolica), Germany (Siegburg, Raeren, Westerwald), Somerset, Devon, Staffordshire and Surrey.

Post-medieval containers in other materials include glass phials, for wine and for medicinal purposes.

For the seventeenth/eighteenth centuries there are also clay tobacco pipes (11.8). They include pipes made in Bristol and the West Country, but there is also one from France.

The evidence for daily life is not as plentiful at Mary-le-Port as for other medieval Bristol sites. This, and the other topics briefly touched on in this section, need to be expanded to include the whole range of resources and materials available to Bristol in the middle ages in a more thorough way than is possible here.

12.5   Trades, crafts and occupations

Evidence for domestic, mercantile and manufacturing activities in the Mary-le-Port area derives principally from two sources: archaeology and written records; a small amount of information can also be gleaned from pictorial sources of the eighteenth century and later. The archaeological evidence is slight and does not include any intact structural features such as furnaces; it does however give some hints of activities along the street well before there is any documentary information. From the thirteenth century onwards, there is increasingly-detailed documentary evidence of what was happening on both sides of Mary-le-Port Street, until, finally, complete plans can be drawn decade by decade. Frances Neale has done precisely this in Chapter 5, so that this section draws heavily upon her work. Only the street area is considered here; there are some possible secular residues under the church, but they are too slight and ambiguous to be discussed further (cf. MF 9.9).

The earliest evidence is for the period up to c.1300. From contexts preceding the hollow way or immediately preparatory to it, there are runnels of lead and ferrous residues (8.6 and 9.7.1 – 2). Iron working (with residues of coal, limestone flux, ore, slags and a ?bloom (SL 34)) seems to have been present from the early stages of the hollow way (8.6.2, 9.7.3 – 4). It is prominent in all parts of the hollow way, and notably *in situ* in association with the Timber Building, which may indeed be both industrial and domestic in function (9.6.2; also see 8.5.2d). There are also cuprous residues and crucible fragments in the levels associated with this property. The metal residues decrease to the west; coal and slag with associated limestone are present as far as the area of the later church porch, but are slight in the westernmost part of the road (MF 9.9), where the hollow way may be of a different character (cf. 12.3 above).

There are also a very few leather residues, preserved in localised conditions, and a possible leather-working tool (8.5.2d, 8.6.2). Numerous spindle whorls may be domestic or possibly may have been associated with industrial production (8.6.2). Quern fragments (from hand querns) and a stone lamp (9.5, 9.7, 3.4) are perhaps more likely to be domestic.

The most prolific material by far is animal bone (8.6.2, 11.21). Barbara Noddle's perceptive analysis suggests evidence of more slaughtering and butchers' waste than consumers' debris. Some bones, including at least some of the horns, appear to be waste from industrial activity; a deposit of horn-cores in MLPS East suggests a horner's place of work (8.5.2d, 8.6.2). There is no direct evidence that metapodials were used for glue or bone working—they may have been consumed as food—but if the former were practised, it may have been at least partly associated with comb making (11.22). Phalanges could be byproducts of tanning, but again there is no direct evidence.

Further evidence of the food industry is provided by a flesh-hook (9.7.6).

While the range of pottery is wide in type and source, there is no evidence of manufacture or retail sale, although wasters were found just beyond the east end of MLPS East, close to St. Peter's (Dawson *et al.*, 1972).

After the thirteenth century and the hollow way deposits, the archaeological evidence is sparse and unreliable; instead the written sources become paramount. There is however an important group of crucibles, dated broadly to the seventeenth century (8.5.4b, 11.10.4aa), which exhibit cuprous residues of bronze casting, possibly associated with bell founding or gunmaking. From a graveslab, we also know of Robert Bush, 'pewterer of this parish', whose wife died in 1794, aged 42 (ST23, table 17.1 MF); and (possibly the same man) a Mr Bush who is recorded on a copper-alloy plate as a churchwarden in 1799 (CA22, table 17.15).

The only possible direct link between the archaeological and documentary evidence is that of apothecary-type phials dated to the late seventeenth – early eighteenth century (11.12) from MLPS East. These (and the associated wine bottle fragments) may have originated from apothecary Robert Meads, who occupied a property on the south side of the street in 1670 (figure 19).

Frances Neale analyses in Chapter 5 the sequence of property holders and their spatial arrangements from the thirteenth–twentieth centuries. The shops in the street are first recorded in 1245. Gardens were still being mentioned in 1387 and 1394 (5.3.12a), but after the fourteenth century Mary-le-Port Street was part of a dense urban environment, as depicted in Ricart's 1479 map and later in that of Millerd in 1673. The parsonage referred to in later sources has been equated with the cellared property attached to the north-east corner of the church. The street was occupied otherwise by a mixed community of merchants, shopkeepers, artisans, and 'persons of substance' (5.3.12i). For the fifteenth century, occupations include those of merchants, a mercer, four brewers, two tailors, a turner, a currier, a baker, a haberdasher, a shoemaker, a draper and a plumber (5.3.12l). There was a Cordwainers' Hall in the fifteenth–sixteenth centuries (5.3.12h); their arms were to be seen later on the chimneypiece at nos. 44–45. In the seventeenth century, the trades of merchant, flaxdresser, grocer, butcher, baker, brewer, cook, ironmonger, tailor, shoemaker, cordwainer, bodicemaker, apothecary and button maker are recorded (5.3.13e). By 1664, two grocers, an ironmonger and a tailor worked in the properties built against the church. Brewers are also represented by their arms displayed on nos. 38 and 40 (5.3.13b).

There are detailed sources for later centuries, including Ashmead's Directory and map of 1828. In the 1860s and 1870s trades include brushmakers, a hosier and draper, an innkeeper, a baker and confectioner; later a chemist, fruiterer and fishmonger, and a bootmaker are listed (5.3.13h and Appendix C). Appendix C (figure 22) is a splendid display of the ninetenth–twentieth-century properties and their trades. Plates 4ff illustrate several of the later shops, notably Jones the brush and basket maker, whose shop was one of the most picturesque in the Bristol of the 1930s.

12.6   Secular buildings and properties

The evidence for the buildings themselves is again principally archaeological for the earlier medieval period; from the fourteenth century onwards, there is some detail in written sources, which is amplified by pictorial maps from the later fifteenth century onwards, by pictures from the eighteenth century onwards, and by photographs in the nineteenth and twentieth centuries.

Sparse evidence for timber buildings or structures was found in MLPS East, consisting of a ?timber slot and post-holes (8.5.2b, 8.5.2d) with a possible hearth and fence (8.5.2e). The principal structure in MLPS West was the Timber Building, to the north of the east end of the church (9.6.2), possibly of two phases. This is dated to the eleventh–twelfth centuries, and is represented by post-holes, possible timber slots and upright plank seatings, and daub with wattle and lath impressions. Associated with this were a hearth, some stone paving, a cesspit and a stone-edged drain, emptying into the hollow way to the north. The building had a ?thresholded entrance onto the Mary-le-Port Street frontage, and was gable-end-on to a predecessor of Buttermarket Passage. It may have combined industrial with domestic use.

Little more can be said of the superstructure of the building or even of its dimensions; the elements of the north and east walls found were probably the greater part of them, but the building must have extended further to west and south. Comparison is made in table 5 with broadly contemporary timber buildings under Bristol Castle (table 5, 9.6.2a).

Timber-based buildings gradually gave way to structures with at least stone footings, even if the superstructure continued in many cases to be largely of wood and other organic materials. Loose 'building' fittings, such as the ceramic chimney louvre fragment (11.10.4x) and roof crests (11.10.4x–y) probably came from such structures. A building with at least stone footings in Tower Lane, Bristol, is suggested to be of twelfth-century date (*Medieval Archaeol.* 25 (1981), 206.

The best-preserved elements of stone buildings found in the present excavations are of course the cellars. It is suggested that cellar excavation, which became such a characteristic feature in Bristol, may possibly have been begun as early as the late thirteenth century (8.5.3a). Certainly by 1480, William Worcestre was able to say that they (together with vaults) were not unusual in Bristol; he recorded no less than fifteen in Mary-le-Port Street—'the cellars made of stone and roofed with boards and timbering' (5.3.12e). This may suggest that stone-vaulted cellars in Bristol are rather later than this. A shop with cellar is recorded in 1443–1446 (5.13.12d). The cellar of the 'cellared property' in the north-east angle of the church, suggested to be the parsonage, has a vaulted stone roof, over which was laid a stone floor; this is dated by its association with the Phase 4 church to the later fifteenth century, but it could be earlier (10.3.4a, 10.6.7).

It is also from the later fifteenth century that detailed records survive for a four-storeyed house in High

Street (for 1472), which Neale uses as an example of what properties were like at this time in Bristol (5.3.12c). This is also the period of the first 'pictorial' map, of Ricart of 1479 (plate 2), which shows buildings in the area with jettied upper storeys, chimneys and apparently with tiled roofs (cf. 5.3.12b).

The fifteenth – sixteenth-century Nos. 44 – 45 Mary-le-Port Street retained into recent times an elaborate ceiling and a stone chimneypiece on which were the Cordwainers' Arms, probably in their hall (5.3.12h).

From the seventeenth century onwards, there is massive documentary evidence for the character of the buildings in the area. Neale discusses those built *c.*1648, 'handsome, five-storeyed, jettied, half-timbered buildings, steeply gabled, and with impressive bay windows' (5.3.13a – b and plates, *passim*). For 1673, we have the pictorial evidence of Millerd's map, though like Ricart's (if less so), its depictions of buildings may not be strictly drawn from life (5.3.13c and 10.3.5a).

This report is no place to discuss the architecture of these post-medieval buildings. Those in Mary-le-Port are part of a much wider study of Bristol's vernacular architecture currently being undertaken by Roger Leech (9.12). They were nevertheless remarkable examples by any standards, not the least because they were only one room deep in the restricted area between the church and street. It is a matter for regret that, having survived for the best part of three centuries, they did not continue to our own day.

12.7   Secular activity in the area of the church

The site of the church may originally have been an area of secular activity, preceding any religious foundation (cf. 12.8 below). Several features among those which survive of pre-twelfth-century date (pit, post-hole or timber slot; burnt soil, hearth, etc., 10.3.1) would in normal archaeological interpretation be regarded as of secular character; and so they may be, if the church is a secondary development in the area. On the other hand, as discussed in Chapter 10, evidence of 'secular' activity is not uncommon *in* churches (10.3.1), and the church could therefore still be primary.

What was happening on the south side of the Phase 1 ?church is totally unknown (as it is later) because of later destruction in this area (10.1). The area to the north of the early church, between it and Mary-le-Port Street, was certainly in secular use, with building which may have been both domestic and industrial. It was only with the expansion of the church northwards in the thirteenth – fourteenth centuries, together with the northern graveyard, that secular activity ceased, but it later regained ascendancy with the construction of domestic or other buildings over the former churchyard in the seventeenth century (Chapters 9 – 10).

The building with stone cellar erected in the angle of the Phase 4 church, between the ?now redundant north-east burial area and the church, is identified with a parsonage, recorded (retrospectively) in 1664 (5.3.13a), although by the seventeenth century it had been entirely absorbed into the church. Its cellar was subdivided, with one half being filled with charnel and rubbish, with a chapel over, the other surviving into modern times as a stoking cellar (10.3.4 – 5, 10.6 – 7).

Such parsonages or priests' houses attached to churches are not it seems uncommon; nor were those built in churchyards (Rodwell, 1981, 110, 135 – 136; see also Drury and Rodwell, 1978, 133 – 151). Another example is Aldermanbury London, where there were intimate links between church and house (Schofield and Dyson, 1980, 42 – 43). Another example that still survives is attached to All Saints' Church, Bristol. It is built into and over the west part of the south aisle; the ground floor equates with the south part of the aisle, the first and second floors being jettied out to the full width of the aisle. This also has a cellar, and the whole may be as early as 1422 (Leech, 10.12).

It is unfortunate that the Mary-le-Port example was so much altered in post-medieval times, and that such evidence of its structure as might have been deduced from its surviving remains was not recovered, beyond the below-ground elements briefly recorded in the present report.

12.8   The churchyard

Urban churchyards are often small and cramped. Space in inner town centres has long been at a premium for secular uses. Thus the northern churchyard of St. Mary-le-Port expanded initially to limits constrained by the street; the church subsequently was enlarged over part of it although there was no room for its own expansion; finally church and churchyard both contracted to their recent small size, hemmed in by buildings as large or larger than the church (Chapters 9 – 10).

Destruction has made it impossible to recover the plan or extent of the churchyard at different times. Very little is known, or can at present be reconstructed from the surrounding street pattern, about its shape and about how the church related to it, although there is as yet no evidence that the church moved around its churchyard as is the case elsewhere (cf. Rodwell, 1981, 137). The level of its surface(s) too is uncertain. There is however no reason to think that the establishment of the churchyard involved raising the existing ground surface, but the extent to which soil may have had to be imported to provide sufficient depth for burial could not be gauged. The recent plan of the churchyard, which is not even on the same orientation as the church, is clearly no reliable guide to its medieval layout. Nor is there any evidence about the extent to which the churchyard and the graveyard were always co-terminous—there were no such obvious clues as areas within its boundary with no burials but indications of medieval secular activities (cf. Rodwell, 1981, 135). In neither Ricart's map of 1479 (plate 2) nor in Millerd's of 1673 (plate 3) is there any clear indication of any substantial space or enclosed area around the church, although some open space is shown in the latter (5.3.13c).

The west side of the church was virtually destroyed, but there is evidence for burial close to and predating the tower (figure 46 and 10.10). There is more archaeological evidence for the ground on the north side of the church (Chapter 9), where there was space between the church and street in Church Phases 1 and 2 (figure 25). The extent of secular activity in this area is unknown (MF 9.9), but grave F76 suggests that there was some space here which was used for burial (9.10, 10.10). The first possible boundary of a north churchyard is represented by the post-holes of a ?fence under the later north porch (9.5), although these might be the boundary of secular properties on the south side of the street. It is their line which is perpetuated by a stone wall, probably during the life of the Phase 4 church (9.6.3, 9.8.4 – 5). The area enclosed extended (eventually) east as far as Buttermarket Passage, but may not have extended west as far as the west end of the church (9.5). The burial area below the north porch was terminated by the paving of the street, if not before (9.5, 9.8.4 – 5). Burials at the north-east end were later than c.1300 (9.6.3), and it was probably this area that was referred to as a churchyard in 1394 (if this does refer to the north side of the church, 5.3.12ii). Burial probably ceased in this area with the construction of the cellared property (9.6.3). Apparently definite limits to graves were found in excavation on the north side of the church, but they were not excavated well enough or over a large enough area to provide reliable data. The street however provided a northern limit at all times.

It was the wedge-shaped north churchyard that was described as having been a 'void space' prior to 1648 (5.3.13a), but this does not mean that burial had ceased before then. The buildings of this period subsequently effectively obscured the north-east churchyard, its forgotten graves being sealed beneath them (5.3.13a).

Burial on the unexcavated east side of the church is unlikely (at least after the eastward expansion of the church in the thirteenth century) as there seems always to have been an alley or passage here (cf. 12.2 above). There was presumably always burial on the favoured south side of the church; references in the late fifteenth and early sixteenth centuries are likely to refer to the south churchyard (5.3.12h), and even if the latter is not explicit by the 1673 map, it is clearly designated as 'burial ground' in Ashmead's map of 1828 (figure 21). Before any south aisle may have been built (10.5), there would clearly have been more room on this side as there was again after its assumed demolition in Phase 5 (10.3.5 and cf. figure 25). The south churchyard is shown in a painting of 1825 (plate 28) with a high (c.3 m.) stone wall. This was capped or replaced by an iron railing with spikes by this century (plate 41). Many burials were observed in the edges of the cutting made by the Norwich Union Building (cf. 10.1). The area between this and the church still remains, and could yield more information about this side.

12.9   Mortuary behaviour and ritual

Non-functional behaviour on the site is represented principally by the church and its internal and external arrangements. Mortuary behaviour in these contexts is an element of Christian ritual, although exhibiting no specifically Christian attributes apart from those expressed on grave memorials. The only other possible evidence for 'ritual' is that of the fossil sea-urchins (11.2.5).

Graves and burial were given scant attention in the 1960s (10.10). The extensive areas of burial were regarded as destructive of archaeological evidence rather than as the 'replacement of one form of evidence by another' (Rodwell, 1981, 105). Present attitudes in contrast regard the archaeology of Christian death as offering opportunities similar to those of pre-Christian periods for demographic studies and in assessing the influence, for example, of patronage, wealth, fashion, or conspicuous display in death (11.2.2; cf. Rahtz 1981).

Human remains were found in the church and in its west, north and south exteriors, in earth graves, cists and vaults. Burial was dense and superimposition very evident. It is probable that many thousand people were at one time or another buried in the church and its graveyards. Although only a tiny fraction of these were seen (if not recorded), perhaps a hundred or so in all, most had long since been destroyed by subsequent building, later grave digging, or vault construction. Each generation paid little regard to the dead of previous times (10.10). Medieval graveslabs were re-used in building certainly within two hundred years (11.2.2 and cf. Rodwell, 1981, 153). Charnel was disposed of in building construction trenches, in stone-lined vaults and in the West Cellar (10.10).

Burial presumably dated from at least the twelfth century if not from pre-Conquest times, possibly from Church Phase 1 (9.10; also cf. CA7 and 8, possible pre-Conquest shroud pins (cf. 12.1 above)). There is no evidence that burial predated the church structural sequence. The earliest definable grave ritual was that of cists lined with slabs of Pennant Sandstone. These, like all subsequent burials, were extended inhumations, orientated west-east, head to west (cf. 10.10).

Some burials were recognised as being medieval from their stratigraphic position. Some (e.g. F76) were earlier than the Church Phase 3 north wall (9.10, 10.10). Others were later than c.1300, possibly laid in specially deposited earth (9.6.3). Some were clearly inside the church, others outside; no grave markers were found for the latter. Although slight attention was given to the medieval dead, their memorial stones and shrines were fully recorded although none was *in situ*. These were of high quality, some with inscriptions (including one in Norman French); sculpture includes a fine angel and a civilian effigy with applied colour (11.2.2). Their presence may reflect factors unchartable by archaeological techniques (and which documentary research in this case has not much elucidated, cf. 5.3.12g)—the possible personal reasons behind church alteration and expansion (cf. Platt, 1981, 20–22).

The post-medieval dead and their mortuary artefacts are still a neglected field of study (cf. Rahtz, 1981). The sixteenth century is represented by the monument in the north wall, what must have once been a more elaborate structure (plate 24 MF). It was originally painted white, purple and red (10.10). The only other pre-eighteenth-century burial of which there is written and pictorial evidence is the well-preserved body found in 1814 in a vault, of seventeenth-century date. It was in a thick lead coffin with an interior of red deal, the interstices stuffed with straw. A full account of this fine example of mortuary behaviour (and indeed with interesting pre- and post-mortem aspects) is given in 11.24.2 (also plates 67 MF and 68). Other post-medieval burial containers were of wood, zinc, and lead; coffin fittings were of brass and base metals—studs, handles (usually six) and plates (figures 88–91, plates 60–62, 64 MF–65 MF, 66; see 11.15 also). Some of the latter were dated and one (William Baylis, died 1803, figure 91) indicated his place of origin or domicile (Stapleton, a suburb of Bristol). Some of the more recent skeletons still exhibited hair (now ginger) and organic residues (10.10).

Burials ceased before 1875, when there was a petition to seal the vaults with concrete, which was done in 1877 (10.3.6, 10.10). The dead were however still not allowed to rest in peace. In less than a century, the church was destroyed, and workmen employed by Bristol Corporation unceremoniously removed most of the coffins and charnel from the vaults for re-burial in cemeteries outside the city limits (10.1).

12.10   St. Mary-le-Port Church

The results of the excavation of the church are meagre by comparison with other investigations where the excavation has been of higher quality, or the building and its stratification have been less destroyed by the combined forces of burial, building and bombing. The record is also deficient in comparison with what it would have been if the work had been done while the church was still in use or at least if it had not suffered an intervening catastrophe after disuse (cf. Hadstock or Barton-on-Humber, Rodwell, 1981).

Rodwell has provided a checklist of all the aspects of a church which should be recorded (1981, 53–56, 109). A comparison of this with the data surviving at St. Mary-le-Port is a salutory reminder of how much has been lost, from altars to dog-tongs, as well as many potential phases of construction and alteration to the fabric and also details of the church as a functioning institution (for the last, cf. Platt, 1981). While excavation would not have been possible before the church's destruction, when it was still a working parish church, a full study done, in say 1939, would have been very valuable as a complement to the post-war work.

In spite of these limitations, the broad history of the church is better known than before. Archaeology has provided an outline phasing (Chapter 10), although major problems still remain, such as that of the south aisle (10.5). Rodwell nevertheless rates 'the elucidation of the complex development plans of relatively minor buildings' as 'one of the most remarkable achievements of post-war archaeology' (1981, 109). Substance has also been given to sparse historical documentary references, such as the 1411 and 1447 mentions of the chapel of St. Katherine (5.3.12g) or that of St. Uncumber, newly built in 1518 (5.3.12g), or William Worcestre's pacing of the 32 m. length of the church in 1480 (5.3.12g). Some portable objects have also been retrieved (3.4), notably worked stone (11.2.2), floor tiles (11.9), fragments of a screen base (11.11), ?vessel glass (11.12), window glass (11.13), a book-clasp (11.15), a bell fragment (11.17) and a commemorative plaque to a churchwarden (11.15). There is also evidence for doorways, floors and their levels (10.8) and wall rendering (10.9).

Many fundamental problems remain unanswered. Where was the font (and its soakaway)? How were the doorways (to west, south and north) at various times related to the church and exterior movements? What was the full extent of the church and the churchyard to the south? How did their size relate to population changes in Bristol? How exactly did its successive phases relate to its cramped urban site? What precisely was its relationship to Mary-le-Port Street before the severance of the seventeenth century?

Particularly disappointing are the failure to find out why the church was in that particular location and the ambiguity of the pre-twelfth-century phases. The structures defined as a possible church or churches before Phase 2B are small (60 m.^{2} and 74 m.^{2}) and are not very convincing in plan. The long narrow shape is unusual, although instances of such 'stretched' layouts can be found. An example is St. Mary Northgate, Canterbury, although in that case the plan was partly determined by special considerations of local topography, and the attachment of the church to the city defences (information Richard Morris). But is the size itself diagnostic of a private church or chapel, too small for a neighbourhood congregation? A further complication is that excavation did not recover the south limit of the early features. The phenomenon of micromobility within churchyards has been noted elsewhere, with rebuildings undertaken alongside earlier churches rather than upon them. So the first suggested church may not therefore be on exactly the same site, to say nothing of other possible structures to the south. If Phase 1 is not a church, what was there before Phase 2 and how and why did it become a church site? There are no obvious reasons such as proximity to springs or to a manor house (at least not in the area of excavation nor in surviving documentation), so was a relationship between the market preserved in the area's early name, St. Mary *in Foro* (5.2) and the church important in this respect (cf. Rodwell, 1981, 140 – 142)?

There is much more that could still be done in the future. St. Mary-le-Port, as now defined in the present report, could be compared in detail with other Bristol churches in their urban environment (cf. 5.2). Bristol's churches have not been well served, and still await definitive study. Most of them are more complete than St. Mary-le-Port; and those that are ruinous (e.g. St. Peter's) deserve better attention when proper resources are available. The surviving superstructure and foundations at Mary-le-Port could be thoroughly examined and dissected. More work on written sources, such as newspaper files, might be profitable.

Further research on parallel material to establish the range and norms of churches contemporary with the various phases would clearly be fruitful, both in terms of the structural sequence and in assessing the plausibility of the interpretative plans suggested in this report, possibly throwing up alternatives; and also in terms of understanding the internal fittings and liturgical arrangements at Mary-le-Port.

12.11 St. Mary-le-Port Church and Street in the urban context

The significance of the work at Mary-le-Port will finally be considered briefly against wider archaeological horizons. The excavation in the 1960s was initiated principally on a local basis. Bristol City Museum sponsored the work, as it had all post-war archaeology to that date in Bristol, and as it continues to do in 1985.

The D.o.E. (now H.B.M.C.E) also supported the work financially and has been the principal provider of the financial resources for the compilaton of this report (3.1).

Urban archaeology in the sense we know it today hardly existed in the 1960s. The opportunities made available by bombing were largely unrealised and resources quite inadequate, as they were for Mary-le-Port. It was not until the 1970s that the threat to urban archaeology by urban renewal was made manifest, notably by the CBA (Heighway, 1972) and by Martin Biddle; the latter pointed out (1968, 109) the low priority given to medieval levels of Roman towns; it may be said that Bristol has been lucky not to have been subject to this particular bias.

Urban archaeology in Britain has in recent years been allocated considerable resources; and urban churches have been accorded a reasonable share of these. Church archaeology ('archaeo-ecclesiology') in general has, however, not attracted universal approval. No less an archaeologist than Martin Carver said as recently as 1978 that 'churches are particularly unedifying as archaeological sites: the structural sequence is difficult to read and usually impossible to date. Artifacts are rare, and the only biological deposits susceptible to analysis are generally those of human bones, normally so numerous . . .' that efforts to understand them and surrounding structures are 'often unrewarding' (Carver, 1978, 11 – 12). The writers of this report feel some sympathy with Carver's view in relation to St. Mary-le-Port. He was however severely taken to task by Rodwell (1981, 35), although the latter still admitted that church archaeology lacks a unifying theoretical framework, a criticism also shared by another major worker in the field, Richard Morris (personal communication). Rodwell's important book has itself done something to remedy this, and he is in general optimistic that archaeo-ecclesiology has now spread out from its art- and architecturally-orientated background (1981, 33 – 34).

The work described in this report may escape some charges of the narrower aspects of church archaeology by including part of the associated urban landscape, Mary-le-Port Street, within its purview; we have indeed been at some pains to emphasise this approach in our report—the church in its environment, however tenuous the evidence may be for either, or for their interrelationships. In this, the present report may be compared with similar studies such as that of St. Peter's Northampton (Williams, 1979), or St. Mary and St. Pancras in Tanner Street, Winchester (*Winchester Studies* 5, forthcoming). We can only hope that future work on Bristol's churches will be equally outward-looking in its integration with the history of Bristol and with wider interests.

Bibliography (including Microfiche)

Addyman, P. V., 1964. 'A Dark Age Settlement at Maxey, Northants'. *Medieval Archaeol.* 8, 20 – 73.

Addyman, P. V. and Hill, D. H., 1969. 'Saxon Southampton: A Review of the Evidence, Part II: Industry, Trade and Everyday Life'. *Proc. Hampshire Fld. Club Archaeol. Soc.* 26, 61 – 96.

Alcock, L., 1966. 'Castle Tower, Penmaen: A Norman Ringwork in Glamorgan'. *Antiq. J.* 96, 178 – 210.

Andrews, D. D. and Milne, G. (eds.), 1979. *Volume I Domestic Settlement, 1: Areas 10 and 6,* in Hurst, J. G. (general ed.), *Wharram: A Study of Settlement on the Yorkshire Wolds.* Soc. for Medieval Archaeol. Mono. Series no. 8. London.

Ashmead, G. C. (with Plumley, J.), 1828. *Plan of the City of Bristol and its suburbs.* Bristol.

Barber, E. A., 1915. *Spanish Maiolica in the Collection of the Hispanic Society of America.* New York.

Barton, K. J., 1960. 'Excavations near Back Hall, Bristol, 1958'. *Trans. Bristol Gloucestershire Archaeol. Soc.* 79, Part II, 251 – 286.

Barton, K. J., 1963. 'A Medieval Pottery Kiln at Ham Green, Bristol'. *Trans. Bristol Gloucestershire Archaeol. Soc.* 82, 95 – 126.

Barton, K. J., 1964. 'The Excavation of a Medieval Bastion at St. Nicholas's Almshouses, King Street, Bristol'. *Medieval Archaeol.* 8, 184 – 212.

Barton, K. J., 1969. 'Two Medieval Vessels from a Pit at the Bon Marché Site, Gloucester'. *Trans. Bristol Gloucestershire Archaeol. Soc.* 88, 209 – 212.

Beachcroft, G. and Sabin, A., 1938. *Two Compotus Rolls of St. Augustine's Abbey.* Bristol Record Soc. 9. Bristol.

Bergquist, H. and Lepiksaar, J., 1957. 'Animal Skeletal Remains from Medieval Lund'. *Archaeology of Lund* I. Lund.

Bickley, F. B. (ed.), 1900. *Little Red Book of Bristol 1.* Bristol and London.

Biddle, M., 1968. 'Archaeology and the History of British Towns'. *Antiquity* 42, 109 – 116.

Biddle, M. and Barclay, K., 1974. 'Winchester Ware', in Evison, V. I., Hodges, H. and Hurst, J. G. (eds.), *Medieval Pottery from Excavations,* 137 – 166. London.

Boore, E. J., 1982. 'Excavations at Peter Street, Bristol, 1975 – 1976'. *Bristol and Avon Archaeology* 1, 7 – 11.

Bramble, J. R., 1884 – 1888. 'Ancient Bristol Documents'. *Clifton Antiquarian Club* I, 138 – 139.

Butler, L. A. S., 1974. 'Medieval Finds from Castell-y-Bere, Merioneth' with contributions by Dunning, G. C. *Archaeol. Cambrensis* 123, 78 – 112.

Carver, M. O. H., 1978. Review of Rodwell, W. and Rodwell, K., 'Historic Churches: A Wasting Asset' in *Bull. CBA Churches Comm.* 8, 10 – 12.

Chaplin, R. E., 1963 – 1964. 'Animal Bone' in Gooder, E., Woodfield, C. and Chaplin, R. E., 'The Walls of Coventry'. *Trans. Birmingham Warwickshire Archaeol. Soc.* 81, 88 – 138.

Chaplin, R. E., 1971. *The Study of Animal Bones from Archaeological Sites.* London.

Clarke, H. and Carter, A., 1977. *Excavations at King's Lynn, 1963 – 1970.* Soc. Medieval Archaeol. Mono. Series No. 7. London.

Clason, A., 1968. 'Animals and Man in Holland's Past'. *Palaeohistoria* 13.

Close-Brooks, J. and Maxwell, S., 1972 – 1974. 'The Mackenzie Collection'. *Proc. Soc. Antiq. Scot.* 105, 287 – 293.

Croney, forthcoming. *Property, Tenure and Rents: Some Aspects of the Topography and Economy at Medieval York.* Unpublished PhD thesis, University of York.

Cunliffe, B. (ed.), 1979. *Excavations in Bath, 1950 – 1975.* Bristol.

Curle, A. O., 1908. 'Accounts of the Earl of Angus' Household, Glasgow and Cannongate 1608'. *Proc. Soc. Antiq. Scot.* 27, 191.

Dallaway, J., 1834. *Antiquities of Bristow in the Middle Centuries.* Bristol.

Davis, D. C., 1972. *English Bottles and Decanters 1650 – 1800.* London.

Davison, B. K., 1972. 'Castle Neroche: An Abandoned Norman Fortress in South Somerset'. *Proc. Somerset Archaeol. Natur. Hist. Soc.* 116, 16 – 58.

Dawson, D. P., Jackson, R. G., Ponsford, M. W. and Jeffrey, R., 1972. 'Medieval Kiln Wasters from St. Peter's Church, Bristol'. *Trans. Bristol Gloucestershire Archaeol. Soc.* 91, 159 – 167.

Drury, P. J. and Rodwell, W. J., 1978. 'Investigations at Asheldham, Essex: An Interim Report on the Church and the Historic Landscape'. *Antiq. J.* 58, 133 – 151.

Dunning, G. C., 1949. 'Report on Medieval Pottery from Selsley Common, near Stroud'. *Trans. Bristol Gloucestershire Archaeol. Soc.* 68, 30 – 44.

Dunning, G. C., 1952. 'Late Saxon Pottery' and 'Late Saxon Metal Objects from Whittington, Gloucestershire', in O'Neil, H. E., 'Whittington Court Roman Villa, Whittington, Gloucestershire. A Report of the Excavations undertaken from 1948 – 1951'. *Trans. Bristol Gloucestershire Archaeol. Soc.* 71, 13 – 87.

Dunning, G. C., Hurst, J. G., Myres, J. N. L. and Tischler, F., 1959. 'Anglo-Saxon Pottery: A Symposium'. *Medieval Archaeol.* 3, 1 – 78.

Eames, E. S., 1971. 'Floor Tiles', in Rahtz, P. A., 'Excavations on Glastonbury Tor, Somerset, 1964 – 6'. *Archaeol. J.* 127, 72 – 78.

Eames, E. S., 1974. 'The Tiles', in MacCarthy, M. R., 'The Medieval Kilns at Nash Hill, Lacock, Wiltshire'. *Wiltshire Archaeol. Natur. Hist. Mag.* 69, 132 – 145.

Ellis, S. E., 1977. 'Spindle-Whorls and Bead', in Clarke and Carter, 315.

Fowler, P. J. and Bennett, J. (eds.), 1973. 'Archaeology and the M5 Motorway, 2nd Report'. *Trans. Bristol Gloucestershire Archaeol. Soc.* 92, 21 – 81.

Fowler, P. J. and Bennett, J. (eds.), 1974. 'Archaeology and the M5 Motorway, 3rd Report'. *Trans. Bristol Gloucestershire Archaeol. Soc.* 93, 101 – 130.

Fryer, A. C., 1925. 'Monumental Effigies made by Bristol Craftsmen (1240 – 1550)'. *Archaeologia* 74, 1 – 72.

Galloway, P., 1976. 'Note on Description of Bone and Antler Combs'. *Medieval Archaeol.* 20, 154 – 156.

Good, G. L., forthcoming. *Excavations at Water Lane, Temple, Bristol, 1971.* BRSMG Monograph series.

Gowenlock, C. E., 1981. *The Chemical Investigation of some Post-Medieval Copper Alloys.* Unpublished MSc Dissertation, University of Bristol.

Greening, P. J., 1966. *North Somerset Miscellany.* Bath and Camerton Archaeol. Soc. Bath.

Grinsell, L. V., 1962. *A Brief Numismatic History of Bristol.* Bristol.

Hallam, A. D., 1950. 'Decorated Medieval Tiles from Taunton'. *Proc. Somerset Archaeol. Natur. Hist. Soc.* 95, 63 – 71.

Hamilton, J. R. C., 1956. *Excavations at Jarlshof, Shetland.* Edinburgh.

Hanschke, G., 1970. *Die Tierknochenfunde aus der Wustung Wullfinger,* 11 die Wiederkauer. University of Munich Dissertation.

Harcourt, R. A., 1969a. 'Animal Remains', in Rahtz, P. A., *Excavations at King John's Hunting Lodge, Writtle, Essex, 1955 – 57.* Soc. for Medieval Archaeol. Mono. Series no. 3, 113 – 115.

Harcourt, R. A., 1969b. 'Animal Remains', in Hurst, D. G. and Hurst, J. G., 'Excavations at the Medieval Village of Wythemail, Northamptonshire'. *Medieval Archaeol.* 13, 201 – 203.

Harcourt, R. A., 1969c. 'Animal Remains', in Mynard, D., 'Excavations at Somerby'. *Lincolnshire Hist. Archaeol.* 4, 78 – 79.

Harvey, J. H., 1961. 'The Origin of the Perpendicular Style', in Jope, E. M. (ed.), *Studies in Building History,* 134 – 165. London.

Harvey, J. H., 1969. *William Worcestre, Itineraries.* Oxford.

Hassall, M. and Rhodes, J., 1974. 'Excavations at New Market Hall, Gloucester'. *Trans. Bristol Gloucestershire Archaeol. Soc.* 93, 15 – 100.

Heighway, C. M. (ed.), 1972. *The Erosion of History.* CBA Urban Research Committee, London.

Hill, D., 1981. *An Atlas of Anglo-Saxon England.* Oxford.

Hochler, C., 1942. 'Medieval Paving Tiles in Buckinghamshire'. *Rec. Buckinghamshire* 45, 1 – 49.

Hodges, R., 1977. 'Trade and Urban Origins in Dark Age England: An Archaeological Critique of the Evidence'. *ROB* 27, 191 – 215.

Hoefnagle, J., 1581. 'Brightstowe', map in Braun and Hohenberg, *Civitates Orbis Terrarum,* 3. Köln.

Hume, I. N., 1961. 'The Glass Wine Bottle in Colonial Virginia'. *J. Glass Stud.* 3, 91 – 117.

Hunt, E. and Co., 1849. *Gloucestershire and Bristol Directory.* London.

Hurst, J. G., 1964. 'Tudor-Green Ware', in Cunliffe, B. (ed.), *Winchester Excavations 1949 – 1960,* 1, 140 – 142. Winchester.

Jackson, R. G. and Price, R. H., 1974. *Bristol Clay Pipes, A Study of Makers and Their Marks.* BRSMG Monograph No. 1. Bristol.

Jope, E. J., 1952. 'Regional Character in West Country Medieval Pottery'. *Trans. Bristol Gloucestershire Archaeol. Soc.* 71, 88 – 97.

Keene, D. J., forthcoming. 'Survey of Medieval Winchester', in *Winchester Studies,* 2. Oxford.

Kunhold, B., 1971. *Die Tierknochenfunde aus Unterregenbach, einer mittelalterlichen Siedlung Wurttembergs.* University of Munich Dissertation.

Lacaille, A. D., 1964. 'Palaeoliths from the Lower Reaches of the Bristol Avon'. *Antiq. J.* 34, 1 – 27.

Leach, P., 1982. *Ilchester Volume I: Excavations 1974 – 1975.* Western Archaeological Trust, Excavation Monograph 3. Bristol.

Lewin, E. M., 1964. *Phase Diagrams for Ceramists.* Ohio.

Little, B., 1954. *The City and County of Bristol.* London.

Lobel, M. D. and Carus-Wilson, E. M., 1975. 'Bristol', in Lobel, M. D. (ed.), *The Atlas of Historic Towns* 2. London.

Lowe, B., 1978. *Medieval Floor Tiles at Keynsham Abbey.* Keynsham.

MacInnes, C. M. and Wittard, W. F. (eds.), 1955. *Bristol and Its Adjoining Counties.* Bristol.

Marshall, K., 1951. 'Excavations in the City of Bristol, 1948 – 51'. *Trans. Bristol Gloucestershire Archaeol. Soc.* 70, 5 – 50.

Medieval Archaeol. Such references = annual references to 'Medieval Britain' section of *Medieval Archaeology.*

Miles, T. J. and Saunders, A. D., 1970. 'King Charles's Castle, Tresco, Scilly'. *Post-Medieval Archaeol.* 4, 1 – 30.

Millerd, J., 1673. *An Exact Delineation of the famous citty of Bristoll and Suburbs.* Bristol.

Moore, D. T., 1978. 'The Petrography and Archaeology of English Honestones'. *J. Archaeol. Sci.* 5, 61 – 73.

Moorhouse, S., 1971. 'Finds from Basing House, Hampshire (c.1540 – 1645): Part 2'. *Post-Medieval Archaeol.* 5, 35 – 76.

Musty, J. W. G., 1958 – 60. 'A Pipe-line near Old Sarum: Prehistoric, Roman and Medieval Finds including Two Twelfth Century Lime Kilns'. *Wiltshire Archaeol. Natur. Hist. Mag.* 57, 179 – 191.

Neale, F., 1974. 'Worship Street, Bristol: A Puzzle Street-name'. *BARG Bulletin* 5.1, 6.

Nicholls, J. F. and Taylor, J., 1881. *Bristol: Past and Present,* 1 and 2. Bristol.

Noddle, B., 1971. 'Animal Bone', in Wade-Martins, P., 'Excavations at North Elmham'. *Norfolk Archaeol.* 35, 25 – 78.

Noddle, B., 1975. 'A Comparison of the Animal Bones from Eight Medieval Sites in Southern Britain', in Clason, A. (ed.), *Archaeozoological Studies,* 248 – 260. Amsterdam.

Noddle, B., 1977. 'Mammal Bone', in Clarke and Carter, 1977, 378 – 399.

Oakley, K., 1965. 'Folklore of Fossils'. *Antiquity* 39, 9 – 16 and 117 – 125.

Parker, J. H., 1853. *Some Accounts of Domestic Architecture in England 2.* London.

Platt, C., 1981. *The Parish Churches of Medieval England.* London.

Ponsford, M. W., 1979a. *Bristol Castle: Archaeology and the History of a Royal Fortress.* Unpublished M Litt Thesis, Univ. of Bristol.

Ponsford, M. W., 1979b. 'A Bearded Face Jug from Wedmore, Somerset, and Anthropomorphic Medieval Vessels from Bristol', in Thomas, N. (ed.), *Rescue Archaeology in the Bristol Area: 1,* 49 – 55. BRSMG Monograph 2. Bristol.

Ponsford, M. W., undated (1975). *Excavations at Greyfriars, Bristol.* Bristol.

Price, R., 1979. 'Survey and Excavations near St. Peter's Churchyard, Bristol, 1972, with a pottery analysis by M. Ponsford and R. Price', in Thomas, N. (ed.), *Rescue Archaeology in the Bristol Area: 1,* 35 – 48. BRSMG Monograph 2. Bristol.

Pritchard, J. E., 1906. 'Bristol Archaeological Notes for 1906'. *Trans. Bristol Gloucestershire Archaeol. Soc.* 29, 265 – 273.

Pritchard, J. E., 1922. 'Bristol Archaeological Notes for 1920 – 23'. *Trans. Bristol Gloucestershire Archaeol. Soc.* 44, 79 – 99.

Rahtz, P. A., 1960. 'Excavations by the Town Wall, Baldwin Street, Bristol, 1957'. *Trans. Bristol Gloucestershire Archaeol. Soc.* 79, Part II, 221 – 250.

Rahtz, P. A., 1974. 'Pottery in Somerset, AD 400 – 1066', in Evison, V.I. *et al.* (eds.), *Medieval Pottery from Excavations,* 95 – 126. London.

Rahtz, P. A., 1977. 'The Archaeology of West Mercian Towns', in Dornier, A. (ed.), *Mercian Studies.* Leicester.

Rahtz, P. A., 1979. *The Saxon and Medieval Palaces at Cheddar.* Brit. Archaeol. Rep. 65. Oxford.

Rahtz, P. A., 1981. 'Artefacts of Christian Death', in Humphreys, S. C. and King, H. (eds.), *Mortality and Immortality,* 117 – 136. London.

Rahtz, P. A. and Greenfield, E., 1977. *Excavations at Chew Valley Lake.* London.

Ralph, E., 1960a. 'St. Ewen's'. *St. Stephen's Review* (August 1960). Bristol.

Ralph, E., 1960b. 'St. Werburgh'. *St. Stephen's Review* (October 1960). Bristol.

Ralph, E., 1961. 'Our City Churches and Their Saints: St. Peter and St. Mary-le-Port'. *St. Stephen's Review* (February 1961). Bristol.

Renn, D. F., 1960. 'The Keep of Wareham Castle'. *Medieval Archaeol.* 4., 56 – 68.

Robinson, W. J., 1915. *West Country Churches,* 3. Bristol.

Rocque, J., 1743. *A Plan of the City of Bristol, 1742.* Bristol.

Rodger, J. W., 1911. 'The Stone Cross Slabs of South Wales and Monmouthshire'. *Trans. Cardiff Natur. Soc.* 44, 26 – 64.

Rodwell, W., 1981. *The Archaeology of the English Church.* London.

Rubinstein, N. (ed.), 1968. *Politics and Society in Renaissance Florence.* London.

Ryder, M. L., 1965. 'Animal Remains', in Bellamy, C. V., 'Pontefract Priory Excavations 1957 – 61'. *Publ. Thoresby Soc.* 49, 132 – 136.

Ryder, M. L., 1971. 'The Animal Remains from Petergate, York'. *Yorkshire Archaeol. J.* 42, 418 – 428.

Schofield, J. and Dyson, T., 1980. 'Aldermanbury: A Possible Case of Continuity?', in *Archaeology of the City of London,* 42 – 43. London.

Shipley, S. P. and Rankin, H., 1945. *Bristol's Bombed Churches.* Bristol.

Shoesmith, R., 1982. *Hereford City Excavations* 2. CBA Research Report 46. London.

Skeel, C., 1926. 'Cattle Trade between Wales and England in the 15th – 19th Centuries'. *Trans. Royal Hist. Soc.* 4th series, 9, 135 – 158.

Smith, M. Q., 1970. *The Medieval Churches of Bristol.* Bristol Branch of the Historical Association Pamphlet 24. Bristol.

Toulmin-Smith, L. (ed.), 1872. *The Maire of Bristowe is Kalendar.* London.

Veale, E. W. W. (ed.), 1931. *The Great Red Book of Bristol—Introduction.* Bristol Record Soc. 2. Bristol.

Veale, E. W. W. (ed.), 1933. *The Great Red Book of Bristol: Text Part I.* Bristol Record Soc. 4. Bristol.

Veale, E. W. W. (ed.), 1937. *The Great Red Book of Bristol: Text Part II.* Bristol Record Soc. 8. Bristol.

Veale, E. W. W. (ed.), 1950. *The Great Red Book of Bristol: Text Part III.* Bristol Record Soc. 16. Bristol.

VCH Somerset 2, 1911. *Victoria County History Somerset 2.* London.

Vince, A. G., 1981. 'The Medieval Pottery Industry in Southern England: 10th to 13th Centuries', in Howard, H. and Morris, E. L. (eds.), *Production and Distribution: A Ceramic Viewpoint,* 309 – 332. BAR International Series 120. Oxford.

Wadley, T. P., 1886. *Notes or Abstracts of the Wills Contained in the Volume Entitled the Great Orphan Book and Book of Wills in the Council House at Bristol.* Bristol Gloucestershire Archaeol. Soc. Bristol.

Walker, D., 1971. *Bristol in the Early Middle Ages.* Bristol Branch of the Historical Association Pamphlet 28. Bristol.

Whitcomb, N., 1956. *Medieval Floor Tiles of Leicestershire*. Leicestershire Archaeol. Hist. Soc. Leicester.

Williams, B., forthcoming a. 'Tiles from Bristol Greyfriars', in Ponsford, M. W., *Excavations at Greyfriars, Bristol, 1973*. BRSMG Monograph.

Williams, B., forthcoming b. 'The Medieval Floor Tiles of the Lord Mayor's Chapel, Bristol'. BRSMG Monograph.

Williams, B., forthcoming c. *A Corpus of Spanish Tiles in the British Isles*.

Williams, J. H., 1979. *St. Peter's Street, Northampton, Excavations 1973 – 1976*. Northampton.

Winchester Studies 5, forthcoming. *The Brooks*.

Winstone, R., 1957. *Bristol As It Was 1914 – 1900*. Bristol.

Winstone, R., 1960. *Bristol in the 1890s*. Bristol.

Winstone, R., 1962. *Bristol in the 1880s*. Bristol.

GENERAL INDEX